Corporate Law

Corporate Law

Naveen Kumar Shelar
Advocate
Delhi High Court

I.K. International Publishing House Pvt. Ltd.
NEW DELHI

Published by

I.K. International Publishing House Pvt. Ltd.
S-25, Green Park Extension
Uphaar Cinema Market
New Delhi–110 016 (India)
E-mail:info@ikinternational.com
Website: www.ikbooks.com

ISBN: 978-93-85909-02-3

Published by Krishan Makhijani for I.K. International Publishing House Pvt. Ltd., S-25, Green Park Extension, Uphaar Cinema Market, New lhi–110 016 and Printed by Rekha Printers Pvt. Ltd., Okhla Industrial Area, Phase II, New Delhi–110 020.

Dedicated to

My Mother, Father and Sister

Preface

The subject "Corporate Law" is an important branch of study in business administration, and after the amendment in the Companies Act, 2013 and the Companies (Amendment) Act, 2015, and various amendments, minor or major, in the Negotiable Instruments Act (NI Act), a new dimension is added to this subject.

Technological advancements, growth of ancillary concepts and responsibilities are constantly attracting the attention of the Legislature and the Judiciary, especially when the question of faith and speedy growth of financial transactions and public interest are involved. Potential risk in the modern business transactions makes even a small business an adventure, and the objective of law is to minimize the uncertainties and to create conducive environment for sustainable business growth, and to impart faith of the common people in businesses. A large number of new concepts and responsibilities, rights and reduction in the number of formalities have been restructured in the new Companies Act and in the NI Act.

The present book is concise, which is well-suited for examinations. Latest case laws are applied in short and analytical views at the appropriate places. Also illustrative examples diagrams charts, comparative tables, general sense of the definitions are incorporated, which gives a smooth and better understanding of the subject. Hopefully, the book will fulfil its purpose of imparting a better understanding of the subject.

Naveen Kumar Shelar

Acknowledgements

It is true that no work can be accomplished without the blessings of God and support of family members. I am thankful to God and all my family members specially my mother and father, Mrs. Maya Devi Shelar and Mr. Moti Ram Shelar, who have been a source of inspiration and a constant support for writing this book. Their recommendations and guidance have been invaluable for the book.

At this juncture I would also like to give special thanks to my sister Poonam Shelar, who helped me in analyzing the judgments of various courts, my daughters Siya & Shrishti who gave their warm love and support for writing this book.

Very special thanks to my dear friend Mr. Deepak Bhatt, who inspired me for legal writing.

I am thankful to my Guru Advocate Jitender Kumar, who inculcated legal knowledge in me and helped me in growing as a successful advocate.

I am thankful to my mentor Advocate Digvijay, who inspires me always.

I cannot forget to thank S. N. Gupta Ex. Additional District & Sessions Judge Delhi, who has always guided and supported me.

Naveen Kumar Shelar

Contents

CHAPTER 1

Features of the Company Bill, 2013

- Introduction
- Key Definitions and Concepts
- Implications on Private Companies
- Sections Notified Till Date and Circulars or Orders Issued
- Revival and Rehabilitation of Sick Industrial Companies

INTRODUCTION

Post-independence there were tremendous changes in the business and corporate environments, globally and domestically, but the Companies Act, 1956 was in existence with the same provisions, to cope up with the international global environment and to keep pace with the economic speed. Voices were raised time and again to overhaul the legislations for better governance of the companies and during this span almost 25 legislations were amended in the Companies Act, 1956.

In the year 2009 there was a major setback to the corporate sector when there was a misdemeanor and gross abandon of legal and compliance requirement by certain companies, which ultimately sped up the demand for rampant changes in the existing Companies Act, 1956.

Minister of Corporate Affairs Salman Khurshid's statement in the Lok Sabha during the Question Hour projected the objective of new Companies Act, 2013. He said, "the Government proposes to introduce the Companies Bill, 2008 as the Companies Bill, 2009, which seeks to have more stringent provisions in case of frauds by companies, their directors and auditors."

"The new Companies Act will give this country a modern legislation, which will contribute to the growth and development of the corporate sector in India. The Act, when enacted, will allow the country to have a modern legislation for regulation of corporate sector in India. The Act, amongst other aspects provides for business friendly corporate regulation / pro-business initiatives, e-governance initiatives, good corporate governance, Corporate Social Responsibility (CSR), enhanced disclosure norms and accountability of management, stricter enforcement, audit accountability, protection for minority shareholders, investor protection and activism and better framework for insolvency regulation and institutional structure."[1]

---

1. Message of D.S. Rawat, Secretary General, ASSOCHAM.

Thus, under such circumstances targeting all such issues so as to reinforce the integrity of India's capital markets and make them a favourite investment destination, a strong regulatory framework was formulated through the Companies Act, 2013.

The Act ensures good governance procedures and practices by shifting the responsibilities on the independent directors to act as a watchdog to look after the function of director and protect the minority shareholders' interest, along with other new unique and mandatory provisions.

The foundation of the new Companies Act, 2013 are based on few broad principles such as:

- Transparency
- Accountability
- Responsibility

The compliance of these three principles are ensured through the mandatory provisions plugged with penalties and prosecution.

COMPANIES ACT, 2013: SIGNIFICANT CHANGES

The present Act brings the unique provisions such as governance, e-management, compliance and enforcement, disclosure norms, auditors, and mergers and acquisitions. It also implements some new concepts such as one-person company, small companies, dormant company, class action suits, registered values, and corporate social responsibility.

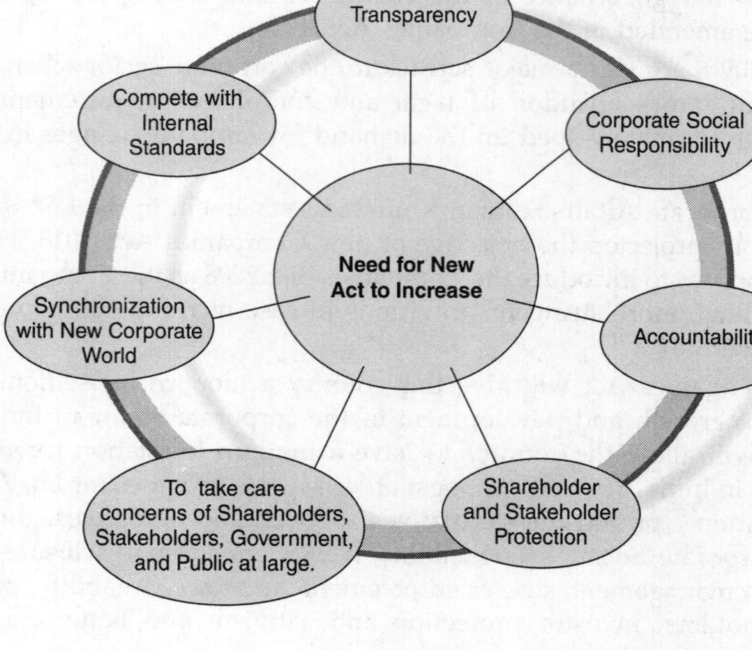

The Companies Act, 2013 passed by the Parliament received the assent of the President of India on 29th August 2013. The Act consolidates and amends the law relating to companies. The Companies Act, 2013 was notified in the Official Gazette on 30th August 2013. Some of the provisions of the Act have been implemented by a notification published on 12th September 2013. The provisions of the Companies Act, 1956 are still in force.[2]

Legislative History of the Companies Act, 2013

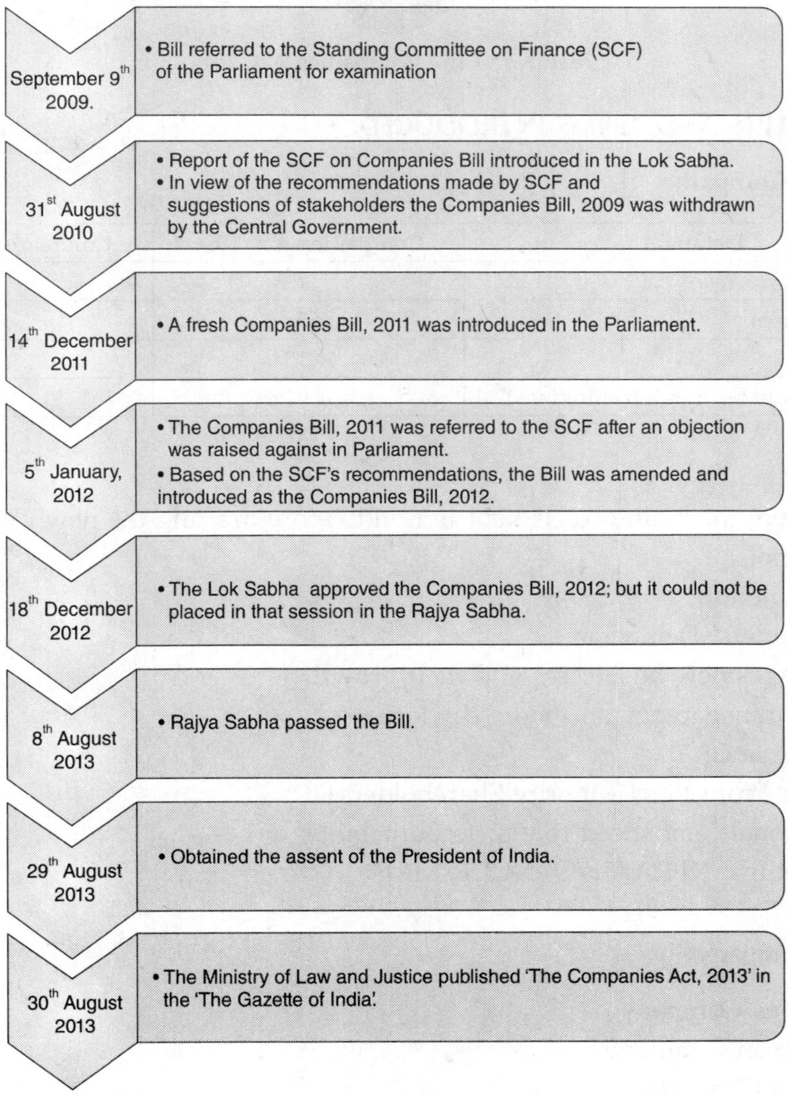

2. http://www.mca.gov.in/MinistryV2/companiesact.html

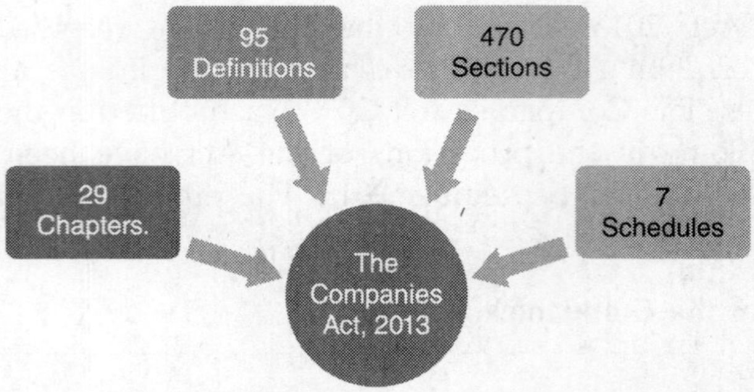

Features of the Companies Act, 2013

NEW CONCEPTS AND TERMS INTRODUCED

One Person Company

Details	Companies Act, 1956	Companies Act, 2013
Parts/Chapters	13	29
Sections/Clauses	658	470
Schedules	15	7
No. of clauses in Section 2 (Definitions)	67	95

Object

Following were the main objects kept in mind before drafting the new Companies Act

- De-controls
- Self-regulation
- Shareholders' Democracy
- Encourages new businesses and their growth
- Higher transparency and more disclosures
- E-Governance
- Investor Protection/Minority Shareholders
- Professionals' enhanced role & accountability
- New Setups: NFRA/SFIO/NCLT/MCP

Nature of Company

- Associates Company
- One Person Company
- Dormant Company

Director

- Independent Director
- Women Director
- Class Action
- CSR
- Register Value
- Private Placement
- Treasury Stock
- Rotation of Auditor
- Nature of Company

Associate Company

Section 2(6) Associate company, in relation to another company, means a company in which the other company has a significant influence, but which is not a subsidiary company of the company having such influence and includes a joint venture company.

Thus, associate company stands for a company having significant influence. It means control of at least 20% of total share capital, or of business decisions under an agreement, and which includes a joint venture company but does not include a subsidiary company.

One Person Company

This is a new concept introduced in this Act to enable the individual as an entrepreneur into the corporate world; if we consider it a most advanced version of sole-proprietor transformed into the 'company' it wouldn't be an exaggeration.

Section 2(62) 'One Person Company' means a company which has only one person as a member.

A person who is a citizen of India is eligible for incorporating such a company. There would be one director. He can himself be a director or appoint anyone else as a director.

Features of One Person Company:

- A person is eligible to incorporate or become nominee only for one 'One Person Company'.
- It can be limited by guarantee or share or be an unlimited.
- Minor is barred to become a member or nominee of the 'One Person Company' or can hold share with beneficial interest.
- In case of limited by share it has to qualify the following requirements as:
  - Minimum paid up capital of Rs 1 lac
  - Restrictions to transfer the share
  - Prohibition to invitation to public for any subscription

- Privilege or Exemption
    - Not required to hold the AGM (Annual General Meeting)

Dormant company

Another classification of company under the new act is Dormant Company under section 455, as when any company registered under this Act for future purpose or to hold an asset or intellectual property and has no significant accounting transaction. Such a company or an inactive one may apply to the Registrar of Companies (ROC) in such manner as may be prescribed for obtaining the status of a Dormant Company. The section says:

455. (1) Where a company is formed and registered under this Act for a future project or to hold an asset or intellectual property and has no significant accounting transaction, such a company or an inactive company may make an application to the Registrar in such manner as may be prescribed for obtaining the status of a dormant company.

Explanation: For the purposes of this section,—

(i) 'inactive company' means a company which has not been carrying on any business or operation, or has not made any significant accounting transaction during the last two financial years, or has not filed financial statements and annual returns during the last two financial years;

(ii) 'significant accounting transaction' means any transaction other than—

(a) payment of fees by a company to the Registrar;

(b) payments made by it to fulfil the requirements of this Act or any other law;

(c) allotment of shares to fulfil the requirements of this Act; and

(d) payments for maintenance of its office and records.

(2) The Registrar on consideration of the application shall allow the status of a dormant company to the applicant and issue a certificate in such form as may be prescribed to that effect.

(3) The Registrar shall maintain a register of dormant companies in such form as may be prescribed.

(4) In case of a company which has not filed financial statements or annual returns for two financial years consecutively, the Registrar shall issue a notice to that company and enter the name of such company in the register maintained for dormant companies.

(5) A dormant company shall have such minimum number of directors, file such documents and pay such annual fee as may be prescribed to the Registrar to retain its dormant status in the register and may become an active company on an application made in this behalf accompanied by such documents and fee as may be prescribed.

(6) The Registrar shall strike off the name of a dormant company from the register of dormant companies, which has failed to comply with the requirements of this section.

COMPANY SECRETARY'S NEW ROLE

Conventionally a Company Secretary was considered being a mere servant or clerk having no authority even to enter into a contract on behalf of the company; gradually he acquires some administrative authorities in the company, but certainly no managerial power.

Company secretary is considered to be the eyes and ears of the Board in the field of corporate governance. Being the expert in this field he is in the true sense natural conscience keeper for the corporate sector by ensuring and authenticating board processes and making sure that companies do the correct things, constantly.

In the new Companies Act, 2013, conceiving a comprehensive Corporate Governance model the Company Secretary's role is significant. It has introduced the concept of Key Managerial Personnel, has significantly elevated the new dimensions in terms of the roles and responsibilities of company secretaries both in employment and in practice. He is not simply to ensure compliance but also as to help the Management in taking a comprehensive view of all the issues that come up in a Company.

The new Companies Act holds the view that 'Company Secretary is not a luxury but a necessity'. Section 205 enunciates twofold functions of a Company Secretary: one is to report to the Board about compliance with the provisions of this Act, the rules made thereunder, and other laws applicable to the company, and two to ensure that the company complies with the applicable secretarial standards.

Section 203 of the new Act establishes mandatory provisions for appointment of whole-time Key Managerial Personnel (KMP) with respect to a certain class of companies to be prescribed by the Central Government. The new term KMP encompasses company secretary

As we have discussed, the Act aims at responsible corporate governance, with individual accountability and disclosures of their management. In such a situation the Company Secretary's role is to ensure compliance with provisions of the law. In case of non-compliance of the provisions of the law by the company, he is also an 'officer-in-default'.

Secretarial Audit Section 204

A new concept of Secretarial Audit has been introduced under the new Act, which is applicable on every listed company and companies belonging to prescribed class or classes of companies. It shall annex a secretarial audit report given by a company secretary in practice with its Board's report in a prescribed form by the Central

Government. The Board in its report shall give details of any qualifications or other remarks made by the Company Secretary in practice. Stringent penal provisions have been provided for non-compliance. If a company or any officer of the company or the company secretary in practice, contravenes the provisions of this section, the company, every officer of the company, or the company secretary in practice, who is in default, shall be punishable with fine which shall not be less than one lakh rupees but which may extend to five lakh rupees.

Secretarial Standards, Section 118

A provision related to Secretarial Standards, issued by the Institute of Company Secretaries of India constituted under section 3 of the Company Secretaries Act, 1980, also incorporated in the new Act by the Central Government under section 118(10) and in default penal provisions thereto as:

> *"Every company shall observe secretarial standards with respect to general and Board meetings specified by the Institute of Company Secretaries of India constituted under section 3 of the Company Secretaries Act, 1980, and approved as such by the Central Government.*
>
> *(11) If any default is made in complying with the provisions of this section in respect of any meeting, the company shall be liable to a penalty of twenty-five thousand rupees and every officer of the company who is in default shall be liable to a penalty of five thousand rupees.*
>
> *(12) If a person is found guilty of tampering with the minutes of the proceedings of meeting, he shall be punishable with imprisonment for a term which may extend to two years and with fine which shall not be less than twenty-five thousand rupees but which may extend to one lakh rupees."*

ROLE OF DIRECTOR

Independent Director

Section 149(6): An independent director in relation to a company, means a director other than a managing director or a whole-time director or a nominee director,

(a) who, in the opinion of the Board, is a person of integrity and possesses relevant expertise and experience;

(b) (i) who is or was not a promoter of the company or its holding, subsidiary or associate company;

(ii) who is not related to promoters or directors in the company, its holding, subsidiary or associate company;

(c) who has or had no pecuniary relationship with the company, its holding, subsidiary or associate company, or their promoters, or directors, during the two immediately preceding financial years or during the current financial year;

(d) none of whose relatives has or had pecuniary relationship or transaction with the company, its holding, subsidiary or associate company, or their promoters, or directors, amounting to two per cent or more of its gross turnover or total income or fifty lakh rupees or such higher amount as may be prescribed, whichever is lower, during the two immediately preceding financial years or during the current financial year;

(e) who, neither himself nor any of his relatives—

(i) holds or has held the position of a key managerial personnel or is or has been employee of the company or its holding, subsidiary or associate company in any of the three financial years immediately preceding the financial year in which he is proposed to be appointed;

(ii) is or has been an employee or proprietor or a partner, in any of the three financial years immediately preceding the financial year in which he is proposed to be appointed, of–

(A) a firm of auditors or company secretaries in practice or cost auditors of the company or its holding, subsidiary or associate company; or

(B) any legal or a consulting firm that has or had any transaction with the company, its holding, subsidiary or associate company amounting to ten per cent or more of the gross turnover of such firm;

(iii) holds together with his relatives two per cent or more of the total voting power of the company; or

(iv) is a Chief Executive or director, by whatever name called, of any nonprofit organization that receives twenty-five per cent or more of its receipts from the company, any of its promoters, directors or its holding, subsidiary or associate company or that holds two per cent or more of the total voting power of the company; or

(f) who possesses such other qualifications as may be prescribed.

(7) Every independent director shall at the first meeting of the Board in which he participates as a director and thereafter at the first meeting of the Board in every financial year or whenever there is any change in the circumstances which may affect his status as an independent director, give a declaration that he meets the criteria of independence as provided in sub-section (6).

Explanation: For the purposes of this section, 'nominee director' means a director nominated by any financial institution in pursuance of the provisions of any law for the time being in force, or of any agreement, or appointed by any Government, or any other person to represent its interests.

In Companies Act, 1956, there were no provisions of an Independent Director, which in the Act of 2013, these new provisions are incorporated.

Insertion of section 149(6): Independent Director is a new concept introduced in the Companies Act (though it is not a new concept for India as Clause 49 of the listing agreement under SEBI establishes mandatory provisions for all listed companies for the appointment of an Independent Director on the Board).

Clinical research of the above-mentioned section reveals that every aspect is being taken care of to keep intact the individual character of independent director for perfect corporate governance and protective measures for preventing the scandals in the company. We can perceive the intention of the phrase as 'a person of integrity and possesses the relevant expertise and experience'.

Rest of the provisions of the section are quite indicative that the legislature wants to save the independent director from any influence, that is why his appointment qualification specifies that he should not be a relative of any other director or there should not be any personal or pecuniary interest in the company. His tenure and remuneration and liability, etc., are the other provisions in the Act which ensure the impartial and independent charter of an independent director.

Women Director

An important feature of the new Act is to recognize the status of women and section 149(1) makes the mandatory provisions of one women director.

CLASS ACTION

Another new feature has been added in the new Companies Act 2013, as Class Action, under the same Section 245 under Chapter XVI on Prevention of Oppression and Mismanagement. This new concept establishes two unique features in the Act: One democracy decision against the majority system and second, a safety device for minority shareholders in the company. The root of the concept can be seen in US, and now it is an integral part of the new Companies Act.

What is Class Action?

Class action is a lawsuit which can be initiated by shareholders against the company as well as the auditors of the company.

Though the provisions are put under the same chapter 'Prevention of Oppression and Mismanagement' as was there in the Companies Act, 1956, but it is not the same as application as against oppression/mismanagement under sections 397 and 398 of the Companies Act, 1956. The objective of the section is not only to empower the minority shareholders or members of the company but also the depositors.

When Can Class Action be Exercised?

As per section 245, *'if they are of the opinion that the management or conduct of the affairs of the company are being conducted in a manner prejudicial to the interests of the company or its members or depositors...'*

Who Can Institute the Class Action?

There are two categories of members qualified by section 245 to institute the class action as:

1. Members
2. Depositors

Members

Section 245(3)(i) specifies that

In case of a company having share capital, member or members:

not less than 100 members of the company or

not less than 10% of the total number of its members, whichever is less or

any member or members singly or jointly holding not less than 10% of the issued share capital of the company.

Provided that the applicants have paid all calls and other sums due on their shares.

b) In case of a company not having a share capital, member or members:

not less than 1/5th of the total number of its members.

Depositors

The number of depositors shall not be less than 100 or

not less than 10% of the total number of its depositors, whichever is less or

any depositor or depositors singly or jointly holding not less than 10% of the total value of outstanding deposits of the company.

What Action Can be Claimed?

Section 245 specifies that

245. (1) Such number of member or members, depositor or depositors or any class of them, as the case may be, as are indicated in sub-section (2) may, if they are of the opinion that the management or conduct of the affairs of the company are being conducted in a manner prejudicial to the interests of the company or its members or depositors, file an application before the Tribunal on behalf of the members or depositors for seeking all or any of the following orders, namely:

(a) to restrain the company from committing an act which is ultra vires the articles or memorandum of the company;

(b) to restrain the company from committing breach of any provision of the company's memorandum or articles;

(c) to declare a resolution altering the memorandum or articles of the company as void if the resolution was passed by suppression of material facts or obtained by mis-statement to the members or depositors;

(d) to restrain the company and its directors from acting on such resolution;

(e) to restrain the company from doing an act which is contrary to the provisions of this Act or any other law for the time being in force;

(f) to restrain the company from taking action contrary to any resolution passed by the members;

(g) to claim damages or compensation or demand any other suitable action from or against –

(i) the company or its directors for any fraudulent, unlawful or wrongful act or omission or conduct or any likely act or omission or conduct on its or their part;

(ii) the auditor including audit firm of the company for any improper or misleading statement of particulars made in his audit report or for any fraudulent, unlawful or wrongful act or conduct;

(iii) any expert or advisor or consultant or any other person for any incorrect or misleading statement made to the company or for any fraudulent, unlawful or wrongful act or conduct or any likely act or conduct on his part;

(h) to seek any other remedy as the Tribunal may deem fit.

(2) Where the members or depositors seek any damages or compensation or demand any other suitable action from or against an audit firm, the liability shall be of the firm as well as of each partner who was involved in making any improper or misleading statement of particulars in the audit report or who acted in a fraudulent, unlawful or wrongful manner.

(3) (i) The requisite number of members provided in sub-section (1) shall be as under:

(a) in the case of a company having a share capital, not less than one hundred members of the company or not less than such percentage of the total number of its members as may be prescribed, whichever is less, or any member or members holding not less than such percentage of the issued share capital of the company as may be prescribed, subject to the condition that the applicant or applicants has or have paid all calls and other sums due on his or their shares;

(b) in the case of a company not having a share capital, not less than one-fifth of the total number of its members;

(ii) The requisite number of depositors provided in sub-section (1) shall not be less than one hundred depositors or not less than such percentage of the total number of depositors as may be prescribed, whichever is less, or any depositor or depositors to whom the company owes such percentage of total deposits of the company as may be prescribed.

(4) In considering an application under sub-section (1), the Tribunal shall take into account, in particular –

(a) whether the member or depositor is acting in good faith in making the application for seeking an order;

(b) any evidence before it as to the involvement of any person other than directors or officers of the company on any of the matters provided in clauses (a) to (f) of sub-section (1);

(c) whether the cause of action is one which the member or depositor could pursue in his own right rather than through an order under this section;

(d) any evidence before it as to the views of the members or depositors of the company who have no personal interest, direct or indirect, in the matter being proceeded under this section;

(e) where the cause of action is an act or omission that is yet to occur, whether the act or omission could be, and in the circumstances would be likely to be –

(i) authorised by the company before it occurs; or

(ii) ratified by the company after it occurs;

(f) where the cause of action is an act or omission that has already occurred, whether the act or omission could be, and in the circumstances would be likely to be, ratified by the company.

(5) If an application filed under sub-section (1) is admitted, then the Tribunal shall have regard to the following, namely:

(a) public notice shall be served on admission of the application to all the members or depositors of the class in such manner as may be prescribed;

(b) all similar applications prevalent in any jurisdiction should be consolidated into a single application and the class members or depositors should be allowed to choose the lead applicant and in the event the members or depositors of the class are unable to come to a consensus, the Tribunal shall have the power to appoint a lead applicant, who shall be in charge of the proceedings from the applicant's side;

(c) two class action applications for the same cause of action shall not be allowed;

(d) the cost or expenses connected with the application for class action shall be defrayed by the company or any other person responsible for any oppressive act.

(6) Any order passed by the Tribunal shall be binding on the company and all its members, depositors and auditor including audit firm or expert or consultant or advisor or any other person associated with the company.

(7) Any company which fails to comply with an order passed by the Tribunal under this section shall be punishable with fine which shall not be less than five lakh rupees but which may extend to twenty-five lakh rupees and every officer of the company who is in default shall be punishable with imprisonment for a term which may extend to three years and with fine which shall not be less than twenty-five thousand rupees but which may extend to one lakh rupees.

(8) Where any application filed before the Tribunal is found to be frivolous or vexatious, it shall, for reasons to be recorded in writing, reject the application and make an order that the applicant shall pay to the opposite party such cost, not exceeding one lakh rupees, as may be specified in the order.

(9) Nothing contained in this section shall apply to a banking company.

(10) Subject to the compliance of this section, an application may be filed or any other action may be taken under this section by any person, group of persons or any association of persons representing the persons affected by any act or omission, specified in sub-section (1).

Section 246. The provisions of sections 337 to 341 (both inclusive) shall apply mutatis mutandis, in relation to an application made to the Tribunal under section 241 or section 245.

CORPORATE SOCIAL RESPONSIBILITY (CSR)

There is no definition of CSR in the Act, though it specifies the areas where to spend under CSR. Section135 of the Act, establishes the mandatory provisions for CSR. Schedule VII suggests the list of activities which a company may opt as CSR. The mandate of the section is that the Corporate must spend 2% of average net profit during three preceding years of profits on social activities as specified in Schedule VII of the Act for social upliftment.

Application of CSR

Section 135 lists the mandatory provisions for the following companies:

- Net worth Rs 500 crore, or
- Turnover Rs 1000 crore, or
- Net profit Rs 5 crore.

Concept

CSR stands for Corporate Social Responsibility. It means a responsibility of the corporate to do something for the society, it is a management self-regulated model whereby the corporate plugs the social responsibilities, for sustainable development.

'Corporate Social Responsibility is the continuing commitment by business to contribute to economic development while improving the quality of life of the workforce and their families as well as of the community and society at large.'[3]

CSR also equalizes with philanthropic or charity model. The aim of CSR is to manage the business in a way which satisfies the ethical, commercial, legal, and public outlook; it is an action for social good beyond the self-interest of company.

3. WBCSD's definition of CSR.

In simple words CSR means that the corporate generate their revenue or profit through society towards which they also have some responsibility. It is considered after Bhopal Gas Tragedy, that the corporate make an impact to the society by their commercial activities, and they should be made responsible for rehabilitation and improvements of society which is being caused or going to be caused or apprehend to be caused by their activities.

CSR in India

Practically, the concept of CSR is not new for India, though it is being integrated with a statute now. If we look at the philosophy of Mahatma Gandhi his belief in 'Trusteeship' which means the capitalist is not the owner of their property but they are the trustees and should work for the well-being of society. Indeed the viewpoint of trusteeship, goodness of human being and ultimately to the society, without destroying the capitalist structure has been a part of Indian culture.

Apart from Gandhi's concept it is the tradition and cultural aspect of India —the service of society. There were a number of corporates who were doing such sustainable development voluntarily, now this concept is backed by the statute and the word 'Responsibility' in the CSR, stands for mandatory provision for it.

Areas Where to Spend Amount Under CSR as Specified in Schedule VII

There are nine broad areas where the amount has to be spent by the corporate as per the mandate of Section 135:

Activities relating to:

(i) eradicating extreme hunger and poverty;
(ii) promotion of education;
(iii) promoting gender equality and empowering women;
(iv) reducing child mortality and improving maternal health;
(v) combating human immunodeficiency virus, acquired immune deficiency syndrome, malaria and other diseases;
(vi) ensuring environmental sustainability;
(vii) employment enhancing vocational skills;
(viii) social business projects;
(ix) contribution to the Prime Minister's National Relief Fund or any other fund set up by the Central Government or the State Governments for socio-economic development and relief and funds for the welfare of the Scheduled Castes, the Scheduled Tribes, other backward classes, minorities and women; and
(x) such other matters as may be prescribed.

Procedure

A CSR Committee should be constituted with three directors out of which one should be an independent director; the committee shall formulate and recommend to the Board about the Corporate Social Responsibility Policy (CSRP), which shall indicate the activities as per Schedule VII, and to recommend the amount of expenditure on the CSR.

REGISTER VALUER

Section 247 under Chapter XVII of the Act makes the provisions for Register Valuer for valuation which is required to be made in respect of any property, stocks, shares, debentures, securities or goodwill, or any other assets, or new worth of a company or its liabilities.

The Central Government or any authority, institution or agency, as may be notified by the Central Government, shall maintain a register to be called the Register of Valuers in which there shall be a register containing the names, addresses and other details of the persons as valuers in pursuance of section 247.

Who are Eligible for Register Valuer

Following are the persons who are eligible to register themselves as a register valuer:

(a) chartered accountant;

(b) company secretary;

(c) cost accountant who is in whole-time practice;

(d) retired member of Indian Corporate Law Service;

(e) any person holding equivalent Indian or foreign qualification as the Ministry of Corporate Affairs may recognize by an order; provided that such foreign qualification acquired by Indian citizen;

(f) Merchant Banker registered with the Securities and Exchange Board of India, and who has in his employment person(s) having qualifications prescribed under (a) above to carry out valuation by such qualified persons;

(g) member of the Institute of Engineers and who is in whole-time practice;

(h) member of the Institute of Architects and who is in whole-time practice;

(i) a person or entity possessing necessary competence and qualification as may be notified by the Central Government from time to time.

Provided that persons referred to in (a), (c), and (d) and qualified person in (b) above shall have not less than five years continuous experience after acquiring membership of respective institutions.

Provided further that in the case of merchant banker the valuation report shall be signed by the qualified person.

Provided also that persons referred to in (a) and (b) shall be in respect of requirement for a 'financial valuation' and the persons referred to in (c) and (d) shall be in respect of requirement for a 'technical valuation' and a person or a firm or limited liability partnership or merchant banker possessing both the qualifications may act in dual capacity.

Explanation: For the purposes of this rule, a person shall be deemed 'to be in whole-time practice', when individually or in partnership or in limited liability partnership or in merchant banker with other persons in practice who are members of other professional bodies, he, in consideration of remuneration received or to be received:

- engages himself in the practice of valuation; or
- offers to perform or performs services involving valuation of any assets with the objective of arriving at financial value of the asset being valued;
- renders professional services or assistance in or about matters of principle or detail relating to valuation.

Nature of the Section

The language of the section is mandatory in nature by using the word "shall" in terms of contravene the provisions of the section and fixing the minimum limit for pecuniary penalty.

If a valuer contravenes any provision of this section or the rules made thereunder, the valuer shall be punished with a fine which shall not be less than rupees twenty-five thousand which may extend to one lakh rupees. And if the intention of the valuer has contravened such provisions with the intention to defraud the company or its member, he shall be punished with imprisonment for a term which may extend to one year and with a fine which shall not be less then one lakh rupees which may extend to five lakh rupees.

The legislature is intended to strict compliance and corporate governance.

PRIVATE PLACEMENT

Private placement of securities is yet another change in the Companies Act, 2013. The provision is different from public fund. The definition of private placement is defined under sub section (ii) of explanation II of section 42 as:

'Private placement means any offer of securities or invitation to subscribe securities to a select group of persons by a company (other than by way of public offer) through issue of a private placement offer letter and which satisfies the conditions specified in this section.'

The offer or invitation to securities is limited to 50 or as may be prescribed; it is also important to note that qualified institutional buyers and employees of the company are to be offered securities under a scheme of employee stock options as per provision under section 62(1)(b).

Bar on Fresh Offer

Sub-section (3) of section 42 bars any fresh offer or invitation under this section unless the previous allotments have been completed or that offer or invitation has been withdrawn or abandoned by the company. It means that through this rider the legislature intended to clear or execute the previous offer or invitation so that any fraud or default may be prevented.

Mandatory Compliance

The mandate of sub-section (4) of section 42 is that any offer or invitation in compliance with the provision of this section shall be treated as a public offer, and it is mandatory under the provisions to comply with Securities Contracts (Regulations) Act, 1956, and the Securities and Exchange Board of India Act, 1992.

Safety Measures

Payment by cash bar

To prevent any type of misdemeanor or fraud certain safety measures have been put in place under section 42 as, all monies payable toward subscription of securities under this section shall be paid through cheque or demand draft or other available banking channels; making payment by cash is barred.

Repayment of money in time-bound manner

The mandate of sub-section (6) of section 42 is that the securities shall be allotted within 60 days from the date of receipt of the application money for such securities, and if the company fails to allot such securities within 60 days, it has to repay the application money to the subscriber within 15 days from the date of completion of 60 days, and if company fails to repay the application money within the aforesaid period (15 days), the company shall be liable to repay that money with 12% p.a. interest.

Separate bank account

Another safety devise is being fitted in the section as there shall be a separate banking account in a scheduled bank, and that will not be utilised for any other purpose other than:

- for adjustment against allotment of securities; or
- for the repayment of monies where the company is unable to allot the securities.

Record of subscriber

Under sub-section (7) of section 42 it is specified that the offer shall be made only to those persons whose names are recorded by the company prior to the invitation to subscribe and that such a person shall receive the offer by name, and the complete record of such person shall be kept by the company, and the complete information about such offer shall be filed with the Registrar within 30 days of circulation of relevant private placement offer letter.

No advertisement to public at large

The mandate of sub-section (8) of section 42 bars any public advertisement or utilizing any media, marketing or distribution channels, or agent to inform the public at large.

Penalty

As per sub-section (10) of section 42, if any company contravenes any provision of section 42, the promoters and directors shall be liable for a penalty which may extend to the amount involved in the offer or invitation or 2 crore rupees, whichever is higher. And the company also returns all monies to subscribers within a period of 30 days of the order imposing the penalty.

TREASURY STOCK

Treasury stock is a share stock that an issuing company repurchases or buys back from its shareholders, or open market, or through merger and acquisition, as there are restrictions that a company cannot hold its own stock and it is provided that as per section 77 of Companies Act, 1956 the company could hold it by way of trust or a special purpose entity.

It has been experienced that the promoters of the companies use the treasury as stocks a way to accumulate their holding in the companies to raise funds and manipulate in voting right, which ultimately ends up increasing the control of the promoters, and to some extent to the minority shareholders. As there was no provision related to treasury stocks in the previous Companies Act, 1956, in the new Act of 2013, it constitutes the restrictive provision related to it.

ROTATION OF AUDITOR

Another important provision has been constituted in the new Companies Act, 2013 is the rotation of auditors. Section 139 gives its mandate on the same as:

> No listed company or a company belonging to such class or classes of companies as may be prescribed, shall appoint or re-appoint—
>
> (a) an individual as auditor for more than one term of five consecutive years; and

(b) an audit firm as auditor for more than two terms of five consecutive years:

Provided that–

(i) an individual auditor who has completed his term under clause (a) shall not be eligible for re-appointment as auditor in the same company for five years from the completion of his term;

(ii) an audit firm which has completed its term under clause (b), shall not be eligible for re-appointment as auditor in the same company for five years from the completion of such term:

Provided further that as on the date of appointment no audit firm having a common partner or partners to the other audit firm, whose tenure has expired in a company immediately preceding the financial year, shall be appointed as auditor of the same company for a period of five years.

The nature of the section is negative which prohibits the re-appointment of individual auditor and auditor firm for more than five consecutive years and two terms of five consecutive years, respectively, for the prescribed companies under the Act. It is also an important feature that such restrictions are also applicable to the common partners of the firm.

INSIDER TRADING

A provision relating to Insider Trading regulated by Securities and Exchange Board of India for listed Indian companies, and Companies Act, 1956 was silent about it.

To remove such difficulties Insider Trading is being comprehensively defined and prohibited under section 195 of Companies Act, 2013.

NEW DEFINITIONS

These are some new definitions that have been introduced in the the Companies Act, 2013 as:

Section 2(16): 'Charge' means an interest or lien created on the property or assets of a company or any of its undertakings or both as security and includes a mortgage.

There was definition of 'Charge' in the Companies Act 1956, earlier.

Section 2 (62) 'One Person Company' means a company which has only one person as a member.

The Companies (Amendment) Act, 2015, has changed the definition 2(68) as

In section 2 of the Companies Act, 2013 (here in after referred to as the Principal Act), –

(i) in clause (68), the words "of one lakh rupees or such higher paid-up share capital" shall be omitted;

It means the minimum paid-up share capital requirement of INR 100,000 in case of a private company under CA 2013 has been done away with.

Section 2(85)* "Small Company" means a company, other than a public company,—

(i) paid-up share capital of which does not exceed fifty lakh rupees or such higher amount as may be described which shall not be more than five crore rupees; or

(ii) turnover of which as per its last profit and loss account does not exceed two crore rupees or such higher amount as may be prescribed which shall not be more than twenty crore rupees.

---

i Ministry of Corporate Affairs order

New Delhi, the 13th February, 2015

S.O. 504(E).—Whereas, the Companies Act, 2013 (18 of 2013) (hereinafter referred to as the said Act) received the assent of the President on the 29th August, 2013;

And whereas, clause (85) of section 2 of the said Act provides for definition of the term "small company";

And whereas, clause (b) of sub-section (11) of section 186 of the said Act provides that the requirements of provisions of section 186 [except sub-section (1) of the said section] shall not apply to any acquisition made by a non-banking financial company registered under Chapter IIIB of the Reserve Bank of India Act, 1934 (2 of 1934) and any other company whose principal business is acquisition of securities;

And whereas, such provisions of clause (85) of section 2 and section 186 of the said Act had come into force on the 1st day of April, 2014;

And whereas, the following difficulties have arisen in giving effect to the above provisions of the said Act:-

(a) According to clause (85) of section 2, a company may be treated as a 'small company' if it meets either of the conditions provided therein thereby making the second limit unrestricted or inconsequential. Difficulties have arisen in this regard as companies which, though, meet one of the criteria but exceed the monetary limit in respect of second criteria excessively are also getting classified as 'small companies'; and

(b) in clause (b) of sub-section (11) of section 186, in the absence of provisions for exemption to a banking company or an insurance company or a housing finance company making acquisition of securities in its ordinary course of business, a difficulty has arisen that such companies cannot make any acquisition of securities in their ordinary course of business;

Now, therefore, in exercise of the powers conferred by sub-section (1) of section 470 of the Companies Act, 2013 (18 of 2013), the Central Government hereby makes the following Order to remove the aforesaid difficulties, namely:-

(1) Short title and commencement.—(1) This Order may be called the Companies (Removal of Difficulties) Order, 2015.

(2) It shall come into force on the date of its publication in the Official Gazette.

2. In the Companies Act, 2013 (hereinafter referred to as the said Act),—

(a) in section 2, in clause (85), in sub-clause (i), for the word "or" occurring at the end, the word "and" shall be substituted; and

(b) in section 186 of the said Act, in sub-section (11), in clause (b), after item (iii), the following item shall be inserted, namely:—

"(iv) made by a banking company or an insurance company or a housing finance company, making acquisition of securities in the ordinary course of its business.".

[F. No. 1/13/2013-CL.V-Part]

AMARDEEP SINGH BHATIA, Jt. Secy.

Provided that nothing in this clause shall apply to—

(A) a holding company or a subsidiary company;

(B) a company registered under section 8; or

(C) a company or body corporate governed by any special Act;

The concept of 'small company' has been introduced for the first time in the Companies Act, 2013. If we analyse the definition with 'One Person Company' it seems that the 'small company' concept is nearer to 'One Person Company'. In terms of privilege and exemption in compliance but small company, under the Companies Act, 2013 enjoy more privilege.

In fact the ideas behind introducing these new concepts are to promote entrepreneurship which ultimately gives movement to the economic growth.

IMPROVEMENT IN RESPONSIBILITIES AND ACCOUNTABILITY ON THE PART OF COMPANIES

Key Managerial Personnel

To achieve the desired objectives, responsibilities and compliance a new concept of Key Managerial Personal (KMP) has been introduced in the Companies Act, 2013, which ultimately amplifies adherence to good corporate governance practices by guiding the Boards to achieve their defined objectives.

Section 2 (51) of the Act defines KPM as:

(51) "Key managerial personnel", in relation to a company, means—

(i) the Chief Executive Officer or the managing director or the manager;

(ii) the company secretary;

(iii) the time director;

(iv) the Chief Financial Officer; and

(v) such other officer as may be prescribed.

Thus, section 2(51) seems to be the substantive provision for KMP, which qualifies the person who can be the KMP, while section 203 of the Act talks about the appointment of the act.

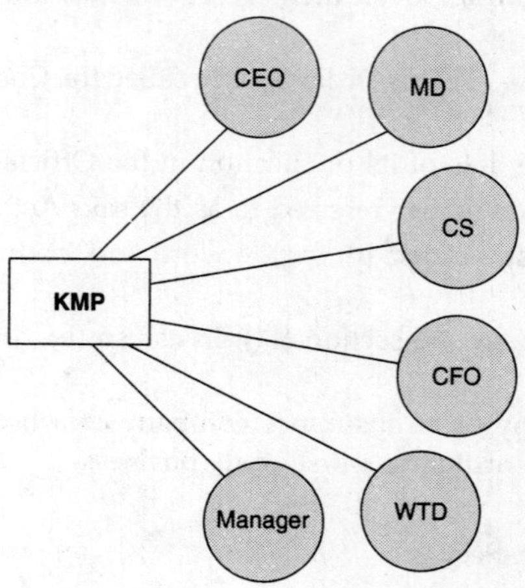

Section mandatory in nature as:

Every company belonging to such class or classes of companies as may be prescribed shall have the following whole-time key managerial personnel,—

(i) managing director, or Chief Executive Officer or manager and in their absence, a whole-time director;

(ii) company secretary; and

(iii) Chief Financial Officer:

Provided that an individual shall not be appointed or reappointed as the chairperson of the company, in pursuance of the articles of the company, as well as the managing director or Chief Executive Officer of the company at the same time after the date of commencement of this Act unless,—

(a) the articles of such a company provide otherwise; or

(b) the company does not carry multiple businesses:

Provided further that nothing contained in the first proviso shall apply to such class of companies engaged in multiple businesses and which has appointed one or more Chief Executive Officers for each such business as may be notified by the Central Government.

(2) Every whole-time key managerial personnel of a company shall be appointed by means of a resolution of the Board containing the terms and conditions of the appointment including the remuneration.

(3) A whole-time key managerial personnel shall not hold office in more than one company except in its subsidiary company at the same time:

Provided that nothing contained in this sub-section shall disentitle a key managerial personnel from being a director of any company with the permission of the Board:

Provided further that whole-time key managerial personnel holding office in more than one company at the same time on the date of commencement of this Act, shall, within a period of six months from such commencement, choose one company, in which he wishes to continue to hold the office of key managerial personnel:

Provided also that a company may appoint or employ a person as its managing director, if he is the managing director or manager of one, and of not more than one, other company and such appointment or employment is made or approved by a resolution passed at a meeting of the Board with the consent of all the directors present at the meeting and of which meeting, and of the resolution to be moved thereat, specific notice has been given to all the directors then in India.

(4) If the office of any whole-time key managerial personnel is vacated, the resulting vacancy shall be filled-up by the Board at a meeting of the Board within a period of six months from the date of such vacancy.

(5) If a company contravenes the provisions of this section, the company shall be punishable with fine which shall not be less than one lakh rupees but which may extend to five lakh rupees and every director and key managerial personnel of the company who is in default shall be punishable with fine which may extend to fifty thousand rupees and where the contravention is a continuing one, with a further fine which may extend to one thousand.

TRANSPARENCY

To achieve transparency in governance certain discloser mechanisms have been put in place under the new Companies Act, 2013 such as:

- Formulation and implementation of risk management policy
- Formulation of Social Responsibility (CSR) policy
- Filing of return with Registrar of Companies, mandatory for every listed company regarding change in shareholding pattern of promoters and top ten shareholders of company.

Protection

- Class action suit
- Exit option to shareholders

Remedy— Regulatory Authorities

- Serious Fraud Investigating Officer (SFIO) has been given statutory status under section 211, to investigate frauds relating to a company.
- Composition of National Company Law Tribunal (NCLT): To give the effect of Supreme Court's judgment on the 11th May 2010, for the composition and constitution of the tribunal.
- Mediation and Conciliation Penal— Section 442 makes the provision for mediation and conciliation as the Central Government shall maintain a panel of experts to be called as the 'Mediation and Conciliation Penal' for mediation between the parties during the pendency of any proceedings before the Central Government or the Tribunal or the Appellate Tribunal.
- Company Prosecutors—Section 443: The Central Government may appoint company prosecutors for the conduct of prosecutions arising out of this Act. The Company Prosecutor shall have all the powers and privileges conferred on Public Prosecutors appointed under the Code on Criminal Procedure, 1973.

Application of Section 203

The application of section 203 on every listed company and every other company having a paid-up share capital of five crore rupees or more shall have whole-time key managerial personnel, by the draft rule 13.6 of Chapter XIII Appointment of Key Managerial Personnel.

AMENDMENT AND CHANGES IN THE COMPANIES ACT, 1956

The objective of the Companies Act, 1956 was to consolidate and amend the law relating to companies and other organizations, and during fifty-five years it was amended almost twenty-five times to accommodate changes at national and international platform. To meet such changes and to make more protection and transparency in company operations and functions a Bill was introduced in 2009 which ultimately became the foundation of The Companies Act, 2013.

Following are some of the salient features of the new Companies Act, 2013:

Governance

- At least one woman director
- At least one Indian resident director
- Independent director (ID) legislated; role and responsibilities defined
- Database of IDs to be maintained; may select IDs from this database
- One-person company permitted unlike minimum two before
- Maximum directors increased to fifteen; any additional director(s) only through special resolution
- Maximum twenty directorships per person; maximum ten public companies
- Stakeholders Relationship Committee introduced
- Mandatory appointment of Key Management Personnel (KMP)
- Directors responsible for design and operating effectiveness of internal financial controls
- Significantly enhanced penalties for directors

Financial Statements and Auditors

- Consolidated financial statements mandatory for all groups, including unlisted/ private companies, with more than one entity; includes associates or joint ventures;
- Mandatory rotation of audit firm for listed companies post 10 years
- Financial year for all companies to be March 31 (exception for subsidiaries of foreign entities)
- Re-casting and re-statement of financial statements can be ordered. Voluntary revision of financial statements for previous periods now permitted
- Auditor to also report on adequacy of internal financial controls system and the operating effectiveness of such controls
- Increased restrictions on non-audit services provided by auditors

- Auditor to be a whistleblower to Central Government, if becomes aware of any fraud
- The maximum limit of 20 companies per partner in an audit firm
- Prescribed companies to appoint internal auditor; manner, period and reporting to be prescribed by the Central Government
- Significant enhancement of penalties for auditors

Mergers and Restructuring

- Restriction on multilayered structures (certain exemptions to foreign acquisitions/ to comply with law)
- Mergers without Tribunal approval permitted between two small companies or between a holding company and its wholly-owned subsidiary
- Merger into a foreign companies introduced
- Valuation report mandatory along with notice to concerned parties in case of proposed mergers
- Scheme of compromise or arrangement must be in line with accounting standards; auditors' certificate attesting needed
- In case of 'reverse merger' of listed company into unlisted company, the transferor may continue to be unlisted
- Holding of treasury shares directly or through a trust, prohibited

Other Miscellaneous Provisions

- 2% of the average net profit of preceding three financial years to be spent annually on Corporate Social Responsibility (CSR) or explain why not; for Companies with net worth of Rs 500 crore or more, turnover of Rs 1000 crore or more, or net profit more than Rs 5 crore
- Valuations for any property, stocks, shares, goodwill or any other assets, net worth of a company, etc., must be performed by a registered valuer
- Class action suits introduced as a remedy for small investors against wrongful acts
- Establishment of a National Financial Reporting Authority (NFRA) with the objective of monitoring and enforcing compliance of auditing and accounting standards
- Establishment of a vigil mechanism (whistle blowing) in the prescribed manner by every listed company
- Deposit accepted (including interest due) to be repaid within one year from enactment or from due date of such payments, whichever is earlier

IMPLICATIONS ON PRIVATE COMPANIES

Companies Act, 2013 seems to suspend the exemptions which were applicable under the Companies Act, 1956. The new Act intends to simplify the commercial behaviour and economic growth for the company, if it complies and works in an honest legal environment.

Increase in Number of Members

Section 2(68)(ii) increased the limit of the number of members/shareholders to a maximum of 200 which were restricted to 50 in the earlier act.

Commencement of Business

Companies Act, 2013, section 11 gives the mandate that before commencement of business or exercising any borrowing power.

It was mandatory to all companies to file the following additional declarations with the Registrar: power:

(i) declaration by a director that minimum paid-up share capital has been paid; and

(ii) company has filed verification of registered office.

In the Companies (Amendment) Act 2015, this section 11 has been omitted, and all the above-mentioned requirements have been done away with.

Further Issue of Share Capital

Under the old Act the private company was not allowed to rights issue and preferential allotment, while such restriction has been suspended in the new Act. The private company can make further allotment only by means of rights issue, ESOP or Private Placement/ Preferential Allotment, subject to compliance of section 62 of the Companies Act, 2013.

Loan to Director

In the old Act the private company was exempted to provide any loan, advances, securities, or guarantees to director and other interested entities, whereas in the Companies Act, 2013, under section 185, such restrictions, are imposed on a private company as well.

Also in the Companies Act, 1956, a company can only receive deposits from its members, i.e., directors of the companies, but under the new Companies Act, 2013 such a restriction to public subscription of shares or debentures has been extended to include all types of securities.

Share Capital and Debentures

Provisions of Section 86 of the Companies Act, 1956, were not applicable on private companies, while Section 43 of the Companies Act, 2013 are applicable on private company with reference to issue shares with differential voting rights.

Appointment of Key Managerial Person

This is a new concept which is applicable on private companies also. Compared to section 269 of the Companies Act, 1956, which mandated a private company, which is a subsidiary of a public company, having a paid-up capital of such sum as may be prescribed, shall have a managing or whole-time director or manager, and further in section 383A, prescribed that every company having such a paid-up share capital shall have a whole-time secretary, and where the Board of Directors of any such company comprises only two directors neither of them shall be the secretary of the company.

As per the mandate of Section 269 & 383A of the Companies Act, 1956, private companies were bound to appoint a managing director or whole-time director or manager except a whole-time company secretary only in the situation when paid-up capital of the company was rupees five crore or more.

While in the Companies Act, 2013, as per the mandate of section 203, every company (means private company also) is required to have the following whole-time key managerial persons, if the company has paid up capital of rupees five crores or more.

(i) Managing Director or Chief Executive Officer or in their absence, a Whole-Time Director

(ii) Company Secretary; and

(iii) Chief Financial Officer.

Company to have Board of Directors (Resident Director)

According to the Companies Act, 2013, under section 149 (3), every company shall have at least one director who has stayed in India for a total period of not less than 182 days in the previous calendar year. The Companies Act, 1956 did not specify such a provision.

Social Corporate Responsibility

This is also a new concept in the Companies Act, 2013, which specifies that every company having a net worth of rupees five hundred crore or more, or turnover of rupees one thousand crore or more, or a net profit of rupees five crore or more during any financial year shall constitute a Corporate Social Responsibility Committee. Such a provision was not available in the Companies Act, 1956.

SECTIONS NOTIFIED TILL DATE AND CIRCULARS OR ORDERS ISSUED

Certain requirements which were applicable only on the Public Companies under the Companies Act, 1956 were extended to the Private Companies also in the new Companies Act, 2014, such as saving sections (Section 90 of Companies Act, 1956) which deal with share capital and voting rights.

Further, the Companies Act, 2013 restricts certain powers of the Board of Directors, such as:

- To dispose of, or sell or lease, or otherwise whole or part the company's undertaking;
- To borrow money more than the aggregate of its paid-up share capital and free reserves.
- To execute such powers, a special resolution should be pass by the Board of the company.

Certain other restrictions which are imposed in the Companies Act, 2013 such as appointment of managerial personnel, requirement related to social corporate responsibilities, appointment of managing director, whole-time director or manager, etc. will discussed in the subsequent chapters.

S. No.	Provisions of Companies Act, 2013 as notified (98 + 1 + 183 = 282 Sections)	Corresponding provisions of Companies Act, 1956	Corresponding provisions of Companies Act, 1956 continue to remain in force
1.	Section 2		
	Clause (1)	2(1)	Nil
	Clause (2)	211(3C)	Nil
	Clause (3)	2(1A)	Nil
	Clause (4)	2(1B)	Nil
	Clause (5)	2(2)	Nil
	Clause (6)	Nil	Nil
	Clause (7)	Nil	Nil
	Clause (8)	Nil	Nil
	Clause (9)	2(5)	Nil
	Clause (10)	2(6); 252(3)	Nil
	Clause (11)	2(7)	Nil
	Clause (12)	2(8)	Nil
	Clause (13)	209(1)	Nil
	Clause (14)	2(9)	Nil
	Clause (15)	Nil	Nil
	Clause (16)	124	Nil
	Clause (17)	Explanation to section 33(2)	Nil
	Clause (18)	Nil	Nil

Contd...

S. No.	Provisions of Companies Act, 2013 as notified (98 + 1 + 183 = 282 Sections)	Corresponding provisions of Companies Act, 1956	Corresponding provisions of Companies Act, 1956 continue to remain in force
	Clause (19)	Nil	Nil
	Clause (20)	2(10) and 3	Nil
	Clause (21)	2(23) and 12(2)(b)	Nil
	Clause (22)	2(23) and 12(2)(a)	Nil
	Clause (24)	2(45)	Nil
	Clause (25)	2(45A)	Nil
	Clause (26)	Nil	428 The term 'Contributory' shall continue for the purposes of winding up.
	Clause (27)	Nil	Nil
	Clause (28)	233B(1)	Nil
	Clause (29)(except sub-clause (iv)	2(11), 2(14), 10	622

To Remember

Reason to revamp the Companies Act, 1956

- Changes in the business and corporate environments
- Old act was not computable with changing commercial environment
- Misdemeanour and gross abandon of legal and compliance requirement

Foundation of new Companies Act, 2013

- Transparency
- Accountability
- Responsibility

Significant Changes

- De-controls
- Self Regulation
- Shareholders' Democracy
- Encourages new businesses and their growth
- Higher transparency and more disclosures
- E-Governance
- Investor Protection/Minority Shareholders

- Professionals' enhanced role and accountability
- New Setups: NFRA/SFIO/NCLT/MCP

Revival and Rehabilitation of Sick Industrial Companies

This chapter deals with procedure for sick companies to make a reference to the Tribunal, order of enquiry by the tribunal to decide whether a company has become sick, preparation and sanction of scheme, rehabilitation and consequences including winding up of sick companies.

J.J. Irani Committee's recommendations on revival and rehabilitation find place in the Companies Act, 2013. It is important to note the Companies Act, 1956 talked only to revival and rehabilitation of "Sick industrial companies" while the Companies Act, 2013 not merely applies to sick industrial companies but all sick companies.

Previous efforts with regards to rehabilitation of companies, such as Sick Industrial Companies Act, 1985 (SICA), or Securitisation and Reconstruction of Financial Assets and Enforcement of Security Interest Act, 2002 (SARFAESI Act) failed to achieve its real objective, with regard to rehabilitation of companies, provisions of the Companies Act, 2013 with regard to rehabilitation of companies, creates a new hope to the secured creditors of the companies.

The Companies Act, 2013, has also modified the definition of the "Sick Company" from **accumulated losses exceed the net, to company has failed to pay the debt within a specified period of 30 days.**

The Companies Act, 2013, also makes penal provisions more stringent, and all other affairs and activities related to revival and rehabilitation are to be completed in time bound manner.

Determination of sickness

Section 253(1)

Where on a demand by the secured creditors of a company representing fifty per cent. or more of its outstanding amount of debt, the company has failed to pay the debt within a period of thirty days of the service of the notice of demand or to secure or compound it to the reasonable satisfaction of the creditors, any secured creditor may file an application to the Tribunal in the prescribed manner along with the relevant evidence for such default, non-repayment or failure to offer security or compound it, for a determination that the company be declared as a sick company.

The determination of sickness of a company depends on the following situation:

- The company has failed to pay the debt within a period of 30 days of the service of the notice of demand made by 50% the secured creditors of a company
- The company has failed to secure or compound the debt to the reasonable satisfaction of the creditors

The Tribunal may determine a company to be sick on application made before it by the creditors of the company or upon any reference made before it.

Under the provision of Sub-section (5) of Section 253 the Central Government or the Reserve Bank of India or a State Government or a public financial institution or a state level institution or a scheduled bank may, if it has sufficient reasons to believe that any company has become, for the purposes of this Act, a sick company, make a reference in respect of such company to the Tribunal for determination of the measures which may be adopted with respect to such company:

Section 253(2 & 4) The secured creditor may also make an application for determination of sickness and for the stay of any proceeding for the winding up of the company or; for execution, distress or the like against any property and assets of the company or; for the appointment of a receiver in respect thereof and that no suit for the recovery of any money or for the enforcement of any security against the company shall lie or be proceeded with. The tribunal may pass an order which shall be operative for one hundred and twenty days.

Section 253(6) proves to secure the interest of creditors as when an application under sub-section (1) or sub-section (4) of section 253 has been filed in such case the company shall not dispose of or otherwise enter into any obligation with regard to its properties or assets except as required in the normal course of business, and the Board of Directors shall not take any steps likely to prejudice the interests of the creditors.

Section 253(7) imposes an obligation on the tribunal that, the Tribunal shall, within a period of sixty days of the receipt of an application under sub-section (1) or sub-section (4), determine whether the company is a sick company or not, with a rider that such determination shall be made in respect of an application under sub-section (1) unless the company has been given notice of the application and a reasonable opportunity to reply to the notice within thirty days of the receipt thereof.

Section 253(8) & (9) says that the tribunal make the decision whether a company is sick after taking into consideration all the available relevant facts and circumstances, and pass an order in writing with this respect within a specific time with any condition or restrictions may deem fit.

Revival and Rehabilitation

Revival and rehabilitation, is a new provision which has been added in Companies Act, 2013. The Companies Act, 1956 did not have such provisions.

Section 254 uses the word Revival and Rehabilitation, which shows the intention of the legislature is not only to revive the sick companies but there should be measures for rehabilitation, the intention can be seen under section 269 by creating rehabilitation and insolvency fund for the purposes of rehabilitation, revival and liquidation of the sick companies, such fund is supported by:

(a) the grants made by the Central Government for the purposes of the fund;
(b) the amount deposited by the companies as contribution to the fund;
(c) the amount given to the fund from any other source; and
(d) the income from investment of the amount in the fund.

A company which has contributed any amount to the fund shall, in the event of proceedings initiated in respect of such company under this Chapter or Chapter XX, may make an application to the Tribunal for withdrawal of funds not exceeding the amount contributed by it, for making payments to workmen, protecting the assets of the company or meeting the incidental costs during proceedings.

The fund shall be managed by an administrator to be appointed by the Central Government in such manner as may be prescribed.

Section 254 says the procedure can be adopted for the same if an application to the Tribunal supported by audited financial statement of immediate financial year of the company along with a draft of revival and rehabilitation of such company or a declaration, within 60 days from the date of determination of the company as a sick company under section 253 of this Act, by the secured creditor or the Company for the determination of the measures with this respect.

However, such reference of scheme for revival and rehabilitation cannot be made before the Tribunal if:

- the secured creditors representing three-fourths in value of the amount outstanding against financial assistance disbursed to the borrower have taken measures to recover their secured debt under sub-section (4) of section 13 of the Securitisation and Reconstruction of Financial Assets and Enforcement of Security Interest Act, 2002: or;
- the financial assets of the sick company had been acquired by any securitisation company or reconstruction company under sub-section (1) of section 5 of the Securitisation and Reconstruction of Financial Assets and Enforcement of Security Interest Act, 2002, no such application shall be made without the consent of the securitisation company or reconstruction company which has acquired such assets.

As per section 254. (1)

"On the determination of a company as a sick company by the Tribunal under section 253, any secured creditor of that company or the company may make an application to the Tribunal for the determination of the measures that may be adopted with respect to the revival and rehabilitation of such company:

Provided that in case any reference had been made before the Tribunal and a scheme for revival and rehabilitation submitted, such reference shall abate if the secured creditors representing three-fourths in value of the amount outstanding against financial assistance disbursed to the borrower have taken measures to recover their secured debt under sub-section (4) of section 13 of the Securitisation and Reconstruction of Financial Assets and Enforcement of Security Interest Act, 2002:

Provided further that no reference shall be made under this section if the secured creditors representing three-fourths in value of the amount outstanding against financial assistance disbursed to the borrower have taken measures to recover their secured debt under sub-section (4) of section 13 of the Securitisation and Reconstruction of Financial Assets and Enforcement of Security Interest Act, 2002:

Procedure

After making the application under section 253, the Tribunal follows the following procedure:

Appointment of interim administrator under section 256

On the receipt of an application under section 254, the Tribunal shall, within seven days fix a date for hearing not later than ninety days from date of its receipt.

Section 256 Appoint an Interim Administrator

Appoint an interim administrator to convene a meeting of creditors of the company in accordance with the provisions of section 257 to be held not later than forty-five days from receipt of the order of the Tribunal appointing him to consider whether on the basis of the particulars and documents furnished with the application made under section 254, the draft scheme, if any, filed along with such application or otherwise and any other material available, it is possible to revive and rehabilitate the application for revival and rehabilitation sick company and such other matters, which the interim administrator may consider necessary for the purpose and to submit his report to the Tribunal within sixty days from the date of the order.

However, if no draft scheme is filed by the company and a declaration has been made to that effect by the Board of Directors, the Tribunal may direct the interim administrator to take over the management of the company; and issue such other directions to the interim administrator as the Tribunal may consider necessary to protect and preserve the assets of the sick company and for its proper management.

Where an interim administrator has been directed to take over the management of the company, the directors and the management of the company shall extend all possible assistance and cooperation to the interim administrator to manage the affairs of the company.

Section 257 Committee of Creditors

The interim administrator shall appoint a committee of creditors with such number of members as he may determine, but not exceeding seven, and as far as possible a representative each of every class of creditors should be represented in that committee.

The holding of the meeting of the committee of creditors and the procedure to be followed at such meetings, including the appointment of its chairperson, shall be decided by the interim administrator.

> The interim administrator may direct any promoter, director or any key managerial personnel to attend any meeting of the committee of creditors and to furnish such information as may be considered necessary by the interim administrator.

Section 258 Order of Tribunal

That the Tribunal on consideration of the report of the interim administrator filed under sub-section (1) of section 256, if the Tribunal is satisfied that the creditors representing three-fourths in value of the amount outstanding against the sick company present and voting have resolved that—

- it is not possible to revive and rehabilitate such company, the Tribunal shall record such opinion and order that the proceedings for the winding up of the company be initiated; or
- by adopting certain measures the sick company may be revived and rehabilitated, the Tribunal shall appoint a company administrator for the company and cause such administrator to prepare a scheme of revival and rehabilitation of the sick company.

The Tribunal may, if it thinks fit, appoint an interim administrator as the company administrator.

Section 259 Appointment of Administrator

The Tribunal may direct the company administrator to take over the assets or management of the company and for the purpose of assisting him in the management of the company, the company administrator may, with the approval of the Tribunal, engage the services of suitable expert or experts.

Section 259 Scheme of Revival and Rehabilitation

Section 259 makes the provision that the company administrator shall prepare or cause to be prepared a scheme of revival and rehabilitation of the sick company after considering the draft scheme filed along with the application under section 254 and provide for any one or more of the following measures, namely:

(a) financial reconstruction of the sick company;

(b) proper management of the sick company by any change in, or by taking over the management of such company;

(c) the amalgamation of—

  (i) the sick company with any other company; or

  (ii any other company with the sick company;

(d) takeover of the sick company by a solvent company;

(e) the sale or lease of a part or whole of any asset or business of the sick company;

(f) the rationalisation of managerial personnel, supervisory staff and workmen in accordance with law;

(g) such other preventive, ameliorative and remedial measures as may be appropriate;

(h) repayment or rescheduling or restructuring of the debts or obligations of the sick company to any of its creditors or class of creditors;

(i) such incidental, consequential or supplemental measures as may be necessary or expedient in connection with or for the purposes of the measures specified in clauses (a) to (h).

Section 259 Sanction of Scheme

Scheme placed before the creditors

The scheme prepared by the company administrator under section 261 shall be placed before the creditors of the sick company in a meeting convened for their approval by the company administrator within the period of sixty days from his appointment, which may be extended by the Tribunal up to a period not exceeding one hundred twenty days.

Submit the scheme before the Tribunal sanctioning the scheme

Then the company administrator shall convene separate meetings of the secured and unsecured creditors of the sick company and if the scheme is approved by the unsecured creditors representing one-fourth in value of the amount owed by the company to such creditors and the secured creditors, representing three-fourths in value of the amount outstanding against financial assistance disbursed by such creditors to the sick company, the company administrator shall submit the scheme before the Tribunal for sanctioning the scheme, however, the scheme relates to amalgamation of the sick company with any other company, such scheme shall, in addition to the approval of the creditors of the sick company under this sub-section, be laid before the general meeting of both the companies for approval by their respective shareholders and no such scheme shall be proceeded with unless it has been approved, with or without modification, by a special resolution passed by the shareholders of that company.

Scheme examination by the Tribunal

The scheme prepared by the company administrator shall be examined by the Tribunal and a copy of the scheme with modifications, if any, made by the Tribunal shall be sent, in draft, to the sick company and the company administrator and in the case of amalgamation, also to any other company concerned, and the Tribunal may publish or cause to be published the draft scheme in brief in such daily newspapers as the Tribunal may consider necessary, for suggestions and objections, if any, within such period as the Tribunal may specify.

The complete draft scheme shall be kept at the place where registered office of the company is situated or at such places as mentioned in the advertisement.

The Tribunal may make such modifications, if any, in the draft scheme as it may consider necessary in the light of the suggestions and objections received from the sick company and the company administrator and also from the transferee company and any other company concerned in the amalgamation and from any shareholder or any creditors or employees of such companies.

(4) On the receipt of the scheme under sub-section (3), the Tribunal shall within sixty days therefrom, after satisfying that the scheme had been validly approved in accordance with this section, pass an order sanctioning such scheme.

(5) Where a sanctioned scheme provides for the transfer of any property or liability of the sick company to any other company or person or where such scheme provides for the transfer of any property or liability of any other company or person in favour of the sick company, then, by virtue of, and to the extent

provided in the scheme, on and from the date of coming into operation of the sanctioned scheme or any provision thereof, the property shall be transferred to, and vest in and the liability shall become the liability of, such other company or person or, as the case may be, the sick company.

(6) The Tribunal may review any sanctioned scheme and make such modifications, as it may deem fit, or may by order in writing direct the company administrator, to prepare a fresh scheme providing for such measures as the company administrator may consider necessary.

(7) The sanction accorded by the Tribunal under sub-section (4) shall be conclusive evidence that all the requirements of the scheme relating to the reconstruction or amalgamation or any other measure specified therein have been complied with and a copy of the sanctioned scheme certified in writing by an officer of the Tribunal to be a true copy thereof shall in all legal proceedings be admitted as evidence.

(8) A copy of the sanctioned scheme referred to in sub-section (4) shall be filed with the Registrar by the sick company within a period of thirty days from the date of receipt of a copy thereof.

Effect and Enforcement of Scheme

No provision of law is useful without its effective enforcement and implementation, Section 263 and Section 264 is important to enforce and implementation of the scheme, the section gives mandate for two things.

- Legal enforceability (scheme to be binding u/s 263)
- Power to implementation of scheme (u/s 264)
- Punishment for certain offences (u/s 267)
- Bar of jurisdiction of any court for appeal (u/s 268)

Scheme to be binding

As per section 263 the scheme to be binding on the sick company and the transferee company or, as the case may be, the other company and also on the employees, shareholders, creditors and guarantors of the said companies.

Power to Implementation of Scheme

Section 264 for the purpose of effective implementation of the scheme, empower the Tribunal to enforce, modify or terminate any contract or agreement or any obligation pursuant to such agreement or contract entered into by the company with any other person.

If it deems necessary or expedient so to do, by order in writing, authorise the company administrator appointed under section 259 to implement a sanctioned scheme till its successful implementation on such terms and conditions as may be specified in the order and may for that purpose require him to file periodic reports on the implementation of the sanctioned scheme.

Where the whole or substantial assets of the undertaking of the sick company are sold under a sanctioned scheme, the sale proceeds shall be applied towards implementation of the scheme in such manner as the Tribunal may direct, the debtors and creditors shall have the power to scrutinise and make an appeal for review of the value before final order of fixing value.

Punishment for certain offences

Whoever violates the provisions of this Chapter or any scheme, or any order, of the Tribunal or the Appellate Tribunal or makes a false statement or gives false evidence before the Tribunal or the Appellate Tribunal or attempts to tamper with the records of reference or appeal filed under this Act, he shall be punishable with imprisonment for a term which may extend to seven years and with fine which may extend to ten lakh rupees.

Bar of jurisdiction

No appeal shall lie in any court or other authority and no civil court shall have any jurisdiction in respect of any matter in respect of which the Tribunal or the Appellate Tribunal is empowered by or under this Chapter and no injunction shall be granted by any court or other authority in respect of any action taken or proposed to be taken in pursuance of any power conferred by or under this Chapter.

Modification of the scheme

When it is difficult to implement the scheme for any reason or the scheme fails due to non-implementation of obligations under the scheme by the parties concerned then the company administrator authorised to implement the scheme, and where there is no such administrator, the company, the secured creditors, or the transferee company in a case of amalgamation, may make an application before the Tribunal for:

- modification of the scheme or
- to declare the scheme as failed and that the company may be wound up.

Order of Winding Up of Sick Company

Winding up of a company can be initiated on two grounds when:

- three-fourths in value of the secured creditors consent to the winding up of the company, the Tribunal may pass an order with this effect, or;
- winding up of company on the report of company administrator.

On the passing of an order the Tribunal shall conduct the proceedings for winding up of the sick company in accordance with the provisions of Chapter XX.

Damages against delinquent directors

If, in the course of the scrutiny or implementation of any scheme or proposal including the draft scheme or proposal, it appears to the Tribunal that any person who has taken part in the promotion, formation or management of the sick company or its undertaking, including any director, manager, officer or employee of the sick company who are or have been in employment of such company, the Tribunal shall be without prejudice to any other legal action that may be taken against the person including any punishment for fraud in the manner as provided in section 447:

(a) has misapplied or retained, or become liable or accountable for, any money or property of the sick company; or

(b) has been guilty of any misfeasance, malfeasance, non-feasance or breach of trust in relation to the sick company, it may, by order, direct him to repay or restore the money or property, with or without interest, as it thinks just, or to contribute such sum to the assets of the sick company or the other person, entitled thereto by way of compensation in respect of the misapplication, retainer, misfeasance, malfeasance, non-feasance or breach of trust as the Tribunal thinks just and proper.

However, if the Tribunal is satisfied on the basis of the information and evidence in its possession with respect to any person who is or was a director or an officer or other employee of the sick company, that such person by himself or along with others had diverted the funds or other property of such company for any purpose other than the purposes of the company or had managed the affairs of the company in a manner highly detrimental to the interests of the company, the Tribunal shall, by order, direct the public financial institutions, scheduled banks and State level institutions not to provide, for a maximum period of ten years from the date of the order, any financial assistance to such person or any firm of which such person is a partner or any company or other body corporate of which such person is a director, by whatever name called, or to disqualify the said director, promoter, manager from being appointed as a director in any company registered under this Act for a maximum period of six years.

To provide a reasonable opportunity of being heard to any person is mandatory before passing any order by the Tribunal under this section against any person.

CHAPTER

2

Company: Origin, Meaning, Features, and Nature

- History of Company
- Meaning and Definition of Company
- Characteristics of Company
- Lifting of Corporate Veil
- Formation of Company
- Classification of Companies
- Promoters
- Pre-incorporation Contracts

ORIGIN OF COMPANY

The concept of Mercantilism is as old as human existence, but there was no formal express or rule of sovereign, except mutual trust, common objective and moral forces.

Under Roman Law

The seed of company can be seen with the term 'corporation', the genesis of Latin word 'Corpus' which means a 'body' or 'body of people'. The concept of corporation was deep rooted in the time of Justinian (527–565). Under the Roman Law we can find certain entities under '*universitas, corpus or collegium*', which possess some rights and liabilities such as right to own property and perhaps make contract, sue and be sued. It seems they perform the act backed by the current law through representatives. It is also an amazing fact that Romans donate an idea of corporation with certain power and capacities, which was enjoyed by a group or collective people, but failed to give birth to any jurist personality which had rights and duties similar to a modern company. But still it was the foundation for modern company.

The concept was carried forward in the Maurya periods as well. Later on, when the Church became the centre of power during the medieval period, it started supporting the financial services industry and representing its interest other than its function of local authority under the City of London Corporation. The Stora Kopparberg, mining community in Falun Sweden, obtained a charter from King Magnus Eriksson in 1347 and alleged the oldest commercial corporation in the world.

Under British Law

The seed was planted by the Romans, but it was not organized, and it is difficult to cite precisely what attributed to the modern company to take its current configuration. However, it is obvious that institutionalized activism and aggressive commercial behaviour, which required collective efforts to generate more profit, was the prime factor to give birth to a modern company.

If we say that modern corporation is the genesis of mutual partnership, it would not wrong as during medieval times traders usually acted under civil law, such as partnership, with the objective of profit. It was the time when European nations chartered corporations to direct colonial ventures. That's how the modern company started getting its present shape.

Initial attempts towards formation of a company were only centralized with merchant adventures for trading overseas. Each member of such groups traded with his own stock and on his own account under the rules thereto, but the liabilities were individual and separate from that of the company. The Royal Charter in 1600 granted by Queen Elizabeth to British East India Company was the milestone in the history of the modern company.

Bubbles Act of 1720

The process of granting the Royal Charter or incorporation of company by the Special Act of Parliament was not adequate to the growing commercial needs. It was expensive and slow, which forced the emergence of partnerships and spontaneous formation of joint stock companies or associations which presumed to act as corporate bodies in England. The problems with such partnerships and joint stocks companies were not in line with rule of law or any legal attributes, and other fraudulent activities were also prevalent. Thus, such associations were not supported by any Royal Charter or any Act of British Parliament, and stood illegal in the eyes of law. Under such circumstances in 1720 the British Parliament passed the Bubbles Act, which enabled the annulment of contracts entered into by those associations.

Modern Company Law

Till 18th century there was a control mechanism either by Royal Charter or Special Act of Parliament. Gradually, the economic activism, intensive desire of profits, and British colonial policy and rapid industrialization gave rise to classical liberalism and a laissez faire economic theory, which supported less government control for best economic growth and private entrepreneurship.

Joint Stock Companies Act, 1844

The Joint Stock Companies Act, 1844 was an effort to minimize the tedious process, without getting any Royal Charter or any Special Act of Parliament. Under this Act a company could be incorporated simply by registration. There was also a provision for Companies House and the office of Registrar of Companies. The Act considered the company as a distinct legal entity, but did not grant to it the privilege of limited liability and members of the company could still be held responsible for unlimited losses by the company.

The Companies Act of 1866

During 1844 to 1866, there were many amendments as Joint Stock Companies Act of 1850, Joint Stock Companies Act of 1857 and Joint Stock Companies Act of 1860. Joint Stock Companies Act of 1866 was a comprehensive piece of legislation for Indian conditions which intended to amend and consolidate the law regarding to incorporation, regulation, and winding up of trading companies and other associations.

Companies Act of 1913

Another attempt was made in the year 1913, to streamline the prevailing Act but it failed to take into account the peculiar features of Indian trade and commerce and some peculiar institution such as 'managing agency.'

Companies Act of 1956

Before 1956 the conventional Act of British regime was enforced. Post independence a need for further revision of the company law was felt. Many changes had taken place. Till 2013 the same piece of legislation was in place and witnessed many amendments with the passage of time.

The Companies Act, 1956 was enacted on the recommendations of the Bhaba Committee set up in 1950 with the objective of consolidating the existing corporate laws and providing a new basis for corporate operations in independent India. With the enactment of this legislation in 1956, the Companies Act, 1913 was repealed. The Companies Act, 1956, has since provided the legal framework for corporate entities in India. The need for streamlining this Act was felt from time to time as the corporate sector grew in pace with the Indian economy, with as many as 24 amendments taking place since 1956. Major amendments to the Act were made through Companies (Amendment) Act, 1988 after considering the recommendations of the Sachar Committee, and then again in 1998, 2000 and finally in 2002 through the Companies (Second Amendment) Act, 2002, consequent to the report of the Eradi Committee. Unsuccessful attempts were made in 1993 and 1997 to replace the present Act with a new law. Companies (Amendment) Bill, 2003; containing important provisions relating to corporate governance was also introduced, the consideration of which has been held back in anticipation of the comprehensive review of the Company Law. While piecemeal reforms continued through amendments, it has not yet been possible to bring about comprehensive, new legislation to replace the existing Act.

The Companies Act, 2013

The Companies Act, 2013 replaced the previous Companies Act, 1956 and was notified on 12 September 2013.

THE COMPANIES (AMENDMENT) ACT, 2015

The Companies (Amendment) Bill, 2014, was passed by the parliament to amend the Companies Act, 2013, and received the assent of the President of India on May 25, 2015 and called the Companies (Amendment) Act, 2015 ("Amendment Act"). The provisions of the Amendment Act have come into force from May 29, 2015 (except sections 13 and 14 of the Amendment Act which will come into force on such date as will be notified by the Central Government).

The Companies Act, 2013 is certainly a chief piece of legislation, most of the gap-fillings in the Act were left in the hands of a subordinate legislation which was supposed to be introduced in the form of Rules, empowering the MCA to mould the law of the land at its discretion. With most of the determining factors left to be decided by way of Rules, in spirit, the Act itself became a subordinated law.

MEANING OF COMPANY

In section 2(20) of the Companies Act, 2013, 'company' means a company incorporated under this Act or under any previous company law.

The section does not give any legal or technical meaning but signifies that any company registered under the Act is considered to be a company. The word 'incorporated under this Act' perhaps denotes the compliance of the said Act. The clinical research of the section shows that it is open-ended, which does not create any periphery for the definition, but intends to recognize a company which will comply with all the provisions of said Act. The reason behind this open-ended definition is that the company is not only a group of persons or a legal or jurist personality, but promulgates social and commercial structure; infiltration to it could destroy the social balance and economic framework.

Chief Justice Marshall in Trs. of Dartmouth Coll. *v.* Woodward, 17 U.S. (4 Wheat.) 518 (1819) discussed the meaning of corporation as 'A company is a person, artificial, invisible, intangible, and existing only in the contemplation of the law. Being a mere creature of law, it possesses only those properties which the character of its creation of its creation confers upon it either expressly or as incidental to its very existence'.

Black's Law Dictionary *defines "corporation" as an "entity having authority under law to act as a single person distinct from the shareholders who own it."*

Creature of Law

Hon'ble Supreme Court in State Trading Corporation of India Ltd. *v.* C.T.O, held:

Under the English Common Law which formed the foundation of the Indian jurisprudence, a company or a corporation aggregate is a national of the State in which it is incorporated and is clothed with a personality given by the law of the land, capable of exercising rights and entitled to protection abroad.

Association of Person

The literal meaning of company draws from the Latin word Com = with or together; panis = bread, means come together for a meal. It referred to an association of persons who come together with a common objective of taking their meals together.

As far as the Companies Act is concerned it defines the company as: 'A company formed and registered under this Act or an existing company.' An 'existing company' means a company formed and registered under any of the former companies acts. This definition does not reveal the real distinctive characteristics of a company. Perhaps a clear definition of the company is given by Lord Justice Lindley:

> By a company is meant associations of many persons who contribute money or money's worth to a common stock and employs it in some trade or business, and who share the profit and loss as the case may be arising therefrom. The common stock so contributed is denoted in money and is the capital of the company and the persons who contribute it, or to whom it belongs, are called as members. The proportion of capital to which each member is entitled is his share which is always transferable although the right to transfer them is more or less restricted. A company thus may be defined as an incorporated association which is an artificial person, having a separate legal entity, with a perpetual succession, a common seal, a common capital comprised of transferable shares and carrying limited liability. It is called an artificial person because of its very nature that law alone can give birth to a company and law alone can put it to an end.[4]

Commercial Objective Tool

Is it easy to conceive that a company is a combination of people who are coming together for their meal? The answer is not strongly affirmative; the company is a legal device for the attainment of any social or economic behaviour or both. It seems to be a combination of social, legal, political, and economic device, which exhibits the commercial conduct of society.

The synonym of company is corporation which is derived from the Latin word 'corpus' which means "body" which indicates a company is also a person, but not a natural person but an artificial or jurist person, who incurs rights and liabilities like a natural person, to attain a social or economic end.

---

4. State Trading Corporation of India Ltd. *v.* C.T.O

Nature and Features of Company

Characteristics of company

The first essential feature of a company comes into existence with the case of Salomon *v.* Salomon and Co. Ltd., (1897) A.C.22, which declared the personality of the Company as Distinct Legal Personality—Jurist Person. The feature underlines the concept 'The right and duty of the company is not the right and duty of the member of the company'.

A principle has been set out in this case that, with a movement the company has been incorporated under the Company Act; it becomes 'a legal person distinct from its members'. It bears its own name and seal. Its assets are separate and distinct from its members: it is also capable of owning property, borrowing money, incurring debts, entertaining contract, sue and can be sued.

The members of the company are its owners but they can be its creditors only, and shareholders can't be held liable for the act of company, because they are not the agent of the company.

The existence of the company arises from a fiction of law. In the case of State Trading Corporation of India Ltd. *v.* C.T.O, it was discussed that:

Unlike an unincorporated company, which has no separate existence and which the law does not distinguish from its members. An incorporated company has a separate existence and the law recognizes it as a legal person, separate and distinct from its members. This new legal personality emerges from the moment of incorporation and from that date the persons subscribing to the memorandum of association and other persons joining as members are regarded as a body corporate or a corporation aggregate and the new person begins to function as an entity.

Further, The Corporation really has no physical existence; it is a mere 'abstraction of law'.

In the case of EBM Co Ltd *v.* Dominion Bank it was discussed as:

'the distinction should be clearly marked, observed and maintained between an incorporated company's legal entity and its action, assets, rights and liabilities on the one hand, and the individual shareholder and their actions, assets, rights and liabilities on the other hand.'

In fact, the managed company in theory retains full legal ownership of its assets and remains "distinct and separate legal entity" as a limited joint stock company. What in effect happens under the managing agency agreement in India is that the managing agent comes to utilize the existing structure of the managed companies organization, to carry on business, earn profits and, in fact, virtually to trade in every possible sphere open to the managed company.[5]

---

5. Commissioner of Income-Tax, ... *v.* Kettlewell Bullen & Co. 1962 46 ITR 39 Cal.

Does it mean the company projects the principle of separation?

The concept of distinct legal personality is not the absolute. The right and duty of company could be considered the right of duty of the members of the company when the person behind the company, directors or shareholder uses the company as a tool for their personal benefits contrary to the objective of the company.

However, 'incorporation' is an act which transforms the company into a jurist person, and confers the legal status with rights and obligations. A juristic person, like any other natural person is in law also conferred with rights and obligations and is dealt with in accordance with the law. In other words, the entity acts like a natural person but only through a designated person, whose acts are processed within the ambit of law.[6]

Company is a citizen of India?

In the case of State Trading Corporation of India Ltd. *v.* C.T.O it was enunciated as: In numerous cases in this Court it was assumed, without contest, that a company is a citizen of India and competent to enforce fundamental rights under Art. 19(1)(f) and (g) of the Constitution. In view of the fact that a company is invested with important fundamental rights under various other Articles of the Constitution and it is recognised as a person capable of holding and disposing of property and carrying on business, commerce and intercourse, it could not be held that the expression 'citizen' in Art. 19 was intended to be restricted to a natural person. A corporation is, however, distinct from its share-holders and even if all the shareholders are Indian citizens.

Halsbury's Laws of England (Vol. 6, 3rd Edition, pages 113–114, paragraph 235) lays down that on incorporation, a company is a legal entity the nationality or domicile of which is determined by its place of registration. Reference was also made to Vol. 9 of *Halsbury's Laws of England*, page 19, paragraphs 29-30, which says that the concept of nationality is applicable to corporations and it depends upon the country of its incorporation.

There is a rule of English Law that a company or an incorporated corporation has a nationality and this nationality is determined by the law of the country in which it is incorporated.

The word 'citizen' is not defined in the Constitution or the General Clauses Act but the word 'person' is defined in the latter to include 'any company or association or body of individuals whether incorporated or not.' The word 'person' therefore, conceivably bears this extended meaning at least in some places in Part III of the Constitution. But it is not necessary to determine where in the Constitution the word 'person' includes a company, etc., because that word has not been used in Article 19.

---

6. Shriomani Gurudwara Prabandhak ... *v.* Shri Som Nath Dass & Ors (Supreme Court of India).

Fundamental rights of company

'The fundamental rights guaranteed by the Constitution are available not merely to individual citizens but to corporate bodies as well except where the language of the provision or the nature of the right compels the inference that they are applicable only to natural persons. An incorporated company, therefore, can come up to this Court for enforcement of its fundamental rights' Though the observations quoted above would seem to lend countenance to the contention raised on behalf of the petitioners, they really do not determine the controversy one way or the other. In that case, a shareholder of the Sholapur Spinning and Weaving Company made an application under Art. 32 of the Constitution for a declaration that the Act impugned in that case was void, as also for the enforcement of his fundamental rights by a writ of mandamus against the Government, and the directors of the company, restraining them from exercising any power under the Act.[7]

The ratio of the State Trading Corporation judgment says that though the company is a jurist person, and exists in the eye of law, but it does not possess the fundamental rights, and it is also important to note that the provisions of Citizenship Act are also not applicable in the case of company.

In Chiranjit Lal Chowdhuri *v.* The Union of India where the learned judge observed obiter: 'The fundamental rights guaranteed by the Constitution are available not merely to individual citizens but to corporate bodies as well except where the language of the provision or the nature of the right compels the inference that they are applicable only to natural persons. An incorporated, company, therefore, can come this Court for enforcement of its fundamental rights and so may the individual shareholders to enforce their own; but it would not be open to an individual shareholder to complain of an Act which affects the fundamental rights of the company except to the extent that it constitutes an infraction of his own rights as well'.

Is company servant of the state?

The question whether a corporation is an agent or a servant of the State must be decided on the facts of each case. In the absence of any statutory provision, a commercial corporation acting on its behalf, even if it is controlled wholly or partially by a Government department, will be presumed not to be a servant or an agent of the State. Where, however, the corporation is performing in substance Governmental, and not commercial, functions, an inference will readily be made that it is an agent of the Government.

---

7. State Trading Corporation of India Ltd. *v.* C.T.O

TRADITIONAL CHARACTERISTIC OF COMPANY

Perpetual Existence = 'a person that never dies.'

A company is the creature of statute, though it considered to be a jurist person, but it is beyond the human characteristics, and unaffected by death or departure of any member of company, and its status is constituted by the Memorandum of Association of the Company, and seems to be the perpetual succession. The word 'perpetual' means continuous without end. It is considered that life does not depend upon the death, insolvency, or retirement of any or all shareholders or directors. The company may be compared with a flowing river where the water keeps on changing continuously; still the identity of the river remains the same. Does it mean the company is immortal which cannot come to an end? The answer is not affirmative, everything its mortal, means nothing more than that 'the corporation lasts until dissolved, principle is also applicable to Company; law creates it and law alone can dissolve it'.

Why Perpetual Existence?

The core objective of any corporation existence is sustainable growth of society, to create financial stability, which cannot be achieved with short-term thinking. Professors Margaret Blair and Lynn Stout used the term 'capital lock-in' which supports long-term capital investment by shareholders of the company and the idea of financial stability. The statutory command gives separate legal entity to plan a perpetual future which is necessary for corporate management.

In Revlon, Inc. *v.* MacAndrews & Forbes Holdings, Inc., 506 A.2d 173 (Del. 1986), it was enunciated that the concept behind the perpetual existence is the long-term value.

Limited Liability

Limited liability is another important feature of company. The phrase comprises two words: limited + liability; which means the liability is limited, or which is strict with some parameter that is shares or limited amount for debt of a company. It is the liability of company to repay not the liability of its members. Members' liability is only limited up to the shares, because the members of the company are neither the owners of the company's undertakings nor liable for its debt. Unlike a partnership firm wherein the liability of the partners for debts are fully and even the personal assets of partner can be attached to discharge the liability of the firm.

The question arises here,

'Why such characteristics are associated with a company?'

Separate legal entity is the fundamental attribute of company, then the obvious is that it is the outspring of its Limited Liability.

In Re London and Globe Finance Corporation Ltd, Justice Buckley discussed as:

> The statues relating to limited liability have probably done more than any legislation of the last fifty years to further the commercial prosperity of the country. They have, to the advantages as well of the investor as of the public, allowed and encouraged aggregation of all sums into large capitals which have been employed in undertakings of great public utility largely increasing the wealth of the country.

Separate Property

When there is a liability there must be right, the same principle is applicable to a company. A company has the liability for its debts and its creditor, in reflection company has some rights, the one which we can see is the right of separate property.

The law makes the company capable of owning, enjoying, and disposing of and managed property on its own name, distinct from its member. The same thing is being discussed in the Case of R.F Perumal V.H.H. John Deavin, A.I.R, 1960 Mad. 43, in which the Hon'ble Madras High Court held that no member of the company can claim during the existence or at the time of winding up of company for the property of company.

Transferability of Shares

This is another feature of a company—transferability of shares of the company, freely transferable without the permission of the company subject to procedures provided in the articles. The shareholders may transfer their shares to another person and this does not affect the funds of the company. In the case of a private company, this right is not absolute but certain restrictions on transfer of its shares are imposed by the act.

Common Seal

As discussed above a company is the jurist person and has no physical existence but exists, and to execute the above-mentioned rights and liabilities it must act through its agents, who can enter into and act on behalf of company, such agents perform such work under the seal of the company. Companies Act, 2013 made requirement of common seal to be affixed on certain documents, as a signature of the company for example bill of exchange, share certificates, etc. Now, the use of common seal has been made optional.

Under **the Companies (Amendment) Act, 2015,** having a common seal of the Company is optional and instead of affixing the common seal on the documents signed by two directors or one director and a company secretary of the company is sufficient.

Accordingly, sections 9, 12, 22, 46, 223 of **the Companies Act, 2012** have been amended accordingly.

Company May Sue and be Sued in Its Own Name

Incorporation gives the power to the company for acquiring legal rights through the principle of separate legal entity, by which the company may sue and be sued in its own name and not its members.

As in the case of Foss *v.* Harbottle it was discussed that, only the company can sue for redress if a wrong has been done to it, not minority shareholders.

LIFTING OF THE CORPORATE VEIL OR DOCTRINE OF PIERCE

Lifting Corporate Veil = Destruction of Separate Legal
Entity or Disregarding Corporate
Entity concept = Holding member liable, not the the Company.
= Denial of protection to shareholder
= Exception to separate legal entity, and limited liability
= Judicial process for treating the rights and liabilities or activities of a company as the rights or liabilities or activities of its shareholders
= Judicial process for looking behind the legal personality to the real controllers

The features of company make it a distinct separate legal personality, who is capable to exercise its rights and liability, i.e., enjoying property , entering into contract, can sue and can be sued in its own name, etc. through its agent.

A company is the creature of law and has no physical existence except the mark of its presence as common seal.

In practice the member of the company controls the affairs of the company. However, there are certain circumstances in which courts will have to look through the corporation, i.e., lift the veil of incorporation, and hold the shareholders of the company directly and personally liable for the obligations of the corporation.

Allahabad High Court in the case of Incan Mutual Fund Benefit Ltd. *v.* Incan Employees Welfare 2006 129 CompCas 977 All, 2004 51 SCL 438 All, held that :

> It is high time to reiterate that in the expanding of horizon of modern jurisprudence, lifting of corporate veil is permissible. Its frontiers are unlimited. It must, however, depend primarily on the realities of the situation. The aim of the legislation is to do justice to all the parties. The veil on corporate personality even though not lifted sometimes, is becoming more and more transparent in modern company jurisprudence. The concept of lifting the corporate veil is a changing concept and is of expanding horizons.

In the case of Subhra Mukherjee *v.* Bharat Coking Coal Ltd. AIR 2000 SC 1203, the Supreme Court rejected the argument that undue emphasis was given to the fact that the directors of the Company were brothers and the appellants are their wives and that the company is a separate legal entity which is independent of its directors and shareholders. On the strength of the decision of Solomon *v.* Solomon the Supreme Court held that 'lifting of veil of incorporation under statutes and decisions of the Courts is equally settled position of law'. The Apex Court further observed. '...To look at the realities of the situation and to know the real state of affairs behind the facade of the principle of the corporate personality, the courts have pierced the veil of incorporation.

Where a transaction of sale of its immovable property by a Company in favour of the wives of the directors is alleged to be sham and collusive, as in the instant case, the Court will be justified in piercing the veil of incorporation to ascertain the true nature of the transaction as to who were the real parties to the sale and whether it was genuine and bona fide or whether it was between the husbands and the wives behind the facade of separate entity of the Company.[8]

For finding out whether or not the buyer and the seller were related persons within the meaning of Customs Valuation (Determination of Price of Imported Goods) Rules, 1988, the Supreme Court permitted lifting of the corporate veil in the case of Collector of Customs *v.* East African Traders [2000] 9 SCC 483.

Why Lifting the Corporate Veil?

The protection of public interests is of paramount importance, when the corporate character is being deliberately used as a cloak for fraud or improper conduct or where the company has been formed to evade obligations imposed by the law, it is necessary to stab the cover of corporate personality, and save the interest of shareholders of or the investors of the company.

The concept of corporate veil comes from the concept of separate legal entity, and limited liability, i.e., shareholders of the are company are liable to till their investment/ share in the company. The separate personality concept is the statutory privilege for legitimate commercial purpose only. The company is the tool to achieve and maintain society's commercial objective, which can be enjoyed only by those who want to make an honest use of the 'Company', contrary; it shall destroy the commercial and ultimately the social structure of the society. Thus, any contrary, fraudulent, dishonest, or illegal use of separate personality immunity cannot be allowed to be used as a shelter. In such circumstances the court comes into the picture and breaks the corporate shell by applying 'lifting the corporate veil.'

A company can only act through its member or agent who actually for their own mala fide intention acts contrary the company, law, state.

When any dishonest, illegal, and fraudulent use of the facility of incorporation takes place, the law lifts the corporate veil and identifies the real person, i.e., members behind the curtain and holds them responsible for the same. This is known as lifting the corporate veil.

The very reason behind this principle is to put a control mechanism or create a legal consequence who tries to use company as a medium to sustain the fraud, or perform contrary objectives.

In the case of Calcutta Chromotype Ltd. *v.* CCE [1998] 3 SCC 681, the Supreme Court held that lifting of veil would depend on facts and circumstances of the case and that even if they are two separate companies under the Companies Act, authorities/court can lift their corporate veil to see whether the persons behind them are the same and if the buyer is found to be associated with the manufacturer, a presumption under

8. supra Incan Mutual Fund Benefit

section 114 of Evidence Act can arise regarding their having interest, directly or indirectly, in the business of each other.[9]

ABSENCE OF CONCEPT LIFTING OF VEIL
The absence of corporate veil piercing would result in a crucial incidence of breached contracts, non-performing debt which ultimately hits the innocent user of the company, and ultimately hit the social structure of society, and creates disbelief in the financial process of the society, and misuse of the corporate entity will increase.

Generally and broadly speaking, we may say that the corporate veil may be lifted where a statute itself contemplates lifting the veil, or fraud or improper conduct is intended to be prevented, or a taxing statute or a beneficent statute is sought to be evaded or where associated companies are inextricably connected as to be, in reality, part of one concern. It is neither necessary nor desirable to enumerate the classes of cases where lifting the veil is permissible, since that must necessarily depend on the relevant statutory or other provisions, the object sought to be achieved, the impugned conduct, the involvement of the element of the public interest, the effect on parties who may be affected, etc.[10]

Theories for Lifting of Corporate Veil

There are two popular theories for of the corporate veil:

1. "Alter-ego" or other self-theory
2. "Instrumentality" theory

Alter-ego or other self-theory

The literal meaning of alter ego is another side of oneself; a second self.

A doctrine used by the courts to disregard the separate entity of a corporate so that they may be held personally liable for their illegal or fraudulent activities and action.

The constituent elements of this theory are:

(i) There is unity of interest and ownership between the company and the interest of shareholder, and the concept of separate legal existence has ceased.

(ii) That separation reveals the fraud and illegal act of shareholder of company.

Instrumentality theory

This theory tries to find out whether the company is being used by its shareholders as an instrument for their personal benefit against the objective of the company, or any fraud is being carried out.

9. Incan Mutual Fund Benefit.

10. Krishi Foundry Employees Union vs Krishi Engines Limited And Ors. 2003 (2) ALD 392, 2003 117 CompCas 340 AP, (2003) IILLJ 798 AP.

Constituent element of this theory

1. The company was only a instrument of shareholder.
2. The shareholder has full control over the company in a way so as to defraud or act contrary to the company objective.

The basic idea behind the concept of corporate veil exhibits that the company is being used by its promoters in a way which gives personal benefits to the promoters of the company contrary to the objective of company.

In nutshell lifting the corporate veil principle is that it is the direct opposite of the limited liability concept, and in the event the veil is lifted, the owners' personal liability arises and their assets are exposed to the litigation, as a sole proprietorship or general partnership as they are conducting the business in their personal capacity.

In Hackbridge-Hewittic and Easun Ltd. *v.* G.E.C. Distribution Transformers Ltd., (1992) 74 Comp. Cases 543 (Mad), a Division Bench of Madras High Court considered the question of lifting the veil and it was observed:

> Indeed, what has come to stay as an organic theory, under which the doctrine has departed from the orthodox approach extending the rule of piercing the veil to know the true character of a person, has in essence made it almost obligatory to make a closer examination as to whether the principal and subsidiary like principal and agent exist for each other or as one mind, thus as organs of each other. It is often said that a corporation is an abstraction. It has no mind of its own any more than it has a body of its own. Its active and directing will must consequently be sought in the person of somebody who for some purposes may be called an agent, but who is really the directing mind and will of the corporation, the very ego and centre of the personality of the corporation. The orthodox approach that a company is a legal entity in itself and thus whether it is a subsidiary of another or not, is of no meaning or consequence for fixing the responsibility of the activities of one upon another.... Thus, on the principle aforementioned, the fact that the subsidiary company has a distinct legal personality does not suffice to dispose of the possibility that its behaviour might be imputed to the parent company. Such may be the case in particular when the subsidiary, although being a distinct legal personality, does not determine its behaviour on the market in autonomous manner but essentially carries out the instructions given to it by the parent company. When the subsidiary does not enjoy any real autonomy in the determination of its course of action on the market, it is possible to say that it has no personality of its own and that it has one and the same as the parent company.

Nature of Lifting of Corporate Veil Principle

In State of U.P. And Ors v. Renusagar Power Co. And Others 1988 AIR 1737, 1988 SCR Supl. (1) 627 the Apex Court observed as follows:

> It is high time to reiterate that in the expanding of horizon of modern jurisprudence, lifting of corporate veil is permissible. Its frontiers are unlimited. It must, however, depend primarily on the realities of the situation. The aim of the legislation is to do justice to all the parties. The veil on corporate personality even though not lifted sometimes, is becoming more and more transparent in modern company jurisprudence. The concept of lifting the corporate veil is a changing concept and is of expanding horizons.

Circumstances under which court lifts the corporate veil

What are the circumstances under which protection under separate legal entity can be suspended by the court, the Supreme Court in the case of Life Insurance Corporation of ... *v.* Escorts Ltd. & Ors 1986 AIR 1370, 1985 SCR Supl. (3) 909, laid down that:

> Generally and broadly speaking, the corporate veil may be lifted where a statute itself contemplates lifting the veil, or fraud or improper conduct is intended to be prevented or a taxing statute or a beneficent statute is sought to be evaded or where associated companies are inextricably connected as to be in reality, part of one concern. It is neither necessary nor desirable to enumerate the classes of cases where lifting the corporate veil is permissible, since that must necessarily depend on the relevant statutory or other provisions the object sought to be achieved, the impugned conduct, the involvement of the element of the public interest, and the effect on the parties who may be affected etc.

The state laws and facts decide the circumstances which can result in a piercing of the corporate veil. However, generally, the following factors are considered by the court that the creation or use of the company to evade fraud and lift the veil:

To Determine the True Character of the Company

As discussed above incorporation of a company is the economic socio-objective for the country, and it is non-default obligation of the company to address the country's economic objective. Sometimes it has been seen that the company may assume a character of an enemy company when persons in de facto control of its affairs are residents of an enemy country.

In famous Case Daimler Co Ltd. *v.* Continental Tyre and Rubber Co. the same thing is being discussed. But as discussed in the case of People's Pleasure Park Co. Vs. Rohleder (1908) 109 Va 439: 61 SE 794, it was discussed that if there is no danger to public interest, the court may refused to pierce the corporate veil.

CASE LAW
Daimler Co Ltd. v. Continental Tyre and Rubber Co. A company was incorporated in England for the purpose of selling tyres manufactured in Germany by a German company. The German company held a larger portion of shares in the English company and all the directors of the company were Germans, resident in Germany. During the First World War the English company commenced an action to recover a trade debt. And the question was whether the company had become an enemy company and should therefore be barred from maintaining the action.
Lord Reading CJ commented that the fact of incorporation was not just a 'technicality', and held that:
'The company is a living thing with a separate existence which cannot be swept aside as a technicality. It is not a mere name or mask or cloak or device to conceal the identity of persons and it is not suggested that the company was formed for any dishonest or fraudulent purpose. It is a legal body clothed with the form prescribed by the legislature…'
On contrary Buckley LJ, held that:
The artificial legal person called the corporation has no physical existence. It exists only in contemplation of law. It has neither body, parts, nor passions. It cannot wear weapons nor serve in the wars. It can be neither loyal nor disloyal. It cannot compass treason. It can be neither friend nor enemy. Apart from its corporators it can have neither thoughts, wishes, nor intentions, for it has no mind other than the minds of the corporators. These considerations seem to me essential to bear in mind in determining the present case.
House of Lords
Lord Parker held that:
I think that the analogy is to be found in control, an idea which, if not very familiar in law, is of capital importance and is very well understood in commerce and finance. The acts of a company's organs, its directors, managers, secretary, and so forth, functioning within the scope of their authority, are the company's acts and may invest it definitely with enemy character… it must at least be prima facie relevant… Certainly I have found no authority to the contrary.

Evade or Circumvent Tax

Tax evasion paralyzes the growth or development of country, and adversely affects the economy of country and fundamentally against the public policy.

It is true that from the juristic point of view the company is a legal personality entirely distinct from its members and the company is capable of enjoying the rights and being subjected to duties which are not the same as those enjoyed or borne by its members. But in certain exceptional cases the court is entitled to lift the veil of corporate entity and to pay regard to the economic realities behind the legal facade. For example, the court has power to disregard the corporate entity if it is used for tax evasion or to circumvent tax obligation.[11]

11. Workmen Employed In Associated ... *v.* Associated Rubber Industry Ltd AIR 1986 SC 1, 1985 (51) FLR 478, 1986 157 ITR 77 SC, (1986) ILLJ 142 SC, 1985 (2) SCALE 321, (1985) 4 SCC 114, 1986 (1) SLJ 218 SC, 1986 (1) UJ 235 SC.

In the case of Juggilal Kamlapat, Kanpur *v.* Commissioner Of Income-Tax 1970 AIR 529, 1970 SCR (1) 720 it was held that:

> In the present case the transaction since the inception appears to be impressed with the character of a commercial transaction entered with a view to earn profit. Large block of shares was purchased at the ruling rates with borrowed money, and soon thereafter the shares were disposed of at a profit in small lots. Some of the shares were sold through brokers to strangers. The story of the firm that some or all the shares were merely 'distributed' to its associates is not proved. The interest which the firm had to pay for the amount borrowed for purchasing the shares was acted in the revenue account and was claimed as a revenue allowance. It was not the case of the firm that Aluminium and J.K. Trust shares were purchased for .acquiring the managing agency. It was claimed that the shares were taken over because the public did not accept those shares. It was one of the objects of the firm to finance its allied concerns and in taking over shares which the public did not subscribe the firm was 'acting' in the course of its business. The firm commenced selling the shares soon after they were purchased. Aluminium shares were purchased between January 26, 1945 and April 5, 1946 (except a few which were retained) and sold at profit. Whereas the first lot was purchased on January 26, 1945, the first sale was made on February 1, 1945. It could not be said that this was an investment in shares independent of the trading activity of the firm. The story that the shares had to be sold on account of financial difficulties is plainly belied by the circumstance that the firm went on purchasing and selling the Aluminium shares. J.K. Trust shares were purchased on February 14, 1945 and were sold on August 22, 1945. Aluminium shares as well as J.K. Trust shares were sold at a profit and through brokers. These transactions were also stamped with the character of commercial transactions entered into with a profit motive and were not transactions in the nature of capital investments.

Same in the case of Sir Dinshaw Manakjee Petit AIR 1927 Bomaby 371, to evade tax Dinshaw became the majority shareholder in all the companies. The companies made investments and whenever interest and dividends were received by the companies, he applied to the companies for loans, and without any objection the loans were granted, which he never repaid. In the decision of court the corporate veil of all the companies was lifted and the income of the companies treated as if they were of Dinshaw.

It was held that:

> The assessee was receiving under the guise of loans or advances the profits which were made by the company which he controlled and in which he held all the shares except three which were held by his subordinates. The company was created by him merely, so that he could make entries in the company's books suggesting that it received the interest and dividends and paid them as loans whilst in reality the receipt of dividends and interest, if it could be called the

business of the company, was its only business and was in fact the business of the assessee himself.

The taxing authority is entitled and is indeed bound to determine the true legal relation resulting from a transaction. If the parties have chosen to conceal by a device the legal relation, it is open to the taxing authorities to unravel the device and to determine the true character of the relationship. But **the legal effect of a transaction cannot be displaced by probing into the substance of the transaction.**[12]

When there is no specific provision for lifting the veil in the Act?

In Meenakshi Mills Commissioner of Income Tax, ... *v.* M/S. Madurai Mills Co. Limited 1973 AIR 1357, 1973 SCR (3) 662, case, while dealing with a situation arising under the Income Tax Act, which does not contain any specific provision regarding lifting of corporate mask, their Lordships of the Supreme Court observed that:

it is well established that in a matter of this description the income tax authorities are entitled to pierce the veil of corporate entity and to look at the reality of the transaction. It is true that from the juristic point of view the company is a legal personality entirely distinct from its members and the company is capable of enjoying rights and being subjected to duties which are not the same as those enjoyed or borne by its members. But, in certain exceptional cases, the Court is entitled to lift the veil of corporate entity and to pay regard to the economic realities behind the legal facade.[13]

Company Acting as an Agent or Trustee of the Shareholder

The identity of company should be its real identity, it should not act as an agent or trustee of the shareholder, or use the corporate facade to cover up that agency or trust.

In the case of R.G. Films Ltd., (1953) 1 Al E.R. 615, 90% of the shares were held by the President of an American Company which financed the production of the film, while the American company produced a film in India technically in the name of a British.

The Board of Trade refused to register the film as a Britsh film on the ground that English company acted merely as the nominee of the American corporation.

The concept of separate legal entity denies the situation. The company exists to become an agent for its shareholders and does not hesitate to lift the veil. Prevention of Fraud or Improper Conduct.

Preventation of Fraud or Improper Conduct

The basic foundation of concept of lifting the veil is based on prevention of fraud, or improper conduct, or legal obligations like defrauding creditors or fraudulent purposes,

12. Commissioner of Income-Tax, *v.* M/S. B.M. Kharwar 1969 AIR 812, 1969 SCR (1) 651.

13. India Waste Energy Development ... *v.* Govt. of NCT of Delhi And Anr 2003 (66) DRJ 224.

or when a company is a sham or a cloak. We have to understand that the main objective of any commercial socio activity is based on two basic foundations – Promotion of justice and prevention of fraud. It is also considered that the term fraud has a wider meaning with lifting the veil, and it is more near to misrepresentation.

It is also considered in the concept of lifting veil that being the non-corporeal existence it cannot sustain the fraud, but the shareholder of the company used the company as a channel to execute their personal benefits and fraud.

Gilford Motor Co. *v.* Horne (1933) is a case when courts treat shareholders and a company as one, in a situation where a company is used as an instrument of fraud.

In the case of Delhi Development Authority *v.* Skipper Construction Company 1996 AIR 2005, 1996 SCC (4) 622, Supreme Court observed that:

> The concept of corporate entity was evolved to encourage and promote trade and commerce: but not to commit illegalities or to defraud people. Where, therefore, the corporate character is employed for the purpose of committing illegality or for defrauding others, the court would ignore the corporate character and will look at the reality behind the corporate veil so as to enable it to pass appropriate orders to do justice between the parties concerned.
>
> The concept of corporate entity was evolved to encourage and promote trade and commerce but not to commit illegalities or to defraud people. Where, therefore, the corporate character is employed for the purpose of committing illegality or for defrauding others, the Court would ignore the corporate character and will look at the reality behind the corporate veil so as to enable it to pass appropriate orders to do justice between the parties concerned.[14]

When a company was formed to avoid welfare legislations

In the case of Workmen Employed In Associated *v.* Associated Rubber Industry Ltd AIR 1986 SC 1, it was held that:

> It is the duty of the court, in every case where ingenuity is expended to avoid taxing and welfare legislations, to get behind the smoke-screen and discover the true state of affairs. The court is not to be satisfied with form and leave well alone the substance of a transaction.
>
> We now live in a welfare state whose financial needs, if backed by the law, have to be respected and met. We must recognise that there is behind taxation laws as much moral sanction as behind any other welfare legislation and it is a pretence to say that avoidance of taxation is not unethical and that it stands on no less moral plane than honest payment of taxation. In our view, the proper way to construe a taking statute, while considering a device to avoid tax, is not to ask whether the provisions should be construed literally, or liberally, nor whether

14. Yella Constructions Limited v. East Coast Railway And 2006 (6) ALD 460, 2006 (6) ALT 714, 2007 73 SCL 112 AP.

the transaction is not unreal and not prohibited by the statute, but whether the transaction is a device to avoid tax, and whether the transaction is such that the judicial process may accord its approval to it.

Public Interest

In company law, separate legal entity of incorporated body, has to be maintained for reasons more than one. Nonetheless, the lifting of corporate veil or piercing the corporate veil is permissible if public interest requires. This is also subject to considerations of permissibility as per the statute. If the company uses any other concern; a firm, society, or association, only to facilitate evasion of legal obligation like payment of direct or indirect taxes or denial of statutory benefits to workmen, the Court has to disregard the separate legal entity of the company. In such an event the question before the Court is one of company law, and the corporate personality of the company is of secondary importance. The important test is whether the method adopted for evasion of legal obligations would subvert public interest.[15]

FORMATION OF COMPANY

Formation of company is not a spontaneous process, it require composite steps for a certificate of incorporation, which gives the company a legal status, or birth to a legal entity. Promoters are persons who visualize the idea of forming a company and execute all the requirements thereto.

Section 2(69) of the Companies Act, 2013 defines the term 'promoter' as under:

'Promoter' means a person

(a) who has been named as such in a prospectus or is identified by the company in the annual return referred to in section 92; or

(b) who has control over the affairs of the company, directly or indirectly, whether as a shareholder, director or otherwise; or

(c) in accordance with whose advice, directions, or instructions the Board of Directors of the company are obliged to act.

Provided that sub-clause (c) shall not apply to a person who is acting merely in a professional capacity.

The above definition clarifies that promoters are the persons who have control over the management of company, directly or indirectly, and board of directors of the company are obliged to act on thier advice. The section excludes the person as director who is acting merely in a professional capacity.

In simple words promoters are like the fathers of the company, who give birth to the company (by conceptualizing and executing the idea), and try to nourish the company thereto.

---

15. Krishi Foundry Employees Union (supra).

In the case of Lagunas Nitrate Co. *v.* Lagunas syndicate (1899)2 Ch. 392, it was discussed that it is not essential that promoter should be associated with the initial formation of the company. Any person who afterwards helps to arrange floating of its capital will be considered a promoter.

Role of Promoter

Certainly promoters play an important role in the company, but they are not considered as agents or a trustee for the company because it is not in existence, but their role is that of a fiduciary in relation to the company and therefore requires making full disclosure of all the relevant facts, including any profit made by them.

In the case of Lidney Wigpool Iron Ore Co. *v.* Bird [1866] 33 Ch. D. 85 it was held that

> Although not an agent for the company, nor a trustee for it before its formation, the old familiar principles of law of agency and of trusteeship have been extended and very properly extended to meet such cases. It is perfectly well settled that a promoter of a company is accountable to it for all monies secretly obtained by him from it just as the relationship of principal and agent or the trustee and cestui que trust had really existed between him and the company when the money was obtained.

Liability of Promoters under the Companies Act, 2013

False information for incorporation of company

Section 7(6): Where, at any time after the incorporation of a company, it is proved that the company has been incorporated by furnishing any false or incorrect information or representation or by suppressing any material fact or information in any of the documents or declaration filed or made for incorporating such a company, or by any fraudulent action, the promoters, the persons named as the first directors of the company and the persons making the declaration shall be liable for fraud under section 447.

Non-compliance

Section 26; The promoters may be held liable for the non-compliance of the provisions of this section:

Section 102(4): Whereas a result of non-disclosure or insufficient disclosure in any explanatory statement annexed to the notice of a general meeting, by a promoter, director, manager, if any, or other key managerial personnel, any benefit accrues to them or their relatives, either directly or indirectly, the promoter, director, manager or other key managerial personnel, as the case may be, shall hold such benefit in trust for the company, and shall, without prejudice to any other action being taken against him under this Act or under any other law for the time being in force, be liable to compensate the company to the extent of the benefit received by him.

The intention of legislature to insert this section is aimed to prohibit the secret profits or any other expense generated by the promoter, as the company cannot be used as a tool for personal profit.

Section 35 has fixed the civil liability of promoter along with other person mentioned in the section, for any misleading statement in the prospectus to a person who has subscribed for any securities of the company on the faith of the prospectus.

Section 36: Punishment for fraudulently inducing persons to invest money: The word 'any person', includes promoter in the preview of this section.

Section 447 Punishment for Fraud: The section establishes the criminal liability in case of any fraud sustained by any person in the company.

Pre-incorporation Contract

When a promoter enters into a contract on behalf of company, being duly prior to it incorporated, to acquire any property or right of the company, is known as 'pre-incorporation' contract or 'preliminary' contract.

The basic rule says a contract made before the company's incorporation cannot bind the company, but it is the personal liability of the promoters who execute the said contract. The exception to this rule is governed by sections 15(h) and 19(e) of The Specific Performance Act, 1963.

The nature of such a contract seems to be a tripartite contract, indeed it is bilateral, and the promoter is not the agent of the company nor he is doing any approved work but he is entering into a contract with a third party on behalf of a non-existing principle. It is important to note here that the company being a legal separate entity, can perform its work only through its agent or members, but before incorporation it is not in existence as in Kelner *v.* Baxter, (1866) LR 2 CP 174, it was held that 'two consenting parties are necessary to a contract, whereas the company, before incorporation, is a non-entity'.

Pre-incorporation Type of Contracts

Pre-incorporation contracts can be classified in two categories—public and private company. A private company can commence its business immediately after obtaining a certificate of incorporation, the concept of provisional contracts is not applicable on a private company.

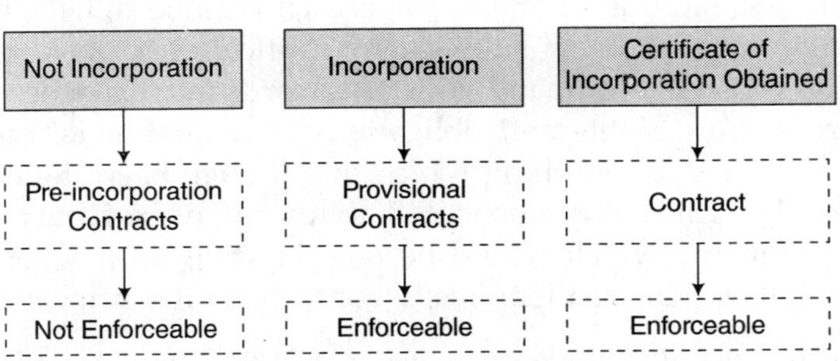

Pre-incorporation contracts

Contracts entered into on behalf of the company by the promoters prior to its incorporation, are known as pre-incorporation contracts.

Provisional Contracts

Contracts entered into after the incorporation of company but prior to obtaining the certificate of incorporation are called provisional contracts.

Before the application of section 11 (commencement of business)* on the company the contract made by the company having a share capital, whether public or private, though made after incorporation but before the company becomes entitled to commence the business, is not binding on the company.

The section specifies certain conditions before commencing the business of company, i.e., a declaration has to be filed by a director in form and verified in such manner as may be prescribed, with the Registrar.

In the case of a company having a share capital, whether public or private, contracts made after incorporation but before the company becomes entitled to commence business in terms of section 11 are provisional and are not binding on the company until the company becomes so entitled after filing of the prescribed declaration by its director and verification of its registered office with the Registrar under that section. But after the company becomes entitled to commence business, such contracts automatically become binding, i.e., without any ratification.

Enforceability of Pre-incorporation Contract

English Law = Promoters are liable not the company

Kelner *v.* Baxter (1866) 2LR 2CP 174[1] was the first English case which enunciated pre-incorporation contracts, and held promoter for it as:

> There was no company in existence at the time, the agreement would be wholly inoperative unless it were held to be binding on the defendants personally. The cases referred to in the course of the argument fully bear out the proposition that, where a contract is signed by one who professes to be signing 'as agent', but who has no principal existing at the time, and the contract would be altogether inoperative unless binding upon the person who signed it, he is bound thereby: and a stranger cannot by a subsequent ratification relieve him from that responsibility. When the company came afterwards into existence it was a totally new creature, having rights and obligations from that time, but no rights or obligations by reason of anything which might have been done before. It was once, indeed, thought that an inchoate liability might be incurred on behalf of a proposed company, which would become binding on it when subsequently formed: but that notion was manifestly contrary to the principles upon which

*Section 11 of Companies Act, 2011, has been omitted in the Companies (Amendamnd) Act, 2015

the law of contract is founded. There must be two parties to a contract; and the rights and obligations which it creates cannot be transferred by one of them to a third person who was not in a condition to be bound by it at the time it was made.

Indian Law

Sections 15(h) and 19(e) of the Specific Relief Act, 1963, govern the pre-incorporation contract.

'When the promoters of a company have, before its incorporation, entered into a contract for the purposes of the company, and such contract is warranted by the terms of the incorporation, the company: Provided that the company has accepted the contract and has communicated such acceptance to the other party to the contract.

Section 15 provides the remedy to the party for specific performance of the contract when a party is reluctant to discharge the obligations of contract, and Section 19 provides the relief against parties and persons claiming under them by subsequent title.

Bare analysis of the sections exhibit that any pre-incorporation contract by the promoters of the company is considered to be the contract of the company or the company has accepted the contract and has communicated such acceptance to the other party of the contract. The contract is warranted by the terms of the incorporation.

'Warranted by the terms of incorporation' means within the scope of the objects of the company as stated in the memorandum or Article of the Company.

To bind the company for pre-incorporation contracts with third parties, the promoters must assume personal responsibility on the face of the agreement itself, the tests of pre-incorporation conditions having been fulfilled and subsequently ratified by the company after its incorporation, there is nothing to doubt the validity of the transfer.

Section 10 of the Companies Act, 2013, supports the same as:

Section 10: Effect of memorandum and articles

(2) Subject to the provisions of this Act, the memorandum and articles shall, when registered, bind the company and the members thereof to the same extent as if they respectively had been signed by the company and by each member, and contained covenants on its and his part to observe all the provisions of the memorandum and of the articles.

(3) All monies payable by any member to the company under the memorandum or articles shall be a debt due from him to the company.

In terms of Section 15(h) of the Specific Relief Act, the promoters of a company before its incorporation could enter into a contract for the benefit of the company and such a contract may be warranted by the terms of incorporation of the company. The said provision is subject to the proviso that the company accepts the said transaction.

While we accept the position that a promoter is neither an agent nor a trustee of the company under incorporation, we are inclined to think that in respect of transactions on behalf of it, he stands in a fiduciary position. For the plaintiff-company Sections 92 and 94 of the Indian Trusts Act, 1882, were relied upon. It seems to us that neither of these sections is of assistance to it. These sections, as we think, contemplate transactions as between persons in existence. In any case, it seems to us that no trust as defined by Section 3 of the Act is brought about by the purchases made by the promoters. The legal position of a promoter in relation to his acts, particularly purchase of immoveable properties on behalf of the company under incorporation, is a peculiar one not capable of being brought into any established or recognized norms of the law as to its character as an agent or a trustee. But, at the same time, it is impossible, to our minds, to deny that he does stand in a certain fiduciary position in relation to the company under incorporation. When he does certain things for the benefit of it, as for instance, purchase of immoveable properties, he is not at liberty to deny that benefit to the company when incorporated. We are prepared to hold that in such a case the benefit of the purchase will pass on to the company when incorporated."[16]

Formation of a Company

Following are the steps involved in forming a company:

- Promotion
- Incorporation or registration
- Capital subscription

Promotion

The formation of company starts with an idea projected by the promoters of the company. It is the process by which the promoters or group of personss, who desire to form a company, project their idea with like-minded persons and bring together men, money, materials, and machinery. Sometimes it is defined as the innovation of business opportunities, and managing subsequent organization of funds, property and abilities into a business concern for the purpose of making profits therefore. In simple words, promotion is transforming an idea into corporate reality.

States of promotion

The promotion can be divided into the following categories:

- Invention of an idea
- Planning and analysis
- Acquisition of requirements
- Financing the proposition

16. Jai Narain Parasurampuria (Dead) ... *v.* Pushpa Devi Saraf & Ors.

Invention of an idea

Every project starts with the invention of an idea, when we conceptualize the potential opportunity in any business. Thereafter the idea is explored with its positive and native side with the help of others.

Planning and analysis

The second state starts when we analyse and do the detailed investigation of idea and constitute the planning for each and every resource to set out the profitability and revenue.

Financing the proposition

The final and important stage is financing – to decide the capital structure of the company, i.e., the shares, the debentures, and other sources of capital generation, such as loans, etc.

Incorporation or registration

Chapter II of the Act enunciates the formation of the company as "Incorporation of Company and Matters Incidental Thereto".

Purpose of the Company Incorporated

Lawful purpose

The intention of the legislature is very clear about the object of the company, by using the word in the section 'A company may be formed for any lawful purpose'. A company can only be incorporated for a lawful purpose only. Although meaning of lawful purpose is not being defined in the act, to understand the meaning of lawful purpose we have to do a clinical analysis.

The objective of any enactment is the projection of the will of the society and it reflects the social behaviour in that particular time. The company is the vehicle to discharge the economic and social behaviour of the society. The object of the section is to formulate a way under which a company can be constructed by the person to uphold not only the requirement of legal provisions but also compete with social structure.

Demarcation of economic freedom

Section 3 of the Act demarcates the adverse object of the company so as to avoid any anomalous situations. The company is the vehicle to discharge the economic objective of the society, which is the final destiny of the company is as reflected in the Memorandum of the Company. In the filtration process, the said word has great importance from the point of view of economic justice, avoidance of hardship to the person associated with company, and it may have affect from any illegal objective of the company.

Otherwise also the law prohibits any association of people for any illegal objective. The section uses the word 'lawful object in the section'. Contrary to such word a company may cease to exist, and under such a situation a great hardship may be caused to the person associated with the company. Using such a word the legislature intended to discourage or bar such incorporation of companies which is contrary to law or economic justice.

Procedure of incorporation of companies

Application to Registrar for Incorporation of Company – Section 4(4) Application for allotment of Desired Name

The first step in the incorporation of a company starts with filing an application before the Registrar within whose jurisdiction the registered office of a company is proposed to be situated, along with requisite document. Form No. INC.1 is used to file the application.

The corresponding section exhibits that the desired name should not resemble or be identical with any other incorporated company or prohibited by government as any word or expression which is likely to give the impression that the company is in any way connected with, or having the patronage of, the Central Government, any State Government, or any local authority, corporation, or body constituted by the Central Government or any State Government under any law for the time being in force.

Documents required for incorporation

(1) Registrar of Companies is the authority who registers the companies. To incorporate a company the following have to be filed:

- (a) memorandum and articles of the company;
- (b) A declaration in the prescribed form by an advocate, a chartered accountant, cost accountant, or company secretary in practice, who is engaged in the formation of the company and by a person named in the articles as a director, manager, or secretary of the company;
- (c) An affidavit from each of the subscribers to the memorandum and from persons named as the first directors, if any, in the articles that he is not convicted of any offence in connection with the promotion, formation, or management of any company, or that he has not been found guilty of any fraud or misfeasance or of any breach of duty to any company under this act or any previous company law during the preceding five years and that all the documents filed with the Registrar for registration of the company contains information that is correct and complete and true to the best of his knowledge and belief;
- (d) the address for correspondence till its registered office is established;
- (e) the particulars of name, including surname or family name, residential address, nationality and such other particulars of every subscriber to the memorandum along with proof of identity, as may be prescribed, and in the case of a subscriber being a body corporate, such particulars as may be prescribed;

(f) the particulars of the persons mentioned in the articles as the first directors of the company, their names, including surnames or family names, the director identification number, residential address, nationality, and such other particulars including proof of identity as may be prescribed; and

(g) the particulars of the interests of the persons mentioned in the articles as the first directors of the company in other firms or bodies corporate along with their consent to act as directors of the company in such form and manner as may be prescribed.

(2) The Registrar on the basis of documents and information filed under sub-section (1) shall register all the documents and information referred to in that sub-section in the register and issue a certificate of incorporation in the prescribed form to the effect that the proposed company is incorporated under this Act.

(3) On and from the date mentioned in the certificate of incorporation issued under sub-section (2), the Registrar shall allot to the company a corporate identity number which shall be a distinct identity for the company and which shall also be included in the certificate.

(4) The company shall maintain and preserve at its registered office copies of all documents and information as originally filed under sub-section (1) till its dissolution under this Act.

(5) If any person furnishes any false or incorrect particulars of any information or suppresses any material information of which he is aware in any of the documents filed with the Registrar in relation to the registration of a company, he shall be liable for action under section 447.

(6) Without prejudice to the provisions of sub-section (5) where, at any time after the incorporation of a company, it is proved that the company has been, incorporated by furnishing any false or incorrect information or representation, or by suppressing any material fact or information in any of the documents, or declaration filed or made for incorporating such company, or by any fraudulent action, the promoters, the persons named as the first directors of the company and the persons making declaration under clause (b) of sub-section (1) shall each be liable for action under section 447.

(7) Without prejudice to the provisions of sub-section (6), where a company has been incorporated by furnishing any false or incorrect information or representation or by suppressing any material fact or information in any of the documents or declaration filed or made for incorporating such company, or by any fraudulent action, the Tribunal may, on an application made to it, on being satisfied that the situation so warrants,

(a) pass such orders, as it may think fit, for regulation of the management of the company including changes, if any, in its memorandum and articles, in public interest or in the interest of the company and its members and creditors; or

(b) direct that liability of the members shall be unlimited; or
(c) direct removal of the name of the company from the register of companies; or
(d) pass an order for the winding up of the company; or
(e) pass such other orders as it may deem fit:

Provided that before making any order under this sub-section,—

(i) the company shall be given a reasonable opportunity of being heard in the matter; and
(ii) the Tribunal shall take into consideration the transactions entered into by the company, including the obligations, if any, contracted or payment of any liability.

Capital Subscription

After the grant of Certificate of Incorporation, it is important for the company to make necessary arrangements for raising the capital of the company, to run its business.

Capital Subscription is the process by which the company collects the funds to run its business.

A private company has the flexibility to start its business immediately after the grant of Certificate of Incorporation, because it is funded by the promoters, however, in the case of Public Limited Company the "Capital Subscription Stage" is important, under which the company can raise the required funds from the public by way of "issue of shares and debentures", which is called "issue a prospectus", which is a sort of invitation to the general public to subscribe to the capital of the company, that is why it is called a "Public Company" and the former one is "Private Company".

The following steps are required for raising funds from the public:

(a) Securities and Exchange Board of India (SEBI) approval
(b) Filling of prospectus
(c) Appointment of bankers/brokers/underwriters
(d) Minimum sub-subscription
(e) Application to stock exchange
(f) Allotment of shares

Securities and Exchange Board of India (SEBI) Approval

Protection of investors are the heights priority in Public Company, SEBI (Securities and Exchange Board of India), is the regulatory authority which monitors and protects the investors, by way of issuing guidelines for the disclosure of information and investor protection.

It is mandatory for the company, before making a public offer for sale of shares and debentures must comply with SEBI guidelines. The fundamentals of SEBI guidelines are:

a company inviting funds from the general public must make adequate disclosure of all relevant information and must not conceal any material information from the potential investors and the companies are required to give information according to 'guidelines for disclosure and investor protection 2009'.

Filling of Prospectus

It is the general rule that a copy of the prospectus or statement in lieu of prospectus is filed with the Registrar of Companies, on the specified date the prospectus will be issued to the public. The purpose of filing the prospectus to the Registrar of Company is to make an invitation to the public to apply for shares or debentures of the company or to make deposits in the company. Investors take a decision to investment in a company primarily on the basis of the information contained in prospectus.

Appointment of Bankers

On the basis of information provided in the prospects if investors want to invest in the company they have to forward their applications for shares along with requisite amount to the company's bankers mentioned in the prospectus. The bankers will then forward all applications to the company and the company takes the decision to allotment of shares.

The reason for appointment of banker for accepting the application is important because raising funds from the public is a tedious task.

Minimum sub-subscription

The main intent of this provision is to avoid companies from commencing business with insufficient resources, the core objective of this provision that the company must receive applications for a certain minimum number of shares before going ahead with the allotment of shares, and in case of insufficient subscription as per prospectus then the received amount shall be refunded within a given time frame.

Section 39 of the Companies Act, 2013 is important with this respect, which prohibits the company to receive the insufficient subscription as:

> "No allotment of any securities of a company offered to the public for subscription shall be made unless the amount stated in the prospectus as the minimum amount has been subscribed and the sums payable on application for the amount so stated have been paid to and received by the company by cheque or other instrument."

The amount payable on application on every security shall not be less than five per cent of the nominal amount of the security or such other percentage or amount, as may be specified by the Securities and Exchange Board by making regulations in this behalf.

Application to stock exchange

Another important step is to make an application at least one stock exchange for permission to deal in its shares or debentures. It is important because if such permission is not granted before the expiry of ten weeks from the date of closure of subscription list, the allotment shall be considered void and all money received from the investor must be returned to them.

Allotment of Shares

If everything goes well as mentioned above, then the last step is to obtain certificate of commencement.

*Certificate of commencement**

In the erstwhile Companies Act, 1956, the date of incorporation of company was not the date of commencement of business, because there was a requirement of obtaining the Certificate of Incorporation from the Registrar of the Company. With the recommendation of J.J. Irani Committee** the requirement of obtaining a certificate of commencement of business has been done away.

CLASSIFICATION OF COMPANIES

Sub-section (1) of section 3 of the Companies Act, 2013 describes three types of companies which can be incorporated as:

I. Public Company
II. Private Company
III. One Person Company
- When there are seven or more persons it is called a Public Company;
- when there are two or more persons it is called a Private Company;
- when there is only one member it is called one person company. It is a new feature which has been added in the Companies Act, 2013 to increase the entrepreneurship.

Further sub-section (2) of section 3 describes that:

(2) A company formed under sub-section (1) may be either

(a) a company limited by shares; or

(b) a company limited by guarantee; or

(c) an unlimited company.

*It appears that issue of a certificate of commencement of business would not be necessary since the present Companies Act prescribes the amount of capital to be paid up immediately after the registration. This should be adequate to establish the borrowing power of the company. In view of this, the requirement of obtaining a separate Certificate of Commencement of business imposes avoidable delay and could be dispensed with.

**Jamshed J. Irani Committee (Expert Committee on Company Law)

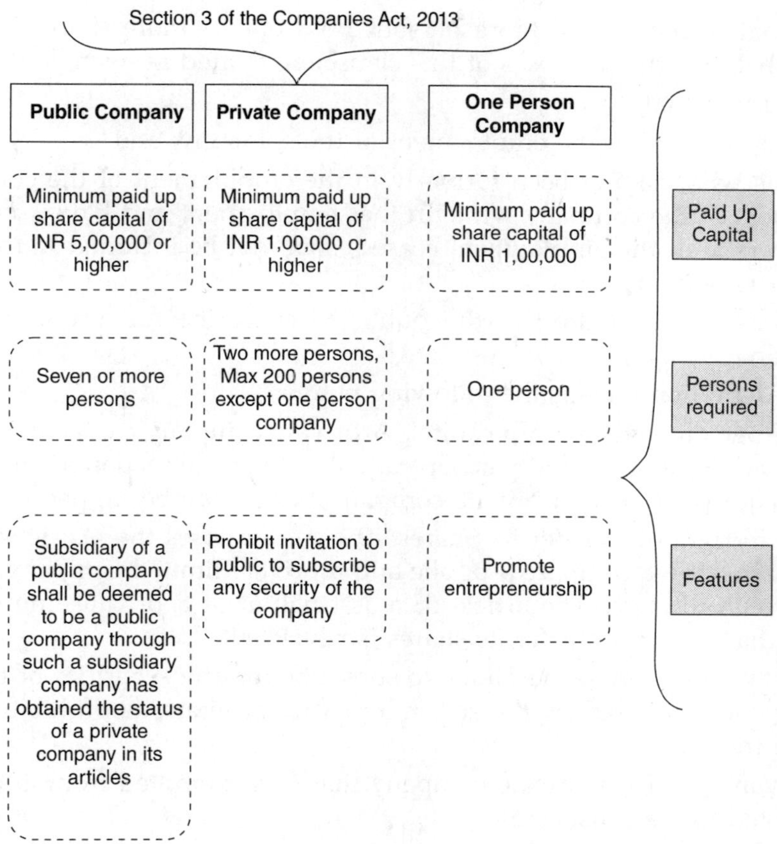

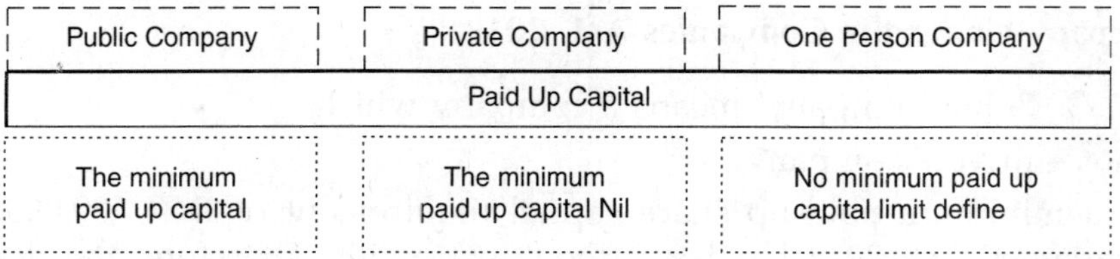

Private Company Under the Companies Act, 2013

It is the most opted choice nowadays in India, because of its characteristics.

Section 2(68) 'private company' is a company that has a minimum paid-up share capital of one lakh rupees or such higher paid-up share capital as may be prescribed, and which by its articles,

(i) restricts the right to transfer its shares;

(ii) except in case of One Person Company, limits the number of its members to two hundred:

Provided that where two or more persons hold one or more shares in a company jointly, they shall, for the purposes of this clause, be treated as a single member;

Provided further that

(i) persons who are in the employment of the company; and

(ii) persons who, having been formerly in the employment of the company, were members of the company while in that employment and have continued to be members after the employment ceased, shall not be included in the number of members; and

(iii) prohibits any invitation to the public to subscribe for any securities of the company.

The above definition reflects the following points:

Number of person, and paid up capital: A private company can be classified on the basis of number of members and paid up capital. As per the section a minimum of two persons are required to form a private company, which can be capped to 200 people.

Restriction to right of transfer its Shares: The Act imposes the restriction to right of transfer of shares. If we compare a public and a private limited company, it is the key attribute between the two. The article of a association of a private limited company, must exhibit that right to transfer its shares is restricted.

Prohibits any invitation to the public to subscribe for any securities of the company: Another restriction imposed by the act on a private company is prohibition to issue a prospectus to the public.

It is an advantage of the private company that it is exempted from any compliance of the act related to the prospectus.

Public Company Under the Companies Act, 2013

Section 2(71)*: 'Public company' means a company which

(a) is not a private company;

(b) has a minimum paid-up share capital requirement of INR 500,000 under the Companies Act, 2013 has been done away with. Therefore, the definitions of private and public companies amended and henceforth, no minimum paid-up capital requirements will now apply for incorporating the company.

Provided that a company which is a <u>subsidiary of a company</u>, <u>not being a private company</u>, shall be <u>deemed to be a public company</u> for the purposes of this Act even where such a subsidiary company continues to be a private company in its articles.

The Section specifies the following points:

1. A public company is distinct from a private company.

*Clause 2(71) in sub-clause (b), the words "of five lakh rupees or such higher paid-up capital," shall be omitted. as per the Companies (Amendment) Act, 2015

2. Certain paid-up capital is required to become a public company, or public company can be classified on the basis of paid-up capital as well.
3. Subsidiary of a company, not being a private company, means a public company, deemed to be a public company, even such a subsidiary company continues to be a private company in its article.

It means there are:

- Public company,
- Private company, and
- Deemed public company.

But Section 2(87) of the Companies Act, 2013 further discussed about the subsidiary company as:

> (87) 'Subsidiary company' or 'subsidiary', in relation to any other company (that is to say the holding company), means a company in which the holding company
>
> (i) controls the composition of the Board of Directors; or
>
> (ii) exercises or controls more than one-half of the total share capital either at its own or together with one or more of its subsidiary companies:
>
> Provided that such class or classes of holding companies as may be prescribed shall not have layers of subsidiaries beyond such numbers as may be prescribed.
>
> Explanation: For the purposes of this clause,
>
> (a) a company shall be deemed to be a subsidiary company of the holding company even if the control referred to in sub-clause (i) or sub-clause (ii) is of another subsidiary company of the holding company;
>
> (b) the composition of a company's Board of Directors shall be deemed to be controlled by another company if that other company by exercise of some power exercisable by it at its discretion can appoint or remove all or a majority of the directors;
>
> (c) the expression 'company' includes anybody corporate;
>
> (d) 'layer' in relation to a holding company means its subsidiary or subsidiaries;

The clinical research of section 2(87) enunciate the following points:

- Subsidiary means in relation to Any Other Company.
- Holding company controls the composition of the Board of Directors. Composition means to appoint and remove all or a majority of directors according to its will.
- Layers (subsidiaries of holding company) shall not have beyond the prescribed numbers of numbers.

When we analyse section 3 and 4(7) of the Companies Act, 1956, it seems the position of a private company was clear. While in the Companies Act, 2013, provisions of section

4 (7) have been repealed, which creates some confusion over the position of an Indian subsidiary's treatment under the Act. Because when we examine section 2(71) in relation with Explanation (c) of section 2(87), simply using the phrase 'not being a private company' is not clear. As a subsidiary company is considered to be a deemed public company if the holding company is not a private company it is pertinent to note here that the holding company could be anything else as well, such as it could be a body corporate.

Further, Explanation (c) establishes that corporate incorporated outside India certainly be considered as a deemed public company by using the expression 'Company' which includes body corporate, though the phrase "for the purposes of this clause' is being used in the section but it may be considered nothing but the definition of a subsidiary.

Other Features of Public and Private Company in The Companies Act, 2013

Section 11

To commence its business or exercise any borrowing power, it is mandatory to pay the value of the shares agreed in the Memorandum by the director, and file a declaration before the Registrar.

Section 203: Appointment of Key Managerial Person

Section says every company, which means private company also requires appointing the following whole time key managerial person

- Managing director , Chief Executive Officer, and in their absence a Whole Time Director
- Company Secretary
- Chief Finance Officer

BASIS OF CLASSIFICATION OF COMPANIES

Incorporation

Statutory companies

When a company is incorporated under the special Act of Parliament or Legislature, it is called a statutory company, public corporation. The special Act defines its powers and functions, rules and regulations governing its employees and its relationship with government departments. The intention to create such companies is to serve a larger public purpose, such as railway, gas, electricity, or any other enterprises of national importance. Life Corporation of India, Reserve Bank of India, Financial Corporation, Unit Trust of India, National Human Rights Commission, Food Corporation of India, Inland Waterways Authority of India, Airports Authority of India, Damodar Valley Corporation, National Highways Authority of India, Central Warehousing Corporation are some such enterprises.

Though it has been created under a special enactment of legislature, but it still comes under the preview of Companies Act, 2013, owned by a government with or without other shareholders, or it might be a body without shareholders.

Key features

Financing and subscription

- Mostly it is funded by the State or Central Government and, it is also authorized to subscribe public subscription.

Autonomous body

It is an important feature of such type of companies that they have the status of an autonomous body and that is why they are free to frame their own policies and procedures subject to their legislature. To provide more flexibility in their work and efficiency, such a status is granted to them, with little government interference.

Registered companies

Companies which are registered under the Companies Act, 2013 (also under the Companies Act, 1956).

Limited

Limited liabilities

Under this category the companies are classified on the basis of their limited liability with reference to their share or guarantee, or during winding up of the company.

Company with limited liability

(a) Limited by Share

When the liability of the members of a company is limited to the amount unpaid on the shares, such a company is known as a company limited by share. Such liability can be enforced during the existence of the company or at time of winding up of the company.

Such liability of company must be mentioned in the Memorandum of the Company as the mandate of section 4 of the Companies Act, 2013, specifies that, in the case of a company limited by shares, that liability of its members is limited to the amount unpaid, if any, on the shares held by them.

(b) Limited by Guarantee

The liability of the members of the company in the event of winding up of the company is limited by a fixed sum which is stipulated in the Memorandum of the Company.

> Application of section 4 of the Companies Act, 2013 specifies that in the case of a company limited by guarantee, the amount up to which each member undertakes to contribute to the assets of the company in the event of its being

wound-up while he is a member or within one year after he ceases to be a member, for payment of the debts and liabilities of the company or of such debts and liabilities as may have been contracted before he ceases to be a member, as the case may be.

It is important to note here that the company is not required to have any share capital, but in case it has the share capital, it can reduce its share capital subject to section 66 of the Companies Act, 2013.

Company with unlimited liability

Section 2(92) defines 'unlimited company' as a company not having any limit on the liability of its members;

Being its characteristic such companies are incorporated in less numbers compared to a limited by shares. The disadvantage of such companies is the liability of members of such companies is not limited.

Other than the limited liability, in an unlimited liability company every member is liable for the debts of the company as in an ordinary partnership, in proportion to their interest in the company. Such type of company may or may not have share capital; if it has share capital, it may be a public company or a private company. Like the partnership firm, its members have a joint and non-limited responsibility to meet any insufficiency in the assets of the company to enable liquidation or winding up liability.

Having many disadvantages, it has certain advantages such as that there is no requirement for share capital for an unlimited company, but when it specifies its share capital in the Memorandum of Association, it can reduce or increase it.

Ownership

Companies can be classified on the basis of their ownership as:

(a) Government Company

Clause 2(45) of the Companies Bill, 2012 defines a 'Government Company' as any company in which not less than 51% of the paid-up share capital is held by the Central Government, or by any State Government or Governments, or partly by the Central Government and partly by one or more State Governments, and includes a company which is a subsidiary company of such a Government Company'.

Sub-section (6) of section 139, immunes the government company for the application of Section 139 which says:

> every company shall, at the first annual general meeting, appoint an individual or a firm as an auditor who shall hold office from the conclusion of that meeting till the conclusion of its sixth annual general meeting and thereafter till the conclusion of every sixth meeting and the manner and procedure of selection of auditors by the members of the company at such meeting shall be such as may be prescribed.

Prohibitions and restrictions regarding political contributions

Section 182 prohibits government companies to contribute any amount directly or indirectly to any political party.

Chapter XXIII defines how to submit the annual reports. Section 394(1) defines: 'where the Central Government is a member of a Government Company, the Central Government shall cause an annual report on the working and affairs of that company', and section 395(1) specifies where the Central Government is not a member of a Government Company, every State Government which is a member of that company, or where only one State Government is a member of the company, that State Government shall cause an annual report on the working and affairs of the company.

(b) Non-Government Company

When any company other than a Government Company is called non-government company, e.g., a Foreign Company Section 2(42) of the Companies Act, 2013 defines a 'foreign company' as any company or body corporate incorporated outside India which (a) has a place of business in India whether by itself or through an agent, physically or through electronic mode; and (b) conducts any business activity in India in any other manner.

Any company incorporated outside the territorial limit of India is known as a foreign company, but the place of conducting the business activity is within the territorial jurisdiction of India.

Provisions of Chapter XXII of the Companies Act, 2013 are applicable to foreign company.

ACCESS TO CAPITAL

Listed Company

When any company's shares are listed on a stock exchange for public trading it is called a listed company.

Section (52): 'Listed company' means a company which has any of its securities listed on any recognised stock exchange.

Unlisted Company

Other then the listed company.

CONTROL

Holding Company

Holding company is determined by two attributes—control and ownership, in which one company is holding and another is a subsidiary company.

Section (46) of the Companies Act, 2013, defines a 'holding company' in relation to one or more other companies. It means a company of which such companies are subsidiary companies.

Subsidiary Company

Section (87) defines 'subsidiary company' or 'subsidiary', in relation to any other company (that is to say the holding company). It means a company in which the holding company

(i) controls the composition of the Board of Directors; or

(ii) exercises or controls more than one-half of the total share capital either on its own or together with one or more of its subsidiary companies.

Provided that such class or classes of holding companies as may be prescribed shall not have layers of subsidiaries beyond such numbers as may be prescribed.

Explanation: For the purposes of this clause,

(a) a company shall be deemed to be a subsidiary company of the holding company even if the control referred to in sub-clause (i) or sub-clause (ii) is of another subsidiary company of the holding company;

(b) the composition of a company's Board of Directors shall be deemed to be controlled by another company if that other company by exercise of some power exercisable by it at its discretion can appoint or remove all or a majority of the directors;

(c) the expression 'company' includes any body corporate;

(d) 'layer' in relation to a holding company means its subsidiary or subsidiaries.

The clinical research of the section shows that, there is a correlation between the holding and subsidiary company; the holding company has control on the number of directors on the board, and controls more the 50% of the total share capital either on its own or together with its other subsidiary.

Another important aspect of a holding company is that it does not have layers of subsidiary companies (layers means subsidiary of subsidiary company), other than specified number in the act. It is also important to note in the definition that it recognises the 'deemed subsidiary' company as well, if the control mentioned in sub-clause (i) and sub-clause (ii) is of another subsidiary company of the holding company.

Associate Company

Section (6) defines 'associate company' in relation to another company. It means a company in which the other company has a significant influence, but which is not a subsidiary company of the company having such influence and includes a joint venture company.

Small Companies

The Companies Act, 2013, introduced a new concept of 'small companies'. The criteria to identify such a company are based on its capital and the turnover; the intention behind it is to provide facilities and exempt such companies from certain formalities.

Section 2(85): "Small company" means a company, other than a public company:

(i) paid-up share capital of which does not exceed fifty lakh rupees or such higher amount as may be prescribed which shall not be more than five crore rupees; or

(ii) turnover of which as per its last profit and loss account does not exceed two crore rupees or such higher amount as may be prescribed which shall not be more than twenty crore rupees:

Provided that nothing in this section shall apply to—

- a holding company or a subsidiary company;
- a company registered under Section 8; or
- a company or body corporate governed by any special Act

After analysing the section following points come into the light:

A small company means other than a public company. It means only a private company can be classified as a small company. There are two basic requirements: maximum paid-up:

(i) share capital should not be rupees fifty lakh and any such higher amount as may be prescribed rupees five crore.

(ii) turnover of which as per its last P&L account should not be more than rupees two crore and any such higher amount as may be prescribed but not exceeding rupees ten crore.

A holding company, subsidiary company, company created for charitable purpose (under section 8), or a company or body corporate governed by a special act are out of the purview of a small company.

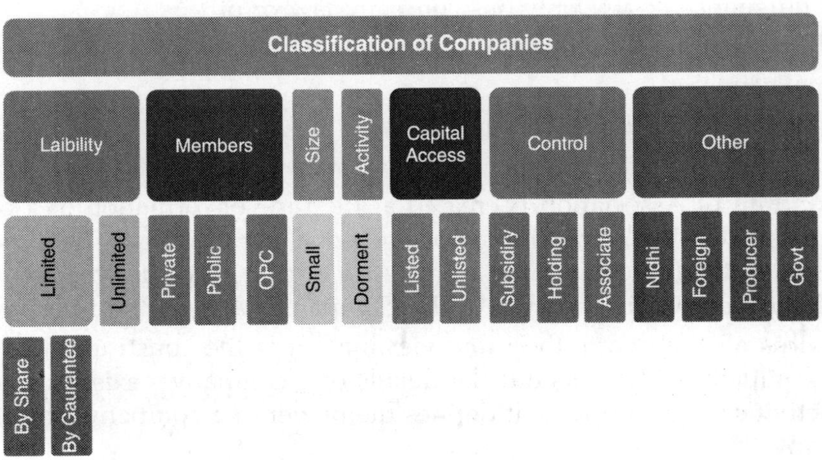

CHAPTER 3

Memorandum of Association & Article of Association

- Constructive Notice
- Indoor Management
- Doctrine of Ultra Vires

MEMORANDUM OF ASSOCIATION

Memorandum of Association is an important document of a company. It is a document that regulates a company's exterior activities and exhibits the formation or incorporation of a company. It reflects the company's name, its shareholders and number of shares held by them, and location of its registered office and also other essential features of the company such as objectives, amount of authorized share capital, liability of its members as limited by shares or by guarantee, and type of contracts the company is allowed to enter into. The memorandum is a public document and may be inspected by anyone, usually at the public office where it is lodged.

Memorandum of Association is the combination of two words Memorandum and Association. Memorandum means a written message in business or diplomacy[17] and association means a group of people. Thus, Memorandum of Association is a written message for a group of persons who are associated for conductiong any business.

Definition of Memorandum: As per section 2(56) 'memorandum' means the memorandum of association of a company as originally framed or as altered from time to time in pursuance of any previous company law or of this Act.

Clinical examination of definition reflects a few points as:

- originally framed
- or as altered from time to time
- in pursuance of any previous company law or of this Act.

Memorandum of Association is created at the time of formation of a company and there is no restriction to alter it. It may be altered as per the need. The important aspect in the definition is MoA, the phrase 'pursuance of any previous company law' reflects the MoA is drafted within the lines of the Companies Act, and not beyond that.

Lord Cairns also supports the same views as: It is the constitution of company or charter of company which sets out the details of a company's existence. It defines the scope of activities of a company, it defines the power of a company, and the limitation of a company.

---

17. http://www.oxforddictionaries.com/definition/english/memorandum

'Memorandum of Association of a company is its charter and defines the limitations of the powers of a company. It contains the fundamental condition upon which alone the company is allowed to be incorporated'.

The definition is not elaborative, except 'as originally framed or altered', while different types of Memorandum of Association are defined in Schedule I.

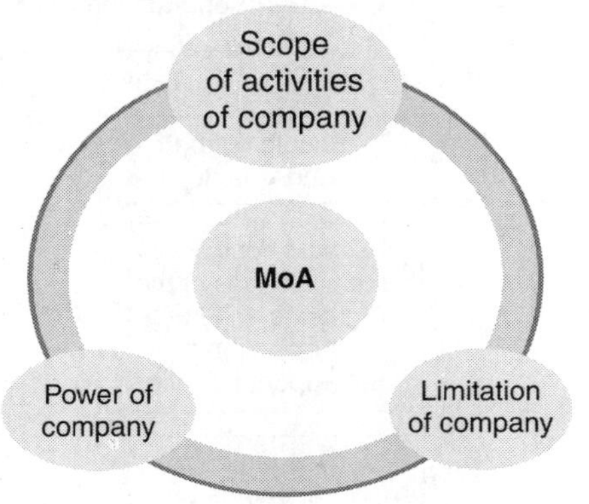

The basic objective of formulation of Memorandum of Association is for the company, and for the public who deals with the company. Actually, it is the relation between a company and the public who deal with the company, which is why it is known as a public document.

As defined by Lord Macmillan

'The purpose of Memorandum of Association is to enable the shareholders, creditors and those who deal with the company to know what its permitted range of enterprise is.'

Thus, the MoA is the object clause of company, for which the company is incorporated. It is also important to note that company cannot do any other business which is not specified in the object clause of MoA.

CONTENTS OF MEMORANDUM OF ASSOCIATION

Section 4(1) of the Companies Act, 2013 states that, the memorandum of a company shall consist of

- Name Clause
- Registered Office Clause
- Object Clause
- Liability Clause
- Share Capital Clause

Name Clause

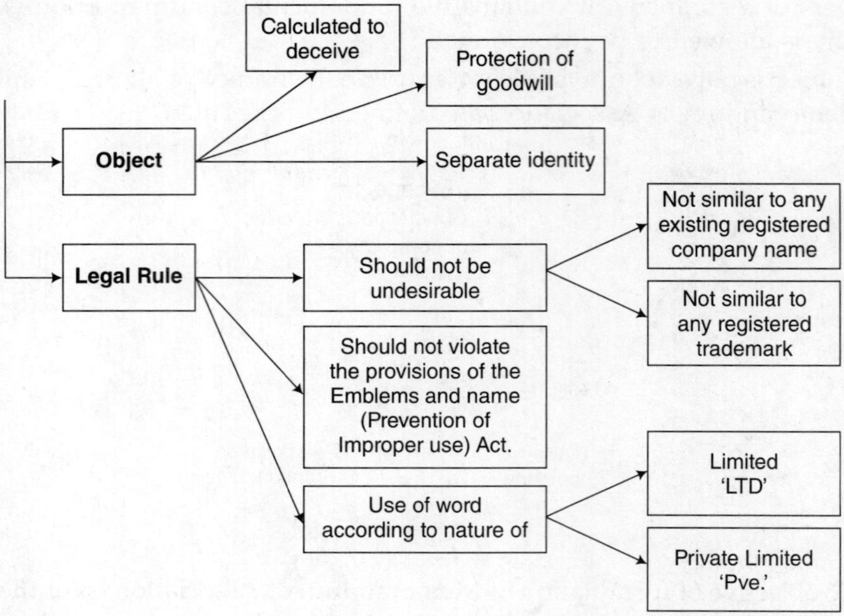

Object of name clause

The company has a monopoly of the use of the name, after registering its name because no other company can be authorized to be registered under a name identical to it, or nearly resembling it so as to be calculated to deceive. The prime objective of name clause in a company is a separate legal identity; therefore it is necessary for its identification.

It means insertion of Name Clause in the MoA based on the following objectives as:

- Protection (protection from calculative deception to general public and the good will of any registered existing company).
- Identity (to create a separate identity for general public).

Separate legal identity

The first clause in the MoA is the Name Clause. Name signifies a separate identity. Being the legal separate identity the company also requires a separate name.

Take the example of a newborn baby; the first thing is giving it a name to establish its identity. The identity of company can only be established when we give a name to it, as in the case of Johnson J in Osborn *v.* Bank of U.S, it is being observed as 'the name of a corporation is the symbol of its personal existence'.

Protection of goodwill

The process of registration of a company, with the name in the MoA protects the goodwill of the company, which often is built around the name.

Avoid-misleading to public or calculated to deceive

Another important aspect of Name Clause in the MoA is to prevent calculated deceit or the intent to misleading the general public with a name that resembles another name. A company's names should not be suggestive of any connection with an unlawful activity or be offensive in form.

To ascertain resemblance between two names, look into the type of product of the companies dealt in, or the type of business of companies, or the location of companies, or the persons involved in the companies.

In the case *of* British Diabetic Association *v.* Diabetic Society, it was held that there was a sufficient similarity between the two names to necessitate a change, even though there was no intention to mislead the public.

Name use in bona fide manner

In Karnataka High Court, in the case of Kirloskar Proprietary Ltd. and ... *v.* Kirloskar Dimensions Pvt. Ltd. AIR 1997 Kant 1, 1999 96 CompCas 726 Kar, ILR 1996 KAR 2957, 1996 (5) KarLJ 446 it was observed that,

> Nothing in this Act, shall entitle the proprietor or a registered user of a registered trademark to interfere with any bona fide use by a person of his own name or that of his place of business or of the name of the place of business, of any of his predecessors in business, or the use by any such person of any bona fide description of the character or quality of his goods.
>
> In the case of Sarabhai International Ltd. *v.* Sara Exports International (1987) PC 269: (AIR 1988 Delhi 134), has held that in case of incorporated company the adoption of the name is by choice whereas in the case of a natural person, the adoption of surname is not by choice and further held, the defence that a man has a right to use his personal name is not available in passing-off action. I am in full agreement with the view taken by the Bombay High Court as stated above. Hence, there is no substance in the argument advanced on behalf of the counsel for the defendants.[18]

Section 4 of the Companies Act, 2013

Sub-sections (2) and (3) of Section 4 signify on which basis the name of the company may be allotted:

---

18. Kirloskar Proprietary Ltd. and (supra).

(2) The name stated in the memorandum shall not

(a) be identical with or resemble too nearly the name of an existing company registered under this Act or any previous company law; or

(b) be such that its use by the company

(i) will constitute an offence under any law for the time being in force; or

(ii) is undesirable in the opinion of the Central Government.

(3) Without prejudice to the provisions of sub-section (2), a company shall not be registered with a name which contains

(a) any word or expression which is likely to give the impression that the company is in any way connected with, or having the patronage of the Central Government, any State Government, or any local authority, corporation or body constituted by the Central Government or any State Government under any law for the time being in force; or

(b) such word or expression, as may be prescribed, unless the previous approval of the Central Government has been obtained for the use of any such word or expression.

Ministry of Corporate Affairs: Name Availability Guidelines, 2011

Legal guidelines for name clause should not be undesirable

The promoters are free to choose any name for the company but the same is subject to certain limitations. The name should not be identical with the name of any existing company. The name should not create an impression that the company is carrying on the business of some other existing company. The name should not be misleading. The Companies Act also specifies that a company cannot be registered with a name which in the opinion of the Central Government is undesirable. The parameters to ascertaining the undesirability are:

- Any other existing registered company with the same or identical or too nearly resembling name.
- The proposed name should not be with an intent to 'calculated deceit'. It means the suggested name should not be connected to any existing registered company.

Name availability guidelines, 2011

Name Availability Guidelines issued by the Government of India, Ministry of Corporate Affairs vide General Circular No. 45/2011:

The proposed name is considered to be undesirable if it is identical with or too nearly resembling with:

(i) Name of a company in existence and names already approved by the Registrar of Companies;

(ii) Name of an a Limited Liability Partnership (LLP) in existence or names already approved by Registrar of LLP; or

(iv) A registered trademark or a trade mark which is subject of an application for registration of any other person under the Trade Marks Act, 1999.

(v) the proposed name(s) is/are not infringing the registered trademarks or a trademark which is subject of an application for registration of any other person under the Trade Marks Act, 1999;

(vi) the proposed name(s) is/are not in violation of the provisions of Emblems and Names (Prevention of Improper Use) Act, 1950 as amended from time to time;

(vii) the proposed name(s) is not such that its use by the company will constitute an offence under any law for the time being in force;

(viii) the proposed name is not offensive to any section of people, e.g., proposed name does not contain profanity or words or phrases that are generally considered a slur against an ethnic group, religion, gender, or heredity.

Emblems and Names (Prevention of Improper Use) Act, 1950

Section 3 of Emblems and Names (Prevention of Improper Use) Act, 1950, Prohibits improper use of certain emblems and names.

Notwithstanding anything contained in any law for the time being in force, no person shall, except in such cases and under such conditions as may be prescribed by the Central Government use, or continue to use, for the purpose of any trade, business, calling or profession, or in the title of any patent, or in any trade mark or design, any name or emblem specified in the Schedule or, any colorable imitation thereof without the previous permission of the Central Government or of such officer of Government as may be authorized in this behalf by the Central Government.

SCHEDULE

1. The name, emblem or official seal of the United Nations Organization.
2. The name, emblem or official seal of the World Health Organization.
3. The Indian National Flag.
4. The name, emblem or official seal of the Government of India or of any State, or any other insignia or coat-of-arms used by any such Government or by a Department of any such Government.
5. The emblems of the St. John Ambulance Association (India), and the St. John Ambulance Brigade (India), consisting of the device of a white eight-pointed cross embellished in the four principal angles, whether or not the device is surrounded or accompanied by concentric circles or other decoration or by lettering.

6. The name, emblem or official seal of the President, Governor, Sadar-i-Riyasat or Republic or Union of India.
7. Any name, which may suggest or be calculated to suggest
   - (i) The patronage of the Government of India or the Government of a State; or
   - (ii) Connection with any local authority or any corporation or body constituted by the Government under any law for the time being in force.
8. The name, emblem or official seal of the United Nations Educational, Scientific and Cultural Organization.
9. The name or pictorial representation of Rashtrapati, Rashtrapati Bhavan, Raj Bhavan.

   9-A. The name of pictorial representation of Mahatma Gandhi, Pandit Jawaharlal Nehru, Chhatrapati Shivaji Maharaj or the Prime Minister of India or the words "Gandhi", "Nehru" or "Shivaji", except the pictorial use thereof on calendars where only the names of the manufacturers and printers of the calendars are given and the calendars are not used for advertising goods.
10. The medals, badges or decorations instituted by the Government from time to time or the miniatures or replicas of such medals, badges or decorations or the names of such medals, badges or decorations or of the miniatures or replicas thereof.
11. The name, emblem or official seal of the International Civil Aviation Organization.
12. The word 'Interpol' which is an integral part of the International Criminal Police Organization.
13. The name, emblem or official seal of the World Meteorological Organization.
14. The name, emblem of the Tuberculosis Association of India.
15. The name, emblem and official seal of the International Atomic Agency.
16. The names 'Ashoka Chakra' or 'Dharma Chakra' or the pictorial representation of Ashoka Chakra as used in the India National Flag or in the official seal or emblem of the Government of India or of any State Government or of a Department of any such Government.
17. The name of the Parliament or the Legislature of any State, or the Supreme Court, or the High Court of any State, or the Central Secretariat, or the Secretariat of any State Government or any other Government Office or the pictorial representation of any building occupied by any of the aforesaid institutions.
18. The name and emblem of the Rama Krishna Math and Ramakrishna Mission consisting of a Swan floating on waters, with a lotus in the foreground and the rising sun in the background, the whole being encircled by a hooded serpent, with the words superimposed on the bottom portion.
19. The names and emblems of the Sri Sarada Math and Ramakrishna Sarada Mission consisting of a swan (facing right) floating on water, with a lotus in the

foreground and the rising sun in the background, the whole being encircled by a wild serpent (facing right) with the words superimposed on the bottom portion.

20. The name of the Bharat Scouts and Guides' with its 'Emblem'.
21. The name and emblem of the International Olympic Committee consisting of five interlaced rings.

Adding the word 'Limited' or Pvt. Ltd

The name of the anticipated company is mentioned in this clause. The name of a company must end with the word 'Limited' in the case of a public company and the words 'Private Limited' in the case of a private company.

The word "Limited" denotes the liability of the members, when the liability of member is limited, the last word of the name must be 'Limited' and in the case of private company 'Private Limited'.

In the case of Basudeo Lal Modi And Ors. *v.* Madanlal Chhapolia And Ors. on 5 November, 1966 AIR 1967 Ori 107, the implication of omitting the word Limited is being discussed as:

Under Section 147 of the Companies Act 1956. corresponding to Sections 73 and 74 of the Act of 1918, the settled position in law is that if a limited company makes a contract without using the word 'limited' the directors who make the contract on behalf of the company are personally liable.

In Atkins and Co. *v.* Wardle, (1889) 58 LJQB 377 the defendant Bamkumar having signed the hand-note without using the word 'limited' after 'Noperam Ramgopal', the defendant Ramkumar is personally liable.

Exception "using the word 'limited'"

Section 8 of the Companies Act, 2013, provides provision that the Central Government may, by licence issued in such manner as may be prescribed, and on such conditions as it deems fit, allows that person or association of persons to be registered as a limited company under this section without the addition to its name of the word 'Limited', or as the case may be, the words 'Private Limited'. The exemption is intended to exempt the liability of the company.

The company registered under this section shall enjoy all the privileges and be subject to all the obligations of limited companies. The object of such exemption is to prohibit the payment of any dividend to its members, when the company intended to apply its profits, if any, or other income in promoting its objects, or has in its objects the promotion of commerce, art, science, sports, education, research, social welfare, religion, charity, protection of environment or any such other object.

The Central Government may, by order, revoke the licence granted to a company registered under this section if the company contravenes any of the requirements of this section or any of the conditions subject to which a licence is issued or the affairs of the company are conducted fraudulently or in a manner violative of the objects of the company or prejudicial to public interest, and without prejudice to any other action against the company under this Act, direct the company to convert its status and change its name to add the word 'Limited' or the words 'Private Limited', as the case may be, to its name and thereupon the Registrar shall, without prejudice to any action that may be taken under sub-section (7), on application, in the prescribed form, register the company accordingly, but not without giving the opportunity of being heard.

Alteration/change in name clause

The mandate of section 13 of Companies Act, 2013, by a special resolution and after complying with the procedure specified in this section alter the provisions of its memorandum, but any such alteration or change in the name of a company shall be subject to the provisions of sub-sections (2) and (3) of section 4 and shall not have effect except with the approval of the Central Government in writing: Provided that no such approval shall be necessary where the only change in the name of the company is the deletion therefrom, or addition thereto, of the word 'Private', consequent on the conversion of any one class of companies to another class in accordance with the provisions of this Act.

It is also important to note here that any change in the name of a company is made under sub-section (2), the Registrar shall enter the new name in the register of companies in place of the old name and issue a fresh certificate of incorporation with the new name and the change in the name shall be complete and effective only on the issue of such a certificate.

No alteration made under this section shall have any effect until it has been registered in accordance with the provisions of this section.

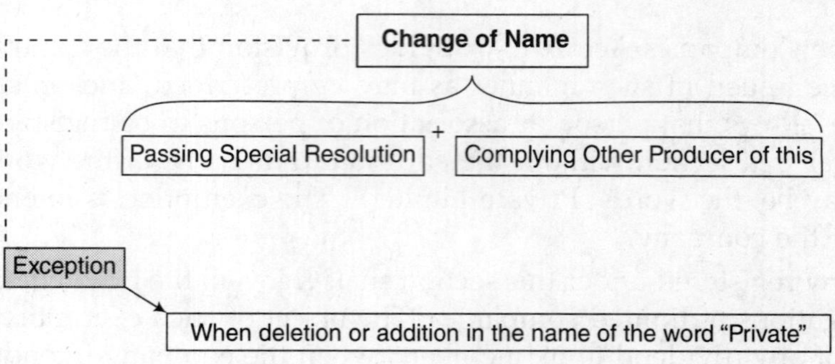

Registered Office Clause

Object of registered office clause

The company is the economic vehicle to achieve the social objective of society, and State, therefore it is necessary to establish the faith among the general public to invest and transaction with the company, contrary to which the whole structure of economic society will collapse. The prime objective of any society or government is to sustain the economic growth by promoting stability and avoiding fraud in the company that is why the new Companies Act, 2013 is equipped with stringent provisions. The MOA authenticates the registered office clause and thereafter it is verified by the ROC, which strengthens the belief that it is going to be a authenticated company.

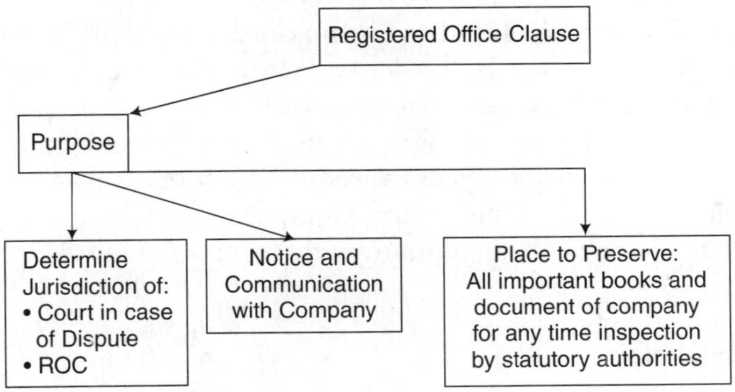

The second clause in the MoA is the registered office clause, which is considered being the domicile of the company, which reflects the name of the 'state' in which the registered office of the company is to be situated. The object of this clause is to determine the jurisdiction of any dispute and where to communicate; as section 2 (29) 'court' means— the High Court having jurisdiction in relation to the place at which the registered office of the company concerned is situated.

The full address of the registered office must be communicated to the Registrar of Companies (RoC) for future communication; however MoA contains only the Place of the Registered Office as sub-clause (b) (1) of section 4 states that only the State in which the registered office of the company is to be situated is to be mentioned.

As per the mandate of section 12 it is declared that all communication or notices to the company is to be sent to the registered office of the company.

It is mandatory as per the mandate of section 12 that a company shall, on and from the fifteenth day of its incorporation and at all times thereafter, have a registered office, and RoC shall verify the address of registered office of the company within 30 days of incorporation of company.

Section 12 further provides that every company shall:

(a) paint or affix its name and the address of its registered office, and keep the same painted or affixed on the outside of every office or place in which its business is carried on, in a conspicuous position, in legible letters, and if the characters employed therefor are not those of the language or of one of the languages in general use in that locality, also in the characters of that language or of one of those languages;

(b) have its name engraved in legible characters on its seal;

(c) get its name, address of its registered office, and the corporate identity number along with telephone number, fax number, if any, e-mail and website addresses, if any, printed in all its business letters, billheads, letter papers and in all its notices and other official publications; and

(d) have its name printed on hundies, promissory notes, bills of exchange, and such other documents as may be prescribed: Provided that where a company has changed its name or names during the last two years, it shall paint or affix or print, as the case may be, along with its name, the former name or names so changed during the last two years as required under clauses (a) and (c): Provided further that the words 'One Person Company' shall be mentioned in brackets below the name of such a company, wherever its name is printed, affixed, or engraved.

Change of registered office

Section 12 of the Companies Act, 2013 provides the situation under which and how a company can change its registered office. Notice of every change of the situation of the registered office, verified in the manner prescribed, after the date of incorporation of the company, shall be given to the Registrar within fifteen days of the change, who shall record the same. As we have discussed earlier, a company is the economic vehicle of society and it is important to establish faith toward the establishment of company in the mind of general public, then it is natural that there must be a stringent procedure that must be followed to change the company's registered office to avoid any fraudulent activity and to protect the interest of creditors or debenture-holders, or any other person concerned with the company. The other aspect is the reduction in the State revenue, that is why shifting office from one State to another State is a tedious job, which requires the amendment in the MoA as well.

Same state different jurisdiction of registrar

As per mandate of section 12(5), special resolution is required in the following cases:

- In the case of an existing company, outside the local limits of any city, town or village where such office is situated.
- In the case of any other company, outside the local limits of any city, town or village where such office is first situated or where it may be situated later by virtue of a special resolution passed by the company.

No company shall change the place of its registered office from the jurisdiction of one Registrar to the jurisdiction of another Registrar within the same State unless such change is confirmed by the Regional Director on an application made in this behalf by the company.

The confirmation referred to in sub-section (5) of section 2 shall be communicated within a period of thirty days from the date of receipt of application by the Regional Director to the company and the company shall file the confirmation with the Registrar within a period of sixty days of the date of confirmation who shall register the same and certify the registration within a period of thirty days from the date of filing of such confirmation.

It is important to note that the certificate referred above shall be considered conclusive evidence that all the requirements with respect to change of the registered office have been complied with and the change shall take effect from the date of the certificate. Sub-section (8) of section 2 specifies that if any default is made in complying with the requirements of this section 12(6), the company and every officer who is in default shall be liable to a penalty of one thousand rupees for every day during which the default continues but not exceeding one lakh rupees.

Different state

The alteration of the memorandum relating to the place of the registered office from one State to another shall not have any effect unless it is approved by the Central Government on an application in such form and manner as may be prescribed.

In the case of different State it is natural there may be concern and doubts of company's creditors, debenture-holders, and other persons concerned with the company: In such a case the Central Government shall dispose of the application of change of registered office within a period of sixty days and before passing its order may satisfy itself that the alteration has the consent of the creditors, debenture-holders, and other persons concerned with the company or that sufficient provision has been made by the company either for the due discharge of all its debts and obligations or that adequate security has been provided for such discharge. Second, it is also mandatory to the company that a certified copy of the order of the Central Government approving the alteration shall be filed by the company with the Registrar of each of the states within such time and in such manner as may be prescribed, who shall register the same, and the Registrar of the State where the registered office is being shifted to shall issue a fresh certificate of incorporation indicating the alteration.

In the case of a different State, the question of loss of revenue and employment opportunity for that State from where the company wants to shift is why the State seems reluctant to allow the company to change it office.

In the case of Minerva Mills Ltd. *v.* Govt. Of Maharashtra 1975 45 CompCas 1 Bom, the alteration of the memorandum so as to change the place of the registered office has been discussed.

> 'On what grounds is a State entitled to oppose the shifting of the registered office of a company from its territory to the territory of another State within the country. The answer to that question would depend on the further question as to in what cases notice should be given to the State from which the registered

office is sought to be transferred to another State. In that connection, I must first refer to the relevant provisions of the Companies Act, 1956, as well as the Industries (Development and Regulation) Act, 1951. Sub-section (1) of section 17, inter alia, provides that a company may, by special resolution, alter the provisions of its memorandum so as to change the place of its registered office from one State to another. Sub-section (2) of that section, however, lays down that such alteration is not to take effect until, and except in so far as, it is confirmed by the court on petition. Sub-sections (3) and (4) of the said section which are material for the purpose of the question I am now considering, are in the following terms:

'(3) Before confirming the alteration, the court must be satisfied

(a) that sufficient notice has been given to every holder of the debentures of the company, and to every other persons or class of persons whose interest will, in the opinion of the court, be affected by the alternation; and

(b) that, with respect to every creditor who, in the opinion of the court, is entitled to object to the alteration, and who signifies his objection in the manner directed by the court, either his consent to the alteration has been obtained or claim has been claim has been discharged or has discharged or has determined, or has been secured to the satisfaction of the court:

Provided that the court may in the case of any person or class of persons for special reasons, dispense with the notice required by clause (a).

'(4) The court shall cause notice of the petition for confirmation of the alteration to be served on the Registrar who shall also be given a reasonable opportunity to appear before the court and state his objections and suggestions, if any, with respect to the confirmation of the alteration.' Sub-section (5) of section 17 enacts that the court can make an order confirming the alteration either wholly or in part, and on such terms and conditions, if any, as it thinks fit, and sub-section (6) lays down that, in exercising its powers under the said section, the court must have regard to the rights and interests of the members of the company and of every class of them, as well as to the rights and interests of the creditors of the company and of every class of them. Sub-section (3) of section 18 of the Companies Act provides for the filing of the court's order with the Registrars of Companies of the two States concerned who would register the same in their records, and section 19 enacts that the alteration of the memorandum in question is not to take effect until it has been so registered."

In the case of In Re: J.L. Morison (India) ... *v.* Unknown, 1999 95 CompCas 907 CLB shifting the registered office, was objected by the employees of the company on the ground that there have been a number of cases pending before the Labour Courts and the High Courts of Karnataka against the company in respect of dearness allowance and bonus for the employees, lay-off of the workmen, closure of the factory at Bangalore, etc. According to him, the employees will be prejudiced by shifting the registered office especially when the pending cases will be transferred to the State of West Bengal. The employees will not be able to realize their dues as and when ordered by the courts in their favour. The proposal of the company is motivated by mala fide intentions.

CLB allowed alteration in the MoA of the company as approved by the special resolution passed at the extraordinary general meeting held and confirmed subject to the conditions that the interests of none of the employees of the company shall be prejudiced either by way of transfer or retrenchment or otherwise and further that pending cases before various courts at Karnataka between the employees of the company and the company shall not be adversely affected.

In the case of Reckitt Benckiser (India) ... *v.* Unknown on 7 June, 2004 55 SCL 437 CLB, it was observed that the decision of shifting of registered office must be left to the domestic decision of the shareholders. The Company is the best judge of how to run its business or where to situate the registered office as

> a resolution of alteration of memorandum of association of the Company for shifting the registered office, I have seen whether the formalities of the Statute have been complied with; looked to the interests of shareholders, creditors, employees and considered objections, taken by such objectors and other persons affected by the shifting of the registered office. It is rather pertinent to observe that none of the shareholders of the Company excepting one (Shri M. Bubna) has objected to the shifting of registered office from the State of West Bengal to the N.C.T. of Delhi. The CLB is neither concerned to consider the wisdom or desirability of the proposed alteration nor to substitute its own wisdom or judgment in the place of the collective wisdom or judgment of the shareholders expressed in the impugned special resolution. These matters must be left to the domestic decision of the shareholders. The Company is the best judge of how to run its business or where to situate the registered office. I drive support for these propositions from the following decisions:
>
> * Parikh Engg. & Body Building Co. Ltd. - (1975) 45 Company Cases 157 (Patna) - to state that 'where the Company finds it will be more economical and convenient if the Company's registered office be situated in a particular city and good reasons have been assigned for this decision, it is the Company which is the best judge of how to runits business.'
>
> * Minerva Mills Ltd. *v.* Govt. of Maharashtra - (1975) 45 Company Cases 1 (Bombay) - to state that 'the shareholders are the best judges of what is good for the Company and the State cannot assume to itself the role of a guardian of their interests, or interfere in the management of the business of the Company which is a matter entirely for the Company itself'.
>
> * Mackinon Mackanzie & Co. Pvt. Ltd. - (1967) 37 Company Cases 516 (Cal) - to state that 'in applying Section 17 of the Companies Act, what the Court has to see whether all the formalities of the Statute have been complied with, and if the safeguards and protection envisaged in the Section have been complied with, the Court will look to the interests of absent shareholders and creditors and consider the objections of the Registrar and decide the matter.'

* Dalmia Cement (Bharat) Ltd. - AIR 1965 Madras 76 - to state that 'whether a company can carry on its business more economically or more efficiently is a matter for the judgment of the directors. They alone are best fitted by reason of their experience in the particular business to decide whether the business can be carried on more economically or more efficiently by adding fresh objects. The Court, of course, on given facts may apply its mind and see whether the directors may reasonably and fairly form that opinion. If the directors consider that under the existing circumstances, it will be convenient and advantageous to combine the new objects with the existing objects, and if it appears that the conclusion may be fairly arrived at, the High Court will not go behind it and hold an Inquiry as to whether the opinion of the directors is well founded or is justified. In the very nature of things, such an inquiry will not be possible for the High court to undertake.'

* Bharat Commerce & Industries Ltd. *v.* Registrar of Companies, West Bengal - Vol.43 (1973) Company Cases 275 (Cal) - to state that 'the loss of revenue to or of employment to the citizens of, a State are not relevant factors for consideration in an application for sanction to alter the Memorandum of a company by removing its registered office from one State to another.'

* Rank Film Distributors of India Ltd. *v.* Registrar of Companies -(1968) 38 Company Cases 487 (Cal) - to state that 'the transfer of a registered office by itself does not affect or appreciably affect, the scope of employment of the people of the State. ... It is, therefore, useless to refuse to confirm the alteration on the grounds of loss of prospect of employment in the State. In any event, taking a broader perspective, the loss of employment in one State will be balanced by employment in another. After all, the country is one and indivisible.'

26. Considering all facts and circumstances of the case, including the specific contentions of various objectors and the legal position explained here in above, the alteration in the Memorandum of Association of the Company, as approved by the special resolution passed at the Extra Ordinary General Meeting held on 29th March 2004, (which Special Resolution is set forth in the Schedule hereto) be and the same is hereby confirmed subject to the following condition:

'that the interests of none of the employees of the Company at its registered office shall be prejudiced by way of retrenchment or otherwise.'

Object Clause

Incorporation of any company is to achieve a certain objective; the object clause is the reflection of the object with which the company is proposed to be established. A company is not legally permitted to do any business other than that specified in its clause. It is also important to note that object of the company chiefly attracts the investor/shareholders, it is natural the fund must be discharged by the company towards the object of company, and not otherwise.

The object of the Company is a protective device or an assurance by the company that the funds raised by the company are not going to be utilized in another company.

Deviation of the object could amount to fraud, as the corporate affairs discharged within a defined business objective for which the company has been established and people choose to interact financially with the company and not otherwise.

The purpose of the object clause in the Memorandum could be pointed out as:

- Information to the Shareholder of Company
- Security to the Creditor
- Limit and Direction of the Company (*ultra vires* act).

The Companies Act, 1956 classifies the object clause in the memorandum as:

- The main object of the company
- Objects incidental or ancillary to the attainment of the main object
- Other objects of the company.

The main clause contains the activities which are part of the company's main business while other objects contain those activities which are not a part of its main business but the company intends to take them in the future.

Section 4(c) of the Companies Act, 2013 defines as, the object clause as 'the objects for which the company is proposed to be incorporated and any matter considered necessary in furtherance thereof'.

The new Companies bill has simplified this requirement of entrepreneurship but discourages fraudulent activities. In the case of Universal Mutual Aid and Poor Houses Association Limited Madras *v.* A.D. Thoppa Naidu and others A.I.R. 1933, it was observed that subscribers to the memorandum are free to choose the object, but it should not be:

- Contrary to the Law of the Land
- Illegal or opposed to the public policy or moral
- In violation of any provision of Companies Act

Alteration in Object Clause

The Companies Act, 2013 seems to be more restrictive on the alteration of the object clause of the memorandum for a company by imposing section 13(8) as a company which had raised money from the public through prospectus but at the time of alteration in the object clause still has an unutilized amount left. The company is restricted to change the object clause unless a special resolution is passed by the company and complies the following two requirements:

1. Publication of the Notice of the aforesaid resolution with justification in the two newspapers which are in the circulation at the place where the registered office of the company is situated, and also place on the website of the company in English and another in vernacular language.

2. An opportunity of exit option can be given to the dissenting shareholders by the promoters and shareholders having control in accordance with the regulations to be specified by the Securities and Exchange Board.

The Companies Act, 2013 lays down certain limits as to the alteration of the object clauses and the natural objective of the legislature in this regard seems to be that the alteration should not be so easy so as to be done by the company bypassing all the laws with an intent to protect the interests of the creditors and the shareholders.

However, if the alteration of memorandum could be put in a straight jacket initially, this could also slow down the industrial peace the memorandum is the constitutional document of the company.

Doctrine of Ultra Vires

The object clause of the memorandum of the company establishes the mission or object for which the company is incorporated. Any act of the company must be confined within the limits of the object clause of company and not go beyond it or else it will be ultra vires.

The word 'ultra vires' consists of two words: 'ultra' and 'vires'. 'Ultra' means beyond and 'vires' means powers. Thus, the expression ultra vires means an act beyond the powers. With regard to a company the doctrine is used as the act of the company which is beyond the powers conferred on it by the object clause of its memorandum. The inherent intention of the legislature is strict compliance of memorandum clauses, and any deviation is considered to be void or invalid as such act is executed without any authority of the memorandum.

The ultra vires can be illustrated like the water of any river – till it flows within the limit it serves its purpose, crossing its limits leads to destruction.

The important aspect of this doctrine is that it cannot be ratified even if all the members wish to ratify it. As it was observed in the case of Indian Steel & Wire Products Ltd. *v.* Commissioner of Income-Tax 1968 38 CompCas 660 Cal, 1968 69 ITR 379 Cal as: 'When a company does an act which is ultra vires, no legal relationship or effects ensue therefrom. Such an act is absolutely void and cannot be ratified, even if all the shareholders agree'.

> The term 'ultra vires' simply means 'beyond powers' or 'lack of power' The term 'ultra vires' signifies a concept distinct from 'illegality'. In the loose or the widest sense every thing that is not warranted by law is illegal but in its proper or strict connotation 'illegal' refers to that quality which makes the act itself contrary to law. The term 'ultra vires' points to the capacity or power of the person to do that act. It is not necessary that an act to be ultra vires must also be illegal. It may be but it may as well, not be. An act may be illegal because it is prohibited

by law or for reasons like fraud, undue influence, or because it may be opposed to public policy. These reasons are not occasioned by the absence of any power in the person to do the act. The essence of the doctrine of ultra vires is that the act is done in excess of the powers possessed by the person in law. This doctrine proceeds on the basis that the person has limited powers.

"In speaking of an ordinary citizen we do not speak of any action being ultra vires. To an ordinary citizen whatever is not expressly forbidden by the law is permitted by the law. It is only when the law has called into existence a person for a particular purpose or has recognised its existence – such as the holder of an office, a body corporate etc – that the power is limited to the authority delegated expressly or by implication and to the object for which it was created. In the case of such a creation the ordinary law applicable to an individual is somewhat reversed. Whatever is not permitted, expressly or by implication, by the constating instrument, is prohibited, not by any express prohibition of the Legislature but by the doctrine of ultra vires."*

If a person exists for a limited purpose alone and that purpose is defined by the law whether expressly or by implication, the doctrine of ultra vires governs him and confines him to that purpose The person can act within the four corners of its constating instrument. The doctrine prevents him from acting beyond the conferred powers.[19]

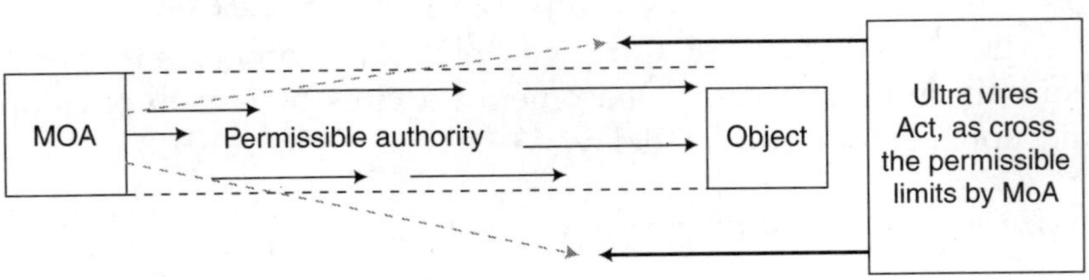

Protection of creditors and investors

The chief objective of the doctrine of ultra vires under company law is to protect the interest of investors and creditors of the company. Interaction and financial affairs of the creditors and investors with the company are attracted with the object for which the company was incorporated. The doctrine ensures the rule that their investment will not be employed for the objects or activities which they did not contemplate at the time of investing their money in the company. The doctrine puts a check over the activities of the company and defines what lines of business company is authorized to conduct.

The memorandum of a company defines its objects and a company's objects are limited to those expressly mentioned and such as are ancillary to the expressed objects. A contract made by the directors upon a matter not within the ambit of the company's

*S.R. Das's *Law of Ultra Vires in British India; Tagore Law Lectures*, 1903

19. Anand Prakash and Anr. *v.* Assistant Registrar AIR 1968 All 22.

objects is ultra vires the company, and, therefore, beyond the powers of the directors. This principle is intended to protect both those who deal with the company, and its shareholders.[20]

In consequence the doctrine of ultra vires is an illusory protection for the shareholders and yet may be a pitfall for third parties dealing with the company"; and that "as now applied to companies, the ultra vires doctrine serves no positive purpose but is, on the other hand, a cause of unnecessary prolixity and vexation.[21]

Difference between ultra vires and illegal

Sometime ultra vires and illegal are considered to be one, but then both are different. Ultra vires defines the limits and beyond those limits any act is considered to be void or invalid, but may not be contrary to law every time, although both are void. An act of the company which is outside its object clause is ultra vires and amounts to void, even if it is legal, Similarly, an illegal act will be void even if it falls within the object clause.

Scope of the rule

The scope of the doctrine itself confines only to those transactions which are beyond the capacity of the company only. To test the doctrine depends upon the terms of the company's MoA which must state the company's objective clearly.

Lord Cairns, LC, in Ashbury Rly. Carriage Co. *v.* Riche observes that 'An ultra vires contract is void ab- initio and cannot become intra vires by reason of estoppels, lapse of time, ratification, acquiescence or delay.'

Construction of the doctrine of ultra vires

Construction is an important rule of interpretation. Construing a memorandum in which there are general words, would be good if constructed within the limit of the object of company, and not otherwise, else objects, clause naturally defeats the very purpose for which it is there.

First time in the Ashbury case, it was observed that any term related to the company must be read in connection with the company's main business, as it was held that the words 'general contractors' must be read in connection with the company's main business.

Lord Selborne in Attorney General *v.* G.E. Rly. Co., (1880) 5 AC 473 (478) laid down the canon of construction of the doctrine of ultra vires as follows:

> I agree with Lord Justice James that this doctrine ought to be reasonably, and not unreasonably understood and applied, and that whatever may fairly be regarded as incidental to, or consequential upon those things which the

20. Cohen Committee in this passage from paragraph 11 of their report
21. Cohen Committee in this passage from paragraph 12 of their report

> Legislature has authorized, ought not (unless expressly prohibited) to be held by judicial construction, to be ultra vires. Referring to these observations of Lord Selborne, Jagannath Dass. J. observed: Bishnu Charan *v.* Stale of Orissa, AIR 1952 Orissa 11 at p. 16.[22]

In the case of Cotman *v.* Brougham, 1918 AC 514, House of Lords had to judge a memorandum which contained an objects clause with thirty sub-clauses enabling the company to carry on almost every possible type of business which a company could adopt. It was observe that:

> The ultra vires doctrine confines corporate action within fixed limits. While it handicaps the ambitious manager, it lays a trap for the unwary creditor. That is why there has been a revolt against it almost ever since its inception. The businessman has always endeavored to evade the limitations imposed by the doctrine on their freedom of action. One of the methods of bypassing ultra vires is the practice of registering memoranda containing a profusion of objects and powers.

Origin and development

The roots of the doctrine of ultra vires could be traced to the case of Ashbury Railway Carriage and Iron Company (Limited) *v.* Hector Riche, (1874–75) L.R. 7 H.L. 653 was decided by the House of Lords. The Ashbury Railway Carriage and Iron Company was incorporated under the Companies Act, 1862. The memorandum clause 3 of this company was 'to make and sell, or lend on hire, railway-carriage, but not to undertake their construction'. But the company agreed to give a loan to build a railway in Belgium, which was in direct contravention of the provisions of the Company Act, 1862.

Blackburn J. said, in this case:

> thought it was at common law an incident to a corporation that its capacity should be limited by the instrument creating it, I should agree that the capacity of a company incorporated under the act of 1862 was limited to the object in the memorandum of association. But if I am right in the opinion which I have already expressed, that the general power of contracting is an incident to a corporation which requires an indication of intention in the legislature to take away, I see no such indication here. If the question was whether the legislature had conferred on a corporation, created under this act, capacity to enter into contracts beyond the provisions of the deed, there could be only one answer. The legislature did not confer such capacity. But if the question be, as I apprehend it is, whether the legislature has indicated an intention to take away the power of contracting which at common law would be incident to a body corporate, and not merely to limit the authority of the managing body and the majority of the shareholders to bind the minority, but also to prohibit and make illegal contracts made by

22. Anand Prakash and Anr (supra).

> the body corporate, in such a manner that they would be binding on the body if incorporated at common law, I think the answer should be the other way.

The doctrine further elaborates and modifies in the case of Attorney General *v.* Great Eastern Railway Co. 4 where it was considered that companies have the power to do things reasonably supplementary to their objects. Care must be taken to differentiate cases where directors violate their authority, but have not acted beyond the capacity or range of the company.

Similar observations of Supreme Court made in the Matajog Dobey *v.* H.C. Bhari AIR 1956 SC 44 (at p. 50) Chandrashekhar Aiyvar J. speaking for the Supreme Court held:

> Where a power is conferred or a duty imposed by statute or otherwise, and there is nothing said expressly inhibiting the exercise of the power or the performance of the duty by any limitations or restrictions it is reasonable to hold that it carries with it the power of doing all such acts or employing such means as are reasonably necessary for such execution.

Doctrine of ultra vires under Indian law

The root of doctrine of ultra vires can be traced from the case of Jahangir R. Modi *v.* Shamji Ladhaand. Some brief facts are given below.

The Directors of a Joint Stock Company purchased shares on behalf of the company in other companies out of the subscribed capital of the company in the ordinary course of its business and not to re-sell them at a profit for the company. A shareholder sued to recover the price of the shares purchased by him, when the company went into losses. The first object of the company was 'purchase and sale of shares on commission' which would exclude purchases by the company on its own account for profit.

Held:

The MoA must authorize the directors to purchase shares in other companies, otherwise the purchase is ultra vires the company. The shareholders can compel such directors to restore the funds of the company employed for such purchase. Courts of Law and Equity have constantly held that no company can purchase its own shares and such a contract is ultra vires. That would be a transfer to an abstraction. Though it would be harsh on some individuals, for companies to flourish in this country, the application of funds of the company must be used for legitimate purposes. Hence, purchase by directors from individual shareholders is ultra vires.

The doctrine is well established and explained by the Supreme Court in the case of Dr. A. Lakshmanaswamy Mudaliar *v.* LIC AIR 1963 SC 1185.

Indian law also supports the aspect that the company has the power to carry out the objects as set out in the objects clause of its memorandum, and also everything which is reasonably essential to carry out those objects.

The doctrine of ultra vires in relation to the powers of a statutory corporation has to be understood reasonably, 'whatever may fairly be regarded as incidental to, or consequential upon, those things which the Legislature has authorised ought not (unless expressly prohibited) to be held by judicial construction, to be ultra vires.'[23]

The MoA of the company is to establish the constitution of the company which further becomes the foundation for making the rules with regard to the authorized limits or range of its object clauses. This is the observation of Supreme Court in the case of Vidya Dhar Pande *v.* Vidyut Grih Siksha Samiti & Ors 1989 AIR 341, 1988 SCR Supl. (3) 442 is important as:

> The doctrine of ultra vires as applied to statutes, rules, and orders should equally apply to the regulations and any other subordinate legislation. The regulations made under power conferred by the statute are subordinate legislation and have the force and effect, if validity made, as the Act passed by the competent legislature.

Test of doctrine

To test the doctrine the following points need to be considered:

- Object of company as mentioned in MoA
- Special power conferred by the MoA
- Things necessary or reasonable for the company, there should be no act which is neither within the main purpose nor the special powers expressly conferred by the MoA.

The doctrine of ultra vires plays an important role in the development of corporate powers. Though largely obsolete in modern private corporation law, the doctrine remains in full force for government entities. An ultra vires act is one beyond the purposes or powers of a corporation. The earliest legal view was that such acts were void. Under this approach a corporation was formed only for limited purposes and could do only what it was authorized to do in its corporate charter.

This early view proved unworkable and unfair. It permitted a corporation to accept the benefits of a contract and then refuse to perform its obligations on the ground that the contract was ultra vires. The doctrine also impaired the security of title to property in fully executed transactions in which a corporation participated. Therefore, the courts adopted the view that such acts were voidable rather than void and that the facts should dictate whether a corporate act should have effect.

Over time a body of principles developed that prevented the application of the ultra vires doctrine. These principles included the ability of shareholders to ratify an ultra vires transaction; the application of the doctrine of estoppel, which prevented the defence of ultra vires when the transaction was fully performed by one party; and the prohibition against asserting ultra vires when both parties had fully performed the contract. The law also held that if an agent of a corporation committed a tort within the scope of the

---

23. V.T. Khanzode & Ors *v.* Reserve Bank of India & Anr 1982 AIR 917, 1982 SCR (3) 411.

agent's employment, the corporation could not defend itself on the ground that the act was ultra vires.

Despite these principles the ultra vires doctrine was applied inconsistently and erratically. Accordingly, modern corporation law has sought to remove the possibility that ultra vires acts may occur. Most importantly, multiple purposes clauses and general clauses that permit corporations to engage in any lawful business are now included in the articles of incorporation. In addition, purposes clauses can now be easily amended if the corporation seeks to do business in new areas. For example, under traditional ultra vires doctrine, a corporation that had as its purpose the manufacturing of shoes could not, under its charter, manufacture motorcycles. Under modern corporate law, the purposes clause would either be so general as to allow the corporation to go into the motorcycle business, or the corporation would amend its purposes clause to reflect the new venture.

State laws in almost every jurisdiction have also sharply reduced the importance of the ultra vires doctrine. For example, section 3.04(a) of the Revised Model Business Corporation Act, drafted in 1984, states that 'the validity of corporate action may not be challenged on the ground that the corporation lacks or lacked power to act'. There are three exceptions to this prohibition: it may be asserted by the corporation or its shareholders against the present or former officers or directors of the corporation for exceeding their authority, by the attorney general of the state in a proceeding to dissolve the corporation or to enjoin it from the transaction of unauthorized business, or by shareholders against the corporation to enjoin the commission of an ultra vires act, or the ultra vires transfer of real or personal property.

Government entities created by a state are public corporations governed by municipal charters and other statutorily imposed grants of power. These grants of authority are analogous to a private corporation's articles of incorporation. Historically, the ultra vires concept has been used to construe the powers of a government entity narrowly. Failure to observe the statutory limits has been characterized as ultra vires.

In the case of a private business entity, the act of an employee who is not authorized to act on the entity's behalf may, nevertheless, bind the entity contractually if such an employee would normally be expected to have that authority. With a government entity, however, to prevent a contract from being voided as ultra vires, it is normally necessary to prove that the employee actually had authority to act. Where a government employee exceeds her authority, the government entity may seek to rescind the contract based on an ultra vires claim.

Effect of ultra vires transactions

Following points need to be remembered for analysing the effect of doctrine.

- An ultra vires transaction cannot be ratified by all the shareholders, even if they wish it to be ratified.
- Estoppel is not applicable when the transaction was fully executed.

- In case of a contract which was fully executory, the plea of ultra vires may be evoked by either party.

Injunction

Injunction may be one applicable remedy when an ultra vires act has been done or likely to be done, any member of the company can get the injunction to restrain that ultra vires act of company.

Personal liability of director

The company is the artificial person, practically the company functions through its directors, who act like the agents of the company and must strictly confine within the limits of the company power, else they are personally liable if they exceed their powers.

Exceptions to the doctrine of ultra vires

There are, however, certain exceptions to this doctrine, which are as follows:

1. An act, which is intra vires the company but outside the authority of the directors may be ratified by the shareholders in proper form.
2. An act which is intra vires the company but done in an irregular manner, may be validated by the consent of the shareholders. The law, however, does not require that the consent of all the shareholders should be obtained at the same place and in the same meeting.
3. If the company has acquired any property through an investment, which is ultra vires, the company's right over such a property shall still be secured.
4. While applying the doctrine of ultra vires, the effects which are incidental or consequential to the act shall not be invalid unless they are expressly prohibited by the Companies Act.
5. There are certain acts under the company law, which though not expressly stated in the memorandum are deemed as implied within the authority of the company and therefore they are not deemed ultra vires. For example, a business company can raise its capital by borrowing.
6. If an act of the company is ultra vires the articles of the association, the company can alter its articles in order to validate the act.

Liability Clause

The fourth clause in the MoA is liability clause which reflects the nature of liability of the members of the company. A simple reading of section 4(d), suggests that the liability of the member can be limited or unlimited, further it can be limited by shares held by the member or limited by guarantee. In case of an unlimited company, the liability clause does not appear in the MoA.

Limited by share

In case of a company limited by shares, members' liability is limited to the amount unpaid, if any, on the share held by them. In simple no member can be called upon to pay more than the amount that remains unpaid on his share value.

Limited by guarantee

In case of a company limited by guarantee, the liability clause must utter the degree of liability of each individual member in the event of its being wound up. It means the amount up to which each member undertakes to contribute to the assets of the company or the cost, charge and expenses of winding up and for adjustment of the right of the contributories among themselves in the event of winding up while he is a member or within one year after he ceases to be a member, for payment of the debts and liabilities of the company or of such debts and liabilities as may have been contracted before he ceases to be a member.

Share Capital Clause

The last clause in the memorandum of association states the total capital of the proposed company. The amount of capital as stated in the memorandum is known as the authorized capital of the company. A company is restricted to collect funds exceeding the authorized capital. It is also mandatory to classify the capital into equity share capital and preference share capital along with number of shares in each category and their value should be given in the memorandum. Ordinary Resolution as stated in section 61 is required for any alteration of the capital clause.

Applicability of section 13

It is important to discuss the application of section 13, as in the new Act it works as a protective device by regulating the process of amendment of MoA. Sub-section (5) of section 13 established that the Central Government shall dispose of the application under sub-section (4) within a period of sixty days and before passing its order may satisfy itself that the alteration has the consent of the creditors, debenture-holders, and other persons concerned with the company or that sufficient provision has been made by the company either for the due discharge of all its debts and obligations or that adequate security has been provided for such discharge.

To Remember

- Alteration in the name clause [Section 13 (2) and (3)]
- Alteration in the Registered Office Clause [Section 13 (4) (5) and (7)]
- Alteration in the Object Clause [Section 13 (8) and (9)]
- Alteration in the Name Clause. Alteration in the Capital Clause [Section 61 read with section 64}

ARTICLES OF ASSOCIATION (AoA)

- By-laws of Company: Rules and regulations for internal affairs of management company
- Govern the internal management and organization of the company
- Second most important document of the company
- It is subordinate to memorandum of association

The articles of association is the document for the company which reflects the rules and regulations of a company for its internal management. It contains regulations for the internal administration of company as section 5(1) of Companies Act, 2013 says: 'The articles of a company shall contain the regulations for management of the company.'

> The articles are formulated to achieve the object of company which is given in the MoA of the Company, as Lord Cairns observed in Ashbury Railway Carriage Co. *v.* Riche that:
>
> The articles play a part subsidiary to the memorandum of association. They accept the memorandum as the charter of incorporation of the company, and so accepting it, the articles proceed to define the duties, the rights and the powers of the governing body as between themselves and the company at large, and the mode and form in which the business of the company is to be carried on, and the mode and form in which changes in the internal regulations of the company may from time to time be made.

The AoA are much flexible then the MoA, which has a fixed format under which it is drafted, while the AoA could be drafted according to the convenience of the company, however, it should not violate any provision of the Companies Act. Lord Justice Bowen enunciated in this regard in Guineness *v.* Land Corporation of Ireland as: 'The memorandum contains the fundamental conditions upon which alone the company is allowed to be incorporated. They are conditions introduced for the benefit of the creditors, and the outside public, as well as of the shareholders. The articles of association are the internal regulations of the company and are for the benefits of shareholders.'

Definition of AoA under section 2(5) of Companies Act, 2013 says 'articles' means the articles of association of a company as originally framed or as altered from time to time or applied in pursuance of any previous company law or of this Act;

After analysing the definition the following points reflect as:

- originally framed or
- as altered from time to time or
- applied in pursuance of any previous company law or of this Act

In the mandate of the definition there is no restriction on alteration of AoA and should be applied within the range of company law.

In the Companies Act, 2013 there is first-time introduction an 'entrenchment provision[24], which facilitates a company to follow a more restrictive procedure than a special resolution for altering a specific clause of articles of association. It is also important to note that this entrenchment provision can be made either on formation of a company or by an amendment in the article by a private company if agreed by all its members and by a special resolution in case of a public company and it shall give notice to the Registrar of such a provision as per the mandate of section 5 of the Companies Act, 2013.

Override Memorandum on Article

As per the mandate of section 6 of the Companies Act, 2013, any provision contained in the memorandum, articles, agreement, or resolution shall, to the extent to which it is repugnant to the provisions of this Act, become or be void, as the case may be.

In case there are any contrary provisions to those of the Memorandum, the provisions of this act will prevail.

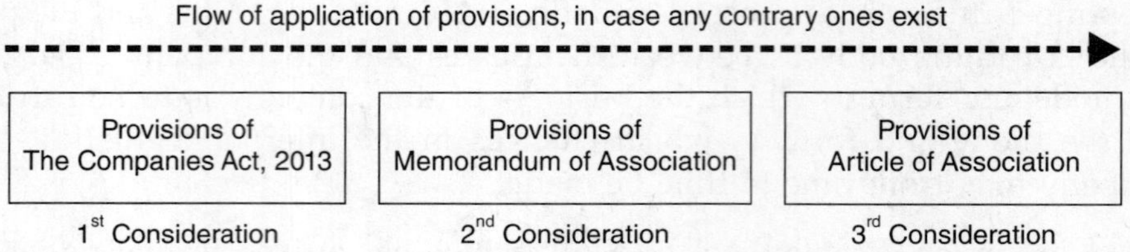

Contents of Articles of Association

Section 5 of the Companies Act, 2013 is positive in nature in the case of a private company as it permits to include such additional matters in its articles as may be considered necessary for its management.

Schedule I, specifies different types of AoA according to the nature of company. A company may adopt all or any of the regulations contained in the model articles applicable to such a company, the broad contents of AoA are as follows:

Company limited by shares	Company limited by guarantee and having a share capital	Company limited by guarantee and not having share capital	Unlimited company and having a share capital	Unlimited company and not having a share capital
TABLE -F	TABLE – G	TABLE – H	TABLE – I	TABLE – J
Interpretation	Interpretation	Interpretation	Interpretation	Interpretation
Share capital and variation of rights	Share capital and variation of rights	Members	Share capital and variation of rights	Members

24. An entrenched clause or provision of a basic law is a provision which makes certain amendments either more difficult or impossible.

Lien	Lien	General meetings	Lien	General meetings
Calls on shares	Calls on shares	Proceedings at general meetings	Calls on shares	Proceedings at general meetings
Transfer of shares	Transfer of shares	Adjournment of meeting	Transfer of shares	Adjournment of meeting
Forfeiture of shares	Forfeiture of shares	Voting rights	Forfeiture of shares	Voting rights
Alteration of capital	Alteration of capital	Board of Directors	Alteration of capital	Board of Directors
Capitalization of profits	Capitalization of profits	Proceedings of the Board	Capitalization of profits	Proceedings of the Board
Buy-back of shares	Buy-back of shares	Chief Executive Officer, Manager, Company Secretary, or Chief Financial Officer	Buy-back of shares	Chief Executive Officer, Manager, Company Secretary, or Chief Financial Officer
General meetings	General meetings	The Seal	General meetings	The Seal
Proceedings at general meetings	Proceedings at general meetings		Proceedings at general meetings	
Adjournment of meeting	Adjournment of meeting		Adjournment of meeting	
Voting rights	Voting rights		Voting rights	
Proxy	Proxy		Proxy	
Board of Directors	Board of Directors		Board of Directors	
Proceedings of the Board	Proceedings of the Board		Proceedings of the Board	
The Seal	The Seal		The Seal	
Dividends and Reserve	Dividends and Reserve		Dividends and Reserve	
Accounts	Accounts		Accounts	
Winding up	Winding up		Winding up	
Indemnity	Indemnity		Indemnity	

Alteration of Articles

Alteration is a natural process in any organization, it allows new changes and more flexibility with the change of time. Alteration is the statutory power conferred by section 14 of The Companies Act, 2013, and no contract can repudiate such power of alteration, as in the case of Melson *v.* National Ins & Guarantee Co. (1874) 1 Ch 200, in which it was observed that if there is a clause in the articles providing that the company would not introduce any change in its original articles, it will be invalid as it contravenes the intention of statute, and no company can deprive itself of the power of alteration. The mandate of section 14 allows alteration or conversion (a private company in to a public company or a public company into a private company) of Articles as:

1. Within the permissible limit of the Companies Act, 2013,
2. Subject to the conditions of Memorandum of Company,
3. By passing a Special Resolution.

Section 14 further specifies that when a private company alters its article in such a manner that they no longer include the restrictions and limitations which are required to be included in the article of a private company under this act, the company is no longer considered to be a private company from the date of such alteration.

Further, the mandate of Section 14, Tribunal approval is mandatory for conversion in the case of conversion of public company into a private company.

And within 15 days such an amended article needs to be submitted in the office of Registrar of Companies.

And the validation of any amended article is only done when it is originally contained in the article.

Comparison between MoA and AoA

Base	MoA	AoA
Object	Fundamental conditions for which the company is incorporated	To frame governing rules to function the company, with regard to its members
Nature	The charter of the company exhibits the nature of its business, company nationality and its capital, and company's relationship with the outside world.	It establishes the rules and regulations for the internal affairs of the company
Limitation	It limits the nature or activity of business of company, beyond which any work is deemed to be ultra vires.	It defines the rules for carrying out the objects of the company as set out in the Memorandum
Status	It supersedes the article if any provision contravenes it.	It is subordinate to the Memorandum. If there is a clash between the Articles and Memorandum then provisions of Memorandum will prevail.
Requirement	Every company must have its own Memorandum	A company limited by shares need not have Articles of its own. In such a case Table A applies

Rectification of Act	Any act of the company which contravenes any provision of MoA, is considered to be ultra vires and cannot be rectified even if all share holders agree	Any act of the company which is ultra vires the articles can be confirmed by the shareholders
Alteration	Stringent process to alter its provisions	Relaxed process to alter its provisions compared to MoA
Functions	It generally defines the relationship of the company to the outsider	It generally defines the relationship of the members of the company

Legal Effect of the Memorandum and Articles

The mandate of section 10 of the Companies Act, 2013, the memorandum and articles shall, when registered, bind the company and the members thereof to the same extent as if they respectively had been signed by the company and by each member, and contained covenants on its and his part to observe all the provisions of the memorandum and of the articles. Also all monies payable by any member to the company under the Memorandum or Articles shall be a debt due from him to the company.

Constructive Notice of Memorandum and Articles

Constructive notice

- Being informed of a case that could affect any one right or interest.
- Knowledge that can be acquired by normal means through a notice given by the public records
- People are presumed to know the contents of which are in public domain

Constructive notice is the legal term which reflects the law and assumes that a person has knowledge of any facts which are in the public records, even though they have no actual knowledge of it. The doctrine discourages the contention if any one denies the knowledge of any fact, which he requires to inquire, being the document in public domain.

For example,

A wants to purchase X property, in such a case A is presumed to know the legal status of the property as the records related to the property are available in the public records.

Notice of a fact means knowledge or cognizance or awareness of such a fact. To give notice of a fact to a person is to bring that fact to his knowledge when the information conveyed is expressed and it brings home knowledge directly to a party the notice is said to be the actual notice. Actual notice embraces all degrees and grades of evidence from the most direct and positive proof to the slightest evidence from which a Court would be warranted in inferring the notice. It is a question of fact and it may be proved by evidence like any other fact. There is no general rule of law because a man has the means of knowledge, he has the knowledge itself. The mere means of knowledge is not the same thing as knowledge. When there is no allegation or proof of direct knowledge, in some cases the law imputes notice to a person and that is called constructive notice. Constructive notice is a notice where knowledge of the fact is presumed from the circumstances of the case. This doctrine of constructive notice had its origin in equity. Subsequently the word notice was often defined in statutes and was defined to include constructive notice. There remained however a number of statutes where even though the word notice was used it was not defined. The question arose if in such cases notice included constructive or imputed notice. It remained in doubt as to how far this doctrine should be extended. Kerr has noted a series of cases in which such eminent Lord Justices as Lords Cotton ham Lyndhurst and L.J. Cranworth Turner, M.R. Jessel, and M.R. Esher have said that the doctrine ought not to be extended one bit further. In Allen *v.* Seckham (1879) 11 Ch.D. 790, Lord Esher observed that the doctrine is a dangerous one. It is contrary to the truth. It is wholly founded on the doctrine that a man does not know the facts and yet it is said that constructively he does know them.[25]

Memorandum and Articles of Association are the two fundamental documents of any company which decide and drive the relationship of company with the outsider, and regulate the internal affair of the company. Section 399 of Companies Act, 2013 makes the AoA and MoA of the company as public documents, which can be inspected by any person by filing nominal fees to the office of Registrar. As per the fundamentals of doctrine of constructive notice, the persons who are dealing with the company had knowledge of contents of the MoA and AoA of the company, and fully understood the documents in public record. Later on he or she cannot deny that he was not aware of it.

Indoor management or Turquand rule

The word indoor management consists of two words: Indoor + Management, which reflect management inside the door, which an outsider cannot see, the doctrine enables a person who is dealing with the company to presume that the internal affairs of the corporation are in order, in accordance with MoA or AoA, and that no irregularities exist.

Exception to the doctrine of constructive notice

This doctrine seems an exception of the Doctrine of Constructive Notice, as outsiders are not required to inquire into the regularity of the internal affairs of the company and will not be affected by irregularities of which they had no notice.

The doctrine of indoor management is in direct contrast to the doctrine or rule of constructive notice, which is essentially a presumption operating in favour of the

25. Hirji Madha *v.* Nagji Kurji And Ors. (1964) 5 GLR 289.

company against the outsider. It prevents the outsider from alleging that he did not know that the constitution of the company rendered a particular act or a particular delegation of authority ultra vires. The doctrine of indoor management is an exception to the rule of constructive notice. It imposes an important limitation on the doctrine of constructive notice. According to this doctrine, persons dealing with the company are entitled to presume that internal requirements prescribed in the memorandum and articles have been properly observed. Therefore, doctrine of indoor management protects outsiders dealing or contracting with a company, whereas doctrine of constructive notice protects the insiders of a company or corporation against dealings with the outsiders. However, suspicion of irregularity has been widely recognized as an exception to the doctrine of indoor management. The protection of the doctrine is not available where the circumstances surrounding the contract are suspicious and therefore invite inquiry.[26]

In the case of M/S. M.R.F. Ltd *v.* Manohar Parrikar & Ors, it was observed that:

The doctrine of indoor management is in direct contrast to the doctrine or rule of constructive notice, which is essentially a presumption operating in favour of the company against the outsider. It prevents the outsider from alleging that he did not know that the constitution of the company rendered a particular act or a particular delegation of authority ultra vires. The doctrine of indoor management is an exception to the rule of constructive notice. It imposes an important limitation on the doctrine of constructive notice. According to this doctrine, persons dealing with the company are entitled to presume that internal requirements prescribed in memorandum and articles have been properly observed. Therefore, doctrine of indoor management protects outsiders dealing with or contracting with a company, whereas doctrine of constructive notice protects the insiders of a company or corporation against dealing with the outsiders. However, suspicion of irregularity has been widely recognized as an exception to the doctrine of indoor management. The protection of the doctrine is not available where the circumstances surrounding the contract are suspicious and therefore invite inquiry.

Origin of doctrine

The doctrine of indoor management is also known as the 'Turquand rule' after Royal British Bank *v.* Turquand. In that case, the directors of a company had issued a bond to Turquand. They had the power under the articles to issue such a bond provided they were authorized by a resolution passed by the shareholders at a general meeting of the company. But no such resolution was passed by the company. It was held that Turquand could recover the amount of the bond from the company on the ground that he was entitled to assume that the resolution was passed.

Exception doctrine of indoor management

This exception was highlighted in the English case of Houghton & Co. *v.* Nothard, Lowe & Wills Ltd., where the case involved an agreement between fruit brokers and a fruit

26. Jasdev Singh & Ors *v.* Unit Trust of India, Delhi High Court.

importing company. There was an allegation that the agreement was entered into by the company's directors without authority. It was held that the nature of transaction was found to have been such as to put the plaintiffs on inquiry. To this effect L.J. Sargant, held: (KB p. 267)

> Cases where the question has been as to the exact formalities observed when the seal of a company has been affixed, such as Royal British Bank *v.* Turquand or County of Gloucester Bank *v.* Rudry Merthyr Steam and House Coal Colliery Co., are quite distinguishable from the present case. In Fireproof Doors Ltd., In re, tends rather against than in favour of the plaintiffs, since if a single director has, as towards third parties, the authority now contended for, the whole of the elaborate investigation of the facts in that case was entirely unnecessary. Perhaps the nearest approach to the present case is to be found in Biggerstaff *v.* Rowatt's Wharf Ltd. But there the agent whose authority was relied on had been acting to the knowledge of the company as a managing director, and the act done was one within the ordinary ambit of the powers of a managing director in the transaction of the company's affairs. It is, I think, clear that the transaction there would not have been supported had it not been in this ordinary course or had the agent been acting merely as one of the ordinary directors of the company. I know of no case in which an ordinary director, acting without authority in fact, has been held capable of binding a company by a contract with a third party, merely on the ground that the third party assumed that the director had been given authority by the Board to make the contract. A limitation of the right to make such an assumption is expressed in Buckley on the *Companies Acts*, 10th Edn, p. 175, in the following concise words: 'And the principle does not apply to the case where an agent of the company has done something beyond any authority which was given to him or which he was held out as having.'
>
> This exception to the doctrine of indoor management has been subsequently adopted in many Indian cases. They are B. Anand Behari Lal *v.* Dinshaw and Co. (Bankers) Ltd. and Abdul Rahman Khan *v.* Mufassal Bank Ltd. Applying the exception to the present scenario, there is sufficient doubt with regard to the conduct of the Power Minister in issuing the Notifications dated 15-5-1996 and 1-8-1996. Therefore, there is a definite suspicion of irregularity which renders the doctrine of indoor management inapplicable to the present case.[27]

Thus, the rule of doctrine of indoor management is still subject to certain exceptions, as:

Knowledge of irregularity

Protection under this doctrine is suspended when a person has knowledge of irregularity in the company. As it has been observed in the case R. Pratt (Bombay) Ltd. *v.* E.D. Sassoon and Co. Ltd. and Anr. AIR 1936 Bom 62 as:

27. Ibid.

If the outside party is put on inquiry by reason of the circumstances under which the transaction was put through, or by the nature of the transaction itself, or by any other surrounding circumstances, and disregards the facts which put him on inquiry as to the irregularity, he cannot get the benefit of the rule.

Forgery

Forgery is another aspect which suspended the protection to outsider under the rule of this doctrine. In the case of Ruben *v.* Great Fingall Ltd (1906) Lord Loreburn observed:

> It is quite true that persons dealing with limited liability Co.'s are not bound to inquire into their indoor mgt. & will not be affected by irregularities of which they have no notice. But this doctrine, which is well established, applies only to irregularities that otherwise might affect a genuine transaction. It can't apply to a forgery.

Suspicious circumstances

Justice Wright in the case B. Liggett (Liverpool), Limited *v.* Barclays Bank, Limited observed:

> the rule proceeds on a presumption that certain acts have been regularly done, and if the circumstances are such that the person claiming the benefit of the rule is really put on inquiry, if there are circumstances which debar that person from relying on the prima facie presumption, then it is clear, I think, that he cannot claim the benefit of the rule.

Negligence

The doctrine cannot be evoked by the person who acted negligently. It is obligatory on the part of the person who is dealing with the company. It may happen that an officer of the company may act outside the power of company, if the person was negligent to enquire about the doctrine, he cannot ask for the protection.

CHAPTER 4

Company Meetings and Proceedings

WHAT IS MEETING?

In general a meeting is a gathering of people for a particular purpose, especially for formal discussion. It can also be defined as a proceeding by a group of people for a common purpose, or for achieving a common goal through interaction with each other, or sharing information and arriving at an agreement.

Since a company is an artificial person it cannot do anything itself without the involvement of the human factor, thus a meeting has an important role in company functioning and governance. As discussed earlier a company is a social vehicle to acquire an economic objective, and sharing of information is required for corporate governance, meeting with regard to company is a gathering of people whose consent is required for something to decide, expressing their consent by consensus of votes.

A meeting reflects as a corporate act, which requires the validity of any resolution, or any proceeding, or transaction of the company. The Companies Act, 2013 exhibits the mandatory requirement of meetings in various aspects the of company proceedings, and without a specified meeting the particular act for which meeting is required cannot have legal force.

Fundamentals of a Valid Meeting

Any meeting under company law is valid if it is constituted under the procedure and manner prescribed by the Companies Act, 2013, else it is void. Following are the fundamentals for constituting the meeting:

1. Duly convened (proper authority and notice)
2. Properly constituted (quorum)
3. Properly conducted (proceeding under this act)

Duly convened

Duly convened means the meeting is called by the proper authority and a proper notice is issued to entitle people to attend the meeting.

Now the question arises: who is the proper authority?

The following persons, under the Companies Act, 2013, can call the meeting:

- Board of directors
- Tribunal the (National Company Law Tribunal)

According to the Act the authority vested to call a general meeting is with the Board of Directors of the Company, and the notice for the meeting is issued under their authority by passing a resolution to that effect. The secretary of the company has no power to call the meeting unless the Board of Directors passes a resolution and authorizes him to do so; likewise the authority cannot be exercised by a single director.

It is important to note here that if the meeting of Board of Directors per se is illegal and the rightful directors are prevented to participate in the said meeting, in that case the resolution passed by the Board of Directors to call the meeting is deemed to be unlawful.

Notice for meeting

A notice is to be issued to all the members who are entitled to attend the meeting by a proper authority of the company. This is another requirement under the Act for constituting valid meeting; section 101 of the Companies Act, 2013 specifies the procedure for it.

Mode of notice

As per section 101(1), the notice can be issued to the entitled persons either in writing or through an electronic mode.

The section does not specify the term electronic mode. This is my assumption to send a notice by email, as it is a common procedure nowadays.

Time of notice

As per the provisions of section 101, the notice should not be less than clear twenty-one days.

In case of an adjourned meeting or of a change of day, time, or place of meeting, clause (1) (a) of section 103 specifies that, the company shall give not less than three days notice to the members either individually or by publishing an advertisement in the newspapers (one in English and one in vernacular language), which is in circulation at the place where the registered office of the company is situated.

Exception

A general meeting may be called after giving a shorter notice if consent is given in writing or by electronic mode by not less than 95% of the members entitled to vote at such meeting.

Contents of notice

Every notice of a meeting shall specify the following:

- Place of meeting,
- Date of meeting,
- Day and the hour of the meeting
- A statement of the business to be transacted

Annexure of notice

In calling the general meeting the company shall attach a statement with the notice which discloses material facts of each item of special business to be transacted at the general meeting as:

1. the nature of concern or interest, financial or otherwise, if any, in respect of each item of:
   (a) every director and the manager, if any;
   (b) every other key managerial personnel; and
   (c) relatives of the persons mentioned in sub-clauses (i) and (ii).
2. Any other information and facts that may enable members to understand the meaning, scope, and implications of the items of business and to take decision thereon.

Other than the above conditions if all business to be transacted therein shall be deemed other than the following:

- the consideration of financial statements and the reports of the Board of Directors and auditors;
- the declaration of any dividend;
- the appointment of directors in place of those retiring;
- the appointment of, and the fixing of the remuneration of the auditors.

In the case of any other meeting, all business shall be deemed to be special:

1. Provided that where any item of special business is to be transacted at a meeting of the company relates to or affects any other company, the extent of shareholding interest in that other company of every promoter, director, manager, if any, and of every other key managerial personnel of the first mentioned company shall, if the extent of such shareholding is not less than 2% of the paid-up share capital of that company, also be set out in the statement.
2. Any document which needs to be referred or considered in the meeting, the time and place should also be mentioned so that the document can be inspected.
3. In every notice calling a meeting of a company which has a share capital, or the articles of which provide for voting by proxy at the meeting, there shall appear with reasonable prominence a statement that a member entitled to attend and vote is entitled to appoint a proxy, or, where that is allowed, one or more proxies to attend and vote instead of himself, and that a proxy need not be a member.

Consequences of non-disclosure or insufficient disclosure in notice

Where, as a result of the non-disclosure or insufficient disclosure in any statement referred to in sub-section (1) of section 101 being made by a promoter, director, manager, if any, or other key managerial personnel, any benefit which accrues to such a promoter, director, manager, or other key managerial personnel or their relatives, either directly or indirectly, the promoter, director, manager, or other key managerial personnel, as the case may be, shall hold such benefit in trust for the company, and shall, without prejudice to any other action being taken against him under this Act or under any other law for the time being in force, be liable to compensate the company to the extent of the benefit received by him.

Consequences of default in complying section 101

If any default is made in complying with the provisions of this section, every promoter, director, manager or other key managerial personnel who is in default shall be punishable with fine which may extend to fifty thousand rupees or five times the amount of benefit accruing to the promoter, director, manager, or other key managerial personnel or any of his relatives, whichever is more.

Notice to whom

The notice of every meeting of the company shall be given to:

- every member of the company;
- legal representative of any deceased member or the assignee of an insolvent member;
- the auditor or auditors of the company; and
- every director of the company;

Effect of omission to give notice to any member

Any accidental omission to give notice to or the non-receipt of such notice by any member or other person who is entitled to such a notice for any meeting shall not invalidate the proceedings of the meeting.

Properly Constituted Quorum

For a meeting to be properly and legally constituted there must be a proper quorum as the mandate of section 103 and section 104 specifies person in the chair and proper compliance with the relevant provisions of the Articles of Association and other provisions of the Act.

Quorum for meeting

The mandate of section 103 specifies the number of persons required to constitute a legal forum, unless article of the company provides any specifies numbers:

In case of a public company

(i) five members personally present if the number of members as on the date of meeting is not more than one thousand;
(ii) fifteen members personally present if the number of members as on the date of meeting is more than one thousand but up to five thousand; or
(iii) thirty members personally present if the number of members as on the date of the meeting exceeds five thousand.

In case of a private company

Two members personally present shall be the quorum for a meeting of the company.

If the quorum is not present

If the quorum is not present within half-an-hour from the time appointed for holding a meeting of the company

(a) the meeting shall stand adjourned to the same day in the next week at the same time and place, or to such other date and such other time and place as the Board may determine; or
(b) the meeting, if called by requisitionists under section 100 (calling of extraordinary general meeting), shall stand cancelled.

Adjournment of meeting

When the meeting is adjourned or there is a change of day, time, or place of meeting, then the time of notice should not be less than three days either individually or by publishing in an advertisement in the newspaper – one in English and one in a vernacular language, which is in circulation at the place where the registered office of the company is located.

Quorum of adjourned meeting is also not present

There may be circumstances when quorum of an adjourned meeting is also not present within half-an-hour, then half-an-hour from the time appointed for holding meeting the members present shall be the quorum.

Who will preside the meeting/chairman of meeting

Section 104 provides that if there is no provision regarding the chairman of the meeting, the members personally present at the meeting shall elect one of them to be the chairman thereof on a show of hands.

In case if a poll is demanded on the election of the chairman, then it will be conducted according to the provision of the act and the chairman elected on a show of hands under sub-section (1) of section 104 shall continue to be the chairman of the meeting until some other person is elected chairman as a result of the poll, and such other person shall be the chairman for the rest of the meeting.

Properly conducted

Proper conduct of the meeting means that proper rules with regard to the meeting are followed. The rules for discussion and order in debate must be observed. The proceedings should also be recorded properly.

Proxies

Literal meaning of proxy is 'near to'. In company law, proxy means an authority given to a person to act for someone else, such as voting.

Appointment of proxy

As per section 105 any member of a company entitled to attend and vote at a meeting of the company shall be entitled to appoint another person as a proxy to attend and vote at the meeting on his behalf.

Right of proxy

But proxies do not have the right to speak at such a meeting and shall not be entitled to vote except on a poll, subject to the provision of the articles of a company otherwise provided. This shall not apply in the case of a company not having a share capital. The Central Government may prescribe a class or classes of companies whose members shall not be entitled to appoint another person as a proxy.

A person appointed as proxy shall act on behalf of such member or number of members not exceeding fifty and such number of shares as may be prescribed.

Notice to proxy

Sub-section (2) of section 105, says,

> In every notice calling a meeting of a company which has a share capital, or the articles of which provide for voting by proxy at the meeting, there shall appear with reasonable prominence a statement that a member entitled to attend and vote is entitled to appoint a proxy, or, where that is allowed, one or more proxies, to attend and vote instead of himself, and that a proxy need not be a member. If default is made in complying with sub-section (2), every officer of the company who is in default shall be punishable with fine which may extend to five thousand rupees.

If any provision of the article of a company requires that a period longer than forty-eight hours before a meeting of the company for depositing any document or any other instrument to the company or with regard to appointing a proxy, the instrument appointing a proxy shall be

- in writing
- signed by the appointer or his attorney duly authorized in writing or, if the appointer is a body corporate, it should be under its seal or be signed by an officer or an attorney duly authorized by it.

If for the purpose of any meeting of a company, invitations to appoint as proxy a person or one of a number of persons specified in the invitations are issued at the company's expense to any member entitled to have a notice of the meeting sent to him and to vote thereat by proxy, every officer of the company who knowingly issues the invitations as aforesaid or willfully authorizes or permits their issue shall be punishable with a fine which may extend to one lakh rupees. But the officer shall not be punishable by reason only of the issue to a member at his request in writing of a form of appointment naming the proxy, or of a list of persons willing to act as proxies, if the form or list is available on request in writing to every member entitled to vote at the meeting by proxy.

KINDS OF MEETINGS

In the Company Act, 1956 there was a provision for three types of meetings– Statutory Meeting, Annual General Meeting, and Extraordinary General Meeting.

The Companies Act, 2013 does not state anything about the Statutory Meetings and there is no provision as such, while in the Companies Act, 1956, section 165 defines the same as the general meeting of members that must be held by a company, limited by guarantee and having a share capital, within a period of not less than one month nor more than six months from the date at which the company is entitled to commence business.

Annual General Meeting (AGM)

The name of the meeting signifies the type of the meeting–Annual General Meeting means a meeting which is held every year in addition to any other meeting. The intention of the meeting is to provide an occasion to the members of the company to express their views on the management of the company's affairs. In this meeting, shareholders of the company may ask any question relating to the acts and affairs of the company, it is a process to enable the shareholders to exercise control over the company.

Legal provisions to AGM

Mandatory to hold AGM

Section 96 of the Companies Act, 2013 provides that every company other than a One Person Company shall in each year hold an AGM in addition to any other meetings. It is mandatory for every company to hold an AGM but a 'one person company' is exempt from holding an AGM.

Notice for AGM is also required as it is the general provision for calling any meeting.

Gap for holding AGM

The time for holding the AGM shall not be more than fifteen months between the date of one AGM of a company and that of the next. However, in case of the AGM, it shall be held within a period of nine months from the date of closing of the first financial year of the company and in any other case, within a period of six months from the date of closing of the financial year. It is also important to note that if a company holds its first AGM as aforesaid, it shall not be necessary for the company to hold any AGM in the year of its incorporation.

The Registrar of Companies has the power, under any special reason, to extend the time within which any AGM, other than the first AGM, shall be held, by a period not exceeding three months.

Time for calling AGM

Every annual general meeting shall be called during business hours, that is, between 9 a.m. and 6 p.m. on any day that is not a national holiday and shall be held either at the registered office of the company or at some other place within the city, town, or village in which the registered office of the company is situated.

The Central Government may exempt any company from the provisions of this sub-section, subject to such conditions as it may impose.

Extraordinary General Meeting (EGM)

A meeting which is called, other than the normal schedule or at short notice, to consider any extraordinary or specific issue is called an extraordinary general meeting.

Section 100 of the Companies Act, 2013 has provisions for the same such as the authority to call the EGM are the Board of Directors of the company.

Legal requisite for holding the EGM

The Board may, whenever it deems fit, call an EGM, at the requisition made by:

- in the case of a company having a share capital—such number of members who hold, on the date of the receipt of the requisition, not less than one-tenth of the paid-up share capital of the company as on that date, carries the right of voting;
- in the case of a company not having a share capital—such number of members who have, on the date of receipt of the requisition, not less than one-tenth of the total voting power of all the members having on the said date a right to vote, call an EGM of the company within twenty-one days from the date of receipt of a valid requisition.

If the Board does not, within twenty-one days from the date of receipt of a valid requisition in regard to any matter, proceed to call a meeting for the consideration of that matter on a day not later than forty-five days from the date of receipt of such requisition, the meeting may be called and held by the requisitionists themselves within a period of three months from the date of the requisition.

CHAPTER 5

Prospectus

A prospectus is a document issued by the company intended to offer securities for sale to the general public. It is a legal document issued by the company, under strict compliance of the Companies Act and Security and Exchange Board of India.

A document that expresses or is issued as a prospectus includes any notice, circular, advertisement, or other information inviting securities or subscription or purchase of shares or debentures from the public.

It is a document containing detailed information about the company and outlines in detail the terms and conditions on which the shares have been offered.

An information booklet or offer document which contains all the information considering an investor to invest in the company.

Notice to the public to invest in the company.

Section 32 has been referred to mean a prospectus which does not include complete particulars of the quantum or price of the securities included therein.

Shelf Prospectus under Explanation to section 31 has been referred to mean a prospectus in respect of which the securities or class of securities included therein are issued for subscription in one or more issues over a certain period without the issue of a further prospectus.

Why Issue the Prospectus?

Incorporation of any company is for a specific objective or objectives, and to execute that objective, the company is required to raise finances for its nourishment, expansion, and organic growth. It helps in creating beneficial rights foundation and broad capacities to create an impact on the national economy. When any one buys securities he is strengthening the company financially to carry on its business using those funds.

We can summarize the object of a prospectus as:

- Invitation to public for investing
- Outline the terms and conditions of investment
- Declaration for the liability of the Director against the terms and conditions stated in the prospectus.

Section 2(70) of Companies Act, 2013:

> *'prospectus' means any document described or issued as a prospectus and includes a red herring prospectus referred to in section 32 or shelf prospectus referred to in section 31 or any notice, circular, advertisement or other document inviting offers from the public for the subscription or purchase of any securities of a body corporate:*

The section exhibits that any documents can be a prospectus. There is no restriction at all for considering the prospectus— it can be any notice, circular, advertisement, or other document if it's described or issued for inviting offers from the public for the payment or purchase of any securities of a body corporate.

The DNA for any prospectus is that it must invite offers from the public to payment or purchase of securities issued by the company. The section also gives place to a red herring prospectus referred to in section 32 or shelf prospectus referred to in section 31.

Section 25 exhibits any document containing offer of securities for sale to be deemed a prospectus as:

'Where a company allots or agrees to allot any securities of the company with a view to all or any of those securities being offered for sale to the public, any document by which the offer for sale to the public is made shall, for all purposes, be deemed to be a prospectus issued by the company; ...'

The ingredients to constitute a prospectus are:

- Invitation to the public
- For subscription or purchase of securities
- It should be issued on behalf of Body Corporate.

After analysing the definitions, it exhibits that a prospectus is an invitation to the public to subscribe to the share capital or debentures of a company, if it fails to do so, it cannot be called a prospectus.

INVITATION TO THE PUBLIC

Prospectus 'must be' an invitation to public, not otherwise.

In the case of Amrutanjan Ltd. *v.* Commissioner Of Income-Tax 1961 41 ITR 21 Mad: Madras High Court enunciated the term Public as:

The term 'public' has not been defined. In the Companies Act, section 2 (37) and section 3 states that a public company means a company which is not a private company. In Nash *v.* Lynde Viscount Sumner, considering the meaning of the word 'public' in section 285 of the English Companies (Consolidation) Act, 1908, which defined the term 'prospectus' as invitation offering to the public, observed at page 169.

> The public, in the definition section 285, is of course a general word. No particular numbers are prescribed. Anything from two to infinity may serve; perhaps even one, if he is intended to be the first of a series of subscribers, but makes further proceedings needless by himself subscribing the whole. The point is that the offer is such as to be open to any one who brings his money and applies in due form, whether the prospectus was addressed to him on behalf of the company or not.

The term 'public' would mean all other members of the company other than the person having a control, that is, more than 50 per cent of the voting power.

In Commissioner of Income-tax *v.* H. Bjordal, the brother of the major shareholder had held shares commanding more than 25 per cent of the voting power. The Privy Council held that the company was one in which the public were substantially interested. We are of opinion that the voting power for the purpose of the explanation would depend on the articles of association. In the present case, there is no distinction between a preference shareholder and an ordinary shareholder, in the matter of voting rights. Therefore, the voting power should be ascertained with respect to both preference and ordinary shares held. Ramayamma has got only about 40 per cent of the total number of shares. She cannot, therefore, be held to be in a position to control the company. Even combining the shares held by Ramayamma, her daughter, her brother and son-in-law, the total percentage is only about 47 per cent. Therefore, even if it were to be held that the third proviso of the section is governed by the explanation thereto in its entirety, the position is that the public are having more than 25 per cent of the voting power and, therefore, the company is one in which the public would be substantially interested.

Prospectus constitutes an office?

The prospectus does not constitute an 'offer' in contractual sense, it is only an initiation to offer, which clearly establishes the definition '*inviting offers*'.

Some scholars consider it a 'discloser statement/document' which is used by the company to use as a selling instrument to subscribe the securities of the body corporate by the public. Further, it can also be the discretion of the board of the company to consider or not to consider the application for opting the security of company by the public. It constitutes the contractual obligation after accepting the application for allotment of shares.

The provisions regarding the prospectus are applicable to both listed and unlisted public limited companies.

Duty of those who issued a prospectus

In the case of Iridium India Telecom Ltd *v.* Motorola Incorporated, the Supreme Court of India held that:

> … observations made by the House of Lords in the case of The Director & c. of the Central Railway Company of Venezuela v. Joseph Kisch 40 which would be of some relevance to the issue under consideration. In this case, the House of Lords examined the duty of those who issued a prospectus inviting investments from the general public and held that they were required to make a true and full disclosure of all the relevant facts. The House of Lords quoted with approval the observations made in the case of New Brunswick and Canada supra.

Railway Company *v.* Muggeridge 41 wherein it has been observed as follows:

> ... those who issue a prospectus holding out to the public the great advantages which will accrue to persons who will take shares in a proposed undertaking, and inviting them to take shares on the faith of the representations therein contained, are bound to state everything with strict and scrupulous accuracy, and not only to abstain from stating as fact that which is not so, but to omit no one fact within their knowledge the existence of which might in any degree affect the nature, or extent, or quality of the privileges and advantages which the prospectus holds out as inducements to take shares.

For Subscription or Purchase

Another ingredient of prospectus is subscribe or purchase the security. It is necessary to understand the meaning of subscribe or purchase. The literal meaning of subscribe is 'promise' or 'agree to', with regard to prospectus the word exhibits the meaning 'agree to purchase the prospectus'.

If we stretc it further it can give us the meaning of 'undertaking for purchase', as in the case of subscription of prospectus.

Purchase meaning

Lord Green M.R. observed in In re V.G.M. Holdings, Limited, (2), (1) (191 1) I.L.R. Ch. 73. 84. (2) (1942) 1 Ch. D. 235. It seems to me that

> the word '**purchase**' cannot with propriety be applied to the legal transaction under which a person' by the machinery of application and allotment, becomes a shareholder in the company. He does not purchase anything when he does that. Mr. Wynn Parry endeavored heroically to establish the proposition that a share before issue was an existing article of property, that it was an existing bundle of rights which a shareholder could properly be said to be purchasing when he acquired it by subscription in the usual way. I am unable to accept that view. A share is a chose (sic) in action. A chose (sic) in action implies the existence of some person entitled to the rights in action as distinct from rights in possession, and, until the share is issued, no such person exists. Putting it in a nutshell, the difference between the issue of a share to a subscriber and the purchase of a share from an existing shareholder is the difference between creation and the transfer of a chose (sic) in action.[28]

Allotment

In Company Law 'allotment' means the appropriation out of the previously inappropriate capital of a company, of a certain number of shares to a person. Till such allotment, the shares do not exist as such. It is on allotment in this sense that the shares come into

---

28. Sri Gopal Jalan & Company v. Calcutta Stock 1964 AIR 250, 1964 SCR (3) 698.

existence. Learned counsel for the appellant has not been able to cite any case where the word 'allotment' has been used to describe a transaction with regard to an existing share, that is, a share previously brought into existence by appropriation to a person out of the authorized capital. In every case the words 'allotment of shares' have been used to indicate the creation of shares by appropriation out of the inappropriate share capital to a particular person.[29]

Golden rule in prospectus

Prospectus is the notice to the public to invest in the company which constitutes the terms and conditions of that investment on the basis of which the public chooses to invest or not to invest in the company. Since prospectus is an invitation to offer, and the genesis of contract. The cardinal principle of contract is that true, fair, and accurate information must be communicated to other party.

Prospectus is the basis of initial communication with the public to invest, as potential investor has no such knowledge about the terms and conditions except this prospectus. It is therefore obligatory on the part of those who issue the prospectus that they disclose only true, fair, and correct information in the prospectus.

The potential investor considers an honest statement of the company's profile; and that there is no ambiguity, or any false, misleading, or erroneous reflection in the company.

The foundation of 'golden rule' is based on true, fair, and accurate. The rule laid down by Justice Kindersley in New Brunswick & Canada Rly. & Land Co. *v.* Muggeridge (1860) is based on three foundations as:

> Those who issue a prospectus holding out to the public the great advantages which will accrue to persons who will take shares in a proposed undertaking, and inviting them to take shares, on the faith of the representations therein contained, are bound to state everything with strict and scrupulous accuracy, and not only to abstain from stating as facts that which is not so, but to omit no one fact within their knowledge the existence of which might in any degree affect the nature, or extent, or quality of the privileges and advantages which the prospectus 'holds out as inducements to take shares'.

The rule propounded that those who issue the prospectus should issue it in utmost good faith and honesty, because it holds out to the public great advantages, and public invest in the company on good faith of the representation contained in it. The golden rule to issue a prospectus is that nothing should be contained in the prospectus which is not true, fair, or correct.

The statement contained in the prospectus should not only be true but it must be true in strict sense, and the prospectus must not miss out or omit any important or correct fact, which becomes the basis of decision of investment in the company.

---

29. Supra.

Discussing the same contention in the case of Pramatha Nath Sanyal *v.* Kali Kumar Dutt (1925) ILR 52 Cal 440, Calcutta High Court it was observed as:

> It is obvious that the preparation of a prospectus necessitates the greatest care; while an attractive statement of the advantages offered is justly permissible, every statement made should be an honest one, no ambiguous phraseology, unfair reservation, or half truths should be allowed to be used or to creep in. On a reference to the sections mentioned above, together with some of the other sections of the Act, e.g., 88, 84 and 100, it is clear that one of the chief aims of the Legislature has been to secure the fullest disclosure of all material and essential particulars as to the state of affairs of a company, and lay the same in full view of all intending purchasers of its shares or participators in its profits. With that object the Legislature has provided that any invitation to the public for that purpose should be subject to the scrutiny of the authorities. It has, therefore, been enacted in Section 92 of the Act that an advertisement of the nature which forms the subject-matter of the present cases should be placed before the Registrar by filing a copy of it before it is issued, and it has also provided that in order to be so filed it must contain essential particulars such as are mentioned in Section 93. That this is so also appears from sub-section (2) of section 93 which makes some exemptions in the case of newspaper advertisements, and sub-section (3) of that section which makes the section inapplicable to a circular or notice inviting existing members or debenture-holders of a company to subscribe either for shares or for debentures. It is clear that an advertisement in the shape in which it has been published would not have been accepted by the Registrar as satisfying the requirements of Section 93; but that only means that it should not have been issued.

Legal requirement regarding issue of prospectus

The Companies Act, 2013 specifies certain legal requirements for issuing the prospectus.

1. Issue of prospectus

After clinical research of chapter III, the prospectus of a company can only be issued after the incorporation of a company, as section 23 states, 'A public company may issue securities and a Private company may issue the prospectus.'

2. Registration of prospectus

As per the mandate of section 389, it is mandatory to register the prospectus with the Registrar of Companies before it is issued to the public as:

> No person shall issue, circulate or distribute in India any prospectus offering for subscription in securities of a company incorporated or to be incorporated outside India, whether the company has or has not established, or when formed will or will not establish, a place of business in India, unless before the issue, circulation or distribution of the prospectus in India, a copy thereof certified by

the chairperson of the company and two other directors of the company as having been approved by resolution of the managing body has been delivered for registration to the Registrar and the prospectus states on the face of it that a copy has been so delivered, and there is endorsed on or attached to the copy, any consent to the issue of the prospectus required by section 388 and such documents as may be prescribed.

Matters to be stated in the prospectus

Section 26 provides the contents of prospectus issued by or on behalf of a public company either with reference to its formation or subsequently, by or on behalf of any person, who is or has been engaged or interested in the formation of a public company, shall be dated and signed stating the following information:

1. Names and addresses of the registered office of the company, company secretary, chief financial officer, auditors, legal advisers, bankers, trustees, if any, underwriters.
2. Dates of the opening and closing of the issue, and declaration about the issue of allotment letters and refunds within the prescribed time.
3. A statement by the Board of Directors about the separate bank account where all monies received out of the issue are to be transferred and disclosure of details of all monies including utilized and unutilized monies out of the previous issue in the prescribed manner.
4. Details about underwriting of the issue.
5. Consent of the directors, auditors, bankers to the issue, expert's opinion, if any.
6. The authority for the issue and the details of the resolution passed therefor.
7. Procedure and time schedule for allotment and issue of securities.
8. Capital structure of the company.
9. Main objects of public offer, terms of the present issue.
10. Main objects and present business of the company and its location, schedule of implementation of the project.
11. Particulars relating to:
    - management perception of risk factors specific to the project;
    - gestation period of the project;
    - extent of progress made in the project;
    - deadlines for completion of the project; and
    - any litigation or legal action pending or taken by a Government Department or a statutory body during the last five years immediately preceding the year of the issue of prospectus against the promoter of the company.
12. Minimum subscription, amount payable by way of premium, issue of shares otherwise than on cash.

13. Details of directors including their appointments and remuneration, and such particulars of the nature and extent of their interests in the company as may be prescribed.
14. Disclosures in such manner as may be prescribed about sources of promoter's contribution.
15. Reports relating to financial information such as auditor reports of the company, profit and loss report, business transactions report.

Types of Prospectus

Shelf prospectus

The word 'shelf' reveals the meaning of shelf prospectus. It is like details contained in a file—first or subsequent securities issued by the company, or any public financial institution, or any schedule or any public sector bank, whose chief objective is financing, may use shelf prospectus.

The main objective is to prepare a standard draft/information which need not be required to be filed every time or afresh. It also saves the cost of issuing the prospectus.

Explanation of section 31 defines shelf prospectus as 'a prospectus in respect of which the securities or class of securities included therein are issued for subscription in one or more issues over a certain period without the issue of a further prospectus'.

It was first introduced under the Companies (Amendment) Act, 2000.

The silent features of it are:

- Shelf prospectus along with the Information Memorandum is to be filed with the registrar at the stage of the first offer of securities.
- The validity of it shall be for a period of 1 year from the date of the first offer.
- No further prospectus is required to be issued if further offer is made during the validity period.

Red herring prospectus

A red herring prospectus contains nearly all the information relating to the company except key details such as particulars on the price of the securities offered and quantum of securities of the issue. The clinical research of section 32, exhibits two words which disclose the meaning of red herring prospects as 'proposing' and 'prior', the company is proposing, not final, and it is the information before issuing the prospectus.

Section 32: When a company 'proposing' to make an offer of securities may issue a red herring prospectus 'prior' to the issue of prospectus.

Explanation of section 32 defines red hearing prospectus as 'a prospectus which does not include complete particulars of the quantum or price of the securities included therein'.

The salient features of it are:

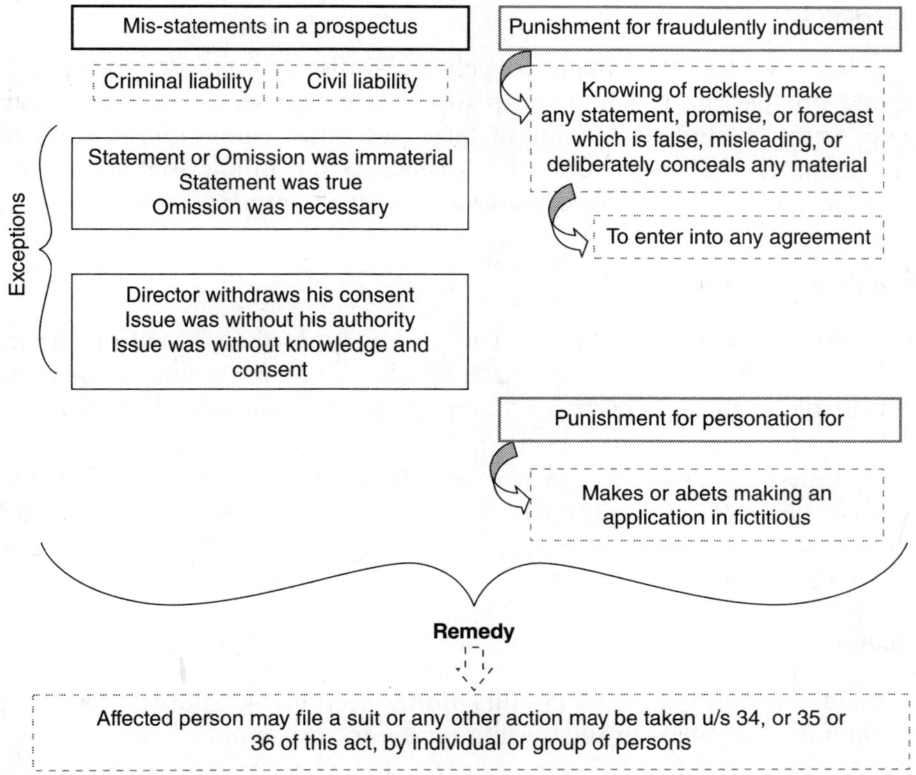

- Red Herring prospectus shall be filed with the Registrar at least 3 days prior to the opening of the subscription list and the offer.
- In case of any variations in the Red Herring prospectus and the prospectus the same shall be highlighted.
- On the closure of the offer the prospectus stating the details of the capital raised, closing price, and other information that was not available on the RHP shall be filed with the Registrar and SEBI.

Abridged prospectus

Abridged prospectus means a shorter version of a prospectus which contains all salient or important features.

According to section 2(1) 'abridged prospectus' means a memorandum containing such salient features of a prospectus as may be specified by the Securities and Exchange Board by making regulations in this behalf.

Its also seems to be a cost saving tool, which reduces cost as compared to issue of full prospectus.

Deemed prospectus

Section 25 exhibits that when a document contains offer of securities for sale to public it is a deemed prospectus. Where a company allots or agrees to allot any securities of the company with a view to all or any of those securities being offered for sale to the public, any document by which the offer for sale to the public is made shall, for all purposes, be deemed to be a prospectus issued by the company.

Mis-statements in a Prospectus

As we observed earlier the foundation of issuing prospectus is based on the true, fair and correct statements as per the golden rule. Thus, it is important to state complete and perfect details in the prospectus, nothing should be omitted and nothing must be untrue.

Stating any untrue statement in a prospectus attracts civil and criminal liability. Every person who is a director or promoter of the company and every person, including an expert at the time of the issue of the prospectus, who has authorized the issue of a prospectus, shall be liable.

Criminal liability

Section 34 talks about the criminal liability under section 447 (punishment for fraud), when any statement is untrue or misleading or any inclusion or omission of any matter, where a prospectus, issued, circulated or distributed, every person who authorizes the issue of such a prospectus, shall be liable for punishment for fraud and shall be punishable with imprisonment for a term which shall not be less than six months but which may extend to ten years and shall also be liable to fine which shall not be less than the amount involved in the fraud, but which may extend to three times the amount involved in the fraud. If the fraud in question involves public interest, the term of imprisonment shall not be less than three years under section 447 of this act.

The section also discusses the exception to it, as when it is proved that such omission or statement was immaterial or statement was true or the omission was necessary.

Civil liability for mis-statements in prospectus

Where a person has subscribed for securities of a company acting on any statement included, or the inclusion or omission of any matter, in the prospectus which is misleading and has sustained any loss or damage as a consequence thereof, the company and every person who was the director of the company at the time of the issue of the prospectus; or who has authorized himself to be named and is named in the prospectus as a director of the company, or has agreed to become such a director, either immediately or after an interval of time; or who is a promoter of the company; or has authorized the issue of the prospectus; and is an expert referred to in sub-section (5) of section 26.

However, the director of the company shall not be liable for civil liability if he withdrew his consent before the issue of the prospectus, and that it was issued without his authority or consent; or the prospectus was issued without his knowledge or consent, and that on becoming aware of its issue, he forthwith gave a reasonable public notice that it was issued without his knowledge or consent.

Where it is proved that a prospectus has been issued with the intent to defraud the applicants for the securities of a company or any other person or for any fraudulent purpose, every person referred to in sub-section (1) shall be personally responsible, without any limitation of liability, for all or any of the losses or damages that may have been incurred by any person who subscribed to the securities on the basis of such a prospectus.

Fraudulently inducing person to invest money

Section 36 also includes punishment under section 447 when any person who, either knowingly or recklessly makes any statement, promise, or forecast which is false, deceptive, or misleading, or deliberately conceals any material facts to induce another person to enter into, or to offer to enter into agreement for, or with a view to, acquiring, disposing of, subscribing for, or underwriting securities; or any agreement, the purpose or the pretended purpose of which is to secure a profit to any of the parties from the yield of securities or by reference to fluctuations in the value of securities; or any agreement for, or with a view to obtaining credit facilities from any bank or financial institution.

Punishment for personation for acquisition

Section 38 includes personation for acquisition for making or abets making of an application in a fictitious name to a company for acquiring, or subscribing for its securities or makes or abets making of multiple applications to a company in different names or in different combinations of his name or surname for acquiring or subscribing for its securities; or otherwise induces directly or indirectly a company to allot, or register any transfer of, securities to him, or to any other person in a fictitious name.

CHAPTER 6

Directors

- Meaning
- Status
- Appointment
- Qualification and Disqualifications
- Removal
- Legal Obligations on Directors

Directors or Board of Directors is the brain of any organization that constitutes and executes the functional aspect, and holds the collective responsibility for drafting and executing the company policies in a right and beneficial manner.

The Companies Act, 2013 under Chapter XI and Companies (Appointment and Qualification of Directors) Rules (2014) defines the provisions with regard to director and matters thereto. The new Act improved the responsibilities and accountability of the director by establishing provisions for certain disclosures like evolution of performance of board, risk policies, whistle-blower mechanism, and CSR policy in the Director Report.

The new Act first time introduced the provisions related to the role of an independent director, duties of directors, increase in minimum number of directors from twelve to fifteen, prohibition for inside trading, penal provisions for non-disclosure, and non-compliance of duties of the director as defined; and the most important is the appointment of women director for certain class of companies.

Director: Meaning

A company is an artificial person and a fiction of law. There is no intangible personality, and does not consist mind and physical body, to execute the functions of the organization. Directors of a company are its eyes, ears, brain, hands, and other essential limbs. As we have discussed earlier the company is the social economic vehicle, which is connected with numerous public purposes so to govern its function and management according to the need and in the interest of company, there must be a living person. A Director is an individual or group of individuals who are elected to act and execute corporate management related policies and to make decisions on major company issues.

A person or group of persons who supervise, control, or manage the company and its affairs, is called Director or Board of Directors.

Section 2 (34): ''director' means a director appointed to the Board of a company'

Definition under section 2(34) defines director who is appointed to the board of the company. It means any person who is appointed to the Board of a company is considered to be a director. The plain reading of the section talks about the appointment by the board. To understand it, it is important to know the definition of Board under section 2(10):

"'Board of Directors" or "Board", in relation to a company, means the collective body of the directors of the company'.

The collective reading of the definition exhibits the core functionary authority who is responsible for achieving the objective of company as mentioned in the MoA and AoA. The Board of Directors of the company is the centre of all functionary processes, and a source of power of a director and management. It is important to note that till the time the Board, by resolution, does not authorise any power to the director he cannot exercise that power. It also establishes the democratic process of election and conferring the power, which is mandatory to attain the social economic objective for which company has been incorporated.

New Provisions Regaled to Directors in Companies Act, 2013

The Companies Act, 2013 made provision for following directors:

- Appointment of women director
- Resident director
- Independent director

Status of Director

It is important to know the status of the director in the company since he is the pivot for the success and direction of the company's success.

Director is the Servant or Clerk of the Company?

It is difficult to understand the status of the director in the company. He may be considered to be the officer or controller of the company, but not the servant of the company. It does not constitute any master–servant relation with company. It would be important to point out the observation made in the case of Lee *v.* Lee's Air Farming Ltd. where the relation between the director and company is considered to be that of an employee.

In the case of **Dwijendra Chandra Chowdhury *v.* Commissioner of Income-Tax, 1966 61 ITR 97 AP, Andhra High Court,** the relationship of the director with the company is:

> Whether a person is a clerk or servant is a question of fact in each case. Some of the determining factors are whether or not the person in question works as the company officer, or is exclusively employed by the company, or is bound to render services generally and in a manner prescribed by the company; and in general a person must have a contract of service with the company in order

> to constitute him a clerk or servant. A managing director is not as such a clerk or servant.

The expression 'clerk or servant' has been given a wide interpretation, it cannot be held to cover a managing director. Reliance was placed by Buckley also on the same decision as reported in In re Newspaper Proprietary Syndicate Ltd.: Hopkinson *v.* Newspaper Proprietary Syndicate. In that case, it was contended that a 'clerk or servant' of a company is entitled to payment, in priority to other creditors, in respect of wages or salary in the winding-up of his company, and it was claimed that the managing director was also entitled to the same benefit. In that connection, the question came to be considered whether a managing director could be held to be a 'clerk or servant'. The following observations are material and may be quoted:

'I think the claim cannot be supported. A managing director is certainly not a clerk of the company. Is he a servant of the company? This proposition was negatived by the Court of Kings Bench in Dunston *v.* Imperial Gas Light and Coke Co., where it was pointed out that a director is not a servant, but a manager; and in Hutton *v.* West Cork Railway Co., L.J. Bowen dealing with a case of a managing director says:

> A director is not a servant. He is a person who is doing business for the company, but not upon ordinary terms.
>
> A managing director is only an ordinary director entrusted with some special powers. It is not relevant to say that he is entitled to remuneration by virtue of a special bargain or that his remuneration is described as a salary. It is sufficient for me to say that he is not, within the meaning of the statue, a servant of the company. So far as I am aware, no such claim has ever been brought forward by a director.
>
> The director of a company as such is not a servant of the company and that the fees he receives are by way of gratuity, but that does not prevent a director or a managing director from entering into a contractual relationship with the company, so that, quite apart from his office of director he becomes entitled to remuneration as an employee of the company. Further that relationship may be created either by a service agreement or by the article themselves.[30]

The control and supervision of the directors was, however, a general control and supervision and within the limits of their authority the appellants as the agents of the company had perfect discretion as to how that work of general management was to be done both in regard to the method and the manner of such work and therefore the circumstances of the case together with the of power of sub-delegation reserved under the Articles of Association established beyond doubt that the appellants were the agents of the company and not merely the servants of the company remunerated by wages or salary.[31]

---

30. Commissioner of Income-Tax, *v.* B. Nagi Reddy 1964 51 ITR 178 Mad.

31. Lakshminarayan Ram Gopal and Son ... *v.* The Government of Hyderabad 1954 AIR 364, 1955 SCR 393

Director is the Agent of the Company?

To determine the relationship between the director and company as an agent, we must understand the meaning of the word 'agent'.

> The agents may regulate and conduct their proceedings in such manner as they may from time to time determine and may delegate all or any of their powers, authorities and discretions as escritoires, treasures and agents of the company to such person or persons and on such terms and conditions as they may think fit, subject to the approval.[32]

The observation made above clearly establishes that the function of an agent is similar to the functions of director in the company; the same was recognized in the case of Ferguson *v.* Wilson[33], and held as.

> What is the position of directors of a public company? They are merely agents of a company. The company itself cannot act in its own person, for it has no person; it can only act through directors, and the case is, as regards those directors, merely the ordinary case of principals and agent. Wherever an agent is liable those directors would be liable: Where the liability would attach to the principal and the principal only, the liability is the liability of the company.

Similar observations are to be found in the judgment of Lord Selborne in -'G.E. Rly. *v.* Turner, (1873) 8 Ch 149 at p. 152. The position thus summed up in Palmer's Company Precedents:

> Where the directors of a company are invested by the regulations with certain powers, the authority thus conferred is to be read subject to the general rules applicable to the exercise by directors of the powers vested in them, and in particular to the rule that the directors are to exercise the powers for the benefit of the company and in the true interests of the company and according to the best of their Judgment, for they stand in a fiduciary position, and must act accordingly.[34]

Director is the Trustee of the Company?

The relationship of director with company is interesting, in some respects they resemble trustees, in others they do not.

Director as trustee of the company: trustees of the company's money and property

In relation to the company's property and its funds in their hands are concerned the director is considered to be the trustee of company. In Regal (Hastings) Ltd. *v.* Gulliver

32. Supra in the case of Dwijendra Chandra Chowdhury.
33. (1866) LR 2 Ch. 77.
34. A. Ananthalakshmi Ammal and Anr. *v.* The Indian Trades and Investments AIR 1953 Mad 467, (1953) IMLJ 275.

[1942] 1 All ER 378, the House of Lords had the occasion to consider this aspect of the case, in another case. In Selangor United Rubber Estates Ltd. *v.* Cradock [1968] 2 All ER 1073 (Ch D) the first question of law discussed was how far the directors are trustees of the company's funds and while answering this question, the discussion proceeded on the assumption that there existed a fiduciary relationship between the director and the company which is clear from the following observation (p. 1091):

> It is clear and not disputed that they owe a fiduciary duty to the company to apply its assets only for the purpose of the company and are, therefore, liable for breach of that duty; but the question how far they are trustees bears on the question how other defendants can be made liable as constructive trustees as claimed.[35]

The following observation In re Forest of Dean Coal Mining Co. [1878] 10 Ch D 450 was noted with approval (p. 453):

Again, directors are called trustees. They are no doubt trustees of assets which have come into their hands, or which are under their control, but they are not trustees of a debt due to the company... A director is the managing partner of the concern, and although a debt is due to the concern I do not think it is right to call him a trustee of that debt which remains unpaid, though his liability in respect of it may in certain cases and in some respects be analogous to the liability of a trustee. So much for the question of unpaid debts.[36]

Director not trustee of the company

Supreme Court of India in the case of Sangramsinh P. Gaekwad & Ors *v.* Shantadevi P. Gaekwad, observed that the director is not the trustee of a company for the individual shareholders as:

It has been held in Percival *v.* Wright [L.R. (1902) 2 Ch. 421] that ordinarily the directors are not trustees for the individual shareholders. Even if the directors owe some duty to the existing shareholders on the footing of there being some fiduciary relationship between them, the relationship is with company: The fiduciary relationship of a director exists with the company: the director is not usually a trustee for individual shareholders. Thus, a director may accept a shareholder's offer to sell shares in the company although he may have information which is not available to that other, and the contract cannot be upset even if the director knew of some fact which made the offer an attractive proposition. So in Percival *v.* Wright a person who had approached a director and sold him shares in the company, afterwards, upon discovering that the director had known at the time of the contract that negotiations were on foot for the purchase by an outsider of all the shares in the company at a higher figure, could not impeach the contract. In his judgment Swinfen-Eady J. said 'there is no question of unfair dealing in this case.

---

35. V.J. Thomas Vettom and K.M.J. ... *v.* Kuttanad Rubber Co. Ltd. and Ors 1984 56 CompCas 284 Ker.
36. V.J Thomas (supra)

The directors did not approach the shareholders with the view of obtaining their shares. The shareholders approached the directors and named the price at which they were desirous of selling.'

Thus, in conclusion, a director is considered to be the trustee of the money of the company but not of the debt due to the company. However, a director is regarded to be the trustee with regard to company's powers which are conferred upon him such as the power of share issue (issuing, allotting, approving transfers, etc.), but such power should be used in the interest of the company and not otherwise.

Qualifications and Disqualifications of Directors

Appointment of director

Section 149 makes provisions for the appointment of director and board of directors.

Number of directors

As per the mandate of the section the minimum requirement of a director as per the nature of the company is:

- Public company: three directors
- Private company: two directors
- One person company: one director

Exception: Any company can appoint more than fifteen directors after passing a special resolution.

The section also makes the provision for appointment of women director in certain class of companies.

Resident director

The section also makes the mandatory provision for one resident director who can stay in India for a total period of not less than one hundred and eighty- two (182) days in the previous calendar year.

Independent Director

There shall be one third (1/3) of independent directors in a listed public company. The independent directors shall be different from the managing director or a full-time director or a nominee director.

Qualification of an independent director

Sub-section 6 of section 149 defines the qualification of an independent director as:

(a) who, in the opinion of the Board, is a person of integrity and possesses relevant expertise and experience;

(b) (i) who is or was not a promoter of the company or its holding, subsidiary, or associate company;

(ii) who is not related to promoters or directors in the company, its holding, subsidiary, or associate company;

(c) who has or had no pecuniary relationship with the company, its holding, subsidiary, or associate company, or their promoters, or directors, during the two immediately preceding financial years or during the current financial year;

(d) none of whose relatives has or had pecuniary relationship or transaction with the company, its holding, subsidiary, or associate company, or their promoters, or directors, amounting to 2 per cent or more of its gross turnover or a total income of fifty lakh rupees or such higher amount as may be prescribed, whichever is lower, during the two immediately preceding financial years or during the current financial year;

(e) who, neither himself nor any of his relatives:

   (i) holds or has held the position of a key managerial personnel or is or has been an employee of the company or its holding, subsidiary, or associate company in any of the three financial years immediately preceding the financial year in which he is proposed to be appointed;

   (ii) is or has been an employee or proprietor or a partner, in any of the three financial years immediately preceding the financial year in which he is proposed to be appointed, of

      (A) a firm of auditors or company secretaries in practice or cost auditors of the company or its holding, subsidiary, or associate company; or

      (B) any legal or a consulting firm that has or had any transaction with the company, its holding, subsidiary, or associate company amounting to 10 per cent or more of the gross turnover of such firm;

   (iii) holds together with his relatives 2 per cent or more of the total voting power of the company; or

   (iv) is a chief executive or director, by whatever name he is called, of any non-profit organization that receives 25 per cent or more of its receipts from the company, any of its promoters, directors or its holding, subsidiary, or associate company or that holds 2 per cent or more of the total voting power of the company; or

(f) who possesses such other qualifications as may be prescribed.

Appointment of independent director

Section 150 says any independent director may be selected from a data bank containing name, address, and qualification of persons who are eligible and willing to act as independent directors, maintained by any body, institute, or association, as may be notified by the Central Government.

The appointment of an independent director shall be approved by the general meeting of the company.

Financial entitlement of independent director

Sub-section (9) of section 149 further bars an independent director to hold any stock option; however he may be entitled to receive remuneration and reimbursement of expenses for participation in the Board and other meetings by way of fee provided under sub-section (5) of section 197.

Term of office of an independent director

Sub-section (10) of section 149, subject to the provision of section 152, the Independent Director shall hold office for a term up to five consecutive years on the board of the company. Section (11) of section 149 bars the independent director, to hold the office for more than two consecutive terms, however he shall be eligible for reappointment only after the expiration of three years. Further, an independent director shall also not be eligible for any other capacity, directly or indirectly to be appointed or associated with the company.

Liabilities of an independent director

He shall be held liable only in respect of such acts of omission or commission by a company which had occurred with his knowledge, attributable through the board process and with his consent or connivance or where he had not acted diligently.

DIRECTOR APPOINTED BY SMALL SHAREHOLDERS

Section 151 makes the provisions for a director who shall be appointed by small shareholders means one who holds the share of nominal value not more than twenty thousand rupees.

The intention to such a provision is to protect the right of small shareholders, and to give them voice and representation in the board.

Legal provisions for appointment and disqualification of director

- A subscriber to the memorandum of a company shall be deemed to be the first director when there is no provision for appointment of the first director in the Article.
- Subject to the provision of this Act, appointment of a director shall be in the general meeting of the company.
- Without allotment of Director Identification Number (u/s 154), no person shall be appointed a director.

- Any person shall not act as a director unless he gives his consent to act as a director.
- An explanatory statement shall be present in the general meeting for appointment of an independent director.
- A person can hold a maximum of twenty directorships including any alternative directorship, in case of a public company it shall be a maximum of ten.
- The disqualification of a director shall not take effect for thirty days from the date of conviction or order of disqualification, or where an appeal or petition is preferred within thirty days as aforesaid against the conviction resulting in a sentence or order, until expiry of seven days from the date on which such an appeal or petition is disposed of; or where any further appeal or petition is preferred against the order or sentence within seven days, until such further appeal or petition is disposed of.

Disqualification for appointment of director

Section 164, states the disqualification, has a threefold pre-appointment and post-appointment provisions.

Pre-appointment

A person is not eligible for appointment as director of a company if:

- he is of unsound mind and stands so declared by a competent court;
- he is an undischarged insolvent;
- he has applied to be adjudicated as an insolvent and his application is pending;
- he has been convicted by a court of any offence, whether involving moral turpitude or otherwise, and sentenced in respect thereof to imprisonment for not less than six months and a period of five years has not elapsed from the date of expiry of the sentence, if a person has been convicted of any offence and sentenced in respect thereof to imprisonment for a period of seven years or more, he shall not be eligible to be appointed as a director in any company;
- an order disqualifying him for the appointment as a director has been passed by a Court or Tribunal and the order is in force;
- he has not paid any calls in respect of any shares of the company held by him, whether alone or jointly with others, and six months have elapsed from the last day fixed for the payment of the call;
- he has been convicted of the offence dealing with related party transactions under section 188 at any time during the last preceding five years; or
- he has not complied with sub-section (3) of section 152.

Post appointment

The second class of disqualifications when person holds the post of director in a company, are when:

- he has not filed financial statements or annual returns for any continuous period of three financial years; or
- he has failed to repay the deposits accepted by it or pay interest thereon or to redeem any debentures on the due date or pay interest due thereon or pay any dividend declared and such failure to pay or redeem continues for one year or more, shall be eligible to be re-appointed as a director of that company or appointed in other company for a period of five years from the date on which the said company fails to do so.

Disqualification by article of company

A private company may, by its articles, provide for any disqualifications for appointment as a director.

Duties of Director

No doubt a director enjoys certain rights which are correlative with duties. The director is required to act in accordance with the articles of the company and shall act always in good faith in order to promote the objective of the company set out for the benefit of the members of the company.

The director is also required to deal with due and reasonable care, skill and diligence, and shall exercise independent judgment, and immune himself from direct or indirect interest that conflict or may conflict with the interest of the company.

The director shall also refrain from any undue gain or advantage either himself or through his relatives, partners, or associates, and he shall not assign his office to anyone.

Resignation and Removal of Director

A director may resign from his office by giving notice in writing to the company, and after taking note on it the board shall intimate to the registrar for the same.

The said resignation shall take effect on the date of resignation or any other date which is mentioned in the resignation.

The company by passing an ordinary resolution can remove the director.

CHAPTER 7

Accounts and Audit

ACCOUNT OF COMPANIES

The account of a company is a set of financial records which shows a written list of transactions for payments, losses, sales, debits, credits, and other monetary transactions. It shows the financial situation of a company.

Sub-section (13) of Section 2 of Companies Act, 2013 states.

'Books of account' include records maintained in respect of:

(i) all sums of money received and expended by a company and matters in relation to which the receipts and expenditure take place;

(ii) all sales and purchases of goods and services by the company;

(iii) the assets and liabilities of the company; and

(iv) the items of cost as may be prescribed under section 148 in the case of a company which belongs to any class of companies specified under that section;

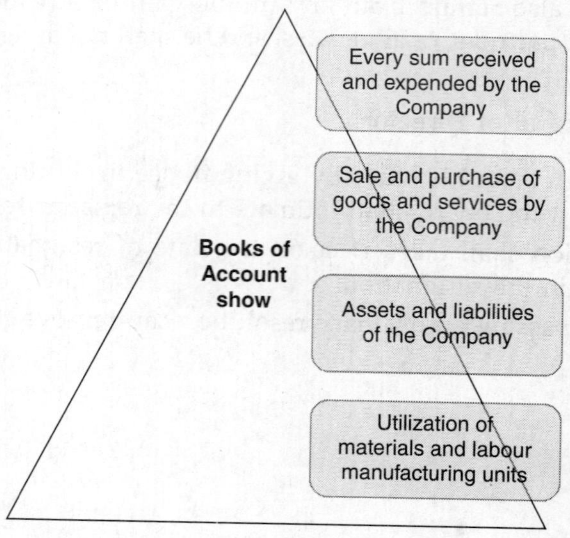

A Record of an Ongoing Relationship, Debt or Obligation

Type

Section 128 of the Companies Act, 2013 says that such books shall be kept on accrual basis and according to the double entry system of accounts. It should be kept at the registered office of the company or any other place where the Board of Directors of the company decides to keep them. They may also be preserved in electronic form.

Statutory Period for Preservation of Record

The books of account of every company relating to a period of not less than eight financial years immediately preceding a financial year, or where the company has been in existence for a period less than eight years, in respect of all the preceding years together with the vouchers relevant to any entry in such books of account, shall be kept in good order:

Provided that where an investigation has been ordered in respect of the company under Chapter XIV, the Central Government may direct that the books of account need to be kept for such longer period as it may deem fit.

Under the Companies Act, 2013

Section 128 of Companies Act, 2013 makes the provision for compulsory preparing the books of account and other relevant books and paper and financial statement for every financial year so as to give a true and fair view of the state of affairs of the company. The Companies Act, 2013 made certain new provisions such as:

Books of Account in Electronic Mode

Rule 3 of the Companies (Account) Rules, 2014 of provides that Company may keep such books of account or other relevant papers in electronic mode.

Financial Statement

Financial statements are a collection of reports about an organization's financial results, financial condition, and cash flows, in a systematic manner, which reflects profitability, operational efficiency, long- and short–term solvency, and growth potential of a company.

It is a formal financial communication between a company and the public, and is considered to be true and fair financial information about the company in accordance with specified standards.

Object of financial statement

The object of accounts of the company is to show a true and fair view of their financial position, which helps the management in decision-making. It helps to:

- Determine the ability of business
- Determine specific business transactions

- Determine cash flow and capability to pay back debts
- Determine the financial ratios
- Assess the various financial activities and financial strength of a company.

Component of financial statement

Sub-section (40) of section 2 says that

"financial statement" in relation to a company, includes:

(i) a balance sheet at the end of the financial year;

(ii) a profit and loss account, or in the case of a company carrying on any activity not for profit, an income and expenditure account for the financial year;

(iii) cash flow statement for the financial year;

(iv) a statement of changes in equity, if applicable; and

(v) any explanatory note annexed to, or forming part of, any document referred to in sub-clause (i) to sub-clause (iv):

Provided that the financial statement, with respect to One Person Company, small company and dormant company, may not include the cash flow statement.

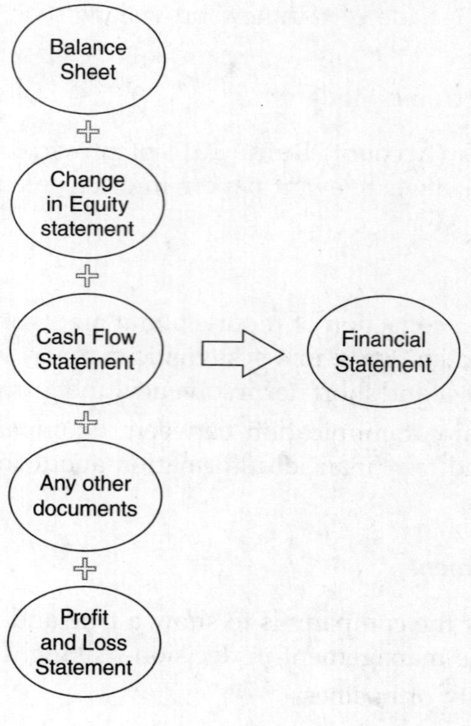

Basic Difference between Record and Report

Books of Account is a record and Financial statement is a report.

Under Companies Act, 2013

There were no provisions for a consolidated financial statement in Company Act, 1956, but under the companies Act, 2013 it is mandatory under Rule 6 of the Companies (Accounts) Rules 2014 where a company has one or more subsidiaries. This expression includes associate companies or joint venture, which is in accordance with the provisions of Schedule III of the Act and the applicable accounting standards.

Audit and Auditor

Audit refers to an inspection of books of account and other relevant documents to ascertain how far the financial statements of the company are true and fair, and to find out whether the books of account are properly maintained or not as required by law.

In general, the audit is an inspection or certification of a company's financial records by an independent body which forms an opinion as to whether the annual accounts of the company are true and fair and its profit or loss is in accordance with the law.

Thus, audit and auditor play an important role in a company. The Companies Act, 2013 made certain new, stricter, and more accountable provisions for the auditor being retained.

Appointment of Auditor

Section 139 of the Companies Act, 2013 talks about the appointment of an auditor in a time-bound manner, under the following mandate:

- It makes mandatory provisions for every company to appoint an individual or a firm as an auditor in the first annual general meeting.
- The auditor shall hold office from the conclusion of that meeting till the conclusion of its sixth annual general meeting and thereafter till the conclusion of every sixth meeting.
- However, the auditor can be replaced through rectification by the members at every general meeting.
- The written consent of the auditor for such appointment is also mandatory.
- Further, auditor should provide certificates that he satisfies all the criteria as prescribed in section 141.
- Information to the Registrar of Companies regarding the appointment of an auditor by the company, within fifteen days is also mandatory.

Appointment and re-appointment and restrictions on auditor and law firm

Listed companies or company which belong to such class or classes of companies as prescribed shall appoint or reappoint:

(a) An individual or firm for more than one term or five consecutive years;

(b) An audit firm as auditor for more than two terms or five consecutive years.

The exception is

- An individual auditor who has completed his term under clause (a) shall not be eligible for reappointment as auditor in the same company for five years from the completion of his term.
- An audit firm who has completed his term under clause (b) shall not be eligible for reappointment as auditor in the same company for five years from the completion of such term.
- As on the date of appointment no audit firm having a common partner or partners to the other audit firm, whose tenure has expired in a company immediately preceding the financial year, shall be appointed auditor of the same company for a period of five year.

It is also important to note here that a retiring auditor shall not be reappointed as per sub-section (4)(i) of section 140.

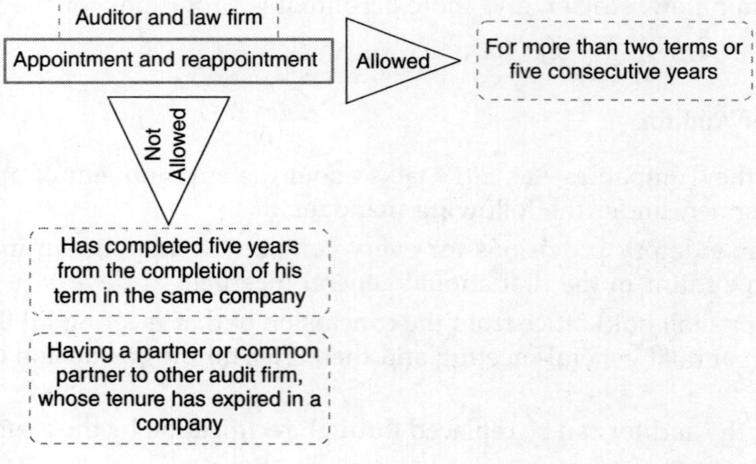

However, the company has the right to remove the auditor and the auditor can also resign.

New provisions introduced in TCA 2013:

- Time-bound appointment and reappointment of auditor in Govt. Companies by CAG (Sec 139).
- Compulsory rotation of auditor for listed companies (Sec 139(2)).

Rotation of auditor

Sub-sections (3) and (4) of section 139 provide that member of the company may resolve to rotate the member or team of auditor, and the Central Government may also do so.

Removal, resignation of auditor

As we have discussed that the auditor is the verifying authority of the company who brings the omissions and errors or any other inconsistencies of the company. It is natural to protect the stability of the company to do their work fairly, and the Act makes a stringent provision for fair and genuine audit. Without prejudice to any action under the provisions of this Act or any other law for the time being in force, the Tribunal either suo motu or on an application made to it by the Central Government or by any person concerned, if it is satisfied that the auditor of a company has, whether directly or indirectly, acted in a fraudulent manner or abetted or colluded in any fraud by, or in relation to, the company or its directors or officers. It may, by order, direct the company to change its auditors. Further that an auditor, whether individual or firm, against whom the final order has been passed by the Tribunal under this section shall not be eligible to be appointed as an auditor of any company for a period of five years from the date of passing of the order and the auditor shall also be liable for action under section 447.

The auditor of the company may be removed from his office before the expiry of his term only by a special resolution of the company after obtaining the previous approval from the Central Government, not otherwise. The mandate of section 140 says, that a reasonable opportunity is provided to the auditor before taking any action against him, i.e., the Principle of Natural Justice is applied here—in simple words a notice should be served upon him.

The auditor may also resign before the expiry of his term, but while doing so he has to furnish a statement in a prescribed form before the company indicating the reasons and other facts as may be relevant to his resignation within a period of thirty days of his resignation, falling to comply such a mandate he shall be punished with a fine.

Rule 3 of Companies (Audit and Auditor) Rules, 2014

Manner and procedure of selection and appointment of auditors

(1) In case of a company that is required to constitute an Audit Committee under section 177, the committee, and, in cases where such a committee is not required to be constituted, the Board, shall take into consideration the qualifications and experience of the individual or the firm proposed to be considered for appointment as auditor and whether such qualifications and experience are commensurate with the size and requirements of the company:

Provided that while considering the appointment, the Audit Committee or the Board, as the case may be, shall have regard to any order or pending proceeding relating to professional matters of conduct against the proposed auditor before the Institute of Chartered Accountants of India or any competent authority or any Court.

(2) The Audit Committee or the Board, as the case may be, may call for such other information from the proposed auditor as it may deem fit.

(3) Subject to the provisions of sub-rule (1), where a company is required to constitute the Audit Committee, the committee shall recommend the name of an individual or a firm as auditor to the Board for consideration and in other cases, the Board shall consider and recommend an individual or a firm as auditor to the members in the annual general meeting for appointment.

(4) If the Board agrees with the recommendation of the Audit Committee, it shall further recommend the appointment of an individual or a firm as auditor to the members in the annual general meeting.

(5) If the Board disagrees with the recommendation of the Audit Committee, it shall refer back the recommendation to the committee for reconsideration citing reasons for such disagreement.

(6) If the Audit Committee, after considering the reasons given by the Board, decides not to reconsider its original recommendation, the Board shall record reasons for its disagreement with the committee and send its own recommendation for consideration of the members in the annual general meeting; and if the Board agrees with the recommendations of the Audit Committee, it shall place the matter for consideration by members in the annual general meeting.

(7) The auditor appointed in the annual general meeting shall hold office from the conclusion of that meeting till the conclusion of the sixth annual general meeting, with the meeting wherein such appointment has been made being counted as the first meeting: Provided that such appointment shall be subject to ratification in every annual general meeting till the sixth such meeting by way of passing of an ordinary resolution.

Explanation: For the purposes of this rule, it is hereby clarified that, if the appointment is not ratified by the members of the company, the Board of Directors shall appoint another individual or firm as its auditor or auditors after following the procedure laid down in this behalf under the Act.

Rule 4 of Companies (Audit and Auditor) Rules, 2014

The auditor appointed under rule 3 shall submit a certificate that:

(a) the individual or the firm, as the case may be, is eligible for appointment and is not disqualified for appointment under the Act, the Chartered Accountants Act, 1949 and the rules or regulations made thereunder;

(b) the proposed appointment is as per the terms provided under the Act;

(c) the proposed appointment is within the limits laid down by or under the authority of the Act;

(d) the list of proceedings against the auditor or audit firm or any partner of the audit firm pending with respect to professional matters of conduct, as disclosed in the certificate, is true and correct. (2) The notice to Registrar about appointment of auditor under fourth proviso to sub-section (1) of section 139 shall be in Form ADT-1.

Eligibility, Qualification and Disqualification of Auditor

To become an auditor a person must satisfy the following conditions. He must be

- a chartered accountant
- a firm whereof majority of partners practicing in India are qualified for appointment as aforesaid may be appointed by its firm name to be auditor of a company.

Following are the disqualifications for appointing as an auditor:

(*a*) a body corporate other than a limited liability partnership registered under the Limited Liability Partnership Act, 2008;

(*b*) an officer or employee of the company;

(*c*) a person who is a partner, or who is in the employment, of an officer or employee of the company;

(*d*) a person who, or his relative or partner:

(*i*) is holding any security of or interest in the company or its subsidiary, or of its holding or associate company or a subsidiary of such holding company: Provided that the relative may hold security or interest in the company of face value not exceeding one thousand rupees or such sum as may be prescribed;

(*ii*) is indebted to the company, or its subsidiary, or its holding or associate company or a subsidiary of such holding company, in excess of such amount as may be prescribed; or

(*iii*) has given a guarantee or provided any security in connection with the indebtedness of any third person to the company, or its subsidiary, or its holding or associate company or a subsidiary of such holding company, for such amount as may be prescribed;

(*e*) a person or a firm who, whether directly or indirectly, has business relationship with the company, or its subsidiary, or its holding or associate company or subsidiary of such holding company or associate company of such nature as may be prescribed;

(*f*) a person whose relative is a director or is in the employment of the company as a director or key managerial personnel;

(*g*) a person who is in full-time employment elsewhere or a person or a partner of a firm holding appointment as its auditor, if such persons or partner is at the date of such appointment or reappointment holding appointment as auditor of more than twenty companies;

(*h*) a person who has been convicted by a court of an offence involving fraud and a period of ten years has not elapsed from the date of such conviction;

(*i*) any person whose subsidiary or associate company or any other form of entity, is engaged as on the date of appointment in consulting and specialised services as provided in section 144.

(*4*) Where a person appointed as an auditor of a company incurs any of the disqualifications mentioned in sub-section (*3*) after his appointment, he shall vacate his office as such auditor and such vacation shall be deemed to be a casual vacancy in the office of the auditor.

Restriction on Auditor

Auditor not to render certain services

The new Act puts restriction on the auditor for directly or indirectly providing the 'other services', i.e., services other than the prescribed statutory services. The new provision u/s 144 is being provided in the act as:

(a) accounting and book-keeping services;
(b) internal audit;
(c) design and implementation of any financial information system;
(d) actuarial services;
(e) investment advisory services;
(f) investment banking services;
(g) rendering of outsourced financial services;
(h) management services; and
(i) any other kind of services as may be prescribed:

The term 'directly or indirectly' shall include rendering of services by the auditor:

(i) in case of auditor being an individual, either himself or through his relative or any other person connected or associated with such individual or through any other entity, whatsoever, in which such individual has significant influence or control, or whose name or trade mark or brand is used by such individual;

(ii) in case of auditor being a firm, either itself or through any of its partners or through its parent, subsidiary or associate entity or through any other entity, whatsoever, in which the firm or any partner of the firm has significant influence or control, or whose name or trade mark or brand is used by the firm or any of its partners.

CHAPTER 8

Prevention and Oppression and Management

WHAT IS PREVENTION?

Dictionary meaning of the word 'prevention' is to 'bar' or 'barrier', and the word oppression means 'the subjugation of one group by another, carried out under conditions of unequal power, and often enforced by threats of or by actual violence'.

WHAT IS OPPRESSION?

The word 'oppressive' is not defined in the Act. The meaning of it is majority shareholders, by an abuse of their predominant voting power, are 'treating the company and its affairs as if it were their property' to the prejudice of the minority shareholders, and in which just and equitable grounds would exist for the making of a winding up order.[37]

In H.R. Harmer, the Court of Appeal, with reference to section 210 of the English Companies Act, 1948 held that the word "oppressive" meant 'burdensome, harsh and wrongful' and that viewing the events proved as a consecutive whole, the affairs of the company if conducted in a manner oppressive to the members, the case for relief under section 210 could be made out.[38]

Viscount Simonds in the House of Lords case of Scottish Co-operative Wholesale Society Ltd. *v.* Meyer, 1958-3 All ER 66 at p. 71 adopted the meaning of oppression as 'burdensome, harsh and wrongful' taking the dictionary meaning of the word.[39]

> In the case of S.P. Jain v. Kalinga Tubes Ltd is defined by the Supreme Court as "the affairs of the company were being conducted in a manner oppressive to some part of the members. The conduct must be burdensome, harsh and wrongful and mere lack of confidence between the majority shareholders and the minority shareholders would not be enough unless lack of confidence springs from oppression of the minority by a majority in the management of the company's affairs, and such oppression must involve at least an element of lack of probity or fair dealing to a member in the matter of his proprietary rights as a shareholder.

In Harmer's case (1), it was held that 'the word "oppressive" meant burdensome, harsh and wrongful'. It was also held that "the section does not purport to apply to every case in which the facts would justify the making of a winding up order under

37. S. P. Jain *v.* Kalinga Tubes Ltd, 1965 AIR 1535, 1965 SCR (2) 720.

38. Maharashtra Power Development v. Dabhol Power Company 2004 (3) BomCR 317, (2004) 3 CompLJ 58 Bom, 2004 52 SCL 224 Bom.

39. Hindusthan Co-Operative ... *v.* Unknown AIR 1961 Cal 443, 65 CWN 69.

the 'just and equitable' rule, but only to those cases of that character which have in them the requisite element of oppression'.

In a leading case, Supreme Court held that to constitute oppressive management it is necessary to examine that the conduct of the majority shareholders was oppressive to the minority as members and this requires that events have to be considered not in isolation but as a part of the majority shareholders, continuing up to the date of the petition, showing that the affairs of the company were being conducted in a manner oppressive to some part of the members. The conduct must be burdensome, harsh, and wrongful and mere lack of confidence between the majority shareholders and the minority shareholders would not be enough unless the lack of confidence springs from oppression of a minority by a majority in the management of a company's affairs, and such oppression must involve at least an element of lack of probity or fair dealing to a member in the matter of his proprietary rights as a shareholder.

Thus, oppression means that a certain group or powerful persons who are enjoying majority shares prevent or constitute oppression and guilty of fraud, misfeasance, or misconduct towards other persons who are not so privileged. It is important to note here that it does not comprise mere domestic disputes between directors and members or lack of confidence between members.

Thus, the basic foundation of operation is harsh and wrongful; oppression involves at least an element of lack of probity and fair dealing to a member in matters of his proprietary right as a shareholder.

What is Mismanagement?

Mismanagement also affects the rights and prejudices and interest of the member and the company and also prejudices the financial and strategic growth of the company. The acts of mismanagement may not necessarily be of the majority but can be by any person in the day-to-day management of the company. It generally related to:

1. Misuse of company assets, finances/funds or dwarfing expenses for personal expenses by the director of the company.
2. Negligence of maintaining the necessary or basic records of the company.
3. Deliberately not filing records with the Registrar of Companies.
4. Absence of basic records of the company with the Registrar of Companies and fail to comply with other statutory obligations.
5. Sale of assets at very low prices.

Prevention of Oppression and Mismanagement

Section 241 provides the tool through which preventive action can be taken by the members of the company in case of oppression.

Application to Tribunal for relief in case of oppression, etc.:

(1) Any member of a company who complains that:

(a) the affairs of the company have been or are being conducted in a manner prejudicial to public interest or in a manner prejudicial or oppressive to him or any other member or members or in a manner prejudicial to the interests of the company; or

(b) the material change, not being a change brought about by, or in the interests of, any creditors, including debenture holders or any class of shareholders of the company, has taken place in the management or control of the company, whether by an alteration in the Board of Directors, or manager, or in the ownership of the company's shares, or if it has no share capital, in its membership, or in any other manner whatsoever, and that by reason of such change, it is likely that the affairs of the company will be conducted in a manner prejudicial to its interests or its members or any class of members, may apply to the Tribunal, provided such a member has a right to apply under section 244, for an order under this chapter.

(2) The Central Government, if it is of the opinion that the affairs of the company are being conducted in a manner prejudicial to public interest, it may itself apply to the Tribunal for an order under this Chapter.

Section 245 Class action: A new provision has been inserted which enables depositors against the company, its director, and auditor if they are of the opinion that the management or conduct of the affairs of the company are being conducted in a manner prejudicial to the interests of the company or its members or depositors, to file an application before the Tribunal on behalf of the members or depositors for seeking all or any of the following orders, namely:

(a) to restrain the company from committing an act which is ultra vires the articles or memorandum of the company;

(b) to restrain the company from committing breach of any provision of the company's memorandum or articles;

(c) to declare a resolution altering the memorandum or articles of the company as void if the resolution was passed by suppression of material facts or obtained by mis-statement to the members or depositors;

(d) to restrain the company and its directors from acting on such a resolution;

(e) to restrain the company from doing an act which is contrary to the provisions of this Act or any other law for the time being in force;

(f) to restrain the company from taking action contrary to any resolution passed by the members;

(g) to claim damages or compensation or demand any other suitable action from or against

(i) the company or its directors for any fraudulent, unlawful, or wrongful act or omission or conduct or any likely act or omission or conduct on its or their part;

(ii) the auditor, including the audit firm of the company for any improper or misleading statement of particulars made in his audit report or for any fraudulent, unlawful, or wrongful act or conduct; or

(iii) any expert or advisor or consultant or any other person for any incorrect or misleading statement made to the company or for any fraudulent, unlawful, or wrongful act or conduct, or any likely act or conduct on his part;

(h) to seek any other remedy as the Tribunal may deem fit.

What Constitutes the Oppression?

Clinical research of section 241 indicates some points to constitute oppression-

- Affairs of the company conducted in a manner which are prejudicial to public interest or oppressive to any other member, or prejudicial to company interest.
- Material changes against the interest of creditor, including debenture holders or any class of shareholder of company.

In various judicial pronouncements oppression is defined as:

Unjust exercise of authority or power

In the case of Mohan Lal Chandumall and Ors. *v.* Punjab Company Ltd., Bhatinda and AIR 1961 P H 485, 1962 32 Comp Cas 937 P H, where a public company amended its articles of association while doing forward contract business to deprive its non-trading members their voting rights, to elect directors, and to call the meeting, and receive dividends, it was held that

> the company's affairs are being conducted in a manner oppressive to any member or members. In this case the non-voting members are being subjected to hardship or burden which may truly be called oppressive. They are subjected to an oppressive conduct in so far as they are being dominated and have to submit to excessive use of authority. Such a conduct amounts to unjust hardship. To oppress, ordinarily means to crush, smother or trample. In this case, their valuable rights are being trampled upon by unjust exercise of authority or power. To take away the right or partaking in dividends earned by their contribution is not merely oppressive but even confiscatory.

Continuous act

It is a debatable question whether the oppression is a one-time act or a continuous process, Division Bench of Calcutta High Court in the case of Tea Brokers P. Ltd. *v.* Hemendra Prosad Barooah (1998) 5 Comp LJ 963 (Cal.) observed that: 'such an act may be even a single act done on one particular occasion if the effect of such an act will be of a continuing nature and the member concerned is deprived of his rights and privilege for all time to come in future'.

> Supreme Court in the case of S.P. Jain *v.* Kalinga Tubes Ltd, observed that: events have to be considered not in isolation but as a part of a consecutive story. There must be continuous acts on the part of the majority shareholders, continuing up to the date of the petition, showing that the affairs of the company were being conducted in a manner oppressive to some part of the members.

Further, the phrase, 'are being conducted in a manner... used in sub-section (a) of section 241 also denotes that oppression must be a continuous process, and not an isolated process.

No domestic quarrel

The action under the shadow of oppression can only be instituted when actual hardship is being caused to the minority shareholder; no domestic quarrel such as decision taken by director of the company against the will of member but in the bona fide interest of company comes under the preview of it.

Prejudicial to public interest

Sub-section (a) of section 241 also denotes that public interest should not be prejudiced, because any act which prejudices the public interest is wrong and against the cardinal principle of welfare of public.

Concept of Oppression and Mismanagement

The concept of Oppression and Mismanagement is an integral part of the present Act and old Act, under the new Act it tries to give a new dimension with class action.

There are certain objectives to establish the principle as:

To maintain shareholders' democracy in the company

Democracy denotes the fair structure of governance in the company, which preserves the rights of every class of member in the company. It is a common phenomenon that the majority prevails over the minority which causes the suppression of the minority shareholder. Aristotle's quotation 'will of the majority is supreme' is very relevant here, because the source of the power is initiated from majority of the members and they always are in an advantageous position and who for their vested interest may misuse the powers and violate the provision of common benefit in the company, ultimately leading to suppression of minority shareholders. To establish the adequate protection for minority shareholders and their rights the Act establishes various provisions to maintain the shareholders democracy in the company.

To prevent ultra vires act of director

It is generaly experienced that the majority shareholders may perform an ultra vires act which prejudices the interest of minority shareholders and is against the interest of the company. To prevent this the minority shareholders enjoy the power under the act to restrain the company under the shadow of court.

Control mechanism

The concept is not only right or liability but is a control mechanism which establishes majority power and minority rights.

CHAPTER
9

Share Capital and Debentures

- What is Capital?
- Nature and Characteristics
- Issue, Allotment, and Forfeiture

WHAT IS CAPITAL?

Capital means the funds provided by the owner or owners to a business, for example, in a proprietary firm the proprietor, in partnership the firm's partners and in a company shareholders provide the funds for business.

Authorized Share Capital

Share capital is the maximum capital that the company is authorized to collect during its lifetime. According to sub-section (8) of section 2 'authorised capital' or 'nominal capital' means such capital as is authorised by the memorandum of a company to be the maximum amount of share capital of the company.

In simple words, authorized capital means the maximum value of securities that a company can legally issue according to the memorandum of association at the time of incorporation of company, which may be changed later on with the consent of shareholders of the company.

It may further be divided into-

(i) Issued Capital – Part of the Authorized Capital which is issued to the public for Subscription is called as Issued Capital, sub-section (50) of section 2 says 'issued capital' means such capital as the company issues from time to time for subscription;

(ii) Paid up capital: Fully paid and received from the shareholders who subscribe to the share of the company. Sub-section (64) of section 2 says 'paid-up share capital' or 'share capital paid-up' means such aggregate amount of money credited as paid-up as is equivalent to the amount received as paid-up in respect of shares issued and also includes any amount credited as paid-up in respect of shares of the company, but does not include any other amount received in respect of such shares, by whatever name it is called;

(iii) Uncalled capital: Remain unpaid by the shareholder for the share they have brought.

Meaning of Share

The share capital is the most important requirement of a business.

A share means a unit of ownership or interest in the company that represents an equal proportion of a company's capital, which entitles the holder of share to an equal claim on the company profit and liability for company debt and loss.

J. Farewell said 'The interest of a shareholder in a company measured by a sum of money, for the purpose of liability in the first place, and of interest in the second, but also consisting a series of mutual covenants entered in to by all the shareholders interest.'

In simple words, a share means a unit of stock that represents ownership in a company, or a number of indivisible units of a fixed amount is known as share.

According to Section 2 (46) of the Company Act, 1956, 'share' means share in the share capital of a company. It includes stock except where a distinction between stock and shares is expressed or implied;

Section 2 (84) of the Companies Act, 2013 'share' is a share in the share capital of a company and includes stock;

The Companies Act, 2013 defines share it is as defined in Company Act, 1956, but the phrase 'except where a distinction between stock and shares is expressed or implied' have been omitted, it means share also includes 'stock'.

Example:

Total capital of a company is 1,00,000 divided in to 10,000 shares of Rs 10 each; each unit of Rs. 10 is called a share.

Total capital of the company is divided into a number of small indivisible units of a fixed amount.

Type of Share

As per section 43 the shares of a company limited by share can be of the following types of share:

1. Equity shares: Equity shares are those shares which are not preference shares. These shares do not enjoy any preferential rights. Equity shares are further divided into two categories as:
   (i) With voting rights; or
   (ii) With differential rights as to dividend, voting, or otherwise.
2. Preference shares: As suggested by the name 'preference share' carries two types of preferences over the equity share as:
   (i) Preferential right in respect of the dividends;
   (ii) Preferential right in regard to the repayment of capital.

Attaching the word 'otherwise' in the section enlarges the range for innovation within the limit of rules. It may be the difference related to managing control, power to appoint a director, or power to appoint proxy, and so on.

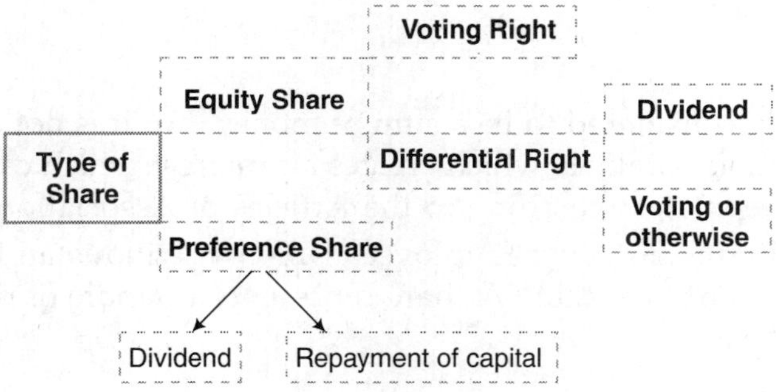

Comparison between Equity Shares and Preference Shares

Basis	Preference Share	Equity Share
Dividend Right	First right on dividend, and dividends are paid before the equity share	Second right, dividends are paid from the balance which remain after dividends are paid to preference share
Dividend Rate	Paid at fixed rate of dividend	Variable year on year depending upon the profit
Arrears of Dividend	Cumulative preference shareholders can get the arrears of past dividend	Equity shareholders cannot get the arrears of past dividend
Repayment/Refund of Capital	In the event of winding up of the company it is paid first before the payment of equity share capital	It paid after the payment of preference share, at the time of winding up of the company
Voting Right	No voting rights except in special circumstances	Attached with voting rights every time.
Convertibility	Convertible into equity share subject to terms of issue	Not convertible
Redemption	May be redeemed	Buyback by company is possible
Right of Participation in Management	No right of participation in management of the company	Have the right to participate in the company

Nature of Shares

Section 44 defines the nature of share or debenture as: 'The shares or debentures or other interest of any member in a company shall be movable property transferable in the manner provided by the articles of the company'.

Share is considered to be a property subject to articles of the company which can be transferred by sale or gift. It reflects a bundle of rights in the company which may vary according to the type of shares acquired.

Bundle of Rights

A share is generally considered to be a sum of money, but it is not a sum of money but a bundle of rights and liabilities which creates an interest which can be measured by a sum of money. It regulates according to the Articles of Association of company.

In the case of Hindustan Lever Employees Union v. Hindustan Lever Ltd. AIR 1995 SC 470), Supreme Court held that: 'A share represents a bundle of rights which include, inter alia, the rights to:

(i) elect directors;
(ii) vote on resolutions at meetings of the company;
(iii) enjoy the profits of the company, if and when dividends are declared and distributed; and
(iv) share in the surplus, if any, on liquidation.

In the case of Bacha F. Guzdar *v.* C.I.T., AIR (1955) SG 74, the position of a shareholder was explained thus:

> There is nothing in the Indian Law to warrant the assumption that a shareholder who buys shares, buys any interest in the property of the company which is juristic person entirely distinct from the shareholders. The true position of a shareholder is that on buying shares he becomes entitled to participate in the profits of the company in which he holds the shares, if and when the company declares, subject to the Articles of Association, that the profits or any portion there of should be distributed by way of dividends among the shareholders. He has undoubtedly a further right to participate in the assets of the company which would be left over after winding up.

Movable Property

The share in a company is a movable property, and the transfer is allowed subject to the provisions provided in the article of the company. The Sale of Goods Act also includes shares in the term 'movable property'. Thus, shares are movable property and can be sold, pledged, assigned, and mortgaged, etc.

In England, a share is regarded as a chose in action. See Harrold *v.* Plenty (1901) 2 Ch. 314. In India, a share is not a chose in action. Section 137 of the Transfer of Property Act says that nothing in Chapter VIII (which deals with transfers of actionable claims) applies to stocks and shares, and section 28 of the Indian Companies Act states that shares constitute movable property. Section 2 (7) of the Sale of Goods Act, 1930, expressly includes shares in the definition given thereof as 'goods'. Before the passing of the Sale of Goods Act, 1930, sales of goods were regulated by the sections comprised in Chapter VII of the Contract Act, but the Sale of Goods Act repealed the whole of the chapter. Section 72 (one of the repealed sections) denoted 'goods' as meaning every kind of movable property; and as shares are movable property, they were goods within the meaning of that section.

In Lalit *v.* Haridas (1916) 24 C.L.J. 335, the Calcutta High Court held that share certificates are neither goods nor documents of title within the meaning of section 178 of the Contract Act, but this decision was given before the enactment of the Sale of Goods Act and, therefore, before the amendment of the Contract Act. On the other hand, the Bombay High Court, long before 1930, held that the term 'goods' used in section 178 of the Contract Act includes shares in joint stock companies and consequently recognized that there could be a valid pledge of shares. See B.D. Sethna *v.* National Bank (1910) 12 Bom.L.R. 870, Fazal *v.* Mangaldas (1921) 46 Bom. 489. and Jamshedji *v.* Maganlal (1925) 27 Bom.L.R. 514. It seems to us that even before the passing of the Sale of Goods Act the Bombay opinion was preferable to the Calcutta opinion, but as the result of the passing of the Sale of Goods Act and the amendment of the Contract Act we consider that the Bombay opinion is not open to dispute. We can see no valid reason for giving the word 'goods' a different meaning in the Contract Act from the meaning which it has in the Sale of Goods Act.

We now come to the question whether a pledge of shares can be created by the mere deposit of the share certificate. A share is not a tangible thing. It is a share in the share capital of the company and is so denoted in section 2 (16) of the Indian Companies Act. Consequently it is necessary for a company to issue 'to a shareholder a certificate showing the number of shares which he holds. As shares are goods and therefore pledgeable, they can only be pledged by the deposit of the share certificate.[40]

In the case of Charanjit Lal Choudhary *v.* Union of India, J. Mukherjee, summarized the rights of a shareholder in a company in the following manner: share is a movable property according to the Indian Companies Act, with all the incidence of such property attached to it.

Issue of Share

Issued at Par: When the share issued is at face value, e.g.,

Share of Rs. 100 is issued at Rs. 100.

Issued at premium: When the share issued is at value above face value, e.g.,

Share of Rs. 100 is issued at Rs. 120.

Issued at Discount: When the share issued is at value below face value, e.g.,

Share of Rs. 100 is issued at Rs. 80.

40. Kannambra Nayar Veettil Valia ... *v.* P.N. Krishna Pattar (1942) 2 MLJ 120.

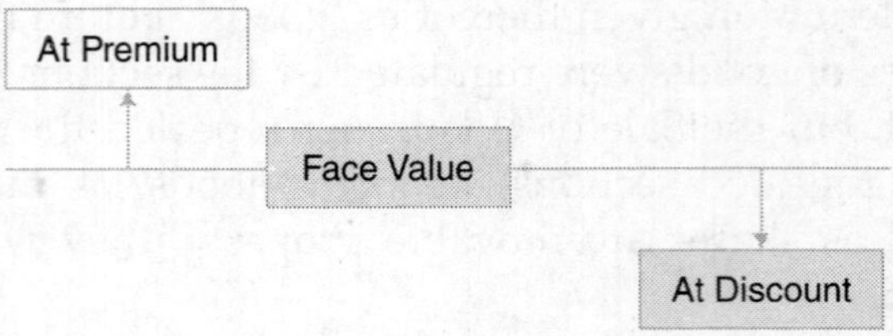

Issue and forfeiture of shares

Issue of shares

Issue of shares means an event or occasion when a company makes available new share for sale or offered shares and held by the shareholder.

In the case of Sri Gopal Jalan & Company *v.* Calcutta Stock ... 1964 AIR 250, 1964 SCR (3) 698.

> Supreme Court held that the process described by Chitty J. is very familiar, in Company Law. Under the Act, a company having share capital is required to state in its memorandum the amount of that capital and the division thereof into shares of a fixed amount: see s. 13(4). This is what is called the authorised capital of the company. Then the Company proceeds to issue the shares depending on the condition of the market. That only means inviting applications for these shares. When the applications are received, it accepts them and this is what is generally called allotment. No doubt there may be an allotment of shares without an application but no instance exists where that word is used to describe a transaction whereby one becomes a share-holder otherwise than by appropriation to him of a share out of the previously unappropriated share capital.

So L.J. Farwell said in Mosely *v.* Koffyfontain Mines Limited (1).

> As regards the construction of these particular articles it is plain that the words 'Creation', 'issue', and 'allotment' are used with the three different meanings familiar to business people as well as to lawyers. There are three steps with regard to new capital; first, it is created; till it is created the capital does not exist at all. When it is created it may remain unissued for years, as indeed it was here; the market did not allow of a favourable opportunity of placing it. When it is issued it may be issued on such terms as appear for the moment expedient. Next comes allotment. To take the words of J. Stirling in Spitzel *v.* Chinese Corporation, 80 L.T. 347, 351, he says: 'What is an allotment of shares? Broadly speaking, it is an appropriation by the directors or the managing body of the company of shares to a particular person'.

Lord Green M.R. observed in In re V.G.M. Holdings, Limited, (2), "it seems to (1) (191 1) I.L.R. Ch. 73. 84.

(2) (1942) 1 Ch. D. 235.

> The word 'purchase' cannot with propriety be applied to the legal transaction under which a person' by the machinery of application and allotment, becomes a shareholder in the company. He does not purchase anything when he does that. Mr. Wynn Parry endeavored heroically to establish the proposition that a share before issue was an existing article of property, that it was an existing bundle of rights which a shareholder could properly be said to be purchasing when he acquired it by subscription in the usual way. I am unable to accept that view. A share is a chose in action. A chose in action implies the existence of some person entitled to the rights in action as distinct from rights in possession, and, until the share is issued, no such person exists. Putting it in a nutshell, the difference between the issue of a share to a subscriber and the purchase of a share from an existing share holder is the difference between creation and the transfer of a chose in action.

Numbering of Shares

The mandate of section 45 is that every share in a company having a share capital shall be distinguished by its distinctive number. However, for shares held by the beneficial owner of shares, which are in the record of a depository such a condition is not mandatory.

Section 46 says: 'A certificate, issued under the common seal of the company, specifying the shares held by any person, shall be prima facie evidence of the title of the person to such shares, and where a share is held in depository form, the record of the depository is the prima facie evidence of the beneficial owner'.

Forfeiture of share

Meaning

The meaning of forfeit is 'to lose the right to hold' or 'deprived of'.

In the legal sense it may be called consequences of breach of contract made with regard to share or contract.

Conditions

Schedule I defines the conditions under which forfeiture of shares can be initiated which are as follows:

> If a member fails to pay any call, or installment of a call, on the day appointed for payment thereof, the Board may, at any time thereafter during such time as any part of the call or installment remains unpaid, serve a notice on him requiring payment of so much of the call or installment as is unpaid, together with any interest which may have accrued.

Requirement/Procedure

Notice

Supplying a notice is required before initiating such a procedure. The notice aforesaid shall bear the following:

(a) name a further day (not being earlier than the expiry of fourteen days from the date of service of the notice) on or before which the payment required by the notice is to be made; and

(b) state that, in the event of non-payment on or before the day so named, the shares in respect of which the call was made shall be liable to be forfeited.

Consequence of non-compliance of notice

If the requirements of any such notice as aforesaid are not complied with, any share in respect of which the notice has been given may, at any time thereafter, before the payment required by the notice has been made, be forfeited by a resolution of the Board to that effect.

(i) A forfeited share may be sold or otherwise disposed of on such terms and in such manner as the Board thinks fit.

(j) At any time before a sale or disposal as aforesaid, the Board may cancel the forfeiture on such terms as it thinks fit.

A person whose shares have been forfeited shall cease to be a member in respect of the forfeited shares, but shall, notwithstanding the forfeiture, remain liable to pay to the company all monies which, at the date of forfeiture, were presently payable by him to the company in respect of the shares.

Liability of Person Whose Shares Cease

The liability of such a person shall cease if and when the company shall have received payment in full of all such monies in respect of the shares.

A duly verified declaration in writing that the declaring person is a director, the manager or the secretary of the company, and that a share in the company has been duly forfeited on a date stated in the declaration, shall be conclusive evidence of the facts therein stated as against all persons claiming to be entitled to the share:

(ii) the company may receive the consideration, if any, given for the share on any sale or disposal thereof and may execute a transfer of the share in favour of the person to whom the share is sold or disposed of;

(iii) the transferee shall thereupon be registered as the holder of the share; and

(iv) the transferee shall not be bound to see to the application of the purchase money, if any, nor shall his title to the share be affected by any irregularity or invalidity in the proceedings in reference to the forfeiture, sale, or disposal of the share.

The provisions of these regulations as to forfeiture shall apply in the case of non-payment of any sum which, by the terms of issue of a share, becomes payable at a fixed time, whether on account of the nominal value of the share or by way of premium, as if the same had been payable by virtue of a call duly made and notified.

http://indiankanoon.org/doc/647270/

Debenture

According to sub-section (30) of section 2 'debenture' includes debenture stock, bond, or any other instrument of a company evidencing a debt, whether constituting a charge on the assets of the company or not.

Clinical research of the section reveals that debenture is an instrument of a company which includes debenture stocks, bond, or any other thing which exhibits the debt of the company and under any charge of the company or not.

In simple words, it is the borrowed capital by the company which issues an instrument under its common seal to acknowledge the debt or borrowing. The debenture holders are the creditors of the company and it generally receives interest at a fix rate.

It has certain feature as:

(a) It is instrument which acknowledges a debt.

(b) The instrument bears the seal of the company.

(c) The instrument exhibits amount and date of repayment of the loan, rate of interest, and date of interest payment.

(d) It is issued against the assets of the company, that is why it is considered to be secured instrument.

Basis	Debenture	Share
Status of Holder	Call debenture holder	Shareholder
Nature	Own funds of the company	Borrowed funds of the company
Exhibit	Capital of the company	Debt of the company
Position of Holder	Owner	Creditor
Income earned	Dividend	Interest
Type of Investment	Secure (issue against the assets of the company)	Not as secure compared to debenture
Voting Right	No Voting Right	Voting Right
Control Management	No power of control the management	Power to control the management
Conversion	Can be converted into share	Cannot be converted into debenture
Repayment	Get first priority over share in the event of winding up of company	Share is repayed after discharging of liability of the company in the event of winding up of company
Interest	Fixed and payable in all circumstances whether profit or loss to company	Dividend depends upon the profit of the company only

CHAPTER 10

Winding Up

- What is Winding Up?
- Modes
- Procedure
- Effect

Meaning

As we discussed in earlier chapters a company has a perpetual character, but it can be wound up under certain circumstances. It involves certain steps as a company denotes economic benefits or a source of benefits to various people, the decision of winding up of companies can also be taken in the interest and for the benefits of its members, creditors, etc.

A legal process by which the life of the company is to come to an end and is considered to be the last breath of the company and the assets of the company are being used for the benefit of its members and creditors.

Now take a look at the meaning given in the Halsburry's Laws of England, 'Winding up is a proceeding by means of which the dissolution of a company is brought about & in the course of which its assets are collected and realized; and applied in payment of its debts; and when these are satisfied, the remaining amount is applied for returning to its members the sums which they have contributed to the company in accordance with Articles of the Company.'

Professor Gower defines winding up of a company as a process whereby its life is ended and its property administered for the benefit of its creditors and members.

In summary, winding up of a company means:

- Last state of the company
- Process of end or dissolved the company
- Winding is the process which ends the life of the company and assets of the company are disposed of. The debts are paid out of those proceeds of assets and distributed among the members and creditors of the company.

Reasons for winding up

Fundamentals believe in the perpetual succession of companies, then why the Act allows the winding up of a company?

The Companies Act formulates or allows to formulate a corporate structure for the movement of economic growth and for the benefits of the company's members. At times the corporate structure collapses and leads to business failure of the company due to any reason – whether fraudulent practice of business, or inadequate capital, or any other managerial or other reason which adversely affects the very purpose of business or eco-social structure. That is why we choose winding up of a company as a last resort, when any revival strategy does not work.

The chief object of winding up of a company is to discharge the debts and liabilities of the company by realizing the assets of the company. The question may arise here whether winding up or dissolution, but both are one and the same thing. The answer is no, but sometimes erroneously the means are considered to be the same. When we analyse the Act it reveals that the legal connotation of both are different.

Basis	Dissolution	Winding Up
Meaning	Dissolution is part of winding up the business affairs of a company; it comes after completing the liquidator activities. The assets are distributed and the board of directors ceases to exist, and affairs of the company have been completely wound up.	Winding up indicates the realizing and collecting the assets of the company and discharging its debts and liabilities, obligations, and distributing its capital and surplus assets among the members of the company, and providing proper time and conditions for dissolution.
Status	Dissolution makes complete dissolution of the company.	Execution of winding up does not cease the existence of the company; the company still remains in existence.
Nature	It is an administrative function.	It is a judicial function.
Role of Liquidator	The liquidator has an important role in the dissolution.	The liquidator has an important role in the winding up, he becomes the representative of the company.
Time of Execution	It is the second stage and final stage after winding up.	It is the preliminary stage before dissolution of the company.
Process	The dissolution of a company is recorded and registered by the Registrar of Companies.	The winding up of a company is heard and judged by the Tribunal.

Modes of Winding Up of Company

There are two basic modes of winding up of a company as per section 270 of the Companies Act. The Act prohibits any other mode except the following modes:

1. Compulsory/By Tribunal
2. Voluntary

Winding up of a company by the Tribunal is the application of the judicial mind: When the winding up petition u/s 272 is being filed it is mandatory for filing a statement of affairs by the director. The tribunal then takes cognizance on that and this mitigates the risk of defraud and protects the rights of members and other persons who are associated with the company and have one or some other interest.

Voluntary winding up lacks the application of the judicial mind, and denotes much chances of defraud and can prejudice the interest of members of the company and other persons who are associated with the company with one or some other interest. In such a case, a stringent process and pre-causation is needed. The act reflects those provisions.

Circumstances for Compulsory Winding Up by Tribunal

- company unable to pay its debts
- Resolved by special resolution
- company has acted against the interests of the sovereignty and integrity of India, the security of the State, friendly relations with foreign States, public order, decency or morality;
- by Tribunal has ordered the winding up of the company under Chapter XIX;
- by the Registrar or any other person authorised by the Central Government by notification if affairs of the company have been conducted in a fraudulent manner or the company was formed for fraudulent and unlawful purpose or the persons concerned in the formation or management of its affairs have been guilty of fraud, misfeasance;
- default in filing with the Registrar its financial statements or annual returns for immediately preceding five consecutive financial years;
- just and equitable ground.

Section 271: Under Part I defines the circumstances under which a company may be wound up by the Tribunal when a company may, on a petition under section 272, be wound up by the Tribunal as:

(a) if the company is unable to pay its debts;

(b) if the company has, by a special resolution, resolved that the company be wound up by the Tribunal;

(*c*) if the company has acted against the interests of the sovereignty and integrity of India, the security of the State, friendly relations with foreign states, public order, decency, or morality;

(*d*) if the Tribunal has ordered the winding up of the company under Chapter XIX;

(*e*) if on an application made by the Registrar or any other person authorized by the Central Government by notification under this Act, the Tribunal is of the opinion that the affairs of the company have been conducted in a fraudulent manner or the company was formed for a fraudulent and unlawful purpose or the persons concerned in the formation or management of its affairs have been guilty of fraud, misfeasance, or misconduct in connection therewith and that it is proper that the company to be wound up;

(*f*) if the company has made a default in filing with the Registrar its financial statements or annual returns for immediately preceding five consecutive financial years; or

(*g*) if the Tribunal is of the opinion that it is just and equitable that the company should be wound up.

(2) A company shall be deemed to be unable to pay its debts,

(*a*) if a creditor, by assignment or otherwise, to whom the company is indebted for an amount exceeding one lakh rupees than due, has served on the company, by causing it to be delivered at its registered office, by registered post or otherwise, a demand requiring the company to pay the amount so due and the company has failed to pay the sum within twenty-one days after the receipt of such a demand or to provide adequate security or re-structure or compound the debt to the reasonable satisfaction of the creditor;

(*b*) if any execution or other process issued on a decree or order of any court or tribunal in favour of a creditor of the company is returned unsatisfied in whole or in part; or

(*c*) if it is proved to the satisfaction of the Tribunal that the company is unable to pay its debts, and, in determining whether a company is unable to pay its debts, the Tribunal shall take into account the contingent and prospective liabilities of the company.

If the company is unable to pay its debts

It is well known that one of the grounds for winding up a company under Indian company law is its incapability to pay 'debts'. Sec. 271(a) clearly indicates. 'if the company is unable to pay its debts' the tribunal may pass the order to wind up the company.

What is 'debt'?

Supreme Court of India in the case of M/s, Vijay Industries *v.* M/s. Natl Technologies Ltd discussed the term 'debt' as: 'debt' refers to an ascertained and definite amount due to the creditor and not a disputed amount. However, it was furthermore held:

(a) The term 'debt' refers to an ascertained and definite amount 'due' and does not refer to a claim for compensation/damages or a claim which requires assessment by a court before it becomes due and payable.

(b) The term 'debt' may refer not only to 'principal' (value of goods or amount advanced), but also to interest due thereon, where there is a contract to pay interest. Where the contract specifically provides for payment of interest, or where there is an admission or promise to pay interest by the company or where in proceedings for recovery of money, a competent court or arbitrator has determined the liability to pay interest, then non-payment of interest (whether with principal or interest alone) may amount to inability to pay debts.

(c) Interest cannot be awarded merely on the basis of a term in a bill or invoice, unless the creditor proves that such provision is based on a contract or agreement on the part of the purchaser to pay interest. This is because a credit bill or an invoice is a unilateral demand by the supplier and is neither a bilateral agreement nor a promise by the purchaser to pay interest. Interest can be awarded on the basis of a provision in a bill/invoice, if it is supported by an agreement or promise to pay interest by the purchaser. Such agreement may be established with reference to correspondence, or by countersigning of the bill by the purchaser, or by acceptance by the purchaser of the term in the bill relating to interest. Where in the absence of an agreement or contract for payment of interest on the value of goods supplied, a notice of demand is sent by the supplier requiring payment of the value of goods supplied with interest thereon and a reply is sent by the purchaser in general terms seeking time to pay the bill amount, such reply cannot be construed as an admission to pay interest. Either an agreement to pay interest or a specific admission or promise to pay interest or an order or decree granting interest by a court or tribunal empowered to award interest, is a condition precedent to hold that interest is a debt due, for the purpose of a winding up petition. In the absence of a contractual or legal liability, nor act as an estoppel in regard to a subsequent denial by the company in legal proceedings.

(d) Where there is a bona fide dispute in regard to interest, the court considering a petition under section 433(e) should not decide the issue, merely to avoid multiplicity proceedings. The purpose of winding up proceedings being completely different from the purpose of proceedings for recovery of a debt, winding up proceedings are not a substitute for a civil suit, and, therefore, relegating parties to a civil suit cannot be considered as resulting in multiplicity of proceedings.

When a company deemed to be unable to discharge its debt, we could find the answer in sub-section (2) of section 271 as:

A company shall be deemed to be unable to pay its debts:

(a) if a creditor, by assignment or otherwise, to whom the company is indebted for an amount exceeding one lakh rupees than due, has served on the company, by causing it to be delivered at its registered office, by registered post or otherwise, a demand requiring the company to pay the amount so due and the company has failed to pay the sum within twenty-one days after the receipt of such demand or to provide adequate security or re-structure or compound the debt to the reasonable satisfaction of the creditor;

(b) if any execution or other process issued on a decree or order of any court or tribunal in favour of a creditor of the company is returned unsatisfied in whole or in part; or

(c) if it is proved to the satisfaction of the Tribunal that the company is unable to pay its debts, and, in determining whether a company is unable to pay its debts, the Tribunal shall take into account the contingent and prospective liabilities of the company.

A mere look at section 434(1) shows that in cases covered by clauses (a) and (b) if the petitioning creditor who files the petition shows to the court even prima facie that his case is covered by the aforesaid provisions, then, of course, the deeming fiction would arise for the court's consideration and in proper cases the court can act upon this presumption and can proceed further with the company petition. However, when we come to clause (c), the court has to be satisfied that the company is unable to pay its debts and that satisfaction will depend upon the proof submitted before the court and to undertake that exercise the court has to take into account the contingent and prospective liabilities of the company also apart from its liability for the debt due to the petitioning creditor, but for which the company petition would not lie at his instance under section 433(e) of the Act. Section 439 deals with the provisions as to application for winding up. So far as the creditors-petitioners are concerned, they are dealt with in section 439(1) which states an application to the court for the winding up of a company shall be by petition presented subject to the provisions of this section, (b) by any creditor or creditors including any contingent or prospective creditor or creditors. Sub-section (8) of section 439 which is heavily pressed for our consideration by Sri Jayaram and other learned counsel for the petitioning creditors reads as under:

On a plain reading of the aforementioned provisions, it is evident that what is necessary for invoking the said provision is that despite service of notice, the company which was indebted in a sum exceeding one lakh rupees than due failed and/or neglected to pay the same within three weeks thereafter or to secure or compound for it to the reasonable satisfaction of the creditor.

Winding up petition is not a legitimate means of seeking to enforce payment of the debt

In Amalgamated Commercial Traders (P) Ltd. *v.* A.C.K. Krishnaswami and Another [(1965) 35 CC 456], wherein it was held:

> It is well-settled that 'a winding up petition is not a legitimate means of seeking to enforce payment of the debt which is bona fide disputed by the company. A petition presented ostensibly for a winding up order but really to exercise pressure will be dismissed, and under circumstances may be stigmatized as a scandalous abuse of the process of the court. At one time petitions founded on disputed debt were directed to stand over till the debt was established by action. If, however, there was no reason to believe that the debt, if established, would not

be paid, the petition was dismissed. The modern practice has been to dismiss such petitions. But, of course, if the debt is not disputed on some substantial ground, the court may decide it on the petition and make the order.[41]

The nature of debt is being defined in the M/s Madhusudan Gordhandas & Co. *v.* Madhu Woollen Industries Pvt. Ltd. [(1971) 3 SCC 632], this Court upon considering Amalgamated Commercial Traders (P.) Ltd. (supra) and various other English cases opined as under:

> Two rules are well settled. First, if the debt is bona fide disputed and the defense is a substantial one, the court will not wind up the company. The court has dismissed a petition for winding up where the creditor claimed a sum for goods sold to the company and the company contended that no price had been agreed upon and the sum demanded by the creditor was unreasonable. (See London and Paris Banking Corporation.) Again, a petition for winding up by a creditor who claimed payment of an agreed sum for work done for the company when the company contended that the work had not been properly was not allowed. (See Re. Brighton Club and Horfold Hotel Co. Ltd.)

The court furthermore opined:

(i) Where the debt is undisputed, the court will not act upon a defence that the company has the ability to pay the debt but did not choose to pay that particular debt.

(ii) Where, however, there is no dispute that the company passed the creditor a debt, entitled him to a winding up order but the exact amount of the debt is disputed, the court will make a winding up order without requiring the creditor to quantify the debt precisely.

(iii) The principles on which the court acts are first that the defence of the company is in good faith and one of substance, secondly, the defence is likely to succeed in point of law and, thirdly, the company adduced prima facie proof of the facts on which the defence depends.

It is also important to note here that section 271 of the Companies Act does not state that the debt must be precisely a definite sum or the statutory interest would come within the purview of the word 'debt'. It is one thing to say that the amount of debt is not definite or ascertainable because of the bona fide dispute raised thereabout or there exists a dispute as regards quantity or quality of supply or such other defences which are available to the purchaser; but it is another thing to say that although the due as regards the principal amount resulting from the quantity or quality of supply of the goods stands admitted but a question is raised as to whether any agreement had been entered into for payment of interest or whether the rate of interest would be applicable or not. In the latter case, in our opinion, the application for winding up cannot be dismissed.

41. M/s Vijay Industries *v.* M/S. Natl Technologies Ltd (supra).

If the company has, by special resolution, resolved that the company be wound up by the Tribunal, it is also considered voluntary winding up. Supreme Court in the case of Neptune Assurance Co. Ltd. & Ors *v.* Union of India & Anr 1973 AIR 602, 1973 SCR (2) 940 held that the expression 'voluntary winding up means a winding up by a special resolution of the company to that effect'.

This option is being provided by the Act in the interest of the shareholder, creditor, or any other person, if they considered that winding up of the company is in their interest or in the interest of company. But it is important to note here that court is not bound by the decision of voluntary winding up. The power of the court is discretionary, and the court may reject the wound-up petition if it is against the company interest or opposed the public policy.

As it has been discussed in the earlier chapters the chief objective of the company is to maintain and sustain the economic socio objective.

No company is allowed to violate or act against the interests of the sovereignty and integrity of India, the security of the State, friendly relations with foreign states, public order, decency, or morality.

If the Tribunal has ordered the winding up of the company under Chapter XIX:

Chapter XIX of the Act talks about 'Revival and Rehabilitation of Sick Companies'. A company is considered to be sick where on a demand by the secured creditors of a company representing 50 per cent or more of its outstanding amount of debt, the company has failed to pay the debt within a period of thirty days of the service of the notice of demand or to secure or compound it to the reasonable satisfaction of the creditors, any secured creditor may file an application to the Tribunal in the prescribed manner along with the relevant evidence for such default, non-repayment, or failure to offer security or compound it, for a determination that the company be declared as a sick company.

On the determination of a company as a sick company by the Tribunal under section 253, any secured creditor of that company or the company may make an application u/s 254 to the Tribunal for the determination of the measures that may be adopted with respect to the revival and rehabilitation of such company.

Thereafter the Tribunal may appoint an interim administrator for formulating the scheme of revival and rehabilitation, and such a scheme is then produced by the administrator before a Committee of Creditor. If such scheme is not approved by the creditors then the administrator shall submit the report to the Tribunal within fifteen days and the Tribunal shall order for winding up of the sick company.

If on an application made by the Registrar or any other person authorized by the Central Government by notification under this Act, the Tribunal is of the opinion that the affairs of the company have been conducted in a fraudulent manner, or the company was formed for a fraudulent and unlawful purpose, or the persons concerned in the formation or management of its affairs have been guilty of fraud, misfeasance, or misconduct in connection therewith and that it is proper that the company be wound up, then it is also a valid and important ground for winding up the company, as no law authorizes any act which is based on a fraudulent or unlawful purpose or the persons who are connected with the company have been guilty of fraud or misfeasance or misconduct, because it would directly hit the chief objective of formulation of company.

If the Company has made a default in filing with the Registrar its Financial Statements or Annual Returns for immediately preceding five consecutive financial years:

Non-compliance of statutory requirements or mandatory requirement is also one of the reasons to wind up the company, because it is considered the health check of the company which secures the interest and financial benefits of members of the company.

If the Tribunal is of the Opinion that it is Just and Equitable that the company should be wound up: The Act specifies the phrase 'just and equitable' on which a company can be wound up. The clinical research of the phrase denotes that the Act provides a wide discretionary power to the court to wind up the company, if it appears it is in the interest of the company, its creditors or members, shareholders or public interest.

> In simple words we can define the affairs of the company are being conducted in illegal, invalid and wrongful manner and in complete violation of the provisions of Articles of Association, the Companies Act and Principles of Natural Justice. The facts would justify the making up of a winding up order on the ground that it was just and equitable that the company should be wound up but such winding up order shall unfairly prejudice the shareholders who have invested substantial funds in the company.

Before granting relief, the court has to satisfy itself that to wind up the company will unfairly prejudice the members complaining of oppression, but that otherwise, the facts will justify the making of a winding up order on the ground that it is just and equitable and that the company should be wound up. The rule as regards the duty of utmost good faith, on which stress was laid by Lord Keith in Meyer, received further and closer consideration in Ebrahimi *v.* Westbourne Galleries Ltd. [1973] AC 360 (HL) wherein Lord Wilberforce considered the scope, nature and extent of the 'just and equitable' principle as a ground for winding up a company.[42]

The legal position is fairly established that in order that the court may make an order under Section 397*, the court must be satisfied, Firstly, the company's affairs are being conducted in the manner oppressive to any member/members; secondly, the facts would justify the making of a winding-up order, on the ground that it was just and equitable that the company should be wound-up; and thirdly, that winding-up order would unfairly prejudice the applicants. For a relief under Section 397, 'a conduct which lacks in probity, conduct which is unfair and which causes prejudice to the petitioner in the exercise of his legal and proprietary rights as a shareholder' must be shown to exist.

42. Maharashtra Power Development *v.* Dabhol Power Company 2004 (3) BomCR 317, (2004) 3 CompLJ 58 Bom, 2004 52 SCL 224 Bom.

* refer section 241 of companies act 2013.

The relevant interests are the interests of the members, not necessarily limited to strict legal rights under the Companies Act or the company's constitution (Articles of Association) but the court may take into account wider-equitable considerations. Put it more analytically: that the oppression complained of must affect a person in his capacity or character as a member of the company; (ii) there must be continuous acts constituting oppression up to the date of the petition; (iii) the events had to be considered not in isolation but as a part of continuous story; (iv) it must be shown as preliminary to the application of section 397 that there is just and equitable ground for winding up the company; and (v) the conduct complained of can be said to be 'oppression' only when it could be said that it is burdensome, harsh and wrongful. Section 397 allows the court to intervene, of course on equitable considerations, where there is visible departure from the standards of fair dealing. While doing so the court may keep in mind the history and particular structure of the particular company and whether the detriment occasioned to the complaining member's interest arises from the acts or conduct of the company complained. 'Oppression' may be due to a desire to obtain power or control. It may also manifest itself in a denial of rights. The position that emerges from catena of cases is that an isolated act which is contrary to law may not necessarily and by itself support the inference that the violation of law was burdensome, harsh, and wrongful, but a series of illegal acts following upon one another, can, in the context lead justifiably to the conclusion that they are part of the same transaction, of which the object is to cause or commit the oppression of person against whom acts are directed.[43]

Who are Entitled to File Winding Up Petition?

Section 272 specifies who can file the petition to the Tribunal for the winding up of a company as:

(a) the company;

(b) any creditor or creditors, including any contingent or prospective creditor or creditors;

(c) any contributory or contributories;

(d) all or any of the persons specified in clauses (a), (b) and (c) together;

(e) the Registrar;

(f) any person authorized by the Central Government in that behalf; or

(g) in a case falling under clause (c) of sub-section (1) of section 271, by the Central Government or a State Government.

(2) A secured creditor, the holder of any debentures, whether or not any trustee or trustees have been appointed in respect of such and other like debentures, and the trustee for the holders of debentures shall be deemed to be creditors within the meaning of clause (b) of sub-section (1).

43. Maharashtra Power Development (supra).

(3) A contributory shall be entitled to present a petition for the winding up of a company, notwithstanding that he may be the holder of fully paid-up shares, or that the company may have no assets at all or may have no surplus assets left for distribution among the shareholders after the satisfaction of its liabilities, and shares in respect of which he is a contributory or some of them were either originally allotted to him or have been held by him, and registered in his name, for at least six months during the eighteen months immediately before the commencement of the winding up or have devolved on him through the death of a former holder.

(4) The Registrar shall be entitled to present a petition for winding up under sub-section (1) on any of the grounds specified in sub-section (1) of section 271, except on the grounds specified in clause (b), clause (d) or clause (g) of that sub-section:

Provided that the Registrar shall not present a petition on the ground that the company is unable to pay its debts unless it appears to him either from the financial condition of the company as disclosed in its balance sheet or from the report of an inspector appointed under section 210 that the company is unable to pay its debts:

Provided further that the Registrar shall obtain the previous sanction of the Central Government to the presentation of a petition:

Provided also that the Central Government shall not accord its sanction unless the company has been given a reasonable opportunity of making representations.

(5) A petition presented by the company for winding up before the Tribunal shall be admitted only if accompanied by a statement of affairs in such form and in such manner as may be prescribed.

(6) Before a petition for winding up of a company presented by a contingent or prospective creditor is admitted, the leave of the Tribunal shall be obtained for the admission of the petition and such leave shall not be granted, unless in the opinion of the Tribunal there is a prima facie case for the winding up of the company and until such security for costs has been given as the Tribunal thinks reasonable.

(7) A copy of the petition made under this section shall also be filed with the Registrar and the Registrar shall, without prejudice to any other provisions, submit his views to the Tribunal within sixty days of receipt of such a petition.

Procedure for Winding Up by Tribunal

The Tribunal may, on receipt of a petition for winding up under section 272 pass any of the following orders, namely:

(a) dismiss it, with or without costs;
(b) make any interim order as it thinks fit;
(c) appoint a provisional liquidator of the company till the making of a winding up order;

(d) make an order for the winding up of the company with or without costs; or

(e) any other order as it thinks fit.

The order under this sub-section shall be made within ninety days from the date of presentation of the petition:

But before appointing a provisional liquidator under clause (c), the Tribunal shall give notice to the company and afford a reasonable opportunity to it to make its representations, if any, unless for special reasons to be recorded in writing, the Tribunal thinks fit to dispense with such notice:

But the Tribunal shall not refuse to make a winding up order on the ground only that the assets of the company have been mortgaged for an amount equal to or in excess of those assets, or that the company has no assets.

Where a petition is presented on the ground that it is just and equitable that the company should be wound up, the Tribunal may refuse to make an order of winding up, if it is of the opinion that some other remedy is available to the petitioners and that they are acting unreasonably in seeking to have the company wound up instead of pursuing the other remedy.

Directions for filing statement of affairs

Where a petition for winding up is filed before the Tribunal by any person other than the company, the Tribunal shall, if satisfied that a *prima facie* case for winding up of the company is made out, by an order direct the company to file its objections along with a statement of its affairs within thirty days of the order in such form and in such manner as may be prescribed.

In a situation of contingency or special circumstances the Tribunal may allow a further period of thirty days, the Tribunal may direct the petitioner to deposit such security for costs as it may consider reasonable as a pre-condition to issue directions to the company.

In case the company fails to file the statement of affairs, the right to oppose the petition shall be forfeited and such directors and officers of the company as found responsible for such non-compliance shall be liable for punishment under sub-section (4) of section 274.

The directors and other officers of the company, in respect of which an order for winding up is passed by the Tribunal under clause (d) of sub-section (1) of section 273, shall, within a period of thirty days of such order, submit, at the cost of the company, the books of account of the company completed and audited up to the date of the order, to such a liquidator and in the manner specified by the Tribunal.

Appointments company liquidators

For the purposes of winding up of a company by the Tribunal, the Tribunal at the time of the passing of the order of winding up shall appoint an Official Liquidator or a liquidator from the panel maintained.

Intimation to company liquidator, provisional liquidator, and registrar

Where the Tribunal makes an order for appointment of provisional Liquidator or for the winding up of a company, it shall, within a period not exceeding seven days from the date of passing of the order, cause intimation thereof to be sent to the Company Liquidator or provisional liquidator, as the case may be, and the Registrar.

Endorsement by registrar and notification in the official gazette

On receipt of the copy of order of appointment of provisional Liquidator or winding up order, the Registrar shall make an endorsement to that effect in his records relating to the company and notify in the Official Gazette that such an order has been made and in the case of a listed company, the Registrar shall intimate about such appointment or order, as the case may be, to the stock exchange or exchanges where the securities of the company are listed.

Notice of discharge

The winding up order shall be deemed to be a notice of discharge to the officers, employees, and workmen of the company, except when the business of the company is continued.

Constitution of a winding up committee

Within three weeks from the date of passing of winding up order, the Company Liquidator shall make an application to the Tribunal for constitution of a winding up committee to assist and monitor the progress of liquidation proceedings by the Company Liquidator in carrying out the function as provided in sub-section (5) of section 277 and such winding up committee shall comprise the following persons, namely:

(i) Official liquidator attached to the Tribunal;
(ii) nominee of secured creditors; and
(iii) a professional nominated by the Tribunal.

Report by company liquidator to the tribunal

The Company Liquidator shall place before the Tribunal a report along with minutes of the meetings of the committee on a monthly basis duly signed by the members present in the meeting for consideration till the final report for dissolution of the company is submitted before the Tribunal. The Company Liquidator shall prepare the draft of the final report for consideration and approval of the winding-up committee. The final report so approved by the winding-up committee shall be submitted by the Company Liquidator before the Tribunal for passing of a dissolution order in respect of the company.

Direction of tribunal on report of company liquidator

The Tribunal on consideration of the report of the Company Liquidator shall fix a time within which the entire proceedings be completed and company be dissolved.

Custody of company properties

Where a winding-up order has been made or where a provisional or Company Liquidator has been appointed the Liquidator shall on order of the Tribunal take the custody or control of all the property assets and actionable claims to which company is or appears to be entitled to take such steps and measures and may be necessary to protect and preserve the properties of the company.

Settlement of list of contributories an application of assets

As soon as may be after the passing of a winding up order by the Tribunal, the Tribunal shall settle a list of contributories, cause rectification of register of members in all cases where rectification is required in pursuance of this Act, and shall cause the assets of the company to be applied for the discharge of its liability.

Dissolution of company by tribunal

When the affairs of a company have been completely wound up, the Company Liquidator shall make an application to the Tribunal for dissolution of the company.

(2) The Tribunal shall on an application filed by the Company Liquidator under sub-section (1) of section 302 or when the Tribunal is of the opinion that it is just and reasonable in the circumstances of the case that an order for the dissolution of the company should be made, make an order that the company be dissolved from the date of the order, and the company shall be dissolved accordingly.

(3) A copy of the order shall, within thirty days from the date thereof, be forwarded by the Company Liquidator to the Registrar who shall record in the register relating to the company a minute of the dissolution of the company.

Circumstances in which company may be wound up voluntarily (section 304)

A company may be wound up voluntarily, if the company in general meeting passes a resolution requiring the company to be wound up:

1. as a result of the expiry of the period for its duration fixed by its articles, or
2. on the occurrence of any event in respect of which the articles provide that the company should be dissolved; or
3. the company passes a special resolution that the company be wound up voluntarily.

Procedure for voluntary winding up

As we have discussed in earlier chapters voluntary winding up requires a more stringent procedure than winding up by the Tribunal. The procedure is based on two things, i.e., time-bound manner, and due diligence of the company's financial health and fraud.

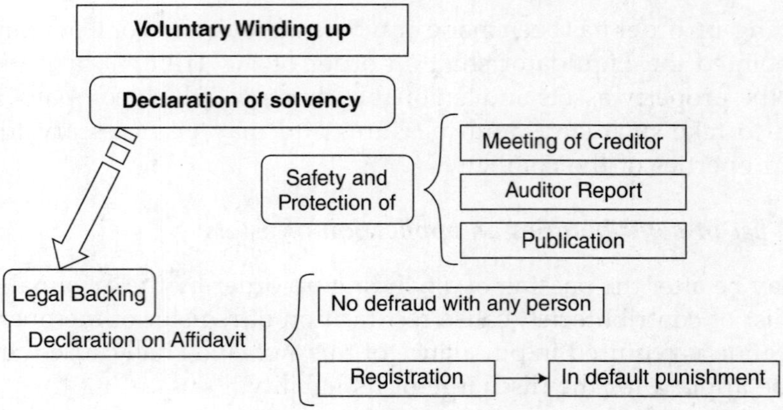

Declaration of solvency in case of proposal to wind up voluntarily

Where it is proposed to wind up a company voluntarily, its director or directors, or in case the company has more than two directors, the majority of its directors, shall, at a meeting of the Board, make a declaration verified by an affidavit to the effect that they have made a full inquiry into the affairs of the company and they have formed an opinion that the company has no debt or whether it will be able to pay its debts in full from the proceeds of assets sold.

The declaration should be made within five weeks immediately preceding the date of the passing of the resolution for winding up the company and be delivered to the Registrar for registration before that date. It should contain a declaration that the company is not being wound up to defraud any person or persons; it is accompanied by a copy of the report of the auditors of the company prepared in accordance with the provisions of this Act, on the profit and loss account of the company for the period commencing from the date up to which the last such account was prepared and ending with the latest practicable date immediately before making of the declaration. The balance sheet of the company made out as on that date should also contain a statement of the assets and liabilities of the company on that date. Any director of a company making a declaration under this section without having reasonable grounds for the opinion that the company will be able to pay its debts in full from the proceeds of assets sold in voluntary winding up shall be punishable with imprisonment for a term which shall not be less than three years but which may extend to five years or with fine which shall not be less than fifty thousand rupees but which may extend to three lakh rupees, or with both.

Meeting of creditors

Meeting of creditors is also required and the notice of such a meeting should be posted to the creditors of the company by registered post. The Board of the Directors in the meeting present a full statement of the position of the affairs of the company together with a list of creditors of the company, if any, along with a copy of declaration under section 305 and the estimated amount of the claims before such a meeting.

In the meeting if two-thirds in value of creditors of the company are of the opinion that:

(a) it is in the interest of all parties that the company be wound up voluntarily, the company shall be wound up voluntarily; or

(b) the company may not be able to pay for its debts in full from the proceeds of assets sold in voluntary winding up and pass a resolution that it shall be in the interest of all parties if the company is wound up by the Tribunal in accordance with the provisions of Part I of this Chapter, the company shall within fourteen days thereafter file an application before the Tribunal.

The copy of the resolution passed in the meeting shall be filed before the Registrar within ten days of the passing thereof. If a company contravenes the provisions of this section, the company shall be punishable with fine which shall not be less than fifty thousand rupees but which may extend to two lakh rupees and the director of the company who is in default shall be punishable with imprisonment for a term which may extend to six months or with fine which shall not be less than fifty thousand rupees but which may extend to two lakh rupees, or with both.

The decision of appointment of the Company Liquidator is also to be taken in this meeting from the panel prepared by the Central Government for the purpose of winding up its affairs and distributing the assets of the company and recommend the fee to be paid to the Company Liquidator.

Appointment of committees

Where there are no creditors of a company, such a company in its general meeting, or where a meeting of creditors is held under section 306, such creditors, as the case may be, may appoint such committees as considered appropriate to supervise the voluntary liquidation and assist the Company Liquidator in discharging his functions.

Publication of resolution to wind up voluntarily

Where a company has passed a resolution for voluntary winding up and a resolution under sub-section (3) of section 306 is passed, it shall within fourteen days of the passing of the resolution give notice of the resolution by advertisement in the Official Gazette and also in a newspaper which is in circulation in the district where the registered office or the principal office of the company is situated.

If a company contravenes these provisions the company and every officer of the company who is in default shall be punishable with fine which may extend to five thousand rupees for each day during which such default continues.

Report of the company liquidator to tribunal for examination of persons

Where the Company Liquidator is of the opinion that a fraud has been committed by any person in respect of the company, he shall immediately make a report to the Tribunal and the Tribunal shall, without prejudice to the process of winding up, order for investigation under section 210. On consideration of the report of such an investigation, the Tribunal may pass such an order and give such directions under this Chapter as it may consider necessary including the direction that such person shall attend before the Tribunal on a day appointed by it for that purpose and be examined as to the promotion or formation or the conduct of the business of the company or as to his conduct and dealings as officer thereof or otherwise.

Final meeting and dissolution of company

As soon as the affairs of a company are fully wound up, the Company Liquidator shall prepare a report of the winding up showing that the property and assets of the company have been disposed of and its debt fully discharged or discharged to the satisfaction of the creditors and thereafter call a general meeting of the company for the purpose of laying the final winding-up accounts before it and giving any explanation thereof.

If the majority of the members of the company, after considering the report of the Company Liquidator, are satisfied that the company shall be wound up, they may pass a resolution for its dissolution.

Within two weeks after the meeting, the Company Liquidator shall

(a) send to the Registrar:

(i) a copy of the final winding-up accounts of the company and shall make a return in respect of each meeting and of the date thereof; and

(ii) copies of the resolutions passed in the meetings; and

(b) file an application along with his report under sub-section (1) in such a manner as may be prescribed along with the books and papers of the company relating to the winding up, before the Tribunal for passing an order of dissolution of the company.

If the Tribunal is satisfied, after considering the report of the Company Liquidator that the process of winding up has been just and fair, the Tribunal shall pass an order dissolving the company within sixty days of the receipt of the application.

The Registrar, on receiving the copy of the order passed by the Tribunal, shall forthwith publish a notice in the Official Gazette that the company is dissolved.

Effect of Winding Up

By tribunal

The order for the winding up of a company shall operate in favour of all the creditors and all contributories of the company as if it had been made out on the joint petition of creditors and contributories.

When a winding up order has been passed or a provisional Liquidator has been appointed, no suit or other legal proceeding shall be commenced, or if pending at the date of the winding-up order, shall be proceeded with, by, or against the company, except with the leave of the Tribunal and subject to such terms as the Tribunal may impose. (2) Nothing in sub-section (1) shall apply to any proceeding pending in appeal before the Supreme Court or a High Court.

Voluntary winding up

In the case of a voluntary winding up, the company shall from the commencement of the winding up cease to carry on its business except as far as is required for the beneficial winding up of its business. However, the corporate state and corporate powers of the company shall continue until it is dissolved.

Provisions applicable to every mode of winding up

Debts of all descriptions to be admitted to proof

In every winding up (subject, in the case of insolvent companies, to the application in accordance with the provisions of this Act or of the law of insolvency), all debts payable on a contingency, and all claims against the company, present or future, certain or contingent, ascertained or sounding only in damages, shall be admissible to proof against the company, a just estimate being made, so far as possible, of the value of such debts or claims as may be subject to any contingency, or may sound only in damages, or for some other reason may not bear a certain value.

Application of insolvency rules in winding up of insolvent companies

In the winding up of an insolvent company, the same rules shall prevail and be observed with regard to:

(a) debts provable;

(b) the valuation of annuities and future and contingent liabilities; and

(c) the respective rights of secured and unsecured creditors, as are in force for the time being under the law of insolvency with respect to the estates of persons adjudged insolvent.

But the security of every secured creditor shall be deemed to be subject to an equal step charge in favour of the workmen to the extent of the workmen's portion therein, and, where a secured creditor, instead of relinquishing his security and proving his debts, opts to realize his security,

(i) the liquidator shall be entitled to represent the workmen and enforce such charge;

(ii) any amount realized by the liquidator by way of enforcement of such charge shall be applied rateably for the discharge of workmen's dues; and

(iii) so much of the debts due to such secured creditor as could not be realized by him or the amount of the workmen's portion in his security, whichever is less, shall rank equal in step with the workmen's dues for the purposes of section 326.

All persons under sub-section (1) shall be entitled to prove and receive dividends out of the assets of the company under winding up, and make such claims against the company as they respectively are entitled to make by virtue of this section but if a secured creditor, instead of relinquishing his security and proving his debts, proceeds to realize his security, he shall be liable to pay his portion of the expenses incurred by the liquidator, including a provisional liquidator, if any, for the preservation of the security before its realization by the secured creditor.

Overriding preferential payments

Workmen's dues and debts due to the secured creditors shall be paid in priority to all other debts, but the sums towards wages or salary referred to in sub-clause (i) of clause (b) of sub-section (3) of section 325, which are payable for a period of two years preceding the winding up order or such other period as may be prescribed, shall be paid in priority to all other debts (including debts due to secured creditors), within a period of thirty days of sale of assets and shall be subject to such charge over the security of secured creditors as may be prescribed. The debts payable under the proviso to sub-section (1) shall be paid in full before any payment is made to secured creditors and thereafter debts payable under that sub-section shall be paid in full, unless the assets are insufficient to meet them, in which case they shall abate in equal proportions.

Preferential payments

In a winding up, subject to the provisions of section 326, there shall be paid in priority to all other debts:

(a) all revenues, taxes, cesses, and rates due from the company to the Central Government or a State Government or to a local authority at the relevant date, and having become due and payable within the twelve months immediately before that date;

(b) all wages or salary including wages payable for time or piece work and salary earned wholly or in part by way of commission of any employee in respect of services rendered to the company and due for a period not exceeding four months within the twelve months immediately before the relevant date, subject to the condition that the amount payable under this clause to any workman shall not exceed such amount as may be notified;

(c) all accrued holiday remuneration becoming payable to any employee, or in the case of his death, to any other person claiming under him, on the termination of his employment before, or by the winding up order, or, as the case may be, the dissolution of the company;

(d) unless the company is being wound up voluntarily merely for the purposes of reconstruction or amalgamation with another company, all amount due in respect of contributions payable during the period of twelve months immediately before the relevant date by the company as the employer of persons under the Employees' State Insurance Act, 1948 or any other law for the time being in force;

(e) unless the company has, at the commencement of winding up, under such a contract with any insurer as is mentioned in section 14 of the Workmen's Compensation Act, 1923, rights capable of being transferred to and vested in the workmen, all amount due in respect of any compensation or liability for compensation under the said Act in respect of the death or disablement of any employee of the company but, where any compensation under the said Act is a weekly payment, the amount payable under this clause shall be taken to be the amount of the lump sum for which such weekly payment could, if redeemable, be redeemed, if the employer has made an application under that Act;

(f) all sums due to any employee from the provident fund, the pension fund, the gratuity fund or any other fund for the welfare of the employees, maintained by the company; and

(g) the expenses of any investigation held in pursuance of sections 213 and 216, in so far as they are payable by the company.

(2) Where any payment has been made to any employee of a company on account of wages or salary or accrued holiday remuneration, himself or, in the case of his death, to any other person claiming through him, out of money advanced by some person for that purpose, the person by whom the money was advanced shall, in a winding up, have a right of priority in respect of the money so advanced and paid-up to the amount by which the sum in respect of which the employee or other person in his right would have been entitled to priority in the winding up has been reduced by reason of the payment having been made.

The debts enumerated above shall—

(a) rank equally among themselves and be paid in full, unless the assets are insufficient to meet them, in which case they shall abate in equal proportions; and

(b) so far as the assets of the company available for payment to general creditors are insufficient to meet them, have priority over the claims of holders of debentures under any floating charge created by the company, and be paid accordingly out of any property comprised in or subject to that charge.

Subject to the retention of such sums as may be necessary for the costs and expenses of the winding up, the debts under this section shall be discharged forthwith so far as the assets are sufficient to meet them, and in the case of the debts to which priority is given under clause (d) of sub-section (1), formal proof thereof shall not be required except in so far as may be otherwise prescribed.

In the event of a landlord or other person distraining or having distrained on any goods or effects of the company within three months immediately before the date of a winding up order, the debts to which priority is given under this section shall be a first charge on the goods or effects so distrained on or the proceeds of the sale thereof, but in respect of any money paid under any such charge, the landlord or other person shall have the same rights of priority as the person to whom the payment is made.

Any remuneration in respect of a period of holiday or of absence from work on medical grounds through sickness or other cause shall be deemed to be wages in respect of services rendered to the company during that period.

Fraudulent preference

Where a company has given preference to a person who is one of the creditors of the company or a surety or guarantor for any of the debts or other liabilities of the company, and the company does anything or suffers anything done which has the effect of putting that person into a position which, in the event of the company going into liquidation, will be better than the position he would have been in if that thing had not been done prior to six months of making winding up application, the Tribunal, if satisfied that, such transaction is a fraudulent preference may order, as it may think fit, for restoring the position to what it would have been if the company had not given that preference.

If the Tribunal is satisfied that there is a preference transfer of property, movable or immovable, or any delivery of goods, payment, execution made, taken or done by or against a company within six months before making winding-up application, the Tribunal may order as it may think fit and may declare such transaction invalid and restore the position.

Transfers not in good faith to be void

Any transfer of property, movable or immovable, or any delivery of goods, made by a company, not being a transfer or delivery made in the ordinary course of its business or in favour of a purchaser or encumbrance in good faith and for valuable consideration, if made within a period of one year before the presentation of a petition for winding up by the Tribunal or the passing of a resolution for voluntary winding up of the company, shall be void against the Company Liquidator.

Certain transfers to be void

Any transfer or assignment by a company of all its properties or assets to trustees for the benefit of all its creditors shall be void.

Liabilities and rights of certain persons fraudulently preferred

Where a company is being wound up and anything made, taken, or done after the commencement of this Act is invalid under section 328 as a fraudulent preference of a person interested in property mortgaged or charged to secure the company's debt, then, without prejudice to any rights or liabilities arising, apart from this provision, the person preferred shall be subject to the same liabilities, and shall have the same rights, as if he had undertaken to be personally liable as a surety for the debt, to the extent of the mortgage or charge on the property or the value of his interest, whichever is less.

The value of the interest of the person shall be determined as at the date of the transaction constituting the fraudulent preference, as if the interest were free of all encumbrances other than those to which the mortgage or charge for the debt of the company was then subjected to.

CHAPTER 11

Social Corporate Responsibility (CSR)

Intersection of section 135's new provisions are indented to change the face of the Indian corporate business. Corporate Social Responsibility (CSR) is an idea that manages and integrates social and environmental concerns; it is based on a self-regulatory mechanism whereby a business monitors and ensures its active compliance with the spirit of the law. Corporate self-regulation is integrated into a the business model.

It is being considered that business activities intentionally or unintentionally affect the environment and also impact the social behaviour. 'Corporate social responsibility' is being used to cover legal and moral responsibility. The term itself denotes 'responsibility' which means self-mechanism towards social empowerment by a corporate.

Sometimes it is considered that the concept of CSR is inspired by the Gandhian philosophy of 'Trusteeship' which says business houses are looked upon as trustees of the resources they draw from society and thus are expected to return them manifold.

Section 2(c) The Companies (Corporate Social Responsibility Policy) Rules, 2014 came into effect from 1 April, 2014. 'Corporate Social Responsibility' means and includes but is not limited to:

(i) Projects or programmes relating to activities specified in Schedule VII to the Act; or

(ii) Projects or programmes relating to activities undertaken by the Board of Directors of a company (Board) in pursuance of the recommendations of the CSR Committee of the Board as per declared CSR Policy of the company, subject to the conditions that such a policy will cover subjects enumerated in Schedule VII of the Act.

Activities Which may be Included in Corporate Social Responsibility Policies

Analysis of the section reveals that it is flexible and provides the place of activities other than those defined in Schedule VII:

(i) eradicating extreme hunger and poverty;

(ii) promoting education;

(iii) promoting gender equality and empowering women;

(iv) reducing child mortality and improving maternal health;

(v) combatting human immunodeficiency virus, acquired immune deficiency syndrome, malaria, and other diseases;

(vi) ensuring environmental sustainability;

(vii) enhancing employment vocational skills;

(viii) social business projects;

(ix) contributing to the Prime Minister's National Relief Fund or any other fund set up by the Central Government or the State Governments for socio-economic development and relief and funds for the welfare of the Scheduled Castes the Scheduled Tribes, other backward classes, minorities, and women; and

(x) such other matters as may be prescribed.

Application of CSR

'Every company' in section 135 means the application of the section by all companies' which satisfy the following conditions:

(a) net worth of the company to be Rs 500 crore or more;

(b) turnover of the company to be Rs 1,000 crore or more;

(c) net profit of the company to be Rs 5 crore or more. Further as per the CSR Rules, the provisions of CSR are not only applicable to Indian companies, but also applicable to branch and project offices of a foreign company in India.

Implementation

Sub-section (2) of section 135 made the provision for the constitution of Corporate Social Responsibility Committee which executes the following functions:

(a) formulate and recommend to the Board, a Corporate Social Responsibility Policy which shall indicate the activities to be undertaken by the company as specified in Schedule VII;

(b) recommend the amount of expenditure to be incurred on the activities referred to in clause (a); and

(c) monitor the Corporate Social Responsibility Policy of the company from time to time.

Responsibility of Board of Director of Company

The board of the company takes into account the recommendations made by the Corporate Social Responsibility Committee, approves the Corporate Social Responsibility Policy for the company and discloses contents of the policy in its report and also places it on the company's website, and ensures that the activities that are included in Corporate Social Responsibility Policy of the company are undertaken by the company.

The Board of every company shall ensure that the company spends, in every financial year, at least 2 per cent of the average net profits of the company made during the three immediately preceding financial years, in pursuance of its Corporate Social Responsibility Policy.

The section also gives the mandate that the company shall give preference to the local area and areas around it where it operates, for spending the amount earmarked for Corporate Social Responsibility activities. If a company fails to spend such amount, the Board shall, in its report made under clause (o) of sub-section (3) of section 134, specify the reasons for not spending the amount.

CHAPTER 12

Company Secretary

- Meaning
- Appointment
- Statues
- Legal Position
- Status under Act
- Function
- Duties

MEANING

The dynamic corporate world redefined the role and scope of company secretary and considered it to be a principle officer in the company for legal affairs and compliance. Conventionally, Company Secretary was considered being a mere servant or clerk having no authority even to enter into a contract on behalf of the company, gradually he acquired some administrative authorities in the company, but certainly no managerial power.

A Company Secretary is considered to be the eyes and ears of the Board in the field of corporate governance being the expert in this field and in a true sense he is the natural conscience keeper for the corporate sector by ensuring and authenticating board processes and making sure that the company does the correct things, constantly.

To understand the meaning of Company Secretary, first we must understand the meaning of term 'Secretary' which denotes a person employed to write or transact business for a company or society. The Latin term for secretary is 'Secretarius' which means 'a confidential writer or notary'.

Sub-section which (24) of section 2 of the Companies Act, 2013 defines 'company secretary' or 'secretary'. A company secretary as defined in clause (c) of sub-section (1) of section 2 of the Company Secretaries Act, 1980 is appointed by a company to perform the functions of a company secretary under this Act; 'Company Secretary' means a person who is a member of the 'Institute'

After analysing the above-mentioned two definitions we come to the conclusion that a 'Company Secretary is one who is qualified to perform certain services under the Companies Act and who is admitted as a member to the Association of Company Secretaries of India, and in general a person who is employed to write or transact business for another person, society, company or a public body'.

Madras High Court in the case of P. Mahamani *v.* Tamil Nadu Magnesite Limited And (1993) 2 MLJ 634 held that:

Under Section 2(45) of the Companies Act, Secretary means a Company Secretary within the meaning of the Clause (c) of sub-section (1) of section 2 of the Company Secretaries Act, 1980 and includes any other individual possessing the prescribed qualifications and appointed to perform the duties which may be performed by a Secretary under this Act and any other ministerial or administrative duties. Clause 45(A) of section 2 of the Companies Act, 1956 reads that Secretary in whole time practice means a Secretary who shall be deemed to be in practice within the meaning of sub-section (2) of section 2 of the Companies Act and who is not in full time employment. Section 2(1)(c) of the Company Secretaries Act, 56 of 1980 defines a Company Secretary as a person who is a member of the Institute which, in turn, is defined in section 2(g) as the institute of Company Secretaries of India constituted under that Act.

Advisor to directors on corporate legislative and compliance matters.

Appointment of Company Secretary

The appointment of company secretary can be linked with the company's paid-up capital and, turnover according to Section 203 of Companies Act, 2013 and Section 8 of Companies (Appointment and Remuneration of Managerial Personnel) Rules, 2014.

Section 203 of Companies Act, 2013: 'Every company belonging to such class or classes of companies as may be prescribed shall have the following whole-time key managerial personnel'.

Section 8 of Companies (Appointment and Remuneration of Managerial Personnel) Rules, 2014: 'Every listed company and every other public company having a paid-up share capital of ten crore rupees or more shall have whole-time key managerial personnel.'

Timeline to Appoint Company Secretary

Time Period: As per Section 203(4), if Company doesn't not have Company Secretary before 01st April, 2014 and provision of Section 203 applicable on such company then such a company has to appoint a Company Secretary within 6 (Six) month till 30th September, 2014 (from 1st April, 2014).

Legal Position

Section 204 says every listed company and a company belonging to other class of companies as may be prescribed shall annex with its Board's report made in terms of sub-section (3) of section 134, a secretarial audit report, given by a Company Secretary in practice, in such form as may be prescribed.

The section made the mandatory duty of the company to give all assistance and facilities to the Company Secretary in practice, for auditing the secretarial and related records of the company.

Status under Act

Company secretary's new role: 'company secretary is not a luxury but a necessity'

In the new Companies Act, 2013, conceiving a comprehensive Corporate Governance model of the Company Secretary to signify his role by introducing the concept of Key Managerial Personnel. This has significantly elevated the new dimensions in terms of their role and responsibilities of company secretaries both in employment and in practice. He is not simply to make sure of compliance but also help the Management in taking a comprehensive view of all the issues that come up in a Company.

The new Companies Act, clarifies the position: 'Company Secretary is not a luxury but a necessity' Section 205 enunciates twofold functions of Company Secretary: one is to report to the Board about compliance with the provisions of this Act, the rules made thereunder, and other laws applicable to the company and second to ensure that the company complies with the applicable secretarial standards.

Sub-section (38) of section 2 of the Companies Act, 2013 defines Company Secretary as an 'expert' who has the power or authority to issue a certificate in pursuance of any law for the time being in force; and sub-section (51) of section 2 of the Companies Act, 2013 defines 'key managerial personnel'.

Functions

Section 205 defines the functions of a Company Secretary as:

(a) to report to the Board about compliance with the provisions of this Act, the rules made thereunder, and other laws applicable to the company;

(b) to ensure that the company complies with the applicable secretarial standards; ('secretarial standards' means secretarial standards issued by the Institute of Company Secretaries of India constituted under section 3 of the Company Secretaries Act, 1980 and approved by the Central Government.)

(c) to discharge such other duties as may be prescribed.

Duties of Company Secretary

Section 10 of Companies (Appointment and Remuneration of Managerial Personnel) Rules, 2014

The Company Secretary shall also discharge the following duties, namely:

(1) to provide to the directors of the company, collectively and individually, such guidance as they may require, with regard to their duties, responsibilities, and powers;

(2) to facilitate the convening of meetings and attend Board, committee, and general meetings and maintain the minutes of these meetings;

(3) to obtain approvals from the Board, general meeting, the government and such other authorities as required under the provisions of the Act;

(4) to represent before various regulators and other authorities under the Act in connection with discharge of various duties under the Act;

(5) to assist the Board in the conduct of the affairs of the company;

(6) to assist and advise the Board in ensuring good corporate governance and in complying with the corporate governance requirements and best practices;

(7) to discharge such other duties as have been specified under the Act or rules; and

(8) such other duties as may be assigned by the Board from time to time.

The Indian Contract Act, 1872

- Contract: Meaning and Essentials
- Competent to Enter into Contract
- Virus in an Agreement for Avoiding Agreement
- Void Agreements

CONTRACT: MEANING AND ESSENTIALS

Contract is the law of 'Obligations', which deals in 'Expectation' arising out of a specific transaction between the contracting parties. It confines preferance of 'Right to performance and cause of breaking the contract'.

Contract is the legal structure of a society. Every day we execute some contract, e.g., when we take an auto rickshaw we extend an offer to him to a particular destination. When he accepts our offer, the contract starts, though it is not in writing and but is not backed up by any statue, it is a form of contract, because it is an agreement which gives the rise of obligations. We can take many illustrations in our daily life, e.g., when we are going to a vegetable market, fruit market, for shopping, by metro or bus, insure our car or our house, and even buying milk are all governed by the law of contract in its different aspects. We experience and execute one or other contract(s) knowingly or unknowingly. If I say, 'Contract is the part of our daily life', it would not be wrong as it affects every person in one way or the other, as all of us enter into some kind of contract everyday.

These are very generic Illustrations of contracts, but what are the stipulations contained in the Indian Contract Act, 1872. In simple words, a contract is 'a rise to obligations which are recognized by law' in which there are certain qualifications attached to parties to contract, and conditions and specific events, etc.

In the modern sense it is the 'mature sense of commercial civilization', which enforces the obligation of individuals. The 'genesis of exact law of contract is enforceable promises'.

THE INDIAN CONTRACT ACT, 1872

The Indian Contract Act, 1872 is an Act which notifies and deals with the principles of the Law of Contract. This Act describes various steps in the construction of a contract, its performance, fundamental ingredients, and remedies in case of breach of contract, and also rules of limitation, qualification, and disqualification for contract.

The underlined idea is to give smooth functioning of society. Sections 10 and 11 of the Act exhibit the intention of the legislature by qualifying that all agreements are contracts. It means the law is ready to provide support to all agreements for becoming a contract, and all persons are capable to enter into a contract, certainly subject to specific qualifications. Thus, the Indian Contract Act is not per se for a special class of people, but as a whole for every one.

Initially, the Indian Contract Act was very diverse in nature but with the passage of time it has been refined and has branched out into separate laws like the Transfer of Property Act, the Sale of Goods Act, and the Specific Relief Act. If I say the history of contract is the history of civilization would be not be wrong.

Law Commission of India in its Thirteenth Report in Part I General states:

> 'The common law of England on which the Indian Contract Act is principally based had its roots in the real property law, which has been described by L.J. Denning, as being "devoid a moral concepts like mathematics", "Right and wrong". Says Denning L.J., did not enter into it nor the redress of grievances; only words and rules and logical dedications from them. In those early days land was the most important kind of property; and the common law lawyers were so absorbed in the land problems that they approached other problems in the same frame of mind. They looked for certainty, and gave justice a second place. In their hands, the law of Contracts and Torts tended to become as technical and rigid as the law of property.

Further, the report specified the intent of legislature to formulate the Indian Contract Act:

> as its Preamble says, the Act of 1872 does not profess to be a complete code dealing with the law relating to contracts. The legislature, while enacting this Act, did not intend to exhaustively codify the whole of the law of contract to be applied by the Courts in India or even any particular sub-division thereof.

It means the legislature wants to limit its application, but later on it has been extended according to the need of the society.

Essential of Contract

1. What is offer?
2. What is Acceptance?
3. Basic Requirements of a Promise and set of Promises?
4. What is Intention?
5. What is Information and Invitation?
6. Difference between Proposal and Intention
7. Difference between Proposal and Information

8. Difference between Proposal and Invitation
9. Difference between Offer and Acceptance
    (a) Price list
    (b) Menu chart
    (c) Tender
    (d) Quotation
    (e) Auction

PROCESS OF FORMATION OF CONTRACT

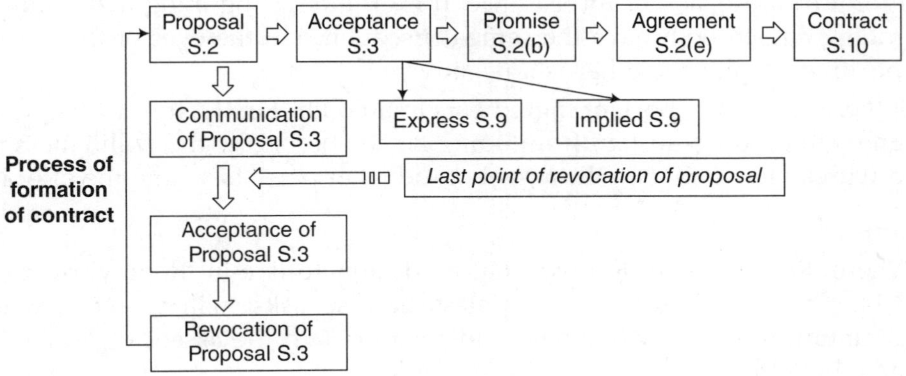

1. What is Offer?

1.1 Meaning of Offer (i.e., Proposal) Section 2(a)

Section 2(a) defines what is offer. The word **'Proposal'** is being used in the section which denotes the initialization of contract, it is the starting point of any contract, which in the later state becomes the Agreement, and with the force of Law it become the Contract. The section says, 'one person signifies to another' means for making the proposal or offer there must be two persons, one who makes or is interested to start the contract, the offer, or initialize to obtain another's willingness, to do or to refrain from doing anything.

(a) Meaning: An offer is a proposal by one person ([44]jus in personam), whereby one expresses his willingness to enter into a contractual obligation in return for a promise, act or forbearance

(b) Offer: The word 'Proposal' used in the 'The Indian Contract Act, 1872' while under the English law the word 'Offer' is used. A Proposal is the primary step in the construction of any contract between two parties or persons – one person to make the proposal and the other person to accept the same.

---

44. *jus in personam* means a 'right against or in respect of a specific person.' Thus, law of contract creates *jus in personam* and *not jus in rem*. A *jus in rem* means 'a right against or a thing'.

1.2 Starting point

Offer is the starting point, or the ignition for a contract. There is no ambiguity in the word 'proposal' and the word 'offer'; they mean one and the same thing and therefore are used interchangeably.

It initializes the construction of any contract, when one is desirous of a performance from the other, while expressing his desire, in the form of an offer or proposal.

In terms of Section 2(a) of the Act 'a person is said to make a proposal when he signifies to another his willingness to do or abstain from doing anything with a view to obtaining the assent of that other to such act or abstinence'. An offer is a proposal by one, whereby he exhibits his willingness to bind himself into a contractual obligation in return for a promise, act, or forbearance. It is an interesting thing that 'doing an act' and 'not doing an act' both have the same consequence in the eyes of the law, though one is a positive act and the other is a negative act.

Hence, there are two important ingredients to an offer. Firstly, it must be expressions of willingness to do or to abstain from doing an act. Secondly, the willingness must be expressed with a view to obtain the assent of the other party to whom the offer is made.

Illustrations

I. Where 'Ram' says to 'Roomy' that he desires to live-in 'Roomy' by the end of 2014. There is no offer made unless he also asks 'will you live with me?', communicating his willingness and act to obtain the assent of 'Roomy' in the same breadth.

II. Where 'X' offers to sell his vehicle to 'Y' he communicates his willingness to do an act. Through this proposal not only his willingness is being conveyed but also an intention to obtain the assent can be seen.

2. Analysis of Section

When **one person signifies** to **another** his **willingness to do** or **to abstain from doing anything**, with a view **to obtaining** the **assent** of that **other person** either **to such act** or **abstinence**, he is said to **make a proposal**.

Look at the words which are in bold and underlined

one person (One Person, a Living Person)

signifies (Indicates or initializes his desire not for all but for a specific person)

another (Not himself or herself but another living person, bilateral process)

willingness (His or her wish to bind another in legal obligations, voluntary)

to do (for an act of doing)

to abstain from (for an act of not doing anything)

doing anything	
to obtaining assent	(To take his consent, or obligation in return)
other person	(the same act as is being communicated)
to such act	
abstinence	(Desirous act for which offer _is being given)
to **make a proposal**	(Proposal complete)

The analysis of the above sections revealed the following points:

(a) **One person:** One person means one living person (it includes artificial person as well, a dead person cannot initiate the contractual proceedings).

(b) **Signifies:** Contract is a two-way process, in which one person indicates or initializes his desire not for all but for a specific person, for his like mind, and it is for a specific person not for all.

(c) **Another:** Contract is a bilateral proceeding, or a two-way communication, it can be initiated by one but completed only when that another, for which it has been signified gives his or her assent to it, in the same nature, same sense, and at the same time.

(d) **Willingness:** identifies the purpose of the contract, or the wish to bind another in legal obligations, for doing or abstaining from doing something. In its deep sense it relates to consideration, when one exhibits his or her desire to bind another in a particular act whether positive or negative, the other to react or give his or her assent thereto for some consideration, only.

(e) **to do:** means an act in reflection of one's desire to bind another for a particular act, the word 'to do' signifies for a positive act, the nature of this act is positive and which can be seen by an overt act only.

(f) **to abstain from doing anything:** while the word 'to abstain from' in nature is a negative act, in a particular sense it is not to reflect to an overt act, but put a bar on the other form to refrain themselves from not doing a particular act, it means not to act.

If we analyse both the words (in 'f' and 'g'), it is very clear that the contract is not confined only for a positive act, it means for doing any thing or an overt act, but contract can be made or initialized for not doing an act, it means not doing something in other words is also an act, but in negative sense.

(g) **to obtaining assent:** The fundamental question here is why the 'one is signifying that another'. The language of the section reveals that the one who is initializing the contract, desirous for a particular action or inaction from 'that another', but his desire or offer may come to an end (complete), only when the another gives his assent thereto, not otherwise. It means it is an action to take another's consent, or obligation in return.

(h) **to such act:** The contract subsists only when it received in the same name and same time as it communicated, the word 'to such act' reflects the same act as is being communicated.

(i) **abstinence:**

(j) **make a proposal:**

Section 2(a) foundation of Indian Contract Act

After analysing section 2(a), we can vehemently say that section 2(a), is the basic foundation of the Law of Contract, it comprises the holistic feature of ICA, as it reflects the basic nature of the law of contract, i.e., when the law of contract initialises, (as it is the bilateral proceedings) and under what circumstances (for the specific person only, not for all), for what object (for obtaining his assent means the volunteer assent without any external force) etc.

On the basis of above analysis of the section these are the following three observations, which make the foundation of any offer:

I. The one must be willing to do something.
II. He should be signified to the other person.
III. He should be made with a view to obtain the assent of that other.

Illustration

X says to Y, 'Will you buy my House for Rs. 500,000?'

X is making an offer to Y.

Mr. X Says to Ms. Y, 'Will you purchase my ice cream at Rs. 20?'

3. Object of the offer?

The object of the offer is to obtain the assent of the other person in two forms: first for a Positive Act (to do) or second in Prohibitions or Negative form (not to do). The analysis of the section reveals, i.e., to do or abstain from doing something. It is also pertinent to note, if some one only that expresses his intention, it does not amount to an Offer for the other. As an intention is an intrinsic desire, and does not constitute any overt act, while an offer results in an overt act by the opposite party (specific person).

Illustration

Z says to Y that he will give a car to any one who will marry his son.

It is the expression of an intention, not the offer.

4. Legal requirement for offer or proposal

4.1 An offer should be unambiguous, specific, absolute, and final.
It must not be ambiguous.

4.2 An offer must be communicated to the specific person for whom it initiated. If it has been communicated to the other person for which it was not initiated it is void or no offer.

4.3 With intent to or capable of making legal relationship between the parties.

I. The offer must be definite specific, complete and not unclear, unambiguous and certain.

Illustration:

Z offered to sell to W. 'a car'. The offer is uncertain as there is nothing to show what kind of car is intended to be sold.

II. Complete offer not in part– Counter offer

Illustration

M offered to sell his car to N for Rs. 3,000. N replied, 'I am ready to pay Rs. 2,000'. On M's refusal to sell at this price, N agreed to pay Rs. 3,000.

This is not the original offer per se but it becomes the counter offer.

III. Offer must be communicated to the specific person

The offer must be communicated to the specific person only; it is successful only when it is communicated to the person for whom it is made. Unless an offer is communicated, there is no recognition and no agreement.

An approval of an offer, in unawareness of the offer it can never be treated as acceptance and does not create any right on the acceptor.

Case law

Gauri Dutta *v.* Lalman Shukla [Lalman Shukla *v.* Gauri Datt (1913) All LJ 489]

Gauri Dutta's nephew has absconded from his home. He sent his servant Lalman Shukla to trace his missing nephew. When her servant had left, then Gauri Dautta announced that anybody who discovered the missing boy would be given a reward of Rs. 500. The servant discovered the missing boy without knowing the reward. When the servant came to know about the reward, he brought an action against Gauri Dutta to recover the same. But his action failed.

It was held that the servant was not entitled to the reward because the offer given by Gauri Dutta was not accepted by her servant.

IV. Offer must be communicated in express words

Offer can be implied by action or expressed but must be communicated in expressed words.

Illustration

- A offers his to sell a pen to B for Rs. 10. It is an express offer.
- A metro going on a definite route from x to y station. This is an implied offer on the part of the owners of the bus to carry passengers at the scheduled fares for the various stages.

V Offer with the object of creating legal relations

An offer without the intention for creating a legal relationship has no value—if a social invite, even if it is accepted does not create a legal relationship because it is not so intended to create a legal relationship.

VI Offer to public at large

In Carilill (*v.*) Carbolic Ball Company, held that:

To increase its sale a company advertised that a reward of Rs.100 would be given to any person who would suffer from influenza after using the medicine (smoke balls) made by the company according to the printed directions.

Mrs Carlill purchased and used the medicine according to the printed instructions of the company but suffered from influenza, she filed a suit to recover the reward of Rs. 100.

The court held that there was a contract as she had accepted a general offer by using the medicine in the prescribed manner and as such was entitled to recover the reward from the company.

VII Definite standing, or open and continuous offer

An offer which remains open for approval over a period of time is known as standing, open, or continuous offer. For example, tender for providing food grain is a kind of standing offer.

Illustration

A offers to B for delivering a weekly magazine. It is a standing or continuous offer.

a. Clear Definite: It is the first and important qualification for an offer that it should be clear and definite, it should not be vague and incomplete. It means the person who is making the offer must communicate his proposal in clear and definite words.

Illustration

A promises to pay the monthly rent to B in the near future.

It is too vague (there is no monthly rent defined nor is it defined what would be the rent).

A promises to pay Rs.100 monthly rent to B from 1, May 2014.

This is not only clear but also definite.

b. Offer must be to a specific person only: The offer is completed only when it has been communicated to a specific person only. Therefore, an offer accepted without the knowledge to whom it was made does not confer any legal rights on the other person for whom it was made. Because only when an offer is made to a specific person then only he can provide his assent to do or abstain from doing anything.

   Constituent elements of an offer:

   - Minimum two parties.
   - Offer must be made to carry legal obligations.
   - Offer must be communicated to the other person.
   - Offer must show the willingness of who makes the offer. Mere telling the plan is not offer.
   - Offer must be made with a view to obtaining the assent of the other person.
   - Offer must be for an act to do or to refrain from doing anything.

5. Mode of communication of an offer

There are two modes of communicating any offer, i.e., express or implied, which includes but is not limited to only by word of mouth, or by advertisement, or by exhibiting a sign or gesture, or by using any other medium of announcement, or even by conduct, and it is not exhaustive that it should always be in writing, while the language of section 3 says that communication is completed only when it comes to the knowledge of the person to whom it is made.

And the section further defines the circumstances under which the communication is deemed to be completed which are:

- as against the proposer, when it is put in a course of transmission to him so as to be out of the power of the acceptor;
- as against the acceptor, when it comes to the knowledge of the proposer;
- The communication of a revocation is complete;
- as against the person who makes it, when it is put into a course of transmission to the person to whom it is made, so as to be out of the power of the person who makes it; as against the person to whom it is made, when it comes to his knowledge.

Illustrations

(a) 'A' proposes, by letter, to sell a house to 'B' at a certain price.
The communication of the proposal is complete when 'B' receives the letter.

(b) 'B' accepts 'A's proposal by a letter sent by post.
The communication of the acceptance is complete, as against 'A' when the letter is posted; as against 'B', when the letter is received by 'A'.

(c) 'A' revokes his proposal by telegram.
The revocation is complete as against 'A' when the telegram is despatched. It is complete as against 'B' when 'B' receives it.
'B' revokes his acceptance by telegram. 'B's revocation is complete as against B when the telegram is despatched, and as against 'A' when it reaches him.

6. *Type of offer*

- Express offer
- Implied offer
- Specific offer
- General offer
- Cross offer
- Counter offer
- Standing, open, and continuous offer

6.1 Specific offer

It is a specific offer when made to a named person. Other than general offer, such a type of offer is made for a particular person.

For example,

'A' makes on offer to 'B' to sell a car owned by 'B' for 22 lakhs to him.

6.2 General Offer/for Public at large (Carlill v. Carbolic Smoke Ball)

First time it is held, those offers which are not communicated to a specific person (as section 2(a), qualify for a specific person only), but to a public at large. It is beyond any time limit, and it remains in force till it is withdrawn, or it can be accepted by anyone at any time.

When the offer is made generally to public at large or is open to all, it is said to be a general offer.

For Example:

An advertisement appears in the newspaper that whosoever finds 'A's missing son would be entitled for an award of Rs. 50,000.

Allahabad HC applied the same provision to the case of Har Bhajan Lal *v.* Harcharan Lal even though the terms of a general offer were not complied with substantially.

A young boy ran away from his father's home. The father circulated a pamphlet, offering a reward. The paper said:

'Anybody who finds the boy and brings him home will get Rs. 500.'

The plaintiff was at Dharmashala railway station, where he happened to see a boy. He overheard a conversation partly in this regard and realized that the boy was the missing boy. He promptly took the boy to the Railway Police Station and sent a telegram to the boy's father that he had found his son. The father denied any obligation towards him.

It was held by the Court that the handbill was an offer open to the whole world and capable of acceptance by any person who fulfilled the condition, and that the plaintiff substantially performed the condition and was entitled to the amount offered.

Carlill *v.* Carbolic Smoke Ball & Co. is a landmark case on general offer.

A company offered by advertisement £ 100 to anyone who would catch influenza, cold, or any such disease after having used the smoke ball according to printed directions. It was said in the same advertisement that £ 1,000 was deposited and the Alliance Bank in this regard showing their sincerity in the matter. Mrs. Carlill used the smoke balls according to the directions but she contracted influenza. The company did not fulfil its promise of reward towards her stating the following reasons:

- that there was no intention to enter into legal relations as it was simply a 'puffy' advertisement;
- that the offer was not made to any one person in particular; and
- that the plaintiff had not communicated her intention to accept.

L.J. Bowen stated the statement was not mere puff, since the company had lodged £ 1,000 with the bank for the purpose. His Lordship refuted the company's argument that an offer could not be made to the world at large.

He observed: 'Why should not an offer be made to all the world which is to ripen into a contract with an offer be made to all the world which is to ripen into a contract with anybody who comes forward and performs the conditions? It is an offer to become liable to anyone who, before it is retracted, performs the condition, and although the offer is made to the world, the contract is made with that limited portion of the public who come forward and perform the condition on the faith of the advertisement.'

She was held entitled to recover the promised reward.

Key Point:

- An offer can be made to the whole world but it ripens into a contract only when a specific person comes forward and accepts it or performs the conditions of the offer.

The principle laid down in this case has been applied by various HCs in various similar cases. The SC in M/s Bhagwati Prasad Pawan Kumar *v.* Union of India[45] observed that it is well settled that an offer may be accepted by conduct.

6.3 General Offer of Continuing Nature

Any general offer is of continuing nature when it is open for acceptance by any number of persons until it is withdrawn.

45. Appeal (civil) 150-151 of 2001

Illustrations

1. For T.V. Show "KAUN BANEGA KORORPATI (KBC), every time a contract would result with the person whosoever sits in the hot seat, answer the questions correctly, subject to their rules and regulations. The producers are under an obligation to pay the promised amount as and when won.
2. In Carlill's case, any number of persons can come forward, consume the smoke balls as per prescription and still catch influenza would be entitled for the reward.
3. In Gauri Dutt's and Harbhajan's Case (as above), the offer stands closed, the moment missing boy is traced by the first person.

Such offers are also called standing or pen offers, e.g., as and when on the basis of a tender, order is placed, a binding contract results. Such an offer may be withdrawn or revoked before the order is placed.

Cross offers

When the offers made by two parties to each other containing almost similar terms of bargain cross each other being communicated, these may be called cross offers. Thus, if the offer of none of the parties was ever accepted by the other, no contract could ever result.

2. What is Acceptance?

Section 2(b) of the Contract Act: When a person to whom the proposal is made signifies his assent thereto, the proposal is said to be accepted. A proposal, when accepted becomes a promise.

As we have seen an offer is the ignition point, the reflection of that ignition is the acceptance of that another from whom the offer is made. In fact, contract comes into existence from the acceptance of an offer, it is an act of assenting by the offeree to an offer.

The offeree is said to have given his acceptance when he gives his assent to the proposal, it may be express or implied. It is express when the acceptance has been signified either in writing, or by word of mouth, or by performance of some required act.

In plain words, a proposal becomes a promise only when it is accepted by the other party to whom the proposal is made. For example:

If A is interested in going in a metro, he has to buy the ticket for an appropriate amount. This is an offer. Issuance of ticket to him is acceptance of the offer.

It is also a established law unless any offer is accepted by the other for that it is made, it creates no legal rights or duties.

Thus, the consent given to the proposal is acceptance.

Anson rightly defined the acceptance as '*Acceptance is to offer what a lighted match is to a train of gunpowder*'. An offer, as such, creates no legal rights or duties unless it has been accepted. Hence, it is acceptance that converts an offer into a contract.

A proposal becomes a promise only after it is accepted by the other party to whom the proposal is made.

Example:

If A is willing to go to watch a football match, he goes to the ticket window and makes the payment of the appropriate amount, it is an offer. Issuance of ticket to him is acceptance of the offer.

Fundamentals of a valid acceptance

To be a valid acceptance, the following qualification are required

1. Communication: Acceptance should be communicated by the offerree to the offeror.

   Illustration

   The manager of Railway Company got a draft agreement linking it to the provision of coal. The manager marked the DD with the words 'Approved' and placed the same in the drawer of his desk and forgot all about it.

   Held, there was no contract between the parties as the acceptance was not communicated.
2. Absolute and unqualified: It should be absolute and unqualified.
3. Mode of communication should be reasonable: It should be made in some usual and reasonable manner unless prescribed.
4. Within the validity of offer: It should be made while the offer is still subsisting.
5. If there is deviation in communication of an acceptance of offer, the offeror may refuse such acceptance by conveyance notice within reasonable time. If the offeror doesn't send a notice of refusal, he has not accepted the offer.

   Example:

   X offers Y by saying that the acceptance be given by telegram. Y sends his acceptance by normal post. It is a legitimate acceptance unless A disputes the acceptance in the prescribed manner.
6. Acceptance of offer must be made by offeror:

   Illustration:

   X applies in a school for the post of a teacher. He was chosen by the authority but the result was not communicated to him. However, someone in his personal capacity informed him about the selection. Afterwards, the appointing authority cancelled its decision.

   X sued the school for breach of contract. The Court discarded the X's action and held that there was no notice of acceptance. 'Information by an unauthorized person is as insufficient as overhearing from behind the door.'

Communication of acceptance

It is an established principle that a contract is a two-way communication, centric to this principle. It is not possible to have acceptance without communication. Look at the definition of acceptance under section 2(b) of the Act. It evidently establishes that for an acceptance to be binding it must be communicated. The word 'signifies' exhibits that willingness and it must be brought to the notice of the other for whom the offer was made. The mere purpose of meeting of minds is not adequate. Some overt act or external manifestation of the intent by any of the following is a must:

- Speech
- Writing or
- Other act

Case law

Powell *v.* Lee: One Mr. Powell applied for a job as headmaster and the school managers decided to appoint him. One of them, acting without authority, told Powell that he had been accepted. Later the managers decided to appoint someone else. Then Powell brought an action alleging that by breach of the contract to employ him he had suffered damages in loss of salary.

The court held that acceptance must be communicated to offeree by the offeror himself or an authorized agent. 'Even if the offerree has his mind to a final acceptance, the agreement is yet not complete. There must be an external manifestation of assent, some words spoken or act done by the offeror or by his authorized agent which the law can regard as the communication of the acceptance to the offeror.'

Ratio

Acceptance must be communicated to the offeree or its authorized agent, not otherwise.

General rule of communication of acceptance

The general rule of acceptance is it should be communicated in the same mode in which the offer is made, or if any other particular way it is prescribed. If it has not been prescribed then a reasonable and proper mode should be adopted under that circumstance.

The mode of acceptance could be written, verbal, telex, fax, telegram, email, cell phones, SMS, internet, and any other electronic medium.

Communication to stranger

Analysis of sections 2(a) and 2(b) attract our attention on the words 'signifies' and 'thereto' means one makes the offer to a particular person, and that particular person has a right to respond to that offer by either accepting or rejecting thereto, not any one else or any stranger. Here we have to remember that an authorized person can also make the acceptance on behalf of that particular person.

The communication of acceptance to a stranger is not a legitimate communication as the same should be made to the offeree himself or his agent. Neither the offeror can impose an obligation of refusal upon the other party nor shall the silence of the offeree be deemed consent. Acceptance may be inferred from the conduct of the parties.

Case law

Brogden *v.* Metropolitan Railway Co., one Mr. Brogden who was the chief of partnership of three, had supplied coal for a number of years to Metropolitan Railway Co. Brogden then suggested that a formal contract should be in place between them for a longer term of coal supply.

After a long negotiation on both sides, Metropolitan's agents drew up some terms of agreement and sent them to Brogden. Brogden wrote in some parts which had been left blank and added an arbitrator who would decide in case any dispute arose. He wrote 'approved' at the end and sent back the agreement documents. Metropolitan's agent filed the documents and did nothing more. After that, both parties acted according to the agreement document's terms. But then a dispute arose, and Brogden argued that no formal contract had actually been established.

The House of Lords held that 'a contract had arisen by conduct and Brogden had been in clear breach, so he must be liable. The word "approved" on the document with Brogden's name was binding on all the partners, since Brogden was the chief partner, even though the standard signature of "B. & Sons" was not used. A mere mental assent to the agreement's terms would not have been enough, but having acted on the terms made it so'.

Ratio: A mere mental assent to the agreement's terms would not have been enough, but having acted on the terms made it so.

3. Basic Requirements of a Promise and Set of Promises?

What is Promise?

When we think about promise, there are number of words that come to our mind to give the meaning of it, and the most relevant ones are:

(a) Commitment
(b) Declaration
(c) Assurance

When we analyse these words in the light of the Indian Contract Act, we come to know that a promise is a commitment by someone for doing or refraining to do anything, in reference to an offer or acceptance, or an assurance or a declaration for an offer or acceptance thereto.

The placement of section 2(b) which defines the promise is also very important as the definition of promise which immediately comes after offer and acceptance means it is synchronzed with the above two, so we can trace the journey of a promise as given below.

The above equation is evident by Section 2(b) of the Contract Act—a proposal when accepted becomes a promise.

The latter states that promise is an agreement, which is binding in nature, if other qualifications attached to it, as mentioned in section 2(e).

Section 2(e): Every promise and every set of promises, forming the consideration for each other, is an agreement

If we further analyse the equation, an agreement itself denotes consensus, and consensus cannot be alone. There are more than two persons to agree on a common purpose. Thus, agreement refers to a situation where meeting of minds is that common objective.

The word 'promise' raises the harmony of obligations one for another which commonly is a link of consideration for each other. After inspecting the section we determine that an obligation for reciprocal compensation is the seed of agreement.

If we think about Anson's view as 'A contract is an agreement enforceable at law, made between two or more persons, by whom rights are acquired by one or more to acts or forbearances on the part of the other or others', then rights can be acquired after enforceability of law? May be not, as mutual return after consensus can give rise to obligations for each other, but in case of a dispute it cannot exist as the energy (i.e., law) which runs this medium is not available. That is why Anson started his view with 'agreement enforceable at law is only contract'.

It is also an interesting fact that the section uses the word 'promise'. It has its importance as proposal that has been accepted becomes a promise, which means that promise is the 'plugging' of the 'common objective' of both the parties who signify their intent to bind themselves for reciprocal compensation.

Another important word in the section is 'forming' which is also a significant word here as it speaks of the binding obligations for each of the parties for the desired positive or negative act.

It is also a reality that there may be situations arise between parties. It is also important there that it is not important that there may be only one obligation, but the set of promises allows the parties to bind themselves to more than one obligation, positive or negative.

The meeting of the minds is called *consensus-ad-idem*, i.e., consent to the matter.

4. What is Intention?

No where intention is defined in the Indian Contract Act, 1872. But the offer is initiated with the intention of the offeror. However, section 2(a) defines a similar word of intention which is 'willingness'. The proposal must be made with willingness to do or refrain from doing anything. Willingness shows that intention to be bound by the proposal when accepted is an fundamental part of the concept of agreement. The party who offers must recognize the legal consequences of the offer. An offer or its acceptance should be made with the intention of creating legal relations. The test of intention is certainly objective, not subjective. The intention of the parties is naturally to know the terms of the agreement and the surrounding circumstances.

'Intention is the primary requisite of a valid offer, which later turns into an agreement, and creates legal relations between the parties.'

Case law

Balfour *v.* Balfour: W and H were husband and wife. H was employed in Sri Lanka. Both went to England for leave. There W became ill and was compelled to stay in England. After completion of his leave H was to go to Sri Lanka. Before going to Sri Lanka H promised to W to send 30 Pounds per month. For initial few months he did so but after that he stopped sending the money. W went to court for the probable expense of maintenance.

Judgment: The court rejected the claim.

Principle: First, it is not an agreement when two parties agree to take a walk together or where there is an offer and acceptance of hospitality.

Second, the parties were not aware that there will be any be legal consequences.

Basic foundation of contract

An offer should be made with an intention to create a legal relationship so as to bind another party. As we consider mens rea a basic element in criminal law, likewise I would consider 'intention to contract' as if the founding pillar or rather basic element in contract law or raising a contractual obligation to bind another party.

Contract law eliminates intention. Once the offer is accepted whether you had the intention or not. Accepting an offer provides qualifying other requisite elements of contract law. Make the contract. What the law requires is that the parties must intend legal consequences.

But there is no provision in the Indian Contract Act to express that an offer or its acceptance should be made with the intention of creating a legal relation while it is an established principle in English law. There are many promises that law does not identify as a contract or those are not enforceable in the court of law.

For example, a promise to go for an outing or lunch with a friend or family. The reason is that there has never been an intention to create a legal relationship in such situations but it does not mean that there can never be a valid contract in family or social matters.

Case law

Intention in family and social relations

In Balfour *v.* Balfour the same is observed: The husband was employed in a government job in Ceylon. He went to England with his wife during vacations. The wife was not in a position to travel back to Ceylon because of certain health issues. The husband promised to pay £30 per month to her towards maintenance for the period she had to live apart. The husband failed to pay the promised amount. She sued him for not fulfilling his promise.

The court held: 'There was no intention to create legal relationship when the husband made that promise and hence he could not be held to be liable.'

> L.J. Atkin observed: 'It is necessary to remember that there are agreements between parties which do not result in contracts within the meaning of that term in our law. The ordinary example is where two parties agree to take a walk together or where there is an offer and an acceptance of hospitality. Nobody would suggest in ordinary circumstances that those agreements result in what we know as a contract, one of the most usual forms of agreements which does not constitute a contract appears to me to be the arrangements which are made between husband and wife.....To my mind those agreements or many of them, do not result in contracts at all...even though there may be what as between other parties would constitute consideration.....They are not contracts because the parties did not intend that they should be attended by legal consequences.

But it does not mean the element of intention in contract law becomes irrelevant; there are certain example which establish that it is an important part, like **Price List, Menu chart, Tender, Quotation, Auction,** which certainly make intention relevant.

L.J. Danckwerts in Jones *v.* Padavatton

In this case one Mrs. Jones lived in Trinidad. Her daughter, a divorcee lady with a baby boy, lived in Washington and was employed with the Indian Embassy there. Mrs. Jones persuaded her daughter to leave her job in Washington and study in England to become a Barrister. Mrs. Jones offered to pay a monthly allowance to her during her studies for the bar in England.

Case law

In Commissioner of Wealth-Tax, ... *v.* Abdul Hussain Mulla Muhammad Ali , (1988)3 SCC 562,569 Hon'ble Supreme Court of India, through the light on Intention in Contract:

'An agreement, even though it is supported by consideration, is not binding as a contract if it was made without any intention of creating legal relations. Of course, in the case of ordinary commercial transactions it is not normally necessary to prove that the parties in fact intended to create legal relations.'

Further it has been observed,

"..... Now it is quite possible for parties to come to an agreement by accepting a proposal with the result that the agreement concluded does not give rise to legal relations. The reason of this is that the parties do not intend that their agreement shall give rise to legal relations. This intention may be implied from the subject matter of the agreement, but it may also be expressed by the parties. In social and family relations such an intention is readily implied, while in business matters the opposite result would ordinarily follow ...."

'... To create a contract there must be a common intention of the parties to enter into legal obligations, mutually communicated expressly or impliedly.'

Onus of Proving Intention in Contract: '..... The onus of proving that there was no such intention is on the party who asserts that no legal effect is intended, and the onus is a heavy one. Where such evidence is adduced, the Courts normally apply an objective test.'

In Balfour v. Balfour, [1919] 2 KB 571 ....."

...Such an intention ordinarily will be inferred when parties enter into an agreement which in other respects conforms to the rules of law as to the formation of contracts. It may be negative impliedly by the nature of the agreed promise or promises, as in the case of offer and acceptance of hospitality, or of some agreements made in the course of family life between members of a family".

In Edwards v. Skyways, [1964] 1 WLR 340 at 355 J. Megaw said:

In the present case, the subject matter of the agreement is business relations, not social or domestic matters. There was a meeting of minds—an intention to agree. There was, admittedly, consideration for the company's promise. I accept the propositions of counsel for the plaintiff that in a case of this nature the onus is on the party who asserts that no legal effect was intended, and the onus is a heavy one.

Intention is the third element under contract law

That in addition to the existence of an agreement and the presence of consideration there is also a third contractual element in the form of intention of the parties to create legal relations.

Test of contractual intention

The examination of contractual intention is forever objective and not subjective. In practical test is 'what a reasonable person would believe under that situation and not what the parties had in minds'.

VENKATACHALIAH J. had referred to chitty on contract in this case and held that:

'... the presumption is that legal obligations are intended. The onus is on the parties asserting the absence of legal relations and the test is not subjective, but is an objective one.'

Case law

In Banwari Lal *v.* Sukh Darshan Dayal, Supreme Court observed:

'Microphones have not yet acquired notoriety as carriers of binding representations. Promises held out over loudspeakers are often claptraps of politics. In the instant case, the announcement was, if at all, a puffing up of property put up for sale'.

Invitation to offer

In general, invitation to treat is an offer to receive or invite offers.

Let's take an example of any advertisement regarding used bike sale or to let the house can't bind the parties making such offers with everyone who responds.

It means when a party, without expressing his final willingness, proposes certain terms on which he is willing to negotiate, he is said to have invited the other party to make an offer on those terms.

Following are the grilling examples of invitation to offer:

- Catalogue of prices
- Announcement to hold auction
- Display of goods with price tags in a shop
- Railway time-table
- Invitation/advertisement to make tenders.

Case laws

In New India Assurance Co. Ltd *v.* Raghvir Singh Narang & Anr.

Special Voluntary Retirement Package (SVRP) (Rationalization of Pay Scales and other Conditions of Service of Development Staff) Amendment Scheme, 2003 was offered as a special option to the Development Officers (D.O.) of the Appellant, i.e., New Indian Assurance Co. The said option was to be exercised within 60 days from commencement of the said scheme. One of the clauses of SVRP stated that once option is made, the Officer cannot withdraw. The Co. had the absolute discretion to accept or reject their request.

Mr. Raghuvir Singh, D.O. opted for SVRP on 3.3.2003. Later, he requested the Co. either to extend the time for exercising the option and if not, his option should be treated as withdrawn as till 31.3.2003. There was no communication from the side of the Co. regarding acceptance of the VR. On 1.4.2003, he was relieved from the service since his VR was accepted.

He filed a writ petition in M.P. High Court seeking a direction to the Co. to reinstate him. The HC allowed the writ following the judgment of the Apex Court in Bank of India *v.* O.P. Swarankar case. This order of the HC was challenged before SC.

It was held that 'Since, SVRP is statutory in nature, so it shall have effect and not Section 5 of the Contract Act. Thus, the provisions of SVRP shall prevail over Contract Law. So, employee cannot withdraw once opted.'

Mcpherson *v.* Appana, Supreme Court of India applied the same principle, where purchase of a lodge was the issue.

The plaintiff made an offer to an agent of the owner to buy defendant's lodge for Rs. 6000 and also mentioned that he was ready to forward any higher price if found reasonable. The agent replied: 'Won't accept less than rupees 10,000.' The plaintiff accepted the same but the defendants refused to sell. A suit of specific performance was brought against the defendants.

It was held that 'there was no concluded contract and that it was merely inviting offers from the side of the plaintiff. The defendants never assented to their offer to buy at Rs. 10,000.'

In Badri Prasad *v.* State of Madhya Pradesh

The divisional Forest Officer wrote to the plaintiff:

'Kindly inform whether you are ready to pay further Rs. 17,000 for the contract of big trees... Which (contract) is under dispute at present?

The contract can be given to you on this compromise only... On receipt of your reply the State Govt. will be informed.'

In reply to the above letter the plaintiff wrote back:

'I am ready to pay Rs. 17,000 provided my claim to have the refund of Rs. 17,000 already paid, from the owner of the village or any other relief consequential to the judgment of that case remains unaffected...'

The Supreme Court held that

> by those letters no contract had been concluded between the plaintiff and the Government. The letter from the Divisional Forest Officer seemed to be merely invitation to offer rather than offer. The letter in reply from the plaintiff was an offer. Further, even if the letter from the Divisional Forest Officer to the plaintiff is treated as an offer, there is no unconditional acceptance from the plaintiff and as such there is no contract in any case.

Harvey *v.* Facey is a established example of invitation to offer where sale of a piece of land was the issue.

The plaintiffs wrote in a telegraph to the defendants:

'Will you sell us Bumper Hall Pen? Telegraph lowest cash price.'

The defendants replied by telegram that stated: 'Lowest price for Bumper Hall Pen, $ 900.' The plaintiffs sent their next telegram stating: 'We agree to buy Bumper Hall Pen 900 asked by you.'

The defendants refused to sell the plot of land at that price later and were sued by the plaintiffs. The plaintiffs contended that by quoting their minimum price in response to the inquiry the defendants had made an offer to sell at that price.

But the Lordships pointed out that the plaintiffs had asked following two questions in their first telegram:

1. their willingness to sell; and
2. the lowest price

The defendants answered only the second and quoted the prices. They never signified their intention to sell. The last telegram of the plaintiffs was an offer to buy but that was never accepted by the defendants. Thus, the defendants reserved their answer as to the willingness to sell, no offer was made.

It was held that 'mere statement of the lowest price at which the vendor would sell contained no implied contract to sell at that price to the person making the inquiry.'

In Bank of India *v.* O.P. Swarankar etc., the nationalized banks with a view to reduce their staff, announced Voluntary Retirement Scheme (VRS).

The SC held that: 'VRS floated by the bank is merely an invitation to treat and not a proposal or offer. In response to the said scheme, the applications filed by the Bank employees constitute on offer. Since the Bank has the power to amend or rescind as well as to accept or reject such applications, it couldn't be termed as an offer.'

In Pharmaceutical Society of Great Britain *v.* Boots Cash Chemists Ltd. It was held that: 'if an intending buyer was willing to purchase the goods at a price mentioned on the tag, he could make an offer to buy the goods. The final decision to accept or reject the offer was that of the shopkeeper. The contract would arise only when the offer was accepted. No customer can force the shopkeeper to sell the goods at the price mentioned on the tag.'

Display of articles

Display of articles on self-service' basis was not an offer but was merely an invitation to treat. When the customer selected an article and brought the same to the cash desk that amounted to an offer to buy the goods. The defendants were, therefore, free to 'accept or reject the offer.'

Nature of offer and Invitation to offer

Offer is a Reactive Process: An offer is a reactive process, once it is ignited, a negative or assertive process comes in response. Let me put it in a more simple way:

When one makes an offer the other party accepts it or rejects it in reaction, it starts as a linear direction and ends in a U turn. It means it is a former process and acceptance is a latter one, but there are situations when to get it initiated we make an offer but actually it is not an offer but an invitation to offer, and by this process we change its nature from linear to U turn.

Invitation to offer is the situation which creates the conditions for offer.

Offer and Acceptance is the Reactive Process

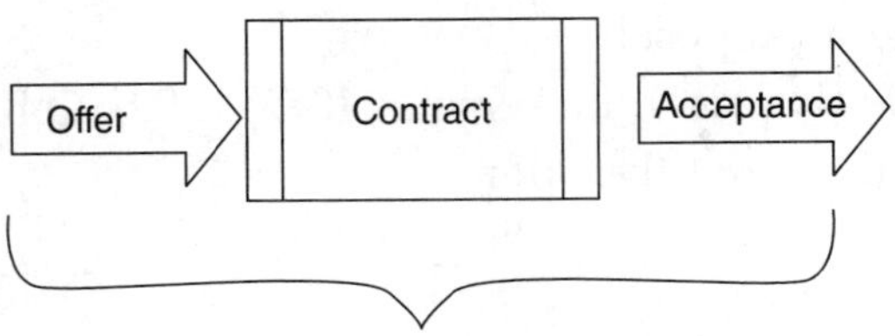

Reactive process

We have read Newton's Laws of Motion in school, which says every action has a reaction; the same thing applies to the Law of Contract, as one signifies to the 'another' to do or to restrain from doing anything (action), its response (reaction) to the other to either accept it or reject it, and that reaction if affirmative, binds the other for a particular act.

It is also a law of physics that through action and reaction emerges a new product, likewise offer and acceptance, results in obligations and liabilities.

Invitation to offer is a reverse process

But there is another situation when it seems that an offer is made by one but actually it is not an offer but an invitation to offer, it is the reverse process in Law of Contract.

Let's see the figure below:

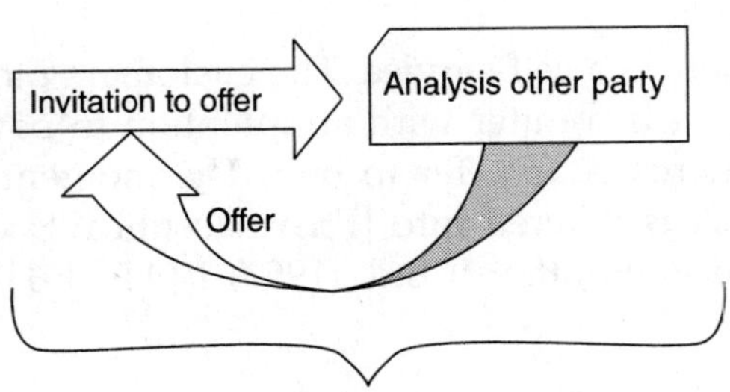

Reverse process

It means a person may create a statement without any intention of creating a binding obligation, which is called a mere declaration of intention but not a proposal.

Examples are many such as Price List, Menu chart, Tender, Quotation, Auction, etc.

Auction

Illustrations:

1. An auctioneer, A advertised that a sale of office cars would take place at an XYZ place. B travelled down about 50 km to join the sale but found the cars were reserved from the sale. B sued the auctioneer for his loss of time and expenses.
2. An auctioneer, at the time of auction, invites offers from the would-be-bidders. He is not making a proposal.

Held: A was not liable [Harris v. Lickerson. (1875) L.R.S. Q.B. 286.]

Ratio: It was an invitation, not the offer.

Prospectus

Illustrations:

3. An offer must be different from an invitation to offer. A prospectus issued by a university for admission to various courses is not an offer. It is only an invitation to offer. A potential student by filling up a purpose form attached to the prospectus is making the offer.

Price list

Illustration:

4. N's display of goods with a price tag on it in a shop window is constructed as an invitation to offer and not an offer to sell. Or it is information about the price of those particular goods.

Menu chart

Illustration

5. In a restaurant, there is a self-service. The customers picking up food items and takes them to the cash counter with an intention to pay. The customer's act in picking up food items is an offer to buy. The moment the cashier accepts the payment a contract is entered into [Pharmaceutical Society of Great Britain v. Boots Cash Chemists (Southern) Ltd. (1953) 1 Q.B. 401].

Quotation

Illustration

6. Likewise, calling the quotation or tender by a company for appointing a water vendor is a mere invitation to offer, not the offer.

The above examples evidently prove that an offer is the final expression of willingness by the offeror to be bound by his offer. While a party, without indicating his ultimate willingness, proposes certain terms on which he is willing to negotiate, he does not make an offer, he only invites the other party to make an offer on purposed terms. This is the basic difference between an offer and an invitation to offer.

Case law

In Harvey *v.* Facie, we find an interesting picture:

A, sends a telegram to B, 'Will you sell us Bumper Hall Pen? Telegraph lowest cash price.'

B replied also by a telegram, 'Lowest price for Bumper Hall Pen £ 900'.

A immediately sends their last telegram stating: 'We agree to buy Bumper Hall Pen for £900 asked by you.'

But B refused to sell the plot of land (Bumper Hall Pen) at that price. A argues that by quoting their minimum price in response to the inquiry, B had made an offer to sell at that price.

It was held that the Judicial Committee rejected A's arguments, by saying that

> In the first telegram, A had asked two questions, first as to the willingness to sell and second, as to the lowest price. They reserved their answer as to the willingness to sell. Thus, they had made no offer. The last telegram of A was an offer to buy, but that was never accepted by B. 5. The offer must be communicated to the offeree. An offer must be communicated to the offeree before it can be accepted. This is true of specific as well as general offer.

Tender

Illustration:

A tender is an offer as it is in response to an invitation to offer. Tenders normally start where, for example, a company invites offers to supply food items. The persons filling up the tenders are giving offers.

Tenders can be classified generally in two categories:

1. specific or definite; where the offer is to supply a definite quantity of goods, or
2. standing or general; where the offer is to supply items occasionally or according to the requirement of tenderee.

Comparison between offer and invitation to offer

Basis	Offer	Invitation to offer
Meaning	One is willing to bind the other in contract by making the offer.	Invites other to make an offer.
Promptness	Shows his readiness to enter into a contract, it is called an offer.	Person invites offer to make an offer to him.
Purpose	Intended to bind other in a legal obligation with the purpose of entering contract.	Intended to invite the proposal and negotiation, promptly not intended to bind other in a legal obligation. Results in offer.
Results	Raises legal obligation instantly; compared to invitation to offer.	Does not raise a legal obligation instantly.
Example	Application filed by the applicant to the college where the applicant seeking admission.	Issuance of prospectus by the college.

5. What is Information and Invitation?

Till now can we understand what the basic qualification of an offer is?

The answer is yes. In simple words an 'offer' is the final expression of willingness by the person who gives it to be bound by his offer. If we put it in plain words it would be:

Final expression of willingness to bind the other.

Now let me test invitation on this ground. Is invitation the final expression of willingness to bind the other?

The answer is no.

What is the intention of invitation?

Where one is devoid of expressing his final willingness proposes conditions on which he is willing to discuss, he does not make an offer but just 'invites' the other party to make an offer on those terms.

For example, a vendor sends a catalogue of medicines indicating prices of various medicines to many persons. This is an 'invitation. The notable part is that the other party may make an offer and the vender may accept or reject the offer.

Thus, an invitation means: A statement or giving some information with a view to inviting others to make offers on that basis.

Offer and invitation appear to be similar but are not similar. See the exhibit below:

Comparison between an offer and an invitation

Basis	Offer	Invitation
Nature	Definite	An intention toward the contract, not definite
Process	Final	An act precedent to make an offer
Binding	Binding after performance of other party means accepted	Not binding, per se accepted
Intention	It is intended to bind other	It is done with intention to induce negotiation
Legal aspect	Give rise to obligation	No power to give rise to legality,
Effect	Initiates the legal obligations	Mere negotiations
Period	Mature	Pre-mature

The basic test for invitation and offer is 'intention to bind'. If there is any intention to bind then it is an offer, contrary to, that it is invitation.

Advertisements for bids/tenders are some basic examples of 'invitation to offer the bid/tender makes the offer which can be accepted or rejected.

Communication of offer

An offer is said to be made when it is communicated to the offeree. Without communication an offer is merely plain and there can be no consensus, and therefore no contract.

In other words, if the offeree acted in ignorance of the offer he will not be entitled to the benefit of the promise.

Illustration

A was cleaning B's property without the knowledge of B, A cannot claim B for cleaning charges as it was not in the knowledge of B.

It establishes a very general rule that without knowledge how can one recognize the other's offer, in a positive or negative way.

Does an agreement exist between the parties (was there an offer and acceptance)?

Communication of offer means transmission of one's will or intention to the other.

The word communication denotes 'an act of transmitting' and the word "offer" denotes 'an expression of readiness to do or give something if desired'.

When we combine these two words, it gives a complete meaning like this:

'An act of transmitting an expression of readiness to do or give something if desired, in return. It may be by any mode: verbal, written, gesture, or song, meaning thereby it is a two-way exchange of act in the affirmative or negative.

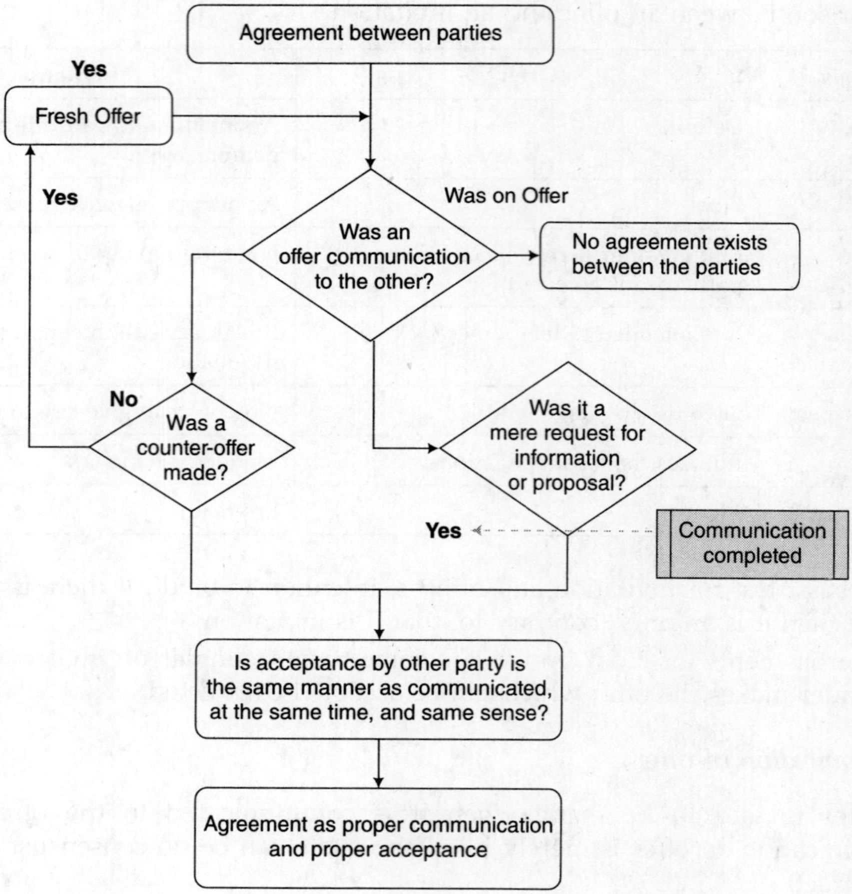

Process of communication

The process of communication initializes when a fact or idea is conceived by one person and the conceiver with intention to a desired act from another transmits into a message, and then transmits the message through some communication medium to another person, the other then must interpret the message and express his intention to do or not to do that desired act communicated by one.

Section 3 of the Indian Contract Act, 1872

Section 3 prescribes how any offer is to be signified or communicated.

Communication, acceptance and revocation of proposals

The communication of proposals, the acceptance of proposals, and the revocation of proposals and acceptances, respectively, are *deemed to be made by any act or omission* of the party proposing, accepting, or revoking, by which he *intends to* communicate such a proposal, acceptance, or revocation, or which *has the effect* of communicating it.

Look at the above italicisized words, which denote when Communication, Acceptance, and Revocation are deemed to be made. The section reveals the answer in the latter party as, it is the deed to be made by an act or omission of the parties, intentions, and effects that make the important ingredients in the same.

Communication, Acceptance, or Revocation are deemed to be made on the Act or Omission of the Parties when they are intended to do so or which have the effect of communicating.

The Section stresses on the following:

- that any act or omission which has the effect of communicating the same, e.g., by words of mouth, by advertisement using any medium, by announcements, or even by conduct, etc.
- communication need not always be express or in writing since the language of sec. 3 does not provide so.

The above-mentioned points are being authenticated under sec. 9, which says communication may be express or implied.

Section 9 promises express and implied: In so far as the proposal or acceptance of any promise is made in words, the promise is said to be express. In so far as such proposal or acceptance is made otherwise than in words, the promise is said to be implied.

Thus, an offer or acceptance when made by words, written or verbal, is said to be express. When the same is made by any other method, it is said to be implied.

Let's take an example of bid in auction or travelling in metro or entering a restaurant is the relevant example of implied communication of offer.

Legal rule regarding communications

For an offer to be valid it must be communicated to the offeree by the offeror, or someone authorized by the offeror.

Communication does not amount to silence, an over act is required: It is an established legal rule that for communicating, accepting, or revocation should not be determined by the mere silence of the parties, as because, it may amount to affirmation or rejection.

Communication of offer when complete

An offer cannot be accepted until and unless it has been brought to the knowledge of the person to whom it is made. This principle is embodied in sec. 4: The communication of a proposal is complete when it comes to the knowledge of the person to whom it is made.

The communication of an acceptance is complete: 'as against the proposer, when it is put in a course of transmission to him so as to be out of the power of the acceptor; or as against the acceptor, when it comes to the knowledge of the proposer.'

Per J. Hidayatullah, (dissenting) (i) In the Entores case Lord Denning no doubt held that acceptance given by telephone was governed by the principles applicable to oral acceptance where the parties were in the presence of each other and that the analogy of letters sent by post could not be applied. But the Court of Appeal was not called upon to construe a written law which brings in the inflexibility of its own language. It was not required to construe the words found in sec. 4 of the Indian Contract Act, namely, 'The communication of an acceptance is complete as against the proposer when it is put in a course of transmission to him, so as to be out of the power of the acceptor.' [667 C-F] Entores Ltd. v. Miles Far East Corporation. [1955] 2 Q.B.D. 327, distinguished.

The communication of a revocation is complete: 'as against the person who makes it, when it is put into a course of transmission to the person to whom it is made, so as to be out of the power of the person who makes it; or as against the person to whom it is made, when it comes to his knowledge.'

Section 5: Revocation of proposals

Section 5 defines revocation of proposal: 'A proposal may be revoked at any time before the communication of its acceptance is complete as against the proposer, but not afterwards.'

Illustration

A proposes, by a letter sent by post, to sell his house to B.

B accepts the proposal by a letter sent by post.

A may revoke his proposal at any time before or at the movement when B posts his letter of acceptance, but not afterwards.

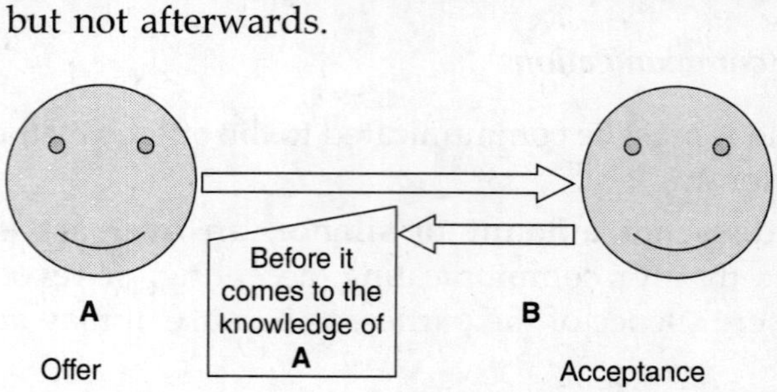

A classic example is that 'a higher bidder can be withdrawn before the hammer fall down in a auction sale.'

Case law

In Bengal Coal Co. *v.* Homee Wadia & Co.: The Bengal Coal Company agreed to supply coal to Homee Wadia & Co. up to a certain quantity at an agreed price for a period of

12 months, as may be required by them from time to time. The plaintiffs placed few orders for the supply of coal and the same were complied with. Before the expiry of the said period of 12 months, the defendants withdrew their offer and refused to comply with the orders placed thereafter. They were sued for the breach of contract.

It was held that 'there was no contract between them and, therefore, there could be no liability for the breach of contract. There was simply a continuing offer to supply coal. They were bound with regards to orders which had already been placed, but were free to revoke their offer for the supply of coal thereafter.'

Similarly in Suraj Besan & Rice Mills *v*. Food Corporation of India, it was held that a person could withdraw or modify his offer of tender before the communication of the acceptance was complete against him and that the Government merely by providing a clause to the contrary in the tender notice could not take away the legal right of a person to revoke the offer.

In Union of India *v*. Maddala Thathaiah Supreme Court of India: The Union of India, as, owners of Railway, invited tenders for the supply of 14,000 maunds of cane jaggery to the railway grain shops. Although the dates by which the supplies were to be made had been mentioned, yet orders for the supply had to be made from time to time.

One of the conditions stipulated in the tender form stated that: 'The Administration reserves the right to cancel the contract at any stage during the tenure of the contract without calling up the outstanding on the unexpired portion of the contract'.

It was held that 'stipulation whereby the appellant could cancel the agreement as regards the supplies of jaggery about which no formal order had been placed was a valid one. The appellants were held to be bound only for the supply of such quantities for which specific orders had already been placed.'

How to make Revocation

The manner in which a proposal can be revoked has been laid down in section 6 of the Act.

As the offer comes into the existence when it comes to the knowledge of the other party, likewise the revocation happens when it comes to the knowledge of other party but before the acceptance by the other party reaches the offeror, not afterwards, as we have seen above and as per the mandate of section 5 of the act.

Now let's examine the process of revocation.

Section 6 Revocation how is it made: A proposal is revoked:

1. by the communication of notice of revocation by the proposer to the other party,
2. by the lapse of the time prescribed in such proposal for its acceptance, or, if no time is so prescribed, by the lapse of a reasonable time, without communication of the acceptance;
3. by the failure of the acceptor to fulfil a condition precedent to acceptance; or
4. by the death or insanity of the proposer, if the fact of his death or insanity comes to the knowledge of the acceptor before acceptance.

Now we can see there are four processes or conditions prescribed by section 6 of the Act, for revocation, i.e.,

1. By Notice of Revocation.
2. By Lapse of prescribed time for acceptance.
3. By failure of condition precedent (terms and conditions).
4. By death or insanity of the proposer.

Revocation by Notice

Case law

Harris (*v.*) Nikerson (1873): An auctioneer advertised in a newspaper that a sale of office furniture would be held. A broker came from a distant place to attend that auction, but all the furniture was withdrawn. The broker thereupon sued the auctioneer for his loss of time and expenses.

It was held that a declaration of intention to do a thing did not create a binding contract with those who acted upon it. So, that the broker could not recover his expenses.

Bank of India *v.* O.P. Swarankar is a relevant judgement on this aspect.

The scheme of Voluntary Retirement Scheme (VRS) offered by the bank to is employees was held to be an invitation to offer. The application of the employee constituted an offer. The employee had a right to withdraw his offer before the same was accepted. A term in the VRS that prevented the employee from withdrawing his application was held to be not binding.

Haridwar Singh *v.* Bagun Sumbrui: While the confirmation of the bid to a bidder below the minimum price was being decided by the department, the bidder agreed to pay the minimum. The department telegraphed its acceptance to the forest officer who was to convey the same to the bidder. The said telegraph was never received by the forest officer. Meanwhile, another bidder offered a higher price and the department accepted. Again, this was communicated to the forest officer, who received it and confirmed to this new bidder.

It was held that no contract was made in the first case as the acceptance was never communicated to the bidder.

Thus, an offer can be revoked by communication of the notice of revocation by the proposer to the other party.

Laps of prescribed time

The acceptance must be made in the prescribed time, but what ill happen if no time is prescribed, then the offer will be considered to have been revoked, as per after the lapse of a reasonable time.

What is 'reasonability' of time?

Reasonability is considered on the basis of facts and circumstances of each case. It means it is not static in nature but dynamic which is fixed according to the nature of goods, e.g., if the goods are perishable in nature such as fruits or the prices change quickly, e.g., gold, even a very small period would be reasonable but not in case of property.

Illustration

A offers to buy stock at a discounted rate before June 2014 to B, but B accepts it in August 2014, the offer is revoked.

Case law **Ramsgate Victoria Hotel Company (*v*.) Monteflore (1886):** On 8 June 'M' offered to take shares in 'R' Company. He received a letter of acceptance on 23 November. He refused to take the shares.

It was held that 'M' was entitled to refuse his offer lapsed as the reasonable period which it could be accepted had lapsed.

Not adherence of conditions precedent or terms and conditions

If there is a condition precedent or specific terms and conditions which are to be fulfilled before the acceptance, then as per section 6(3), the proposal would stand revoked. Sec. 6 (4) provides that the proposal stands revoked by the fact of death or insanity of the proposer if that fact is brought to the knowledge of the acceptor before acceptance.

Illustration

X offer Y to sell his house if Y joins Lawyers club before June 2014. Y. does not join the same, the offer is revoked.

Destruction of subject matter

It is also an important condition of revoking of offer, when the subject matter disappears or becomes illegal or the proposer dies or becomes insane. It is important and pertinent here that under the Indian law death of the proposer will not have any effect of revocation of the proposal. This is the opposite of English law.

Apart from the above-mentioned four conditions there are other conditions also which revoke the offer.

Counter-offer

Counter-offer amounts to rejection of the original offer, meaning thereby the original offer stands revoked. Counter-offer initializes the original process of offer and acceptance, or overrides the previous offer.

In literal meaning, counter-offer means when offerer modifies the qualification of offer.

Case law

In Hyde *v*. Wrench (1840) the above-mentioned principle has been discussed: 'W' offered to sell a farm to 'H' for L 1000 (pounds). 'H' offered L 950 (pounds) 'W' refused the offer. Subsequently, 'H' offered to purchase the farm for L 1000 (pounds).

It was held that there was no contract as 'H' by offering L 950 (ponds) had rejected the original offer.

Change in law

An offer comes to an end if the law is changed so as to make the contract contemplated by the offer illegal (or) incapable of performance.

Accepted other than the prescribed mode

If the offer is not accepted in accordance with the prescribed mode the offer stand revokes, for example,

A offers B a sale 100 box of rice and communicates to reply via written letter. B replies orally, the offer stands revoked.

Postal communication rules

When communication takes place in person then it constitutes a valid contract without giving any trouble. The difficulty arises when the promisor is situated at one place and the promisee is at a remote place. As time is the important element in contractual obligations, but communication of acceptance by post raises a question mark on contractual timing and when the acceptance is complete, because there may be changes of lapse of time between the posting of a letter and it reaching the recipient. Therefore, the 'postal rule' has been developed.

The rule that acceptance is completed on posting, other than the conventional rule that acceptance is completed when it is communicated to the offeree has an exception that acceptance is not completed until it is communicated to the offeree.

Final and unqualified expression

Acceptance is a final and unqualified expression of assent to the terms of an offer; it is like a bullet which once shot cannot take the defence that it was without intention to bind the contract.

Chitty on Contract said that 'An acceptance is a final and unqualified expression of assent to the terms of an offer, and the objective test of agreement applies to an acceptance no less than to an offer.'

Qualification of acceptance

To raise the contractual obligations certain necessary qualifications are required.

- Communication
- Mirror image
- Absolute and express
- Communication of acceptance

An offer is accepted when the acceptance is communicated. The communication must be made to the offeree and a communication of acceptance made to a third person creates no contract. The communication of acceptance may be by words spoken or written or implied from the conduct of the parties; if any particular method of acceptance is prescribed it should be communicated accordingly.

Acceptance is the mirror image of offer

"It is a well settled law that acceptance must be at the same sense, same time, and with the same intention,". That is why it is sometimes called the mirror image rule, the exact replica of offer. Deviation to that and not the acceptance, but a counter-offer, can supersede the original offer.

But an interesting criticism may arise here: mirror image is not exactly the same, as it seems the same per say but change of sides means which is right is actually left in the mirror and vise versa. Does it also apply to the 'mirror image rule', is a question of debate.

Absolute and express

Acceptance must be unqualified and absolute and must correspond with all the terms of the offer.

The mandate of section 7 says:

Acceptance must be absolute: In order to convert a proposal into a promise the acceptance must be absolute. In order to convert a proposal into a promise the acceptance must—'

(1) be absolute and unqualified;

(2) be expressed in some usual and reasonable manner, unless the proposal prescribes the manner in which it is to be accepted. If the proposal prescribes a manner in which it is to be accepted, and the acceptance is not made in such manner, the proposer may, within a reasonable time after the acceptance is communicated to him, insist that his proposal shall be accepted in the prescribed manner, and not otherwise; but, if he fails to do so, he accepts the acceptance.

Competence to Enter into Contract

Unsoundness of mind, minority, incapacity of person of law, insolvency, etc.

Analysis of Section 11: Indian contract act defines certain qualifications for formulating a valid contract, competency of parties to contract are also an important aspect. Section 11 exhibits the capacity of the party for raising the legal obligations under the law of contract.

Section says:

Who are competent to contract: '**Every person** *is competent to contract who is of the* **age of majority** *according to the law to which he is subject, and who is of* ***sound mind*** *and is* ***not disqualified*** *from contracting by any law to which he is subject.*'

Supreme Court of India

Ramanlal Bhailal Patel & Ors *v.* State of Gujarat

Anatomy of section

Look at the bold and underlined words in the section, which indicate the intention of the legislature as:

Who are competent to contract:

- Every person
- age of majority according to the law to which he is subject,
- who is of sound mind
- not disqualified from contracting by any law to which he is subject.

Who are Competent to Contract: Every Person

The section starts with who are competent to contract, and with the very next word the legislature answers the quest: Every Person means legislature intended to make every person qualify for raising the contractual obligation, and forming the contract, as contract is a social phenomena, and legislature are not at all intended to qualify certain persona, but to all who are intended to contract, and who possess certain prerequisite qualifications.

Age of majority, sound mind

Application of a valid agreement results in rights and liabilities of both the parties to contract, and an applicable agreement requires that both the parties should recognize the legal consequences of their conduct, and it can only be achieved when both the parties have a mature mind. The legal yardstick to measure maturity, by the law of contract is, that both the parties should be major and of sound mind and if not, contrary to the law would presume that the maturity of their minds has not reached the extent of forecasting the pros and cons of their acts. Hence, a bar on minors and lunatics competency to contract.

Not disqualified by any law

There are many laws which disqualify certain types of persons, to be in line with the legal obligation refers to other applicable laws which exist; the persons who are contracting should also qualify to these conditions.

1. Who are competent?

There are three types of persons who qualify to the section 11 test and they are:

- Major
- Sound mind
- Competent by relevant law

2. *Who are incompetent to contract?*

- Minor
- Unsound mind
- Idiot
- Lunatic
- Drunken and intoxicated
- Alien enemy
- Foreign sovereign
- Convict
- Insolvent
- Company incorporation

3. *Minor's contract in India*

Minor is not qualified under section 11, contract with a minor is void per se. Here two questions arise:

First, who is minor?

Second, why minor is disqualified by section 11?

First, who is minor under Indian Laws, and Religion?

The answer of the first question is in Section 3 of the Indian Majority Act, 1875,

Section 3. Age of majority of persons domiciled in India:

Subject as aforesaid, {Subs.by Act 8 of 1890, s. 52, for 'every minor of whose person or property a guardian has been or shall be appointed by any Court of Justice, and every minor under the jurisdiction of any Court of Wards'} [every minor of whose person or property, or both, a guardian, other than a guardian for a suit within the meaning of Chapter XXXI of the Code of Civil Procedure {See now the Code of Civil Procedure, 1908 (5 of 1908), (4 of 1882), Sch. I, Order XXXII}, has been or shall be appointed or declared by any Court of Justice before the minor has attained the age of eighteen years, and every minor of whose property the superintendence has been or shall be assumed by any Court of Wards before the minor has attained that age] shall, notwithstanding anything contained in the Indian Succession Act {See now the Indian Succession Act, 1925 (39 of 1925)} or in any other enactment, be deemed to have attained his majority when he shall have completed his age of twenty-one years and not before.

Subject as aforesaid, every other person domiciled in {Subs.by Act 3 of 1951, s. 3 and Sch., for 'Part A States and Part C States'} [India] shall be deemed to have attained his majority when he shall have completed his age of eighteen years and not before.

Likewise the definition of minor is defined in

Section 2(e) of The Indian Succession Act, 1925, as:

'minor' means any person subject to the Indian Majority Act, 1875 (9 of 1875.), who has not attained his majority within the meaning of that Act, and any other person who has not completed the age of eighteen years; and 'minority' means the status of any such person.

i. The Hindu Minority and Guardianship Act (HMGA), 1956, in Section 4 (a), defines a 'minor' as a person who has not completed the age of 18 years.

Iv The Prohibition of Child Marriage Act, 2006 says that a male has not reached majority until he is twenty-one years of age and a female has not reached majority until she is eighteen years of age.'

V Muslim, The Muslim Personal Law (Shariat) Application Act, 1937 in section 3(b) That he is competent to contract within the meaning of section 11 of the Indian Contract Act, 1872:

But the age of marriage in Muslim personal law is the age of puberty (around 14 years). It is an important fact that if the marriage of a Muslim girl has been performed while she was minor, the marriage cannot be void per se as it is the social phenomenon, but the persons who participated in the marriage are not held liable for punishment u/s 4, 5 and 6 of the Child Marriage Restraint Act. In fact, a Muslim girl can marry on attaining the age of puberty [46]which is considered to be the age of majority, and her marriage cannot be declared void because she is below the age of 18, according to the Child Marriage Restraint Act.

Christian and Zoroastrian personal laws also uphold the age of minor as below eighteen.

4. *Exception*

Almost all the enactments notify the age of majority of 18 years for all practical purposes. Christians and Parsis also attain the age of majority at 18. It also important to know that under the Child Marriage Restraint Act, 1929, which is a substance law, the age of marriage is 21 years for males and 18 years for females.

Under Indian Majority Act, 1875, age of majority is 21 years when a guardian of a minor's person or property is appointed under the Guardian and wards Act, 1890.

And under Muslim law the age of majority is 14 years which is the age of puberty.

5. *Consideration received by a person during his minority can be a good consideration?*

'Whether consideration received by a person during his minority can be a good consideration for a fresh promise by him after his attaining majority. No doubt under section 2 a past consideration may be a good consideration, but that past consideration must be an existing one and a valid one. Section 25 is the only section which declares

46. Age of Puberty means age of majority under Muhammadan Law, which is 14 years.

that an agreement made without consideration is void. The whole question is whether such a transaction falls within section 25, sub-clause (2).'[47]

Effect when Minor Attained the age of Majority: In the case of Narain Singh *v.* Chiranji Lal A.I.R. 1924 All. 730, it was remarked that if a minor, when of full age, takes it upon himself to pay a previous debt, there is no reason either in law or equity why his agreement should be deemed to be 'unlawful'. Of course there is no question of unlawfulness, but one of want of consideration. This also was a case of a further advance after majority. There is no question of ratification in such cases. The case of Gregson *v.* Rajah Sri Sri Aditya Deb [1890] 17 Cal. 223 was distinguishable on the ground that the transaction of a disqualified proprietor was voidable. But the language of section 37, Court of Wards Act, is similar to that of section 11, Contract Act, and it is difficult to hold that a contract by a disqualified proprietor is 'only voidable and not void. The real ground on which the Privy Council case is distinguishable is that although the contract had commenced during the period of disqualification, it had been continued and performed after the disqualification had ceased and fresh advances also had been made by the creditor.

Contract for marriage

Option of puberty—khiyar al-buloogh

There is no bar between men and women in terms of contract, they can conclude the contract between themselves. Imagine a case where both are minors, more specifically if they are subject to Muhammadan law, and below the age of puberty, they might be entered into by their respective guardians. Under Islamic law, there is a notion called *khiyar al-buloogh*, which means 'the option of puberty'. Under this concept the marriage of an immature daughter (below the age of puberty or minor as per Islamic law which is 14 years) can be arranged by an elder, she has the right to annul the marriage at the age of puberty.

The same question was examined in **Yousuf Rawther** *v.* **Sowramma on 24 June, 1970, AIR 1971 Ker 261** as

> Before the Act 8 of 1939 (The Dissolution of Muslim Marriages Act, 1939) a minor girl given in marriage by the father or the father's father, had no option to repudiate it on the attainment of her puberty but this has now been changed. The contract of the father or the father's father stands on no higher footing than that of any other guardian and the minor could repudiate or ratify the contract made on his or her behalf during the minority, after the attainment of puberty. 'Puberty' under Muhammadan law is presumed, in the absence of evidence, on completion of the age of 15 years. It would, therefore, necessarily follow that the minor should exercise the option after the age of 15 years unless there was evidence to the contrary that the puberty had been attained earlier and the

47. Allahabad High Court in the case of Suraj Narain Dube *v.* Sukhu Aheer and Anr. on 6 July, 1928 AIR 1928 All 440.

burden of proving this shall lie upon the person so pleading. Anything done by the minor during the minority would not destroy the right which could accrue only after puberty. The co-habitation of a minor girl would not thus put an end to the 'option' to repudiate the marriage after puberty.'

Right of minor accrues after age of puberty

In the case of Ghulam Lakina *v.* Falak Sha Allah Baksh, AIR 1950 Lah 45 an effort to protect the right of minor, against the thing which has been done by him or her, under the age of puberty as:

Any thing done by the minor during the minority would not destroy the right which could accrue only after puberty. The cohabitation of a minor girl would not thus put an end to the option to repudiate the marriage after puberty. The assent should come after puberty and not before, for the simple reason that the minor is incompetent to contract, nor should the consummation have taken place without her consent.

Effect of minor's agreement: liability of minor under tort

In any law there is a system for check and balance, if one side you are immune to certain thing, it does not mean a protection layer cannot be penetrated; certainly the law seems to bias towards children and women, as they belong to vulnerable sections of the society. As the Law of Contract provides the immunity to a minor by making a minor's contract void, but on the other hand for the benefit of minor and for the stability of society and apart from that Public Policy is the centric idea for any enactment, because the law is the will of society, therefore, if a minor makes a breach of an agreement he cannot be made liable for the same. On the other hand, when a minor commits a tort he is liable for that, like any other mature people are.

For example, a minor misrepresents his age and fraudulently stating that he is of the age of majority takes lend from another person, according to the mandate of section 11, the minor cannot be asked to repay as minor's agreement is void, but on the other hand, he has also committed fraud. In the case of a deceptive misrepresentation of his age other party when the enters into a contracts the court may award damages to that other party under sections 30 and 33 of the Specific Relief Act, 1963.

No estoppel against minor

First we need to understand the meaning of estoppel, 'A rule of law that when person A, by act or words, gives person B reason to believe a certain set of facts upon which person B takes action, person A cannot later, to his (or her) benefit, deny those facts or say that his (or her) earlier act was improper.'[48]

Now look at what Section 115 in The Indian Evidence Act, 1872 says:

'115 Estoppel: When one person has, by his declaration, act or omission, intentionally caused or permitted another person to believe a thing to be true

48. http://www.duhaime.org/LegalDictionary/E/Estoppel.aspx

and to act upon such belief, neither he nor his representative shall be allowed, in any suit or proceeding between himself and such person or his representative, to deny the truth of that thing.

Illustration

A intentionally and falsely leads B to believe that a certain land belongs to A, and thereby induces B to buy and pay for it. The land afterwards becomes the property of A, and A seeks to set aside the sale on the ground that, at the time of the sale, he had no title. He must not be allowed to prove his want of title.

There are a few words in both the definitions that are important, which are '**intention**' '**act**', it means with a malafide intention conceive the true facts to achieve certain benefits, and both the definitions say the person cannot deny the truth of that, but the said principle of estoppel is also not applicable to minor case.

Take an example, if a minor misrepresenting his age to induce another for deriving the benefit out of contractual obligations, will there be any estoppel against him?

The answer is no such estoppels will be there against the minor; the reason is simple as we have discussed earlier the protection by law to infant.

Mental capacity in contract

Sound mind: anatomy of section 12 in the Indian Contract Act, 1872

What is a sound mind for the purposes of contracting: A person is said to be of sound mind for the purpose of making a contract, if, at the time when he makes it, he is *capable of understanding* it and of *forming a rational judgment* as to its *effect upon his interests.*

A person, who is *usually of unsound mind,* but *occasionally of sound mind,* may make a contract when he is of sound mind.

A person, who is *usually of sound mind,* but *occasionally of unsound mind,* may not make a contract when he is of unsound mind.

Illustrations

(a) A patient in a lunatic asylum, who is, at intervals, of sound mind, may contract during those intervals.

(b) A sane man, who is delirious from fever, or who is so drunk that he cannot understand the terms of a contract, or forms a rational judgment as to its effect on his interests, cannot contract whilst such delirium or drunkenness lasts.

Perusing the section there are three attribute to qualify the test of sound mind which are:

- capable of understanding
- forming a rational judgment
- effect upon his interests

The section seems to be in positive approached, as initiated by section 10 (all agreements are contracts) and section 11 (every person is competent), the same convention is followed in this section as well, it seems that the legislature does not want to emit the negative aspect, that is why the positive approach is being depicted, and rather than who is of unsound mind, the section qualifies the persons who are of sound mind. But to understand who are of sound mind we have to analyse the bilateral approach, sound and unsound mind.

As the section qualifies the following three persons as of sound mind:

- Capable of understanding
- Forming a rational judgment
- Effect upon his interests

Capable of understanding

What is the meaning of the phrase is 'Capable' and 'Understanding'

The literal meaning of capable is 'competent', means the 'power or the energy to execute an act'.

If we link the word capable to section 12 then the word 'capable' denotes the opposite word of madness, lunatic, idiot, ill in sense, under the influence of any substance (alcohol or any other drug or any substance which ceases his mind and rational logical power), or under the influence of intoxication.

In reference to law of contract the capability is synonymous with the following attributes:

- Capability of contractual obligations
- Capability to contractual rights and duties
- Capability of legal consequence

And the word 'understanding' denotes the sense of rational thinking in terms of contractual obligations with respect to the above-mentioned three attributes.

The combination of words capable of understanding exhibits the complete sense that a person who is mad, lunatic, idiot, ill, insane, under the influence of any substance (alcohol or any other drug or any substance which cease his mind and rational logical power), or under the influence of intoxication, he deprived to take a rational judgement so the person is out of this qualities is sound mind.

Forming a rational judgement

Forming a rational judgement is the state of mind in which a person draws inference or analyses the consequences of an act. The word rational denotes the balancing approach of mind in which a person to contract draws a lucid reference which is opposed to the judgement of a person who are mad, lunatic, idiot, ill, insane, under the influence of any substance (alcohol or any other drug or any substance which ceases his mind and rational logical power), or under the influence of intoxication. These are the states of mind which prevent normal perception, behaviour, or social interaction; seriously mentally ill. The last word judgement is a conclusive state in which a person to contract takes a verdict of the contractual obligations and consequences.

Delhi High court in the case of K.R. Raghavan *v.* Union of India (UoI) and Ors defined the word 'Decision' as 'Indeed the very word "decision" has a different meaning in the one sphere of activity and the other. When a person resolves to act in a particular way, the mental step may be described as "decision". Again, when a judge determines an issue of fact upon conflicting evidence, or a question of low upon forensic argument, he gives a "decision". But the two mental acts differ.'

Effect upon his interests

Both the above two attributes ultimately is the destination of interest of the person to contract, which seems that the enactment is beneficiary legislature.

The word effect upon his interests is to denote that a person who is entering into a contract must be a person who understands what he is doing and is able to from a rational judgement for his personal interest and benefits, not contrary to his benefits. It means there are two important aspects of it first, the person to a contract is supposed to be able to understand the nature and content of the contract, and after the understanding the nature and content of the contract he or she should be able to formulate a rational judgment about the effect of the contract on his interest. So the legislature states that not only the person has interest but he should understand the nature and content of the contract, and must form a beneficial or rational judgement thereto.

And the people who are not qualified on these two aspects are not capable of entering into the contract because they cannot understand the content and simultaneously they cannot formulate a rational judgment.

At the time he makes it

Legislature is more serious about the duration in which he behaves in a rational manner, and the legislature being intended with an affirmative aspect adopting positive aspects and ignoring the period in which the person to contract are with unsoundness of mind. It seems the mandate of the legislature is beneficial legislature, not prohibitory, and it is in line with social policy to maintain the social order and structure.

After analysing, we can categorize two categories of competence of persons as per section 12, competent and non-competent, on the basis of mental capacity to analyse the contractual obligations

What is sound mind and unsound mind?

Soundness or unsoundness of mind as inability to enter into a contract is the question of degree of incapability. Sir J. Hannen in Boughtson *v.* Knight 'unsoundness of mind is a question of degree'.

It is a fundamental postulate that a 'mentally disordered person cannot give that rational consent which is necessary to the validity of a contract'.

The same question is being discussed by the Delhi High Court in the case of

Idiot (Permanent inability)

First of all we have to understand what is the meaning of idiot? An idiot is a person incapable of managing his affairs; it is a defect or sterility of the intellectual power. 'A person who has been without understanding from his nativity and whom the law, therefore, presumes never likely to attain any.'[49] And it is to be considered that an idiot is incapable of forming a rational judgement by birth, and lost his mental faculty.

As per the mandate of section 12, a sound mind person must formulate the rational judgement to its effect upon his interests, and an idiot is deprived this quality, because it is a permanent inability of a person, so a contract by an idiot is void.

Lunatic (Temporary Inability)

The dictionary meaning of lunatic is 'a person whose actions and manner are marked by extreme eccentricity or recklessness.' Lunatic is a person whose mind fluctuates in situations, means sometimes become sound and sometimes becomes unsound.

So during the period of lunacy when his mind was unsound and he or she enters into the contract that contract will be void.

Drunk/Intoxicated/Illness (Temporary inability)

Drunkard is a person who has drunk to an extent where he loses the balance of mind. It is also deviation of the mental sense of rational judgement for a particular period when the person, is under the effect of liquor or intoxication. It does not mean that who forever enjoys liquor, his mind is always unsound. If any person is consuming alcohol he becomes permanently disabled though he is consuming liquor but his mind is sound. Contractual obligation raised by him till a level where his mind becomes unsound and during that period if he enters into the contract that contract will be void. The same situation happens with deviation of soundness of mind under the effect of any intoxication, or for any illness, or old infirmity.

Incompetent by law

In the previous pages we have discussed mental or physical incapacity of parties to contract the following persons are disqualified under statutory disqualifications

- Alien enemy
- Foreign sovereign
- Convict
- Insolvent
- Company incorporation

---

49. Law Dictionary

An alien enemy is an individual who, due to permanent or temporary allegiance to a hostile power is regarded as an enemy in wartime. In general terms an alien residing in a country at war with the one of which he or she is a citizen.

It is obvious that an enemy cannot propose a contrary contract against the interest of the country, which is why the contract with alien enemy is void.

Indian Contract Act bars contract with alien enemy before or during the war, and the alien enemy can neither contract with an Indian citizen nor can be sued in any Indian Court, he can sue only after the due approval of Government of India.

Foreign sovereign or any accredited representatives of foreign sovereign are also barred under Indian Law of Contract to contract. They cannot sue unless they choose to submit themselves to the jurisdiction of an Indian court. But it does not mean that they are not capable of entering into contract and enforce those contracts within the jurisdiction of an Indian Court, but they cannot be proceeded against in Indian courts without the sanction of the Central Government. But the agent of foreign sovereign can be held liable for the contract.

However the Indian Contract Act, 1872 does not say anything about the contracts of foreign sovereigns, but the Code of Civil Procedure qualifies the foreign sovereign to sue and to be sued in Indian Courts, under section 83 to section 87(b), but subject to Central Government.

Convict: A convict is also disqualified to enter into a contract, during the terms of sentence of imprisonment.

An exception to this rule is that he can enforce a contract when he is on parole or he is being pardoned by the court or after expiry of his term of impression.

Insolvent: As we have seen so far the foundation of contractual obligations is based on reciprocal promises which raises obligations and liabilities. The whole act of law of contract moves around the consideration, the benefit of one and another derived by contractual parties, that is why the rule of capacity is being drafted and attributed to the law of contract, to the better and absolute performance of contractual obligations.

Insolvency is a situation when an individual, corporation, or any other organization fails to meet its financial obligations for repaying the debts which are due on him, means he is incapable of discharging his obligations.

Under the law of contract an insolvent cannot enter into a contract relating to his property, if his property is subject to adjudged insolvent and his property stands vested in the official assignee appointed by the court.

The exception to this rule is that an insolvent has a right to make contracts which are necessary for his reasonable maintenance and that of his family.

Company or corporation: Language of section 11 of Indian Contract Act, said, 'Every Person' is competent to contract. The section does not say about human being or natural person, rather competent to every person for contractual obligations.

The definition of 'person' under section 3(42) of General Clauses Act, 1897 as 'Person' shall include any, company or association or body of individuals, whether incorporated or not.'

Virus in an Agreement for Avoiding Agreement

- Coercion
- Undue influence
- Misrepresentation
- Fraud

The heading of the chapter 'Virus in Agreement' exhibits the nature of the chapter that the agreement due to virus is voidable not void, as the virus is a disease, or bug, if not cured within time it could hurt the object.

Sections (13-18) are descriptive, which relate to the substantive sections.

John Bouvier's *Bouvier's Law Dictionary* Volume II (8th edn West Publishing Company 1914) describes that Freedom of contract can be understood as 'having the ability at will, to make or abstain from making, a binding obligation enforced by sanctions at the law'.

As we have discussed in earlier chapters a contract is mutual consent of the parties, that is why it is synonymous to *consensus ad idem,* means at the free will of the parties, where parties give their assent to bind each other for doing and from abstaining to do anything, without any external force or pressure. We see the virus of the contract in the form of coercion, which destroys the free will and the power to analyse its benefit or there is no sense of analysing its benefits out of the contractual obligations, but the party who caused by coercion, is not executing its free will to contract, but it is exercising the will of the other, which violates the basic principle of acceptance by the same party at the same sense for which the offer is given. In other words, the contract under coercion is with contract without acceptance though the acceptance that comes from the party, to some extent it is yes, but it seems to give the acceptance to the offer. But legislature, through section 19, does not make such a contract that is caused by coercion as void ab initio, but voidable at the instance of the party whose consent caused it. That is why it is put under the category of virus. What is the reason for it? The simple answer is that there are changes that the party to the contract may take adverse advantage of the situation, if it makes it ab initio void. We can also underline the idea behind it to save the social structure of contract and performance of the contract per se.

It is important to understand coercion more concisely, for that we must first analyse consent and free consent.

Free consent

The legal enforceability as we have discussed earlier, conceives the element of free consent, which is the combination of two words 'free' and 'consent'.

It means a consent which is free. Now the question arises, what is the meaning of consent, and what it should be free from?

Consent

In a general sense consent denotes parties to the contract should think about the subject matter in the same sense.

Section 13 defines Consent, 'Two or more persons are said to consent when they agree upon the same thing in the same sense.'

Section 13 says that the agreement between two persons or more as it is bilateral proceeding as discussed in the earlier chapters. Further, the section says that the persons are said to consent when, they agree upon the same thing in the same sense. What does it mean? The meeting of minds on consensus ad idem, the perfect identity of mind over the subject matter. The word same thing denotes the subject matter of the agreement, and same thing denotes the perfect identification of mind, deviation from the offeror's sense does not amount to a contract. If we take it further in respect to the law of contract it is *Consentire est facere* which is to consent to a thing is to do a thing.

Consent without knowledge is no consent

Knowledge and communication is the founding pillar in contract law, as without communication and knowledge to the other party (offeree), there is no binding obligation to each other likewise, as Jessel said, 'You cannot consent the thing unless you have knowledge of it'.

Does it mean that consent comprises two elements: 'knowledge' and 'approval of the parties', the answer is in the affirmative, as both the words are correlated. When something comes to the knowledge of the party concerned then only it gives its approval or its consent.

Word 'Free' defined

The phrase free consent is used in section 10. As we already have discussed about the consent, indeed, the law of contract also defines the word consent under section 13, but the word 'free' has not been defined anywhere in the Act. To understand it is necessary to understand both the words.

The word free, in section 10, is not used in its general sense or literal mining, but a deep meaning attached to it. Free means freedom from any encumbrance which disqualifies the consent, or is voluntary in nature. The word free is the qualification of consent, it means what type of consent is required for a valid contract.

As the legislature advocates freedom of contract without any restrictions, if any restriction is attached to it in terms of free consent, then there is no contract at all, because there would be violation of the principle of meeting of mind. And the legislature intends the agreement to be freely made and not obligatory. It should be real not imaginary, and without any false representation. A compromised consent has no place in law.

Consent should be a free consent as it is sine qua non of a valid agreement.

The word 'free' is correlated to section 14, which says consent is free when it is not caused by: (a) coercion, as defined in section 15, or (b) undue influence, as defined in section16, or (c) fraud, as defined in section 17, or (d) misrepresentation as defined in section 18, or (e) mistake, subject to the provisions of section 20, 21, and 22.

Effect of

Absence of consent: void – ab – initio

When there is no consent at all, the agreement is **void - ab - initio** and it is not enforceable at the option of either party, as it violates the basic rule of contract, of valid acceptance, because consent comprises two things, knowledge and approval of the parties to the contractual obligations. If there is no knowledge, there could not be a qualified acceptance, and if there is no qualified acceptance there could not be valid contractual obligations.

Absence of free consent: voidable at the option of parties

While any of the parties to contract is caused by coercion, undue influence, fraud, misrepresentation, or mistake, it is not a free consent and does not constitute a valid contract and the contract is voidable at the option of the party whose consent was so caused.

The mandates of section 19 are so in line with the idea as

Section 19 in the Indian Contract Act, 1872, voidability of agreements without free consent: When consent to an agreement is caused by coercion, 1[***] fraud or misrepresentation, the agreement is a contract voidable at the option of the party whose consent was so caused.

A party to contract, whose consent was caused by fraud or misrepresentation, may, if he thinks fit, insists that the contract shall be performed, and that he shall be put in the position in which he would have been if the representations made had been true.

Exception: If such consent was caused by misrepresentation or by silence, fraudulent within the meaning of section 17, the contract, nevertheless, is not voidable, if the party whose consent was so caused had the means of discovering the truth with ordinary diligence.

Explanation: A fraud or misrepresentation which did not cause the consent to a contract of the party on whom such fraud was practised, or to whom such misrepresentation was made, does not render a contract voidable.

After scrutinizing the section it reveals three things:

- the agreement is a contract voidable at the option of the party whose consent was so caused;
- whose consent was caused may be if he thinks fit, insist that the contract shall be performed and that he shall be put in the position if the representations made had been true.

- the legislature is not considering the agreement without free consent is void ab-into, while the agreement is a contract, mens an enforceable contract, but it may be voidable at the option of the party because the benefits of the caused party may be prejudiced.

And the latter part of the section provides a choice to the caused party that if he thinks fit that the contract may be in line with his benefits he shall perform the contract, instead of the contract repugnant.

If, however, the consent is caused by mistake the agreement is void.

Now let's examine the elements of free consent as defined under section 14 as:

Coercion

Definition

Essential elements

Difference between duress and coercion

Doctrine of economic duress

Effects of coercion

Exterritorial jurisdiction

Burden of proof

Definition

In simple words coercion means an act against the free will of the party or forcing another party to act in a particular manner by use of any external force such as intimidation or threat or some other pressure.

It is basically a fear to save one self or his property from the external force which is put by other. It is a sort of threat or force used by one upon another to compel another to enter into a contract.

Based on the definition the attribute to contract as threat to murder, rape, shoot, destroy the property, attempt to commit suicide.

The rules regarding coercion are explained in the section 15 of the Indian Contract Act.

Coercion = Force Compulsion

According to section 15, 'Coercion' is the committing or threatening to commit any act forbidden by the Indian Penal Code, or the unlawful detaining, or threatening to detain, any property, to the prejudice of any person whatever with the intention of causing any person to enter into an agreement. Coercion is 'forced compulsion'.

Section 15 'Coercion' defined: Coercion' is the committing, or threatening to commit, any act forbidden by the Indian Penal Code (45 of 1860) or the unlawful detaining, or threatening to detain, any property, to the prejudice of any person whatever, with the intention of causing any person to enter into an agreement." Explanation: It is immaterial whether the Indian Penal Code (45 of 1860) is or is not in force in the place where the coercion is employed."

Illustrations

A, on board an English ship on the high seas, causes B to enter into an agreement by an act amounting to criminal intimidation under the Indian Penal Code (45 of 1860). Tc

A afterwards sues B for breach of contract at Calcutta.

A has employed coercion, although his act is not an offence by the law of England, and although section 506 of the Indian Penal Code (45 of 1860) was not in force at the time when or place where the act was done.

It is considered that nothing could be 'coercion' under the Indian Law unless it satisfies the definition of 'coercion' which is found in sec. 15 of the Indian Contract Act.

After analysing the above definition we can say that the definition of coercion is exclusively a definition which applies to the thought whether there has been a free consent to an agreement so as to render it a contract under section 10. That is why the definition of 'coercion' is narrowed down to an unlawful act done 'with the intention of causing the person to enter into an agreement'.

Essential element of coercion and analysis of section

After analysing section 15, the following points which are underlined are to be the considered committing, or threatening to commit, any act forbidden by the Indian Penal Code (45 of 1860) or the unlawful detaining, or threatening to detain, any property, to the prejudice of any person whatever, with the intention of causing.

The application of coercion is twofold, committing or threatening to commit means the coercion actually is in existence or has not actually been done but threat to be done in future.

A threat to commit suicide (an act which could be done in future), or whether coercion could be caused by a threat to commit suicide.

Act forbidden by the indian penal code

The words (act forbidden by the Penal Code) make it clear that the court must decide whether the alleged act of coercion is such as to amount to an offence. It means that coercion does not always mean to commit an offence or not cross the boundary of offence, for instance:

A threatens to blow up the Red Fort unless B gives C a pronote for Rs. 50,000 and B is a man of such fine artistic feelings that to save the noble structure, he gives the pronote to C.

Is it coercion?" Certainly the answer is no, because the nature and gravity of the threat is not practical or possible, and does not amount to any offence, though there was a coercion.

While if a person commits or threatens to commit an act forbidden by the Indian Penal Code with a view to obtaining the consent of the other person to some agreement, the consent is considered to have been obtained by coercion.

For example:

A threatens to shoot B, if B does not agree to sell his property to A at a stated price. B's consent in this case has been obtained by coercion.

It is also an important aspect that for coercion to be there it is not necessary that the Indian Penal Code should be applicable at the place where the consent has been so caused.

Explanation to section 15 makes it apparent that to comprise coercion, 'it is irrelevant whether the Indian Penal Code is or is not in force in the place where the coercion is employed.'

Effect of coercion

Where the consent of a contracting party has been obtained by some form of pressure which the law regards as improper, and for this reason the victim of such pressure may be entitled to relief, that is why section 19 exhibits the remedy for the agreement is a contract voidable at the option of the party whose consent was so caused.

What is duress

The literal meaning of duress is 'threats, violence, constraints, or other action used to coerce someone into doing something against their will or better judgement.'

Dictionary meaning of duress is:

'Unlawful pressure exerted upon a person to coerce that person to perform an act that he or she ordinarily would not perform.'[50]

The bare perusal of the literal meaning and definition shows that duress is closely related to coercion, as both in coercion and duress there is a forced act against the will of any person to enter into a contract, or a threat of violence to a person to enter into a contract.

Lord Scarman: 'Duress, whatever form it takes, is a "coercion of the will" so as to vitiate consent.'

Duress under English and Indian Law:

It is said that duress is the approximate term of coercion under English law. 'What the Indian Law calls coercion is called in English law Duress or Menace. Duress is said to consist in actual or threatened violence or imprisonment of the contracting party or his wife, parent or child, inflicted or threatened by the other party or by one acting with his knowledge and for his advantage. But coercion as defined in sec 15 is much wider and includes the unlawful detention of property. Further, it may be committed by any person, not necessarily a party to the contract. Again, it need not be directed against the contracting party or his parent, wife or child but it may be against any person, even a stranger. While in English law, duress must be such as to cause immediate violence and also to unnerve a person with ordinary firmness of mind, these requisites are not necessary in Indian law.'[51]

50. http://legal-dictionary.thefreedictionary.com/

51. Karuppayee Ammal *v.* Karuppiah Pillai and Anr. (1987) 2 MLJ 138.

Comparison between coercion and duress

S.No.	Analysing Factor	Coercion	Duress
1	Meaning	Coercion in India means committing or threatening to commit an act forbidden by the Indian Penal Code, or unlawful detaining or threatening to detain the property	Threats, violence, constraints, or other action used to coerce someone into doing something against their will or better judgement
2	Against	Person and Property, Can be aimed at a stranger to contract also	Against person, not against his property; duress is applied to the party to the contract only

Fraud: Section 17

Definition

Essential elements

suppressio veri, suggestio falsi

When does silence amount to fraud?

Active concealment of truth

Importance of intention

Definition

Section 17 in The Indian Contract Act, 1872

17. 'Fraud' defined: 'Fraud' means and includes any of the following acts committed by a party to a contract, or with his connivance, or by his agent, with intent to deceive another party thereto or his agent, or to induce him to enter into the contract:

(1) the suggestion, as a fact, of that which is not true, by one who does not believe it to be true

(2) the active concealment of a fact by one having knowledge or belief of the fact;

(3) a promise made without any intention of performing it;

(4) any other act fitted to deceive;

(5) any such act or omission as the law specially declares to be fraudulent.

Explanation: Mere silence as to facts likely to affect the willingness of a person to enter into a contract is not fraud, unless the circumstances of the case are such that, regard being had to them, it is the duty of the person keeping silence to speak, or unless his silence, is, in itself, equivalent to speech.

(a) A sells, by auction, to B, a horse which A knows to be unsound. A says nothing to B about the horse's unsoundness. This is not fraud by A.

(b) B is A's daughter and has just come of age. Here the relation between the parties would make it A's duty to tell B if the horse is unsound.

(c) B says to A, 'If you do not deny it, I shall assume that the horse is sound.' A says nothing. Here, A's silence is equivalent to speech.

(d) A and B, being traders, enter upon a contract. A has private information of a change in prices which would affect B's willingness to proceed with the contract. A is not bound to inform B.

If we summarize the above section in one line 'fraud is act or omission with an intention to deceive the other. Fraud means when one party intentionally or deliberately or with the intention to deceive the other party, enters into the contract. It is a dishonest assertion to deceive other. If one party has knowledge about the thing that a statement or thing is not true and but with a deliberate intention induces other to enter into the contract.

The section exhibits that a party to the contract or his connivance or his agent, it is not required that a party directly involved in making a deceitful statement or act or omission but the other person can also help him in making an intentional or deliberate presentation to another party to enter into the contract. The paramount element in fraud is intention to deceive the other. The word 'induce' in the section clarifies the character of fraud creating such circumstances through their untrue statement by which another party is being provoked to enter into the contract. It means the proceeds of fraud may wrongful loss to other party and wrongful gain to the party who influences the other to enter into the contract by using a deceitful statement or assertion.

Fraud and misrepresentation

It is also well settled that misrepresentation itself amounts to fraud. Indeed, innocent misrepresentation may also give reason to claim relief against fraud. A fraudulent misrepresentation is called deceit and consists in leading a man into damage by wilfully or recklessly causing him to believe and act on falsehood. It is a fraud in law if a party makes representations, which he knows to be false, and injury enures therefrom although the motive from which the representations proceeded may not have been bad.[52]

Under English law

The position of fraud has been discussed by the Gauhati High Court in the case of Smt. Best Morning Khongthohrem *v.* Nirmalendu AIR 1987 Gau 63 as 'Fraud in English common law implies absence of honest belief. Fraud in common parlance is a somewhat comprehensive word that embraces a multitude of delinquencies differing widely in turpitude, but the types of conduct that give rise to an action of deceit have been narrowed down to rigid limits. As was held in Le Lievre *v.* Gould, (1893) 1 QB 491, a charge of fraud is such a terrible thing to bring against a man that it cannot be maintained in any Court unless it is shown that he had a wicked mind.'

52. Commissioner of Customs, Kandla *v.* M/S Essar Oil Limited & Ors.

Element

It was held in Deny *v.* Peek, (1889) 14 AC 337 that absence of honest belief is essential to constitute fraud.

Suggestion of false fact with knowledge

To constitute a fraud it is important that the person who is making the representation knows the falsity of the statement.

Fraud means a false statement 'made knowingly, or without belief in its truth, or recklessly, careless whether it be true or false'. In testing the honesty of the petitioner's belief, his statement must not be considered according to its ordinary meaning, but according to its meaning as understood by him. At common law, nothing less than a want of honest belief, or, nothing less than a lie suffices to found an action of deceit. The course of equity has given a more extended meaning to the word 'fraud' and has developed a doctrine of constructive fraud including class of cases of fraud which did not necessarily import the element of *dolus malus* and tried to prevent a man from acting against the dictates of conscience and had tried to grant injunction in anticipation of injury, as well as relief where injury had been done. A man who concludes a transaction under such circumstances that he is not a free agent and not equal to protecting himself is entitled to the protection of the Court. The doctrine has been applied to a wide field of human activities where a confidential or fiduciary relation exists between the two parties to a contract or other transaction. Whenever the relation between the parties to a contract is of a confidential or fiduciary nature, the person in whom the confidence is reposed and who thus possesses influence over the other cannot hold that other to the contract unless he satisfies the Court that it is advantageous to the other party and that he has disclosed all material facts within his knowledge. Even silence in such a case constitutes misrepresentation.[53]

In fact, fraud is committed where one man induces another to act on a false belief by a representation which he does not himself consider to be true. He need not have specific knowledge or credence that it is not true.

Illustration

A wanted to buy a used computer from B; B knows that the computer is virus infected, but asserted that the computer is free form virus.

As the material aspect of buying the computer free from virus, B asserted that it is free from virus having knowledge, that it is a false statement to induce A to enter into a contract of buying the virus infected computer.

In the case of RC Thakkar *v.* Bombay Housing Board AIR 1973 Guj 34 (DB) it was examined by the Gujarat High Court that, to constitute the falsity of a representation it should be found false in substance as well as in fact. It is further observed what is false as if the material circumstances are incorrectly stated, that is to say, if the discrepancy between the facts as represented and the actual facts as represented and the actual facts

53. Smt. Best Morning Khongthohrem *v.* Nirmalendu AIR 1987 Gau 63.

is such as would be considered material by a reasonable representation, the representation is false.

Illustration

A tells B to buy his cow knowing it to be false it is pregnant. On this suggestion A agrees to buy the cow Rs. 5,000.

Active concealment of fact

The language of the act says active concealment of the fact having knowledge. It means the concealment must be active and not passive, because active concealment is different from passive concealment amounting to keeping mum about the material fact. But it is also important to know if the person whose consent is so caused by fraud is in the position of discovering such truth by due diligence or prudence then it does not amount to active concealment and thus fraud.

Illustration

A's marriage with B is fixed. At the time of marriage B was pregnant by some person other than A. Though B was aware of the fact of her pregnancy but she concealed it from A. This is active concealment and thus constitutes fraud.

A purchases the land from B, who has already sold his land to X and he did not tell B that he has already sold this land to X.

Negligence is not Fraud

'Fraud' is a conduct either by letter or words, which induces the other person or authority to take a definite determinative stand as a response to the conduct of the former either by words or letter. Although negligence is not fraud but it can be evidence on fraud as observed in Ram Preeti Yadav *v.* U.P. Board of High School and Intermediate Education(2003 (8) SCC 311).

Silence-Explanation of Section 17

Mere silence is not fraud:

Look at the Explanation of section 17 as " Mere silence as to facts likely to affect the willingness of a person to enter into a contract is not fraud, unless the circumstances of the case are such that, regard being had to them, it is the duty of the person keeping silence to speak, or unless his silence, is, in itself, equivalent to speech."

The explanation reveals that mere silence as to facts likely to affect the willingness of a person to enter into a contract does not amount to fraud. It means every silence does not constitute the fraud under section 17, except the person under a duty to speak or silence equal to speech. The underlined idea of the present exception is making responsible to the person who are entering into the contract that he must be aware about the contract while entering into it, it seems to the principle of Caveat Emptor, which establishes "Let the Buyer Be Aware". But it is also the fundamental fact that it is the duty of both the parties to disclose the material fact, to qualify the mandate of section.

Illustration

A sells by auction to B, a horse which A knows to be unsound, A says nothing to B about the horse's unsoundness. It is not fraud.

Exception- When does silence amount to fraud

1. Duty to speak:

There are certain circumstances and situations where a person under the duty to speak, and if he does not speak it amounts to fraud. Now the question arises when the duty to speak does arise? The answer of this question is where one party reposes trust and confidence in the other, or where necessary to speak or the willingness of the party is likely to be affected. There are certain contracts, and such contracts are considered to be Uberrimae fidei, i.e., contracts requiring utmost good faith.

Following are some circumstances where it is the duty of the person keeping silence to speak.

uberimae-fide (Contracts of insurance)

In contracts of insurance, the insured is under the duty to disclose all material facts relating to the insurance which are possible to affect the risk and thus the willingness of the insurer.

Contract of immovable property

Under Sec. 55(i) (a) of the Transfer of Property Act, 1882, says 'to disclose to the buyer any material defect in the property 1[or in the seller's title thereto] of which the seller is, and the buyer is not, aware, and which the buyer could not with ordinary care discover'; the seller is under an obligation to disclose to the buyer any material defect in the property or in the seller's title of which the seller is aware and the buyer is not aware, nor he (buyer) could know with ordinary care.

Example

1. A knows that the foundation of his house is weak. He sells this house to B but does not disclose this defect to B. It is fraud.

   B can avoid the sale when he comes to know of the defect.

   Likewise, contracts of fiduciary relations, contract of guarantee, customary contract are a few examples where a person is under duty to speak.

2. Where silence is equivalent to speech:

   Where silence is equivalent to speech, silence amounts to fraud.

   For example, B says to A, 'If you do not deny it, I shall assume that the vehicle is sound.' A says nothing. Here A's silence is equivalent to speech and as such, it is fraud.

3. Half truths

   Silence may constitute fraud where a person discloses only the half truth and then keeps silent. A person may become guilty of fraud by non-disclosure also if he voluntarily discloses something and then stops half-way. A person may keep silent. But if he speaks, he is duly bound to disclose the whole truth.

Intention and fraud?

The literal meaning of intention is an aim or plan, the section bears the phrase 'with intent to deceive another party' manifests that intention to deceive the other is the important element in fraud. The section used the above phrase with the application of mind to deceive. Thus, intentional deception to cause a person is the constituent element of fraud, and its a pivot element when we scrutinize the section, the word 'intent' comes in substantive part.

By 'fraud' is meant an intention to deceive; whether it is from any expectation of advantage to the party himself or from the ill will towards the other is immaterial. The expression 'fraud' involves two elements—deceit and injury to the person deceived. Injury is something other than economic loss, that is, deprivation of property, whether movable or immovable or of money and it will include any harm whatever caused to any person in body, mind, reputation, or such others. In short, it is a non-economic or non-pecuniary loss. A benefit or advantage to the deceiver will almost always call loss or detriment to the deceived, even in those rare cases where there is a benefit or advantage to the deceiver, but no corresponding loss to the deceived. Section 17 of the Contract Act defines fraud as an act committed by a party to a contract with intent to deceive another. From the dictionary meaning or even otherwise fraud arises out of deliberate active role of representator about a fact which he knows to be untrue yet he succeeds in misleading the representee by making him believe it to be true. The representation to become fraudulent must be of the fact with knowledge that it was false.[54]

In the case of Dr. Vimla *v.* Delhi Administration the Supreme Court observed: We have, however, come to the conclusion that this is too narrow at view. While, no doubt, in most cases of an intention to defraud the intention is to cause an economic loss' there is no reason to introduce any such limitation. Provided that the intention is to cause the person deceived to act to his real detriment, it matters not that lie suffers no economic loss. It is sufficient if the intention is to deprive him of a right or to induce him to do something contrary to what it would have been his duty to do, had lie not been deceived.

Effect of fraud

Any act based on fraud vitiates the entire action taken. Effect of fraud on any proceeding or transaction is that it becomes nullity. In Lazarus Estate Ltd. *v.* Beasley (1956) 1 QB 702, Lord Denning observed at pages 712 & 713, 'No judgment of a Court, no order of a Minister can be allowed to stand if it has been obtained by fraud. Fraud unravels everything.' In the same judgment Lord Parker LJ observed that fraud vitiates all transactions known to the law of however high a degree of solemnity. In the case of Ram Preeti Yadav *v.* U.P. Board of High School and Intermediate Education(2003 (8) SCC 311), it was observed as:

54. The State of Andhra Pradesh & Anr *v.* T. Suryachandra Rao.

I cannot accede to this argument for a moment "no Court in this land will allow a person to keep an advantage which he has obtained by fraud. No judgment of a Court, no order of a Minister, can be allowed to stand if it has been obtained by fraud. Fraud unravels everything". The Court is careful not to find fraud unless it is distinctly pleaded and proved; but once it is proved it vitiates judgments, contracts and all transactions whatsoever.

Misrepresentation: section 18

Definition

Misrepresentation is another element of free consent. It is the combination of two words Mis + Representation, means the demonstration which is deviated from facts. It refers to a situation where a person is induced to enter into a contract entirely or partly by a false declaration of fact, not opinion or intention made by the other. It means misrepresentation is an assertion or manifestation through words or conduct which is not true or in accordance with the fact. When the person making a false statement believes the statement to be true and does not intend to mislead the other party to the contract it is known as 'misrepresentation'.

It means misrepresentation is when a party (person) asserts something which is not true while he believes it to be true, in fact a false representation is made innocently.

Section 18 in the Indian Contract Act, 1872

'Misrepresentation' defined: 'Misrepresentation' means and includes—'

(1) the positive assertion, in a manner not warranted by the information of the person making it, of that which is not true, though he believes it to be true

(2) any breach of duty which, without an intent to deceive, gains an advantage of the person committing it, or any one claiming under him, by misleading another to his prejudice, or to the prejudice of any one claiming under him; or

(3) causing, however innocently, a party to an agreement, to make a mistake as to the substance of the thing which is the subject of the agreement.

The underlined idea after analysing the section is that misrepresentation is not influx with intention, but the one who makes the assertion is of the belief that it is true, and there is no intention to deceive but it is done in innocence. It means innocent mis-statements of the fact which are substances for the configuration of the contract, and material of the fact. Though the statement is not true, it is false but party who is asserting it ignorant of this fact and is innocently exhibiting the same. The basic element is that there is no intention to cheat the other.

Delhi High Court in the case of Joginder Singh *v*. The Bar Council Of India AIR 1975 Delhi 192, 1975 RLR 15 discussed that non-disclosure of the convictions did not amount to fraud as:

that the appellant had gained admission as an advocate by fraud or misrepresentation in that he had refrained from disclosing that he had previously been convicted of offences. The facts on which that conclusion rested were admitted by the appellant. Merely because the certificate was referred to in the interrogation of the appellant, or in the argument of his counsel, does not mean that the Bar Council relied on it, or the surrounding circumstance, for the purpose of reaching its decision. (33) These were all the contentions raised on behalf of the appellant.

Elements of misrepresentation

- Unjustified statement of facts – positive assertion – believe true, really not true-no basis of misrepresentation
- Breach of duty, without any intent to deceive
- Causing inducing other, however innocently, to make mistake as to quality or nature of subject matter

Unjustified statement of facts

If we analyse the above-mentioned statement it reveals that misrepresentation is an untrue statement of fact made by one party to the other which was intentional and persuaded the latter to enter into the contract, and the one party positively asserted, while it is not warranted.

In the case of, Avon Insurance plc. *v.* Swire Fraser Ltd. (2000), the test of falsity is being discussed as

What, however, is the test of truth or falsity, and how difficult is it to rebut the inference of inducement? Is a representation true if in substance it is true, even if to some extent, let us assume some real and more than trivial extent, it is false? Moreover, where the transaction is complex and the representations are manifold, much may depend on how they are categorized. If the representations are chopped into small slices, and the microscope is turned up to investigate each slice, it may be easier to establish the inaccuracy of a representation than if the matter is looked at more broadly. On the other hand it may be that the smaller the slice, even on the assumption of materiality, the weaker is the inference of inducement. So these questions are interlinked.

The section is not discussing about negative assertion but a positive assertion in a innocent manner, ignorant of the fact that the information is not true.

The basic element at the time of making the positive assertion is the person who is making it, does not have bad intentions or is not concealing any mala fide intention to induce the other.

Positive assertion

Positive assertion of a fact is true while the information does not warrant it to be so, though the person making it believes it to be true amounts to misrepresentation.

Illustration

A asserted to B that a vehicle certainly not more than 500 tonnage was registered. In fact the vehicle was not there and the maker was unknown to A, and it is contrary to the statement of A.

In the case Edgington *v.* Fitzmaurice (1885), it examined intention at the time of making the statement, and it was held that intentions can count as an actionable misrepresentation. It is also discussed that the claimant should prove that statement made was false, and it was within the knowledge of defendant and he was not aware whether it was true or false.

If we examine this case in the light of section 18, the section is in line with the decision as there is positive assertion and the person who is making it believes it is true and not in ambiguity or containing that it is false.

Misrepresentation and ambiguity

Misrepresentation and ambiguity in a contract may bring them closer to overlie in certain cases and many a time seems to be an act of the same genesis, but there are differences between misrepresentation and ambiguity. Ambiguity means when there is more than one way of understanding, but in misrepresentation there is positive assertion and no scope of doubts.

Misrepresentation of fact and law

Statement of Fact Material Facts

As we have discussed in previous chapters to execute the mandates of law of contract it is essential that both the parties must agree to the same thing in the same sense. If there are deviations in conceiving the material fact differently by both the parties to contract, the contract stands void.

Misrepresentation of facts relates to the positive assertion of any material facts with regards to contractual obligations during negotiations, when the representation is untrue for some existing fact or any past event. The constituent requirement of the section is positive assertion about the material fact in a manner that is not warranted. If the statement of fact is not related to material fact it does not amount to misrepresentation. Now the question arises: what is the meaning of material fact? In the case of Baker *v.* Asia Motor Co Ltd, (1962)MLJ425, the question was examined as: 'a fact is said to be material if it would affect the judgement of a reasonable person in deciding whether to enter into the contract and, if so, on what terms'.

Illustration

A wanted to buy an used car of B, while showing the car, B represented the car as five years younger than its actual age. (This is a material fact, and amounts to misrepresentation.)

A applied for job in B's company. As per company policy they prohibit persons who have been convicted, A is previously convicted. (This is a material fact.)

Example

A wanted to buy B's car and inquires about the engine, and B positively asserted that the engine of the car was in good condition, while the information was not true.

Thus, it constitutes a misrepresentation. It is also called actionable misrepresentation, when it comprises a false statement. One must differentiate between statements of fact, which are actionable if false, and statements of opinion or belief; statements of law and cases of silence or non-disclosures which are not in general actionable. There are two basic elements of actionable misrepresentation: one, there must be false statement of fact which is material to contract and second, future conduct or intention.

Statement of opinion or belief

A statement of opinion or belief is the assumption or personal knowledge of one who is making such representation. He may not be aware about the true facts or material facts which are required for raising the contractual obligations. And it is not considered a statement of fact except it is in the knowledge of the person who is making the representation. The question was analysed in the case of Bisset *v.* Wilkinson [1927] AC 177 by Privy Council. In this case one purchased a piece of farmland to use as a sheep farm. He enquired of the seller how many sheep the land would hold. The seller had not used it as a sheep farm but estimated that it would carry 2,000 sheep. Believing the statement the claimant purchased the land. The estimate turned out to be wrong and the claimant brought an action for misrepresentation.

The Privy Council held that the statement was only a statement of opinion and not a statement of fact and therefore not an actionable misrepresentation.

Likewise in the case of Smith *v.* Land and House Property Corporation (1884) where a vendor lied about the tenant being 'most desirable', although he knew this was not true. It was held that there was a misrepresentation of fact as the vendor was in a position to know the true facts.

Statements of future conduct

In the case of Esso Petroleum Co Ltd *v.* Mardon (1976) QB 801, the company was held liable for damages for making an inaccurate sales forecast.

In the case of Edgington *v.* Fitzmaurice (1885) 29 Ch D 459, a company raised money from the public by saying that the invested amount will be used for the expansion of the business, while the real motive was to utilize the money for clearing the company's debts. It was held to be a fraudulent misrepresentation of fact.

> There must be a misstatement of an existing fact; but the state of a man's mind is as much a fact as the state of his digestion. It is true that it is very difficult to prove what the state of a man's mind at a particular time is, but if it can be ascertained, it is as much a fact as anything else. A misrepresentation as to the state of a man's mind is, therefore, a misstatement of fact.

But it was also examined in the case of Edgington *v.* Fitzmaurice (1885) 29 Ch D 459 that a future statement regarding the conduct or act of the person who is making it, except the statement, is incorporated into a contract.

Statements of law

Making a false statement as to what the law is, is not a misrepresentation, for example:

A made the representation to B that a lease agreement does not need to be in writing and registered.

In the case Oudaille *v.* Lawson it was discussed that where there is a duty of the carer to ensure that any advice or information should be supplied in accuracy and it is fundamental for the person who is making the representation, and the other party to rely on it, it must be supplied accurately.

Active concealment

As we have discussed earlier making false representation with knowledge amounts to actionable misrepresentation, likewise the active concealment of fact also amounts to misrepresentation.

Examples:

A wanted to buy a horse. He asked B who is the owner of horse, the health of the horse. B knows the health of horse is not good but he actively conceals this material fact. This amounts to misrepresentation.

A wanted to marry B, who was married before and widow at the time of marriage, B concealed this fact. This amounts to active concealment of fact and to misrepresentation.

Non-Disclosure

Non-disclosure of statement does not amount to misrepresentation, except when it is requested to disclose, as in the case of Hands *v.* Simpson Fawcett (1928) 44 TLR 295, it was held that a commercial traveller who kept quiet, at a job interview, about his serious motoring convictions was not guilty of misrepresentation. While if he had been asked directly whether he had such conviction and then asserted negatively he would have been liable for it.

Silence

Silence does not amount to misrepresentation but when you are duty bound to disclose voluntarily, it may be. It is also regarded that a deliberate physical action such as a nod or wink or shake of the head, or even a smile can amount to misrepresentation, but we have to conceive that a simple reticence does not amount to a legal action as there are exceptions to this general rule.

Half-truth

Half-truth means representing in part, it is a statement which, although it is factually true, creates a false impression in the mind of the representee because some information is not disclosed. It is generally a half-cooked story that has no substance, it is like making a representation on the basis of half-truth which creates serious doubts; it is neither yes nor no. Thus, if the silence is used to cover a half-truth, then it may be considered a misrepresentation.

As in the case of Tapp *v.* Lee (1803) B & P 367, where a property vendor who asserted that the property had planning permission for business purposes but fails to add that the permission is a temporary one and is shortly due to expire would be guilty of misrepresentation.

In the case of Jennings *v.* Zihali-Kiss, where the requisite information was intentionally concealed, amounts to misrepresentation.

Change of circumstances

Sometimes a statement is asserted and is true but due to a change of circumstances or lapse of time it changes or becomes false. In such a case it is the duty of the person who asserted that statement to make the other party aware of the correct statement. Contrary to it will amount to a misrepresentation.

uberrimae fidei

Contracts which are formulated on 'utmost good faith' is called uberrimae fidei. Such types of contracts impose a duty to disclose all the material facts which are essential for the contract, e.g., a contract like insurance.

Fiduciary relationship

Where fiduciary relationship exists, it is the duty of the party to disclose material facts which are necessary to a contractual obligation or which can change the ultimate decision of the parties to contract.

Comparison between fraud and misrepresentation

Contentions	Fraud	Misrepresentation
Section of ICA	17	18
Meaning	Wrongful representation is made wilfully to deceive the party	Innocently without any intention to deceive the other party
Nature	Intention to cheat	Misstatement made innocently
Thin line	Falsity	Innocent
Mental Element	False statement deliberately or recklessly made to deceive another, INTENTIONAL MISREPRESENTATION	False statement without any INTENTION to deceive; it is an innocent representation, believing to be true.
Effect	The agreement is voidable but also the aggrieved party can claim damages	The agreement can be void at the option of party whose consent is so caused and no damages can be claimed

VOID AGREEMENT

The chapter falls under the category of Void Agreement and *ab intio void,* means not enforceable by law and 'to be treated as invalid from the outset,' or in plain words from the beginning, i.e., unenforceable from the very beginning. Thus, the chapter covers those agreements which are void from the beginning. Void agreements fall under these categories:

1. Agreement under mistake of matter of facts
2. Agreement defective legality of object
3. Agreement without consideration
4. Agreement restrain of marriage
5. Agreement restrain of trade
6. Contingent contract

What is Valid Agreement?

An agreement which qualifies all the essential elements of a contract, i.e., offer, acceptance, consideration, competency of parties, object, etc., is called a valid contract. A valid contract can be enforced by law. It means a valid contract has no infirmity of law and it is enforceable with its initialization.

What is Voidable Contract?

If we analyse, section 2(i) 'An agreement which is enforceable by law at the option of one or more of the parties thereto, but not at the option of other or others, is a voidable contract.'

However, the contract continues to be good and enforceable when it made but it is liable to be repudiated or set aside on the instance of party by the court. As we have seen void contracts which are not invalid at the threshold, but void at the option of the parties whose consent is caused by virus of the contract (see chapter V), it does not mean that it has legal enforceability till the time the party whose consent so caused has not made it void. Under Chapter II of Indian Contract Act, 1872, it is being discussed which contracts are voidable. For the sake of refreshing memories, contracts which are caused by virus, i.e., coercion, undue influence, fraud, or misrepresentation fall under this category.

A thing is void which was done against law at the very time of doing it, and no person is bound by such an Act; but a thing is only voidable which is done by a person who ought not to have done it, but who nevertheless cannot avoid it himself after it is done; though it may by some Act in Law be made void by his Heir, etc.[55]

55. Martin *v.* Cowles, 18 N.C. 29, 32 (1834).

What is Void and Void Ab Initio?

There is thin line between 'void' and 'ab initio void'. Ab initio is a Latin word which means 'from the beginning' and the word 'void' means invalid or having no legal force, no sanity in law, or a lack of existence. It does not mean it is void at the threshold or from the beginning as an agreement, which was legal and enforceable when it was entered into, but it may subsequently become void due to impossibility of performance, change of law, or other reasons. When it becomes void the agreement ceases to have its legal effect. If we analyse section 2(g) it says 'an agreement not enforceable by law is said to be void' means in a void contract there is no existence of legal enforceability. When we club these words with agreement it reflects the meaning as 'void' could just mean it's void now, it might not have been before and 'void ab initio'. It is void from the beginning, so it was never valid.

Example

Annulment of marriage, when there are some legal infirmities in the marriage

Remarriages are not void but if any enactments were passed which restrain remarriage then it becomes void.

The void contract does not provide a remedy to breach of promise or set of promises and nor does it oblige the promisor. The clinical feel of this definition is that the term 'void contract' includes only those bargains that were not contracts at all, the phrase becomes nothing more than a contradiction and an intellectual fake passion. However, we should not underline the elegance of this definition, on the foundation that it fails to confess the possibility that a bargain might not give rise to a remedy or a legally-recognized duty, but might still have some legal effect.

Expressly Declared Void Agreement

There are certain agreements, which are expressly declared to be void. They are as follows:

(1) Agreement by a minor or a person of unsound mind. [Sec (11)]
(2) Agreement of which the consideration or object is unlawful. [Sec (23)]
(3) Agreement made under a bilateral mistake of fact material to the agreement. [Sec (20)]
(4) Agreement of which the consideration or object is unlawful in part and the illegal part cannot be separated from the legal part. [Sec (24)]
(5) Agreement made without consideration. [Sec (25)]
(6) Agreement in restraint of marriage. [Sec (26)]
(7) Agreement in restraint of trade [Sec (27)]
(8) Agreement in restraint of legal proceedings. [Sec (28)]
(9) Agreements the meaning of which is uncertain. [Sec (29)]

(10) Agreements by way of wager. [Sec (30)]
(11) Agreements contingent on impossible events. [Sec (36)]
(12) Agreements to do impossible acts. [Sec (56)]

Reason Making Certain Agreement Voidable, Void and void ab initio

We must understand the basic philosophy behind the Indian Contract Act, 1872 which governed the contract in India. It is an interesting fact that Contract Act does not purport to codify the complete law relating to contracts in India, but it provides the rooms and indeed preserves any usage or custom of trade or any incident of any contract and tries to create a system so that any custom or trade or usage is not inconsistent with the provisions of the Act.

The early courts classified the term 'void' with the magnitude as acts are:

- absolutely void as to all purposes
- void as to some purposes only
- as to some persons only
- void by operation of law

The basic structure of the Indian Contract Act, 1872 is founded on two basis – principal civil obligations, and public policy, which shield to govern the society. Any shake or infiltration on these two basic principles can collapse the structure of society. It is rightly observed by a scholar that 'a public policy is supposed to be the application of the fundamental ethical, political, and social principles which guide the legal evolution both in legislation and in the administration of justice'. Perhaps that is the reason the Indian Contract Act, 1872 is unable to hold every kind of agreement, there are certain agreements which remain untouched by it. As we have discussed previously agreements are the 'social behaviour of society' and society cannot remain without them. The opinion of Lord Atkin seems justifiable 'The doctrine should only be invoked in clear: cases in which the harm to the public is substantially incontestable' and the public policy is policy of law. The second principle of civil obligation gives the momentum of social behaviour and synonyms of contractual obligations, in line with the social structure and will of the society.

Comparison between void agreement and voidable contract

Contentions	Void agreement	Voidable contract
Enforceability	No legal enforceability. As per section 2(g) an agreement not enforceable by law is said to be void.	Remains in force till it is rejected. As per section 2(h) an agreement enforceable by law is a contract.
Defects	It is ab-initio and its defects cannot be removed.	Not void ab-initio void, only voidable at the instance of the party, so its defects can be removed.

Rights of Third Party	Third party is not entitled to acquire any rights.	When party acting under good faith for consideration into a contract and before the contract is rejected, they acquires the right.
Compensation	Non-performances of such contracts do not stand for compensation, if any loss sustained.	Compensation for loss arising due to non-performance of the contract, can be claimed.
Collateral Agreement	A collateral agreement to void agreement is a void contract.	A collateral agreement to a voidable contract is not a void contract.
Lapse of Time	Expiry of reasonable time is not the element of void contract.	It may become a valid contract if the aggrieved party does not reject it within a reasonable time.
Free Consent	It is void due to lack of any essentials of a valid contract except free consent.	It is voidable because the consent of a party is not free.

Comparison between illegal agreement and void agreement

Contentions	**Illegal Agreement**	**Void Agreement**
Prohibition	Prohibited by law	Not prohibited by law
Punishment	Punishable under law	Not punishable under law
Nature	Void ab inito, all illegal agreements are void agreements	Remain in force till rejection, all void agreements are not illegal agreements.
Object	Object is prohibited by law and illegal	The object is not illegal, but not qualifying the fundamental of Contract Act and void
Collateral Agreement	A collateral agreement to an illegal agreement is not enforceable	A collateral agreement to a void agreement is enforceable
Restoration	Restoration of benefit exchange cannot be restored	Restoration of benefit applicable

Agreement Under Mistake

Definition of mistake

The literal meaning of mistake is an error in comprehending facts. If we examine this definition under contract then it reflects one party or both parties to enter into a contract one or both the parties are erroneous. Law of contract recognizes different types of mistakes, as mistake of fact, when both the parties are at error on material aspects of contract affecting the rights of one of the parties to a contract. Further, it is considered that the mistake can be at any stage of contract such as at the time of negotiation. It can be mistake of motive, or it may be mistake of identity with whom the contract is executed, or a mistake related to the subject matter, and finally it may be mistake of fact and law.

As we have examined earlier, contract is the social behaviour and the foundation laid on the principle of performance, and not under the shield by any party of contract.

Under Indian Contract Act, 1872, three sections, i.e., S.20, S.21, and S22 are related to mistake as:

As it has been clear by the above diagram that the effect of mistake in relation to contract vary from valid to ab-inito void, and which ultimately provide damage and compensation and sometimes rectification respectively.

Section 20. Agreement void where both parties are under mistake as to matter of fact. Where both the parties to an agreement are under a mistake as to a matter of fact essential to the agreement the agreement is void.

Explanation: An erroneous opinion as to the value of the thing which forms the subject-matter of the agreement, is not to be deemed a mistake as to a matter of fact.

Illustrations:

(a) A agrees to sell to B a specific cargo of goods supposed to be on its way from England to Bombay. It turns out that, before the day of the bargain the ship carrying the cargo had been cast away and the goods lost. Neither party was aware of these facts. The agreement is void.

(b) A agrees to buy from B a certain horse. It turns out that the horse was dead at the time of the bargain, though neither party was aware of the fact. The agreement is void.

(c) A, being entitled to an estate for the life of B, agrees to sell it to C. B was dead at the time of agreement, but both parties were ignorant of the fact. The agreement is void.

Analysis of section

The clinical research of the section in nutshell shows that mistake is related to **matter of fact essential to the agreement.**

Both the parties to an agreement are under a mistake

If we examine the underlined words above, it says both the parties to an agreement are under a mutual mistake such as would render a contract void within the meaning of Section 20 depends upon facts which must be pleaded and proved. The section is buttress mutual mistake as the phrase 'both the parties', unilateral mistake does not substantiate the agreement void.

Unilateral mutual and common mistakes of fact

In the case of U.P. Government Through The ... *v.* Lala Nanhoo Mal Gupta **AIR 1960 All 420,** it has been discussed that mistakes in the formation of contracts may be of three kinds, namely, unilateral mistake, mutual mistake, and common mistake.

Indeed, English contract law also recognizes three types of mistakes:

- **Unilateral mistake:** Where only one party is mistaken
- **Common mistake:** Where both parties make the same mistake
- **Mutual mistake:** Where the parties are at cross purposes.

Unilateral mistake

The word 'unilateral' itself discloses its meaning: mistake by one party only, means where only one party is mistaken. Unilateral mistake consists of two categories:

1. Mistake of Terms and Conditions of Contract
2. Mistake of Identity

Mistake of Terms and conditions of Contract

When one party to the contract has the knowledge of the mistake or the circumstances related to it, it is considered to be a Mistake of Terms and Conditions of Contract.

Common mistake

'Common' means which is on both sides; in common mistake both parties to the contract make the same mistake. The categories of common mistake are obstructive elucidation, and directly hitting the essential components of a contract that may inadvertently lead to a failure of the contract. That is why the contract falls under the category of void.

There are three categories to a common mistake which are as follows:

- Res extincta: the subject matter of the contract does not exists
- Res sua: where the goods already belong to oneself
- Mistake as to quality of subject matter

Res extincta is the Latin phrase which comprises two words *Res* means *Thing* and *Extincta* means *cease to exist*. The applications of res extinct apply the when there is common mistake, and parties to the contract believe the subject matter existing at the time of contract, but actually it does not exist. (See the illustration of section 20.)

Mistake as to quality: When both the parties are under a mistake to a particular quality of the subject matter. Lord Atkin examines in the case of Bell *v.* Lever Bros Ltd [1931] that 'Mistake of both parties about the existence of some quality which makes the thing without the quality essential different from the thing as it was believed to be'.

Mutual mistake

Though there is a meeting of the minds in the mutual mistake, but the parties to the contract are at cross-purposes. A mutual mistake occurs when parties to a contract are both mistaken about the same material fact.

For example, A wanted to buy a blue carpet and he contracts to B to buy the same. B sells the carpet conceiving the blue carpet. Later it was revealed that the carpet was of sky colour. Hence, the contracts are void due to a mutual mistake.

In a case of mutual mistake the contracting parties misunderstand each other and there is no real correspondence of offer and acceptance. The parties are really not consensus ad idem and there is in fact no agreement at all. In this case also the contract is void.[56]

---

56. U.P. Govt. (supra).

Section 20 is concerned with common mistake of fact and not mutual mistake: A common mistake is there where both parties are mistaken about the same vital fact although both parties are ad idem, e.g., the subject matter of the contract has already perished. A contract in such a case is void. Where each party is mistaken as to the other's intention, though neither realises that the respective promises have been misunderstood, there is mutual mistake.

A mistake will not affect assent unless it is the mistake of both parties, and is as to the existence of some quality which makes the thing without the quality essentially different from the thing as it was believed to be. Neither party can rely upon his own mistake to say that it was a nullity from the beginning, no matter that it was a mistake which to his mind was fundamental, and no matter that the other party knew that he was under a mistake. A fortiori, if the other party did not know of the mistake but shared it. The question is not what the parties had in their minds, but what reasonable third parties would infer from their words or conduct. The court has to ascertain the "sense of the promises".

(a) Mistake of Non-existence of Subject Matter

The mandate of the section is only the mutual mistake for a matter of fact essential to the agreement and not otherwise. Now the question arises: What is the fact essential to the agreements, essential means which is core or fundamental or necessary to the agreement, without which the agreement cannot be sustained, or for which the agreement is formulated.

Illustrations of section 20 signify the essential facts to the agreement as:

(a) A agrees to sell to B a specific cargo of **goods** supposed to be on its way from England to Bombay. It turns out that, before the day of the bargain the ship conveying the cargo had been cast away and the goods were lost. Neither party was aware of these facts. The agreement is void.

(b) A agrees to buy from B a certain **horse**. It turns out that the horse was dead at the time of the bargain, though neither party was aware of the fact. The agreement is void.

The bold and underline words in the above illustrations are the essential facts to the agreement as without it the agreement is nothing. In fact the nature of promise or the link between the parties to contract which raises the contractual obligations are the essential facts to the agreement such as:

(i) **Existing Fact:** The mistake must be related to essential facts only this includes the existing fact and not the speculative facts. If the mistake is related to any future event in the contract the contract may be set aside on non-happening of such a specified future event, but such a mistake does not make the contract void ab inito, till the time the specified time/date of such a specified event the contract remains in force and on the specified time of that event the event must be in existence.

(ii) **Material Fact:** As we have discussed earlier essential fact to the contract means the core of the agreement without which the contract cannot exist. The statement denotes the material fact of the contract which, means the substantial nature or quality of facts; the term 'material fact' under refers to every fact or information which has a bearing on the decisions with respect to the contract.

(iii) **Mistake of Identity of Parties:** As we have seen the offer and acceptance is the communication to signify the person only as per section 2(a) and 2(b), else the contract does not substantiate the fundamental principle of the contract and is void. The attributes of mistake of identity are as follows:

- assumption of a false name
- taking over a business
- fraud

Effect of mistake of fact

> Thus, a mistake as to an essential and integral element in the subject-matter of the contract will void the contract. A mistake will not affect assent unless it is the mistake of both parties, and is as to the existence of some quality which makes the thing without the quality essentially different from the thing as it was believed to be. A distinction, therefore, should be drawn between a mistake as to the substance of the thing contracted for, which will void the contract and mistake as to its quality which will be without effect. According to circumstances even a mistake as to the substance of the thing contracted for may not necessarily render a contract void.[57]

Section 23 in the Indian Contract Act, 1872

The word object denotes the reason behind the contractual obligations; the word 'consideration' has been distinguished from the word 'object' but the clinical research enunciated that consideration may be the object for the other side, which constitutes the purpose or design for raising the contractual obligations. As in the case Jaffer Meher Ali *v.* Budge-Budge Jute Mills Co. ILR 33 Cal 702, discussed 'consideration' and 'object' used in section 23 of the Contract Act do not mean two different things, but 'two different views of the same thing'.

Illustrations:

(a) A agrees to sell his house to B for 10,000 rupees. Here B's promise to pay the sum of 10,000 rupees is the consideration for A's promise to sell the house, and A's promise to sell the house is the consideration for B's promise to pay the 10,000 rupees. These are lawful considerations.

(b) A promises to pay B 1,000 rupees at the end of six months. If C, who owes that sum to B, fails to pay it, B promises to grant time to C accordingly. Here the

57. I.T.C. Limited *v.* George Joseph Fernandes & Anr AIR 839, 1989 SCR (1) 469.

promise of each party is the consideration for the promise of the other party and they are lawful considerations.

(c) A promises, for a certain sum paid to him by B, to make good to B the value of his ship if it is wrecked on a certain voyage. Here A's promise is the consideration for B's payment and B's payment is the consideration for A's promise and these are lawful considerations.

(d) A promises to maintain B's child and B promises to pay A 1,000 rupees yearly for the purpose. Here the promise of each party is the consideration for the promise of the' other party. They are lawful considerations.

(e) A, B, and C enter into an agreement for the division among them of gains acquired, or to be acquired, by them by fraud. The agreement is void, as its object is unlawful.

(f) A promises to obtain for B an employment in the public service, and B promises to pay 1,000 rupees to A. The agreement is void, as the consideration for it is unlawful.

(g) A, being agent for a landed proprietor, agrees for money, without the knowledge of his principal, to obtain for B a lease of land belonging to his principal. The agreement between A and B is void as it implies a fraud by concealment, by A, on his principal.

(h) A promises B to drop a prosecution which he has instituted against B for robbery, and B promises to restore the value of the things taken. The agreement is void, as its object is unlawful.

(i) A's estate is sold for arrears of revenue under the provisions of an Act of the Legislature, by which the defaulter is prohibited from purchasing, the estate. B, upon an understanding with A, becomes the purchaser, and agrees to convey the estate to A upon receiving from him the price which B has paid. The agreement is void, as it renders the transaction, in effect a purchase by the defaulter, and would so defeat the object of the law.

(j) A, who is B's mukhtar, promises to exercise his influence, as such, with B in favour of C, and C promises to pay 1,000 rupees to A. The agreement is void, because it is immoral.

(k) A agrees to let her daughter to hire B for concubinage. The agreement is void, because it is immoral, though the letting may not be punishable under the Indian Penal Code. (45 of 1860).

23. What consideration and objects are lawful, and what not:

The consideration or object of an agreement is lawful, unless

- It is forbidden by law; or
- Is of such a nature that, if permitted, it would defeat the provisions of any law; or
- Is fraudulent; or
- Involves or implies, injury to the person or property of another; or
- The Court regards it as immoral, or opposed to public policy.

Object of section 23

The object of section 23 is to formulate a way under which a contract can be constructed by the parties to the contract which uphold not only the requirement of legal provisions but also compete with social structure.

Object and Consideration Must be Legal

The periphery of section 23 not only touches the motives or action but hits also the object and considerations. What is the meaning of object and consideration here?

Pertinent to the context of investigation of the questions let us see the diagram below:

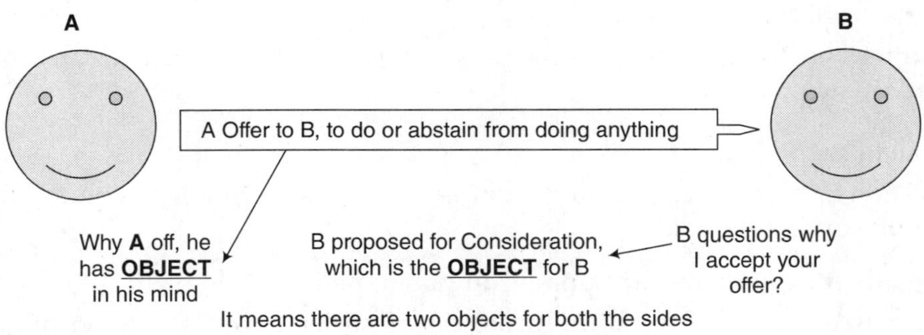

Object is the soul of any agreement, for which an agreement is constituted, or for achieving the same any contract is made.

Section 23 in the Indian Contract Act, 1872

> 23. What consideration and objects are lawful, and what are not. The consideration or object of an agreement is lawful, unless it is forbidden by law; or is of such a nature that, if permitted, it would defeat the provisions of any law; or is fraudulent; or involves or implies, injury to the person or property of another; or the Court regards it as immoral, or opposed to public policy. In each of these cases, the consideration or object of an agreement is said to be unlawful. Every agreement of which the object or consideration is unlawful is void.

In each of these cases, the consideration or object of an agreement is said to be unlawful. Every agreement of which the object or consideration is unlawful is void.

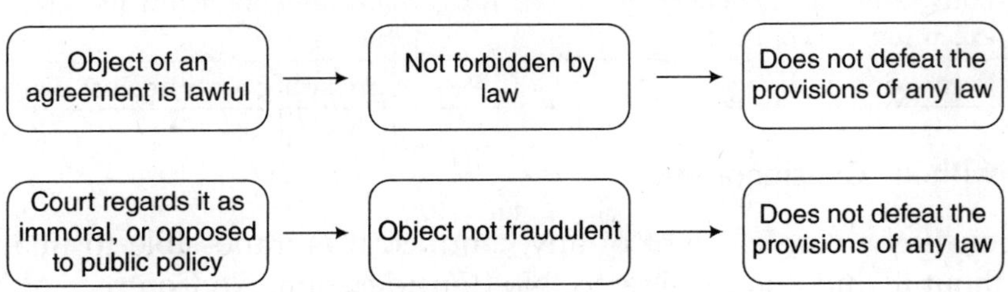

Act forbidden by law or defeat the provisions of any law

Law is the guiding principle of society, which controls the structure of society, and prohibits those acts which are contrary to the structure of society. The section includes the words 'forbidden by law' and 'defeat the provisions of any law' denotes if any contract's object contravenes any provision or prohibited by any law or statue, is void contact.

The express 'forbidden by law' broadly covers acts which are punishable under Indian penal code.

For example:

X does an agreement with Y to rob an divide the property equally which they would receive after robbery.

The expression "defeats the provisions of any law" covers an act which violates any provision of law.

If it is fraudulent

When parties to contract execute any contract with the intention to commit any fraud with any person is also void.

Court regards it as immoral, or opposed to public policy

As we discussed earlier, law is the protector of society. Any attack on morality and public policy which are the basic elements of civil society are the direct concern of any court. If any contract which imposes immorality or is against the public policy is considered by court as void.

The ambit of public policy is very wide. It covers economic, social, political, or moral, or any other thing which is in contravention of society in general.

For example, agreement for sexual immorality, women trafficking, or any agreement for past cohabitation, etc.

Comparison between object and consideration

Base	Object	Consideration
Meaning	Purpose for which agreement is made	An act or abstinence or the promise made at the desire of promisor or payment of promise
Nature	Collective Both parties act to achieve the object for executing the contract	Individual Consideration is the individual gain for the parties
Example	Purchasing a car	Purchasing a car against drugs

Agreement without Consideration

Consideration is the core element of any contract, it is impossible to imagine a valid contract without it, and it is considered 'No Consideration, No Contract' although there are certain exceptions to this rule.

The cardinal principle of Indian Contract Act, 1872 seems in section 2(e) which says that *"every promise and every set of promises that form a consideration for each other is an agreement."*

What is consideration?

In simple words it is the 'benefit that each party gets or expects to get from the contractual transaction'. It is like a driving force which sparks the parties for a contractual transaction, which is based on a promise or set of promises to do or not to do something under the legal boundaries. It is a legal bargain tool which is used to formulate a contract according to the wish of the parties. It may consider pre-existing duties for each of the parties, to execute a legal contract.

Consideration is not only equal to money, it can be anything of value in the form of money, physical objects, services, promise actions, abstinence from a future action, promised to another party in the formation of contract or anything else.

In the case of Bank of Baroda *v.* Kayenkay Agencies And Ors. 2003 114 Comp Cas 431 Delhi: The consideration should be something which not only the parties regard but the law can also regard as having some value. It must be real and not illusory.

In Currie *v.* Misa (1875) LR 10 Ex 153; (1875-76) LR 1 App Cas 554. J. Lush gives the definition of consideration in English law as: 'A valuable consideration, in the sense of the law, may consist either in some right, interest, profit, or benefit accruing to the one party, or some forbearance, detriment, loss or responsibility, given, suffered, or undertaken by the other'.

'An act or forbearance of one party, or the promise thereof, is the price for which the promise of the other is bought, and the promise thus given for value is enforceable.' (Pollock on Contracts, 8th ed., p. 175.)

Payment of Promise: In the case of Dunlop *v.* Selfridge what one party must 'pay' (it is not requiring in financial term only) for promise of other party such that promise becomes legally binding.
QUID PRO QUO ACTION IN RETURN FOR PROMISE
NOT THE MOTIVE OR REASON FOR CONTRACTING

Consideration under English law

Under English law, there are number of interpretations of consideration which are confusing such as practical benefit, legal benefit, factual benefits, or detriment of a person is consideration or not, is a question mark. When we analyse the English system of law there is no statutory existing law in order to define consideration and it rests on the discretion of court whether an act amounts to a consideration or not.

Pre-existing duty

A pre-existing duty of a person is considered to be the exception of consideration. Conversely, there is no precise criterion to define pre-existing duty. In some cases, English common law compounds the pre-existing duty with consideration.

Consideration and the Indian Contract Act, 1872 (S. 2(d) r/w S.25)

To understand consideration under the light of the Indian contract act, we have to analyse the cardinal principle of contract.

Section 2(a) of the Contract Act provides as follows:

When one person signifies to another his willingness to do or to abstain it from doing anything, with a view to obtaining the assent of that other to such act or abstinence, it is said to make a proposal.

The words 'to do' in Section 2(a) signify two things: a proposal and an undertaking that another party shall, at the request of the proposer, do something. The very next section 2(b) exhibits a proposal which, when accepted becomes a promise. Section 2(d) tells how consideration is formed when, at the desire of the promisor, the promisee or any other person has done or abstained from doing, or does or abstains from doing, or promises to do or to abstain from doing, something, such act or abstinence or promise is called a consideration for the promise. Section 2(e) further specifies amalgamation of consideration which lays a foundation of legal agreement as every promise and every set of promises, forming the consideration for each other, is an agreement. Section 2(f) displays that promises which form the consideration or part of the consideration for each other are called reciprocal promises and finally section 25 gives the mandate that except under certain conditions an agreement made without consideration is void.

Purpose of consideration

'Reason' for the enforcement of a promise

Consideration is normally an objective or a service that can be seen in the form of a promise. To enforce promise or agreement it is essential to establish that there was a return for that promise.

It is considered a foundation in law of contract: 'no consideration no contract'. It means consideration plays a cardinal role in any legally binding contract. But what is the purpose of having the consideration as a basic element in any contract, avoiding exception to it?

The purpose of consideration in contract is based on following elements:

- Purpose or caution: The first and foremost purpose is to conceive prudently why they are raising the contractual obligations.
- Proof or evident: It can be utilized as proof to execute and discharge the contractual liabilities and rights.
- Utilize or channelling requirement: Prudently satisfy their desire with available resources during the process of forced bargain.

Essentials of valid consideration

This definition contains three ingredients:

1. At the desire of the promisor
2. The promisee or any other person
3. Has done or abstained from doing something

Such act, abstinence, or promise is called consideration.

Present consideration or executed consideration is consideration given simultaneously with promise

Section 2(d) uses the word 'does' to notify present consideration, also known as executed consideration which means parties to the contracts perform their part of the promise, which comprises the consideration for the promise by other party.

Illustrations

1. A agrees to sell his car to B for a sum of Rs 10,000. B pays money to A at the time of making the contract the consideration will be taken as 'present' for A.
2. A receives Rs. 5,000 in return for which he promises to deliver goods to B. The money A receives is the present consideration for the promise he makes to deliver the goods.

Future consideration

The beauty of the Indian Law of Contract is that it gives place to every type of consideration—past, present, and future. The words 'for doing' in section 2(d) exhibits future consideration. It is also known as Executory when one party makes a promise in exchange of the promise made by other party. The performance of this promise is to be done after making the contract, at any future date. This is called future consideration.

Illustration

1. X promises to deliver certain goods to Y after a week. Y promises to pay the price after a fortnight. This is consideration.
2. A promises to deliver a car to B after a week. B promises to pay the price after a month. The promise of A is supported by the promise of B. The consideration in this case is future.

Comparison among past consideration, present consideration and future consideration

Basis	Past Consideration	Present Consideration	Future Consideration
What is	Promisor had received the consideration before the date of the promise,	Promisor receives consideration along with his promise	Promisor has to receive consideration in future for his promise
Denoted by word u/s 2(d)	Is done	Does	For doing

Recognition under Indian law	Recognized under the Indian Contract Act, 1872	Recognized under the Indian Contract Act, 1872	Recognized under the Indian Contract Act, 1872
Recognition under English law	Not recognized, past consideration no consideration	Recognized	Recognized

Such act, abstinence or promise is called consideration

Consideration need not be adequate, but legally of sufficient value

This part of section 2(d) exhibits the nature and type of consideration, the section does not provide its mandate only in terms of money or monetary benefits, it is confined with the words 'Act, Abstinence or Promise' which may be adequate, equal, or justified in the eyes of law sometimes and sometimes not. Does it mean there are no protective devices provided by the Indian Contract Act, for the type and nature of consideration?

To answer this question let's take an example:

A promises to give his luxurious house, if B opens the door for him.

Certainly, the word used in the definition does not hold the spirit, thought completes the definition. Whereas when we compare the English Law of Contract, always intended to 'consideration must be of some value in the eyes of law' as it has been propounded in the case of Currie *v.* Misa (1875) LR 10 Ex 153; (1875-76) LR 1 App Cas 554. As 'A valuable consideration, in the sense of the law, may consist either in some right, interest, profit, or benefit accruing to the one party, or some forbearance, detriment, loss or responsibility, given, suffered, or undertaken by the other.'

Test of consideration: Real or Not

In order to test whether a consideration provided for in a document is real or not, the following tests have been laid down by Sir William Anson in his Law of Contract on p. 90.

(a) Did the promisee do, forbear, suffer, or promise anything in respect of the promise to him;

(b) Was his act, forbearance, sufferance, or promise of any ascertainable value;

(c) Was it more than he was already legally hound to do, forbear, or suffer?

On the answer to these questions depends the reality of the consideration.[58]

It is also important to note that inadequacy of consideration does not lie with excessive or less consideration, it may be correlated with fraud or mistake or any influence or inducement, but what is important to note is it should not be turn the contract to impossibility.

When a court is satisfied that a promisor has entered into an agreement with his free will and with knowledge of consideration, the consideration in agreement cannot be held inadequate and agreement considered to be valid even without less consideration.

58. Madras High Court Kulasekaraperumal *v.* Pathakutty Thalevanar and Ors

Natural love and affection

It is a commonly established fact of human behaviour, that natural love and affection provide no room for any obligation or consideration generally, and sometimes there are some elements of influence which may be the outspring of love or affection or some inclination in relationship and it is based on giving and not receiving. The same human attribute has been tried to be accommodated in the section with the following safety devices:

1. Agreement in writing
2. Registered under law

Family settlement

The object of family settlement is to settle existing or future disputes regarding properly amongst members of a family. The word 'family' in the context is not to be understood in a narrow sense of being a group of persons who are recognized in law as having a right of succession or having a claim to a share in the property in dispute.

Compensation for past voluntary service

Section 25(2) acknowledges the past voluntary service, but when we go in clinical research of past consideration we find that there are two conditions for it as:

- Voluntary service
- Service rendered at request without promise, at the time of service

Voluntary service

A promise to wholly or partly compensate a person who has already voluntarily done something for the promisor is enforceable. Section 25, sub-clause (2) applies when there is a promise to compensate wholly or in part a person who has already voluntarily done something for the promisor. The word 'compensate' has been used advisedly and does not connote the same idea as repayment of a loan. The word 'voluntarily' also indicates to my mind that something has been done without any promise of compensation. It may or may not have been done out of one's own accord without any request of the other person, but there should not be any understanding between the parties that compensation would be given for the act in future.[59]

Agreement in Restraint of Marriage and its Exceptions

Section 26

With reference to the cardinal principle of promoting agreements which intend to restrain the freedom of marriage and not the restrain of marriage, the mandate of section 26 of the Indian Contract Act agreement in restraint of marriage is void. This section says that every agreement in restraint of marriage of any person, other than a minor, is void.

The exception to the section referring to any restriction of a minor's marriage is not void. This promotes the public policy. The fundamental idea behind this principle is

59. Suraj Narain Dube (supra).

'social welfare' because marriage is considered to be a social and emotional tie and an essential function of life, and private freedom and happiness. Any restriction is certainly a direct hit on personal freedom: The exception is based on public policy and minor's welfare though there is a separate enactment which protects their rights.

Section 26 is not merely referring to total restraint of marriage but every agreement in restraint of marriage, however partial the restraint may be.[60]

The same observation was in the case of Moharrum Ali *v.* Aysha Khatun, (1915) 9 CWN 1226, in such a case there was a condition if the husband married another woman the first wife would divorce him, which was upheld and court held that 'The nature of restraint may be absolute or partial, the party may be restrained from marrying at all or from marrying for a fixed period, or from marrying a particular person, or a class of persons, the agreement is void'.

Under the light of the above cases and mandate of section 26 whatever may be the nature of restraint in agreement, it is void, whether absolutely restrained from marrying, or from marrying for a fixed period, or partially restrained from marrying a particular person or a class of persons. The language of the section is direct and mandatory—there is no difference in absolute restraint or restraint of the freedom of marriage.

There is only one exception—the restraint of marriage of a minor is valid.

In the case of Rao Rani *v.* Gulab Rani, there was an agreement between the two co-widows to the effect that if any of them remarried she should forfeit her right to her share in the deceased husband's property. It was held that the agreement provides that if a widow elected to remarry, she would be deprived of her rights. The court pointed out that no restraint was imposed upon either of the two widows for remarriage. A penalty on remarriage may not be construed as a restraint of marriage.

In the case of Badu *v.* Badarnessa, there was a provision in the *Kabilnama* wherein the husband authorized his wife to divorce him and to get maintenance for the period of *iddat*, in the event of his remarrying a second wife. It was held that the agreement was valid because it was not a restraint of marriage.

Likewise in the case of Latafatunnissa *v.* Shaharbanu, an agreement that upon remarriage, the widow would lose the right to maintenance, was upheld by the court.

In Rao Ram *v.* Gulab, (A.I.R., 1942, Alld. 351) the Allahabad High Court analysed on the issue whether partial or indirect restraint on marriage can be brought under the purview of this section, and it was denoted that there is no difference between the two and partial or indirect restraint on marriage shall also be covered by this section.

We should also consider the view of the English law on this point which covered partial or indirect restraint on marriage and did not consider it void. Only those agreements which imposed total restraint shall be declared void.

---

60. Khorshed Maneck *v.* The Official Trustee (1948) 50 BOMLR 108.

Agreement in Restraint of Trade

Section 27

What constitutes restraint of trade is summarized in Halsbury's *Laws of England* (3rd edition), Volume 38, at page 15 and onwards. It is a general principle of the Common Law that a person is entitled to exercise his lawful trade or calling as and when he wills and the law has always regarded jealously any interference with trade, even at the risk of interference with freedom of contract as it is public policy to oppose all restraints upon liberty of individual action which are injurious to the interests of the State. The court takes a far stricter view of covenants between master and servant than it does of similar covenants between vendor and purchaser or in partnership agreements. ...This principle is based on the footing that an employer has no legitimate interest in preventing an employee after he leaves his service from entering the service of a competitor merely on the ground that he is a competitor. (Kores Manufacturing Co., Ltd. *v.* Kolak Manufacturing Co., Ltd. [1959] Ch.[61]

> Section 27 Agreement in restraint of trade is void, 'Every agreement by which anyone is restrained from exercising a lawful profession, trade or business of any kind, is to that extent void.'
>
> Exception 1: Saving of agreement not to carry on business of which goodwill is sold – One who sells the goodwill of a business may agree with the buyer to refrain from carrying on a similar business, within specified local limits, so long as the buyer, or any person deriving title to the goodwill from him, carries on a like business therein, provided that such limits appear to the court reasonable, regard being had to the nature of the business.'

The language of the section is very clear – any restriction of trade is void. Any restraint on trade shall violate the fundamental principle of Public Policy and violate the provision of the Constitution of India, Article 301 Freedom of trade, commerce and intercourse as 'Subject to the other provisions of this part, trade, commerce and intercourse throughout the territory of India shall be free.'

Object of section

Under the common law in England a man is entitled to exercise any lawful trade or calling as and where he wills. The law has always regarded jealously any interference with trade, even at the risk of interference with freedom of contract, as it is public policy to oppose all restraints the liberty of individual action which are injurious to the interests of the State. A person may be restrained from carrying on his trade by reason of an agreement voluntarily entered into by him with that object and in such a case the general principle of freedom of trade must be applied with due regard to the principles that public policy requires for persons of full age and understanding, the utmost freedom to contract.

61. Niranjan Shankar Golikari *v.* The Century Spinning And Mfg. Co.1967 AIR 1098, 1967 SCR (2) 378.

Contingent Contract

Contract can be classified into two categories on the basis of performance attributes, as

- Absolute Contract
- Contingent Contract

Absolute Contract: A contract which has no qualifications to perform or where there is no condition, it is called Absolute Contract, and which can be performed under all circumstances.

Contingent Contract: A contract which is performed on the basis of any condition or where there is condition, then such contract is called Contingent Contract.

Meaning

Therefore, Contingent Contract means Conditional Contract. Validity of the contract depends upon the performance of imposing conditions if fulfilled, the contract becomes valid and the parties are bound to perform their obligations. If imposed and the condition is not fulfilled, the contract become void and need not be performed.

Thus, contingent contracts depend upon the happening or not happening of the some uncertain event of the future. It is also called a conditional contract. All indemnity contracts, guarantee contracts, and insurance contracts are contingent contracts.

Literal meaning of the word according to legal-dictionary.thefreedictionary.com/

'Contingent' is 'fortuitous' and depends upon the possible occurrence of a future event, and the existence is not assured.

The word contingent denotes that there is no present interest or right but only a conditional one which will become effective upon the happening of the designated condition. A contingent remainder is the right to possess property after the death of a person who holds a life estate in the part of land provided a specified condition is fulfilled. An owner of land who grants a life estate to a son with the remainder to a daughter if she marries, has created a contingent remainder, the contingency being the daughter's marriage.

In brief it means uncertain or unsure, condition possible, but not assured upon the occurrence of some future event which is itself uncertain, or questionable.

Section 31: 'Contingent contract' defined: A 'contingent contract' is a contract to do or not to do something, if some event, collateral to such contract, does or does not happen.

If we analyse the definition it has two dimensions 'to do' and second 'not to do' something. It means the section includes positive act and a negative act. The section seems to be the same genesis of section 2(a) 'to do' or 'abstain from doing' anything, but section 2(a) does not signify any condition while the execution of section 31 is dependent upon some event or collateral condition which generally is a future event.

The backbone of continent contract is 'happening or non-happening of an uncertain event'.

Essentials

Following are the essentials of the conditional contract:

(i) It is a contract to do or not to do something

(ii) Dependent on happening or non-happening of an event

(iii) One event is a collateral event

(iv) The event is uncertain

The core of contingent contract is uncertainty of the future stipulated by the party and obligations or rights start from the point of that happening or non-happen of a stipulated future event.

It is a contract to do or not to do something

The DNA of a contingent contract clearly seems in this section **'to do** or **not to do something'** is primarily like any other contract, the genesis of section 2(a) seems to do or not to do something. However, this is an absolute and unconditional one, without any qualification or conditions, which is to be performed under any event. Its performance whether positive (to do) or negative (not to do) is dependent on some event's happening or not happening – the contingency.

Illustration

A contracts to B to pay Rs. 1,000 if her father dies next month

A contracts to pay B Rs 2,000 if B house is burnt

A promises to pay B Rs. 500 if a certain ship does not return within a year

Dependent on happening or non-happening of an event

The attribute of 'to do' or 'not to do' or performance of the contract, or obligations or rights arise on the basis of some future, uncertain event. If the performance of obligation is dependent on a certain (must happen) future event which has to occur, the contract will not be a contingent contract. Mere delay of the time of performance will not make the contract contingent at some future time. The focal point is event has to be very futuristic and uncertain, and it must be happen or non-happen.

On event is a collateral event

Contingent contract is based on uncertainty for a collateral event, and can be executed only at the fulfilment of a collateral event, not otherwise. For example:

A insures his house against earthquake, A can claim only when there is a earthquake. Earthquake is the collateral event in this case.

Pollock and Mulla say 'a "collateral event" means an event which is neither a performance directly promised as a part of the contract, nor the whole of the consideration for a promise'.

Thus, the collateral event is the integral part of the contingent contract for example:

A agreed to sell B if B makes 50% payment within one week to A.

Here making the 50% payment is the collateral event.

The event is uncertain

The word 'contingent' itself denotes the uncertainty and such uncertainty should not be dependent on promisor. It should be futuristic, without any discretion of promisor. Section 32 used the word 'uncertain' for enforcing the contingent contract. It means contingent contract does not talk about a certain event but a uncertain future event.

For example,

A agrees to make the payment of B if B succeeds in the litigation.

Enforceability

Enforceability of contingent contract depends on certain factors:

When

Such a contract under section 32 of the Contract Act, becomes enforceable by law when the future event contemplated in the contingent contract had happened.

Mandate of section 32: Contingent contract cannot be enforced by law until that event has happened. It means the ignition point for contingent contract is the happening of that uncertain future event, and if such an event becomes impossible, the contract becomes void.

The impossibility of performance of contract attracts the doctrine of frustration.

Illustrations

(a) A makes a contract with B to buy B's horse if A survives C. This contract cannot be enforced by the law unless and until B dies in A's lifetime.

(b) A makes a contract with B to sell a horse to B at a specified price, if C, to whom the horse has been offered, refuses to buy him. The contract cannot be enforced by law unless and until C refuses to buy the horse.

(c) A contracts to pay B a sum of money when B marries C. C dies without being married to B. The contract becomes void.

In the case of Satyabrata Ghose *v.* Mugneeram Bangur & Co. 1954 AIR 44, 1954 SCR 310, the Supreme Court held

Section 32 of the Indian Contract Act which deals with contingent contracts or similar other provisions contained in the Act. In the large majority of cases however the doctrine of frustration is applied not on the ground that the parties themselves agreed to an implied term which operated to release them from the performance of the contract.

At what time

Collateral event becomes impossible

A agrees to pay B a sum of money if a certain ship does not return. The ship sinks. The contract can be enforced when the ship sinks.

As section 33 says: Contingent contracts to do or not to do anything if an uncertain future event does not happen, can be enforced when the happening of that event becomes impossible, and not before.

The relief is given by the court on the ground of subsequent impossibility when it finds that the whole purpose or basis of a contract was frustrated by the intrusion or occurrence of an unexpected event or change of circumstances which was beyond what was contemplated by the parties at the time when they entered into the agreement. Here there is no question of finding out an implied term agreed to by the parties embodying a provision for discharge, because the parties did not think about the matter at all nor could possibly have any intention regarding it[62].

Expiration of Fixed Time

Section 35 says expiration of fixed time of makes contract void.

Contingent contracts to do or not to do anything, if a specified uncertain event happens within a fixed time, becomes void, if, at the expiration of the time fixed, such an event has not happened, or if, before the time fixed, such an event becomes impossible.

When contracts may be enforced, which are contingent on specified event not happening within fixed time: Contingent contracts to do or not to do anything, if a specified uncertain event does not happen within a fixed time, may be enforced by law when the time fixed has expired and such an event has not happened, or before the time fixed has expired, if it becomes certain that such event will not happen.

Illustrations

(a) A promises to pay B a sum of money if a certain ship returns within the year. The contract may be enforced if the ship returns within the year and becomes void if the ship is burnt within the year.

(b) A promises to pay B a sum of money if a certain ship does not return within a year. The contract may be enforced if the ship does not return within a year, or is burnt within the year.

It means the enforceability of contingent contract is only possible within the time specified for happening of contingent event, not after that.

When the event is considered impossible

Section 34 includes the future conduct of a living person, the contingent contract is void when such person does something to make that event void.

If the future event on which a contract is contingent is the way in which a person will act at an unspecified time, the event shall be considered to become impossible when such a person does anything which renders it impossible that he should so act within any definite time, or otherwise than under further contingencies.

---

62. Satyabrata Ghose *v.* Mugneeram Bangur & Co (supra).

Illustration

A agrees to pay B a sum of money if B marries C. C marries D. The marriage of B to C must now be considered impossible, although it is possible that D may die and that C may afterwards marry B.

Exception of Section 27

Sale of goodwill

The exception of section 27 relates to sale of goodwill. This section is not applicable to restraint of goodwill. One who sells goodwill of a business with a buyer to refrain from carrying on a similar business, within specified local limits so long as the buyer, or any person deriving title to the goodwill from him, carries on a like business therein provided that such limits appear to the court reasonable, regarding the nature of business.

The section provides the discretionary power to court. If the court appears reasonable to restrain the buyer of goodwill on the basis of the nature of business the object is to protect the interest of a purchaser of a goodwill.

Meaning of goodwill: There is no specific definition of goodwill, it is not easy to define. However, 'goodwill' being an abstract property is an intangible asset. It is not a physical asset like buildings or equipment. In plain words it is a favour or advantage that a business has acquired especially through its brands and its good reputation, which give a competitive edge to the competitors and there is increase of a business, especially as part of its purchase price. It actually increases the probability that the old customer will resort to its old place.

'Goodwill is an intangible asset as held in many cases and as per the Accounting Standard 26 on intangible assets issued as per the Indian Companies Act, 1956 and also by the Institute of Chartered Accountants of India, goodwill is an intangible asset.'[63]

Lord Macnaghten defines 'goodwill' as: 'Often it happens that goodwill is the very sap and life of the business, without which the business would yield little or no profits. It is the whole advantage, whatever it may be, of the reputation and connection of firm, which may have been built up by years of honest work or gained by lavish expenditure of money.'

Allahabad High Court in Smt. Vindoor Bai *v.* Controller of Estate Duty, 1981 132 ITR 421 All, defines 'goodwill' very elaborately as Lord Lindley dealing with the concept of goodwill on p. 235 spoke thus:

> 'Goodwill regarded as property has no meaning except in connection with some trade, business, or calling. In that connection I understand the word to include whatever adds value to a business by reason of situation, name and reputation, connection, introduction to old customers, and agreed absence from computation, or any of these things, and there may be others which do not occur to me. In this wide sense, goodwill is inseparable from the business to which it adds value,

63. Income Tax Appellate Tribunal: Delhi in Cyber India Online Ltd., New Delhi *v.* Assessee

> and, in my opinion, exists where the business is carried on. Such business may be carried on in one place or country or in several, and if in several there may be several businesses, each having a goodwill of its own....
>
> The goodwill of a business usually adds value to the land or house in which it is carried on if sold with the business...'

Lindley on Partnership, 13th Edn., on p. 463, discussing the concept of 'goodwill', states:

> The term goodwill can hardly be said to have any precise signification. It is generally used to denote the benefit arising from connection and reputation; and its value is what can be got for the chance of being able to keep that connection and improve it. Upon the sale of an established business its goodwill may have a marketable value, whether the business is that of a professional man or of any other person, but whether or not the goodwill has a saleable value is a question of fact to be determined in each case. But it is plain that goodwill has no meaning except in connection with a continuing business; it may have no value except in connection with a particular premises, and may be so inseparably connected with it as to pass with it under a will or deed without being specially mentioned.

Certain Relations Resembling Those Created by Contract

Quasi contract

The fundamental principle of law of contract is voluntarily binding for mutually agreed obligations and rights, the word quasi denotes 'apparently but not really'. The meaning itself exhibits an obligation of one party to another where no actual contract exists. It means the contract is seemingly a contract between the parties but not mutually, it is an obligation of one party to another imposed by law independently of an agreement between the parties.

A quasi-contract is the act of a person, allowed by law, by which he obligates himself towards the other party, or by which another binds himself to him, without any agreement between them.

In other words a quasi-contract is not a legally-binding document, but a legal alternate for a contract that is shaped to inflict equity between two distinct parties.

In simple words the definition of quasi-contract reflects in word 'quasi' itself which means 'apparently but not really; seemingly' or "being partly or almost'. The contract which 'resembling,' 'having some, but not all of the features of'.

The quasi contract does not come into existence by itself, except by order of the court, by which the court tries to avoid the unjust enrichment of a party in a dispute on any payment or for a good or services, or agreement of the parties.

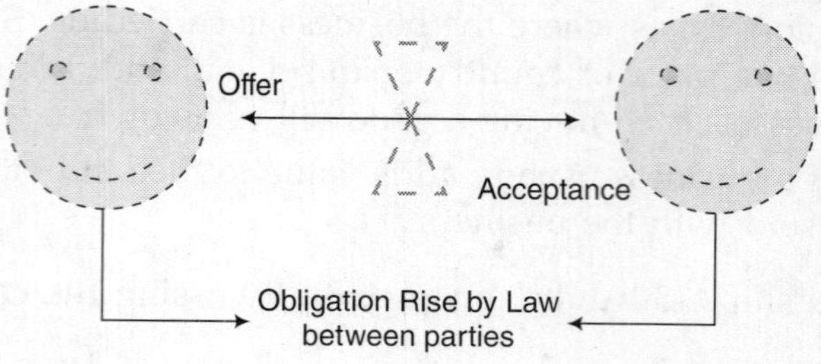

Object

The prime object of imposition such obligation to one party is to avoid unjust enrichment, which means one person is unjustly or by chance enriched at the expense of another. And law considers 'a person who has been unjustly enriched at the expense of another is required to make restitution to the other.' Thus, through quasi-contract which was created by law to promote equitable treatment, seems to be a fiction of law.

The basic elements of a quasi-contract requires three fundamental principles.

(i) One has been enriched by another benefit: A furnished valuable goods/rendered services to B with a reasonable expectation of being compensated; B failed to meet these expectations.

(ii) The enrichment is at the expense of the other: A knowingly accepted the aforementioned goods/services and obtained a direct benefit through this acceptance.

(iii) The retention of the enrichment is unjust: B receives benefits by the goods/services as unfair in situations where the plaintiff received no compensation.

Comparison between contract and quasi-contract

Basis	Contract	Quasi Contract
Definition	Initiated upon the will of the parties to contract with a view to create an obligation	Is not a contract except a legal fiction
Nature	Is an agreement	Is not an agreement
Object	It is created to raise the obligations and rights	It is created to avoid unjust enrichment
Execution	Act of parties	Act of court or parties

In a normal contract, both parties agree to the stipulations of the agreement and the surrounding issue. To affirm the agreement and to make the contract binding, the parties enter into an oral or written agreement prior to execution by way of exchange of goods or services.

In a quasi-contract no mutual assent is achieved between the parties, the court creates a contract to promote fairness to avoid unjust enrichment between the parties.

Negotiable Instruments Act, 1881

INTRODUCTION

The Negotiable Instruments Act was enacted in India in 1881, preceding which the English Negotiable Instrument Act was applicable in India. The roots of the present Act can also be seen with certain modifications in the English Act. The application of the present Act is valid in whole of India except in the State of Jammu and Kashmir.

The operative foundation of this Act lies under the provisions of 'Section 31: Issue of demand bills and notes' which says,

> No person in India other than the Bank or, as expressly authorized by this Act, the Central Government shall draw, accept, make or issue any bill of exchange, hundi, promissory note or engagement for the payment of money payable to bearer on demand, or borrow, owe or take up any sum or sums of money on the bills, hundis or notes payable to bearer on demand of any such person:
>
> Provided that cheques or drafts, including hundis, payable to bearer on demand or otherwise may be drawn on a person's account with a banker, shroff or agent.
>
> Notwithstanding anything contained in the Negotiable Instruments Act, 1881, no person in India other than the Bank or, as expressly authorized by this Act, the Central Government shall make or issue any promissory note expressed to be payable to the bearer of the instrument.

The plain reading of above section exhibits as:

MEANING, CHARACTERISTICS AND KINDS OF NEGOTIABLE INSTRUMENTS

1.1 Meaning of Negotiable Instrument

Negotiable Instruments have a pivotal role in the business world. It is not only important for interstate trade, but it plays an important role for cross borders' business and trade. It wouldn't be wrong to say it is the life line for the modern business world. A negotiable instrument plays a major role in different parts of the world in raising the economy.

Transferable quality in mercantile law refers to negotiability. In a general sense, a Negotiable Instrument is an instrument capable of being transferred by endorsement or delivery when it passed on to the holder who has the right to sue in his own name and take fee of equities against the assignor payee.

Definition of negotiable instruments

Negotiable = Transferable

Instrument = Written documents

= A written document which is transferable in nature

A written document or written order or promise to pay a sum of money transfers between two parties or from one person to the bank or from the bank to the person or from one bank to another bank.

In very simple words, negotiable refers to the term transferability of right and instrument refers to a tool (document) through which the right is being transfer from one person to another.

The word 'negotiable' means 'transferable by delivery' and the word 'instruments' means a 'written document by which a right is created in favour of a person'.

A document becomes negotiable when it contains an unconditional promise to pay a sum of money and is payable on demand.

Thus, the term negotiable instrument plainly refers to a document containing rights that can be transferred by delivery or any document that constitutes a right to an entitlement in such a manner that it is not achievable to enforce or transfer the right separately from the instrument.

In a very generic sense it can be considered a piece of paper which entitles a person to a sum of money and which is transferable from one person to another merely by delivery or by endorsement and delivery. The instrument exhibits an obligation of payment of money by one who issues it. The person to whom it is so transferred becomes entitled to the sum mentioned therein and also to the right to further transfer it, without a formal assignment but by mere endorsement and delivery.

Thus, it means any written instrument which is capable of being transferred by endorsement and delivery which vest the legal title of the holder and enables him to sue?

The answer is yes.

Section 13. Negotiable Instruments Act, 1881 defines:

11[(1) A 'negotiable instrument' means a promissory note, bill of exchange, or cheque payable either to order or to bearer.

Explanation 1: A promissory note, bill of exchange, or cheque is payable to order which is expressed to be so payable or which is expressed to be payable to a particular person, and does not contain words prohibiting transfer or indicating an intention that it shall not be transferable.

Explanation 2: A promissory note, bill of exchange, or cheque is payable to the bearer which is expressed to be so payable or on which the only or last endorsement is an endorsement in blank.

Explanation 3: Where a promissory note, bill of exchange, or cheque, either originally or by endorsement, is expressed to be payable to the order of a specified person, and not to him or his order, it is nevertheless payable to him or his order at his option.]

12[(2)] A negotiable instrument may be made payable to two or more payees jointly, or it may be made payable in the alternative to one of two, or one or some of several payees.

The definition is not elaborative, it includes what comes under negotiability, nothing else.

Thus, the term 'negotiability' and 'instrument' have a separate consideration, which requires more attention as Professor Goode defines 'instrument is a document of title of money'.

So we can say that an instrument is a document which 'physically expresses the payment obligation'. It can only be enforced when the instrument signed by the possessor or it should be with the authority of that person.

A negotiable instrument is a written promise or request for the payment of a certain sum of money to order or bearer.

A written document by which a right is given to a person and which is transferable in accordance with provisions of NI Act, 1881.

A signed writing (record) that can be used either as a substitute for money or as a means of extending credit.

1.2 Making of Negotiation?

Chapter IV 'of Negotiation' defines the mode of negotiation as:

i. Negotiation by delivery
ii. Negotiation by endorsement
    (a) Effect of endorsement

By delivery

Section 47 Negotiations by delivery.

Subject to the provisions of section 58, a promissory note, bill of exchange or cheque payable to bearer is negotiable by delivery thereof. (Instrument obtained by unlawful means or for unlawful consideration. When a negotiable instrument has been lost, or has been obtained from any maker, acceptor or holder thereof by means of an offence or fraud, or for an unlawful consideration, no possessor or endorsee who claims through the person who found or so obtained the instrument is entitled to receive the amount due thereon from such maker, acceptor or holder, or from any party prior to such holder, unless such possessor or endorsee is, or some person through whom he claims was, a holder thereof in due course.)

Exception: A promissory note, bill of exchange, or cheque delivered on condition that it is not to take effect except in a certain event is not negotiable (except in the hands of a holder for value without notice of the condition) unless such event happens.

Illustrations

(a) A, the holder of a negotiable instrument payable to bearer, delivers it to B's agent to keep for B. The instrument has been negotiated.

(b) A, the holder of a negotiable instrument payable to bearer, which is in the hands of A's banker, who is at the time the banker of B, directs the banker to transfer the instrument to B's credit in the banker's account with B. The banker does so, and accordingly now possesses the instrument as B's agent. The instrument has been negotiated, and B has become the holder of it.

When delivery of Negotiation happen?

Section 46 of Negotiable Instrument Act, 1881 says 'Delivery of Negotiation' happens when on the acceptance or endorsement of a promissory note, bill of exchange, or cheque is completed by delivery, actual or constructive. As between parties standing in immediate relation, delivery to be effectual must be made by the party making, accepting, or endorsing the instrument, or by a person authorized by him in that behalf. As between such parties and any holder of the instrument other than a holder in due course, it may be shown that the instrument was delivered conditionally or for a special purpose only, and not for the purpose of transferring absolutely the property therein. A promissory note, bill of exchange, or cheque payable to bearer is negotiable by the delivery thereof. A promissory note, bill of exchange, or cheque payable to order is negotiable by the holder by endorsement and delivery thereof.

Negotiation by endorsement

Negotiation by Endorsement, section 48: Subject to the provisions of section 58, a promissory note, bill of exchange or cheque payable to order, is negotiable by the holder by endorsement and delivery thereof.

Effect of endorsement

The endorsement of a negotiable instrument followed by delivery transfers to the endorsee the property therein with the right of further negotiation; but the endorsement may, by express words, restricts or excludes such right, or may merely constitute the endorsee an agent to endorse the instrument, or to receive its contents for the endorser, or for some other specified person.

Illustrations:

B signs the following endorsements on different negotiable instruments payable to bearer: (a) 'Pay the contents to C only.' (b) 'Pay C for my use.' (c) 'Pay C or order for the account of B.' (d) 'The within must be credited to C.'

These endorsements exclude the right of further negotiation by C. (e) 'Pay C.' (f) 'Pay C value in account with the Oriental Bank.' (g) Pay the contents to C', being part of the consideration in a certain deed of assignment executed by C to the endorser and others." These endorsements do not exclude the right of further negotiation by C.

1.3 Who May Negotiate?

Section 51 defines the capacity of parties who may negotiate as:

Every sole maker, drawer, payee or endorsee, or all of several joint makers, drawers, payees or endorsees, of a negotiable instrument may, if the negotiability of such instrument has not been restricted or excluded as mentioned in section 50, endorse and negotiate the same.

Explanation: Nothing in this section enables a maker or drawer to endorse or negotiate an instrument, unless he is in lawful possession or is holder thereof; or enables a payee or endorsee to endorse or negotiate an instrument, unless he is holder thereof.

Illustration: A bill is drawn payable to A or order. A indorses it to B, the endorsement not containing the words 'or order' or any equivalent words. B may negotiate the instrument.

1.4 Characteristics of Negotiable Instruments

A negotiable instrument has the following characteristics.

Acquisition of Property

The possession of negotiable instruments, by any person entitles him to become its owner and entitled to the sum of money contained in it. If It is payable to the bearer, the property in it passes from one holder to another by mere delivery, no formal assignment is required. In the case when it is payable to order, the property passes by endorsement, i.e., by the signature of its holder on its back and its delivery. In the words of J. Blackburn 'The transferee being a bon afide holder for value can acquire a better title to it than that of his transferor.'

Title

The transferee of a negotiable instrument is known as 'holder in due course'. A legitimate transferee for value is not affected by any defect of title on the part of the transferor or of any of the previous holders of the instrument. As in the words of Justice Willis, 'A negotiable instrument is one, the property in which is acquired by anyone who takes it bona fide and for value notwithstanding any defects of the title in the person from whom he took it'.

Exception to Nemo dat quod non habet

The presumption in favour of holder of the negotiable instrument is the owner of the property contained therein. However, the legal rule 'Nemo dat quod non habet,' means 'no one gives what he doesn't have'. A negotiable instrument does not merely give possession of the instrument but right to property also as the exception of this legal rule. The property in a negotiable instrument can be transferred without any formality and the property passed by mere delivery to the transferee, even bearer. On the other hand, property is required for the transfer of property. That the bona fide transferee is not affected by any defect of title on the part of the transferor, the holder of the negotiable instrument is considered to be the holder in due course. The general rule of 'nemo dat quod non habet, does not apply to negotiable instruments.

Rights to sue

In case of dishonour of the instrument, the transferee of the negotiable instrument can sue in his own name. According to J. Blackburn a negotiable instrument is transferable like cash, so that the transferee can enforce the rights embodied in it in his own name.

Contractual obligations

The instrument clearly states the contractual right to payment and the right will be transferred only after the complete delivery. The person who has that entitlement and possesses the instrument is considered its true owner.

1.5 Kinds of Negotiable Instruments

Section 13 of Negotiable Instruments Act, 1881 specifies:

11[(1): A 'negotiable instrument' means a promissory note, bill of exchange, or cheque payable either to order or to bearer.

SALIENT FEATURES OF NEGOTIABLE INSTRUMENTS

I. Liability of parties to negotiable instruments and discharge of parties from such liability
II. Types of Negotiable Instruments

Liability of Parties to Negotiable Instruments and Discharge of Parties from Such Liability

The expression 'parties to the cheque' or 'bill of exchange' is not defined under the Act. But Chapter III of the Act deals with the same. Under the various Sections of Chapter III, Legislature defines the liability of the various persons dealing with the bills of exchange, cheques etc. Section 26 of the Act declares that every person who makes, draws, accepts, endorses, delivers, or negotiates may bind himself and be bound. Section

28 of the Act deals with agent signing a negotiable instrument on behalf of any person making, drawing, accepting, endorsing, delivering, or negotiating the negotiable instruments. Similarly, Section 29 of the Act deals with the liability of the legal representative of any of the persons mentioned above when he signs a negotiable instrument. Section 30 deals with the liability of the drawer. The liability of everyone of the persons who would have an occasion to deal with a cheque/bill of exchange, in various capacities is clearly spelts out by the Legislature in the succeeding sections. The Legislature also spelt out the various circumstances under which such liability accrues to such a person. Therefore, from any one of the persons, who deals with a negotiable instrument, contemplated under Chapter III of the Act, who are the parties to the negotiable instrument, the amount can be recovered subject to the limitations imposed under the relevant provision ... Section 35 of the Act stipulates that any person who endorses and delivers a negotiable instrument is bound himself thereby to the subsequent holder to compensate such holder for any loss or damage caused to him, in case, the instrument eventually is dishonoured by that person who is legally liable to make the payment. Of course, the section itself provides that the endorsee may at the time of endorsement expressly exclude or make his liability conditional ... Section 35 of the Act stipulates that any person who endorses and delivers a negotiable instrument is bound himself thereby to the subsequent holder to compensate such holder for any loss or damage caused to him, in case, the instrument eventually is dishonoured by that person who is legally liable to make the payment. Of course, section itself provides that the endorsee may at the time of endorsement expressly exclude or make his liability conditional.

Discharge of parties from such liability

Section 40 of the Act talks about the discharge of endorser's liability as:

Where the holder of a negotiable instrument, without the consent of the endorser, destroys or impairs the endorser's remedy against a prior party, the endorser is discharged from liability to the holder to the same extent as if the instrument had been paid at maturity.

Illustration: A is the holder of a bill of exchange made payable to the order of B, which contains the following endorsements in blank:

First endorsement, 'B.'

Second endorsement, 'Peter Williams.'

Third endorsement, 'Wright & Co.'

Fourth endorsement, 'John Rozario.'

This bill A puts in suit against John Rozario and strikes out, without John Rozario's consent, the endorsements by Peter Williams and Wright & Co. A is not entitled to recover anything from John Rozario.

Special Rules of Evidence in Negotiable Instruments Act

Chapter XIII specifies certain Special Rules of Evidence in Negotiable Instruments such as:

Sections 118–119 Presumptions

Sections 120 to 122: Estoppel

(a) Presumptions

Sections 118 and 119 of the Act deal with certain presumptions which the court presumes in regard to negotiable instruments. Such presumptions need not be proved as they are presumed to exist in every negotiable instrument until the contrary is proved. The following presumptions shall be made.

(a) Of consideration

That every negotiable instrument was made or drawn for consideration, and that every such instrument, when it has been accepted, endorsed, negotiated, or transferred, was accepted, endorsed, negotiated or transferred for consideration:

In the case of

Section 118(a) of the Negotiable Instruments Act which is relevant runs as follows:

'Until the contrary is proved, the following presumption shall be made: that every negotiable instrument was made or drawn for consideration...'

In view of this provision it has to be presumed that every negotiable instrument was executed for consideration, the result whereof will be that whenever a claim is made on any negotiable instrument the onus of proving want of consideration is on the defendant. So far as this aspect of the matter is concerned, it could not have been seriously disputed nor it has been disputed. What was, perhaps, urged on behalf of the defendants in the court below was that as soon as it is shown that consideration mentioned in the negotiable instrument or alleged in the plaint is not established, the presumption under Section 118 of the Negotiable Instruments Act is rebutted.

(b) As to date

That every negotiable instrument bearing a date was made or drawn on such date.

(c) As to time of acceptance;

That every accepted bill of exchange was accepted within a reasonable time after its date and before its maturity.

(d) As to time of transfer

That every transfer of a negotiable instrument was made before its maturity.

(e) As to order of endorsements

That the endorsements appearing upon a negotiable instrument were made in the order in which they appear thereon.

(f) As to stamp

That a lost promissory note, bill of exchange, or cheque was duly stamped.

(g) That holder is a holder in due course

That the holder of a negotiable instrument is a holder in due course:

Provided that, where the instrument has been obtained from its lawful owner, or from any person in lawful custody thereof, by means of an SP offence or fraud or has been obtained from the maker or acceptor thereof by means of an offence or fraud, or for unlawful consideration, the burden of proving that the holder is a holder in due course lies upon him.

(b) Section 120 to 122 Estoppel

Section 120 Estoppel against denying original validity of instrument

Section 120 creates an Estoppel as :

"No maker of a promissory note, and no drawer of a bill of exchange or cheque, and no acceptor of a bill of exchange for the honor of the drawer shall, in suit thereon by a holder in due course, be permitted to deny the validity of the instrument as originally made or drawn".

There is a bar to put a question of original invalidity of the instrument it cannot be present, against the holder in due course by the drawer of a bill of exchange or cheque or by an acceptor for the honor of the drawer.

Except when the instrument is void on the face of it, for example, promissory note made payable to "bearer", or forge signature or any other legal deformity even the holder in due course cannot recover the money.

Section 121 Estoppel against denying capacity of payee to endorse

"No maker of a promissory note, and no acceptor of a bill of exchange payable to order shall, in suit thereon by a holder in due course, be permitted to deny the payee's capacity at the date of the note or bill, to endorse the same".

Section 122 Estoppel against denying capacity of payee to endorse

"No endorser of a negotiable instrument shall, in a suit thereon by a subsequent holder, be permitted to deny the signature of a capacity to contract of any prior party to the instrument"

The plain reading of sections 121 and 122 creates a strict liability of the maker of promissory note or acceptor of a bill of exchange; they cannot deny the instrument on the ground that they are not capable enough of payee to endorse or on the basis of admissibility of signature.

Except in the case of forgery or any legal infirmity on the instrument.

Types of Negotiable Instrument

(i) Promissory notes
(ii) Bill of exchange
(iii) Cheques

As we discussed in earlier chapters, section 13 of the NI Act defines the type of negotiable instrument as:

Promissory note

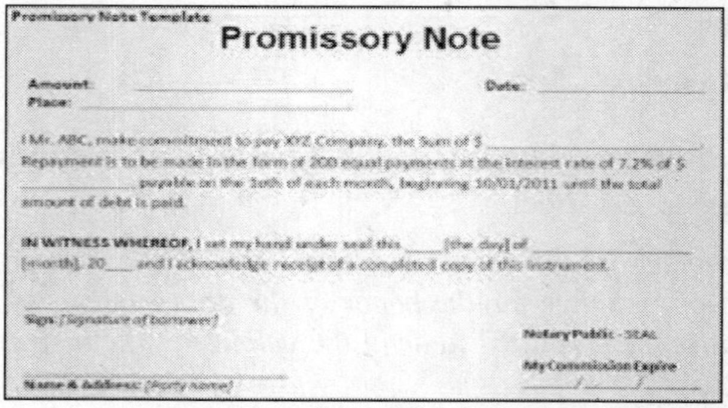

Promissory Note Template

Promissory Note

Amount: ______________ Date: ______________
Place: ______________

I Mr. ABC, make commitment to pay XYZ Company, the Sum of $ ______________
Repayment is to be made in the form of 200 equal payments at the interest rate of 7.2% of $ ______________ payable on the 1oth of each month, beginning 10/01/2011 until the total amount of debt is paid.

IN WITNESS WHEREOF, I set my hand under seal this _____ [the day] of ______________ [month], 20___ and I acknowledge receipt of a completed copy of this instrument.

____
Sign: *[Signature of borrower]*

Notary Public - SEAL
My Commission Expire
_____/_____/_____

____
Name & Address: *[Party name]*

In a simple words a promissory note is a signed document containing a written promise to pay a stated sum to a specified person or the bearer at a specified date or on demand.

Definition of promissory notes in section 4 of NI Act:

'A promissory note is an '**instrument in writing**' (note being a bank-note or a currency note) containing an "**unconditional undertaking**, **signed by the maker**, **to pay a certain sum of money"** to or to the "**order of a certain person"**, or to the "**bearer of the instruments**."

Illustrations

A signs instruments in the following terms:

(a) 'I promise to pay B or order Rs. 500.'
(b) 'I acknowledge myself to be indebted to B in Rs. 1,000 to be paid on demand, for value received.'
(c) 'Mr. B, O U Rs. 1,000.'
(d) 'I promise to pay B Rs. 500 and all other sums which shall be due to him.' (e) 'I promise to pay B Rs. 500, first deducting thereout any money which he may owe me.'
(f) 'I promise to pay B Rs. 500 seven days after my marriage with C.'
(g) 'I promise to pay B Rs. 500 on D's death, provided D leaves me enough to pay that sum.'

(h) 'I promise to pay B Rs. 500 and to deliver to him my black horse on 1st January next.'

The instruments respectively marked (a) and (b) are promissory notes. The instruments respectively marked (c), (d), (e), (f), (g), and (h) are not promissory notes.

Essential elements

Karnataka High Court in the case of Raghunath Balakrishna Deshpande *v.* Biharilal Krishnaprasad Dave AIR 1972 Kant 159, AIR 1972 Mys 159 specified the essential elements of promissory notes as:

The document will be a promissory note if it fulfils the following conditions specified in section 4:

(1) It must be in writing and signed by the maker;

(2) It should not be a bank note or a currency note;

(3) It must contain an unconditional promise to pay a sum certain in money only;

(4) It must be payable on demand or at a fixed or determinable future time;

(5) It must be payable

(i) to a specified person;

(ii) or to the order of a specified person;

(iii) or to the bearer of the instrument.

Clinical research of the above definition specifies the following elements of promissory note as:

1. It must be in writing and signed by the maker

The word 'instruments' denotes written documents, mere verbal promise to pay is not a promissory note. The reason behind it must be in any form that cannot be altered easily as it carries a financial obligation.

Signature of the person who promises to pay is the essential requirement even though it might have been written by the promisor himself. Signature binds the maker of promissory note, and specifies his identity and intention to pay by the terms of the agreement. It is important to note here that a pronote can be signed by the authorized agent of the maker, however, the agent must expressly state as to on whose behalf he is signing, else he personally be held liable as a maker.

2. It should not be a bank note or a currency note

The bank note or a currency note is different from a promissory note, though it has some similarity, such as the promise to pay, unconditional promise, signed by the maker, to pay a certain sum of money, but they are not for a specific person.[1]

It is necessary to note that the fifth condition requires that the amount must be payable to a specified person or to the order of a specified person, or to the bearer. It is, therefore, clear that even if there are no recitals in the document that the amount is payable to the order of a specified person or to the bearer, the document will still be a promissory note if the amount is payable to a specified person.

3. It must contain an unconditional promise to pay a certain sum in money only to a certain person

The above definition defines that there should not be any qualification (dependent upon the happening of some outside contingency or event) attached to pay the sum of money as contained in the promissory note; it must be an unconditional undertaking and be payable absolutely to pay, and a mere acknowledgment is not enough.

The promise to pay must be for a certain sum of money, which clearly specifies identity of the person in the promissory note, no ambiguity or unclear amount constitutes a promissory note.

Thus, a promise or order to pay is not 'conditional' to the time for payment of the amount or any instalment thereof being expressed to be on the lapse of a certain period after the occurrence of a specified event, which according to the ordinary expectation of mankind is certain to happen, although the time of its happening may be uncertain.

The sum payable may be 'certain', within the meaning of sections 4 and 5, although it includes future interest or is payable at an indicated rate of exchange, or is according to the course of exchange, although the instrument provides that on default of payment of an instalment, the balance unpaid shall become due.

The person to whom it is clear that the direction is given or that payment is to be made may be a 'certain person', within the meaning of this section and section 4, although he is misnamed or designated by description only.

4. It must be payable on demand or at a fixed or determinable future time

There is no automatic execution of a promissory note, it must be executed on demand and the said demand should be raised at a fixed or determinable future time, the word determinable exhibits that time should be real in sense, it must not be vague or imaginary.

Example:

On demand (or six months after date) I promise to pay Peter or order the sum of rupees one thousand with interest at 8 per cent per annum until payment.

5. It must be payable

(i) to a specified person;

(ii) or to the order of a specified person;

(iii) or to the bearer of the instrument.

Bill of exchange

Rs. 10,000 | Guwahati
June 12,2009

Three months after date pay Mr. .... or order a sum of'
Rs. 10.000 value received.

To

Mr. .... | Sd/- ....

Barpeta. | *Slamp*

A three-party negotiable instrument in which the first party, the drawer presents an order for the payment of a certain sum on a second party, the drawee, for payment to a third party, the payee, on demand or at a fixed future date. A bill of exchange is distinguishable from a promissory note, since it does not contain a promise and the drawer does not expressly pledge to pay it. It is similar to a note, however, since it is payable either on demand or at a specific time.

Section 5 of the Act defines, 'A bill of exchange is an instrument in writing containing an unconditional order, signed by the maker, directing a certain person to pay a certain sum of money only to, or to the order of a certain person or to the bearer of the instrument.'

Section 2(2) of The Indian Stamp Act, 1899 defines a 'Bill of exchange' as a bill of exchange as defined by the Negotiable Instruments Act, 1881 (26 of 1881), and includes also a hundi, and any other document entitling or purporting to entitle any person, whether named therein or not, to payment by any other person of, or to draw upon any other person for, any sum of money.

A bill of exchange, therefore, is a written acknowledgement of the debt, written by the creditor and accepted by the debtor. There are usually three parties to a bill of exchange—drawer, acceptor or drawee, and payee. The drawer himself may be the payee.

Difference between promissory note and bill of exchange

To determine the character of the document, we must look to the provisions of the document itself. From the definitions of promissory note and bill of exchange it will be seen that the essential character of a promissory note is that 'it shall contain a promise', and the essential character of/a bill of exchange is that it shall contain an order. In this particular case each one of these instruments contains a promise. It is contended, however, that the word 'accepted' over the signature of the makers changed the character of the document from a promissory note to a bill of exchange. Certainly, it is not usual for the maker of a promissory note to write 'accepted' across it, but it is sometimes the case that the maker of a bill of exchange writes 'accepted' across it. But that in my view is not conclusive. The word 'accept' simply means, with regard to bills of exchange, to take responsibility for or to agree to meet. That is according to common language. That indicates what acceptance means according to the Negotiable Instruments Act. It means assent, but it means assent on the part of the drawee.[6465]

Comparison between a promissory note and a bill of exchange

Basis	Promissory Note	Bill of Exchange
Character	It shall contain a promise.	It shall contain an order.
Word 'accepted'	It is not usual for the maker of a promissory note to write 'accepted' across it.	It is sometimes the case that the maker of a bill of exchange writes 'accepted' across it.
Number of parties	In a promissory note there are only two parties – the maker (debtor) and the payee (creditor).	In a bill of exchange there are three parties; drawer, drawee, and payee; although any two out of the three may be filled by one and the same person.
Promise	A promissory note contains an unconditional promise.	In a bill of exchange there is an unconditional order to the drawee to pay according to the direction of the drawer.
Liability	The mandate of section 32 of NI Act fixed the primary and absolute liability of the maker of promissory note.	According to the mandate of section 30 of NI Act the liability of the maker of Bill of Exchange is secondary and conditional which arises when the drawee fails to make the payment, and after the notice of dishonour.
Relationship with the payee	According to section 44 of NI Act the relationship with the payee is immediate.	Same as the case.
Nature	Can be conditional.	It can also not be drawn conditionally, however, it can be accepted conditionally with the consent of the holder.
Made Payable to	The maker and the payee cannot be the same person. It means it cannot be made payable to the maker himself.	This can be made to himself also.
Notice of dishonour	Not required.	Requried.

64. Dada Silk Mills and Ors. *v.* Indian Overseas Bank.

65. Calcutta High Court in C.C. Sinha *v.* Bidhu Bhusan De and Anr. Equivalent citations: AIR 1955 Cal 562.

Hundi is also a bill of exchange

A 'bill-of-exchange' is defined as meaning a bill-of-exchange by the Negotiable Instruments Act, 1881 and includes a hundi, and any other document entitling or purporting to entitle any person, whether named therein or not, to payment by any other parson of, or to draw upon any other person for, any sum of money.[66]

In the case of Fisher v. Calvert [1879] 27 W.R. 301, where a person entitled to a sum of money under a will signed a document purporting to authorize and direct the trustee of the will to pay a certain sum of money to a creditor, it was held that although that instrument was within the literal meaning of the wider language used by the English Stamp Act, the case was not one which could be intended to be covered by the expression 'bill-of-exchange' even for the purpose of a Stamp Act. The instrument in question in that case was really in the nature of an equitable assignment by way of charge of the right to receive a sum of money under the will; in other words, it was not a document of the general character which was in the contemplation of the legislature while using the wide language to which I have referred to. On the other hand, in the case of Rothschild & Sons v. Commissioners of Inland Revenue [1894] 2 Q.B. 142, we have an illustration of an instrument which was not a bill-of-exchange in the technical sense, but was held to come within the extension of the usual definition which is operated by the Stamp Act. In that case a certain foreign Government had issued bonds and had issued interest coupons for ten years. As part of the same document, there was what was called talon, namely, a document stating that interest coupons for another ten years would be forthcoming at the end of ten years. The question arose whether these interest coupons were liable to duty as being bills-of-exchange and it was held that, although the documents merely stated that interest would be paid at a certain time and place and were not bills of exchange. Within the legal definition of that phrase, nevertheless they did come within the more general language by which the Stamp Act had extended the definition.[67]

Comparing the definition in section 19 of the Negotiable Instruments Act, 1881 with the definition in section 2(3) of the Indian Stamp Act, 1899, it would be apparent that the Indian Stamp Act, 1899 provides an extended definition of the expression 'Bill of Exchange payable on demand'. In so far as the present case is concerned, the Learned Counsel for the Plaintiff emphasized that 'Bill of Exchange payable on demand' includes an order for the payment of any sum of money by a Bill of Exchange or Promissory Note or for the delivery of Bill of Exchange or Promissory Note in satisfaction of any sum of money or for the payment of any sum of money out of any particular fund which may or may not be available or upon any condition or contingency which may or may not be performed or happened. In the present case, the first two Bills of Exchange

66. Stamp Act *v.* Unknown on 12 June, 1928 AIR 1928 Cal 566.
67. Stamp Act *v.* Unknown (supra)

were drawn at sight, while the third Bill of Exchange was payable 70 days on sight after the estimated time of arrival. The Learned Counsel appearing on behalf of the Plaintiff submitted that in any event, the first two Bills of Exchange were payable at sight and the modification which was brought about was only in the terms of collection upon the request of the defendants that they may be granted some additional or extended time to pay the amount due under the two Bills of Exchange. The submission was that even if the terms of collection of the two Bills of Exchange and the terms of the third Bill of Exchange are taken into consideration, it would be apparent that what they provide is that the Bill of Exchange is payable 70 days sight from the estimated time of arrival. The payment of the amount due under the Bill of Exchange was, it was submitted, thus conditional upon the estimated time of arrival and if the goods did not arrive, there was no question of the contingency for the payment of the goods coming into existence. The payment under the Bill of Exchange was, therefore, according to the submission conditional or contingent upon arrival which was an event which may not in a given case have happened or come into existence. In these circumstances, it was argued that the Bills of Exchange in the present case are all Bills of Exchange payable on demand within the meaning of that expression contained in the Indian Stamp Act, 1899, and that being the position, the three Bills of Exchange were not liable to be stamped under the provisions of the Indian Stamp Act, 1899. On the other hand, the Learned Counsel for the defendants submitted that clauses a, b, and c of sub-section (3) of section 2 deals with instruments which are not in themselves Bills of Exchange. Consequently, since the instruments in the present case are Bills of Exchange, the Plaintiff cannot rely upon clause (a) to sustain the submission that the Bills were an order for payment conditional on the happening of an event and were hence payable on demand ... Sub-section (2) of section 2 of the Indian Stamp Act, 1899 provides a definition of the expression 'Bill of Exchange'. Besides a Bill of Exchange as defined by the Negotiable Instruments Act, 1881, the expression has also been defined to include a hundi and any other document entitling or purporting to entitle any person, whether named therein or not to payment by any other person or to draw upon any other person for, any sum of money. Sub-section (3) of section 2 provides a definition of the expression 'Bill of Exchange payable on demand'. The definition is an inclusive definition and is hence not an exhaustive enumeration. Clauses (a), (b), and (c) of sub-section (3) extend the ordinary connotation of the meaning of that expression. That is indeed clear from clause (c) which includes even a letter of credit within the meaning of what constitutes a Bill of Exchange payable on Demand. Clause (a) includes (i) an order for the payment of any sum of money by a Bill of Exchange or Promissory Note; (ii) an order for the delivery of any Bill of Exchange or Promissory Note in satisfaction of any sum of money; (iii) an order for payment of any sum of money out of any particular fund which may or may not be available; and (iv) an order for the payment of any sum of money upon any condition or contingency which may not be performed or happen. Similarly, an order for the payment of any sum of money—weekly, monthly, or at any other stated period is considered to be a Bill of Exchange payable on demand under clause (b) of sub-section (3). These provisions of sub-section (3) would demonstrate that for the purposes of the fiscal enactment which the Stamp Actis, the Legislature adopted an extended definition of what constitutes a Bill of Exchange payable on demand. This definition extends the ordinary meaning of the expression as known in common parlance or for that matter as adopted by the Negotiable Instruments Act, 1881. No stamp duty is payable on a Bill of Exchange payable on demand.[68]

Bill of Exchange = a written acknowledgement of the debt, written by the creditor and accepted by the debtor. There are usually three parties to a bill of exchange—drawer, acceptor or drawee, and payee. Drawer himself may be the payee.

Cheque Meaning, Nature and Legal Characteristics

Meaning of cheque

ABC Bank

Date____________

Pay 'A; ____ or the bearer
sum of rupees ____________________________________ only.

Rs ------/-

A/c No---------LF------

Sd/-

No--------------------

The cheque is an order to a bank to pay a specific amount of money from a person's account to the person in whose name the cheque has been issued, it is a type of bill of exchange and was developed with an idea to remove the hassle to carry large amounts of money. It is regularly used in the financial transactions, and makes the financial transactions more convenient and safe.

The origins of cheques can be seen in the ancient banking system, in which bankers would issue orders at the request of their customers, to pay money to recognized payees. Such an order was referred to as a bill of exchange.

Section 6 of NI Act defines cheque as:

A 'Cheque' is a bill of exchange drawn on a specified banker and not expressed to be payable otherwise than on demand and it includes the electronic image of a truncated cheque and a cheque in the electronic form.

Explanation I: For the purposes of this section, the expressions (a) 'A cheque in the electronic form' means a cheque which contains the exact mirror image of a paper

---

68. M/S Wolstenholme International ... *v.* Twin Stars Industrial AIR 2001 Bom 409, 2001 (4) BomCR 114, (2001) 3 BOMLR 777.

cheque, and is generated, written, and signed in a secure system ensuring the minimum safety standards with the use of digital signature (with or without biometrics signature) and asymmetric crypto system; (b) 'A truncated cheque' means a cheque which is truncated during the course of a clearing cycle, either by the clearing house or by the bank whether paying or receiving payment, immediately on generation of an electronic image for transmission, substituting the further physical movement of the cheque in writing.

Explanation II: For the purposes of this section, the expression 'clearing house' means the clearing house managed by the Reserve Bank of India or a clearing house recognized as such by the Reserve Bank of India.

The literal meaning of cheque is 'a printed form, used instead of money, to make payments from your bank account'.[69]

In simple words 'Cheque is an instrument in writing containing an unconditional order, addressed to a banker, bearing the signature of the owner or holder of such account with the, to pay on demand a certain sum of money to the order of certain person or to the bearer of instrument.'

Nature of cheque

Genesis of bill of exchange

The application of section 5, of NI Act as signed by the drawer must contain an unconditional order on a certain banker to pay a specified sum of amount to or the order of the specified person or to the bearer of the instrument. It is also applicable on a cheque as it falls under with the character of Bill of Exchange.

Written contract

A cheque is a contract in writing with the trait of negotiability with a reasonable cause in order to be valid and enforceable. It means if the fundamental contract for which the cheque was given is voidable, illegal, or is impossible to perform, the claim for enforcement by the payee of the cheque will be unsuccessful. It is mandatory to enforce the cheque obligations, the validity of the primary transaction will be relevant.

Legal characteristics

Relevant provisions with respect to dishonour of cheque

Sections 138 to 142 of chapter XVII, of the negotiable Instrument Act, 1881, deals with dishonouring of cheques. This chapter has been inserted by the Act 66 of 1988, which comes into force w.e.f. 01.04.1989, as the Banking Public Financial Institutions and

69. http://dictionary.cambridge.org/dictionary/english/cheque

Negotiable Instruments Law (Amendment), Act, 1988, amending Negotiable Instruments act 1881 by amending sections 80 to 117 with a new chapter XVII. The chief objective to insert this chapter was to promptitude and remedy against defaulters and to ensure credibility of the holders of the negotiable instrument.

Statement of Objects and Reasons

The Negotiable Instruments Act, 1881 was amended by the Banking, Public Financial Institutions and Negotiable Instruments Laws (Amendment) Act, 1988 wherein a new Chapter XVII was incorporated for penalties in case of dishonoured cheques due to insufficiency of funds in the account of the drawer of the cheque. These provisions were incorporated with a view to encourage the culture of the use of cheques and enhancing the credibility of the instrument. The existing provisions in the Negotiable Instruments Act, 1881, namely, sections 138 to 142 in Chapter XVII have been found deficient in dealing with dishonoured cheques. Not only the punishment provided in the Act has proved to be inadequate, the procedure prescribed for the courts to deal with such matters has been found to be cumbersome. The courts are unable to dispose of such cases expeditiously in a time-bound manner in view of the procedure contained in the Act.

2. A large number of cases are reported to be pending under sections 138 to 142 of the Negotiable Instruments Act in various courts in the country. Keeping in view the large number of complaints under the said Act pending in various courts, a Working Group was constituted to reveiw section 138 of the Negotiable Instruments Act, 1881 and make recommendations as to what changes were needed to effectively achieve the purpose of that section.

3. The recommendations of the Working Group along with other representations from various institutions and organizations were examined by the Government in consultation with the Reserve Bank of India and other legal experts, and a Bill, namely, the Negotiable Instruments (Amendment) Bill, 2001 was introduced in the Lok Sabha on 24 July, 2001. The Bill was referred to Standing Committee on Finance which made certain recommendations in its report submitted to Lok Sabha in November 2001.

4. Keeping in veiw the recommendations of the Standing Committee on Finance and other representations, it has been decided to bring out, *inter alia,* the following amendments in the Negotiable Instruments Act, 1881, namely:

(i) to increase the punishment as prescribed under the Act from one year to two years;

(ii) to increase the period for issue of notice by the payee to the drawer from 15 days to 30 days;

(iii) to provide discretion to the court to waive the period of one month, which has been prescribed for taking cognizance of the case under the Act;

(iv) to prescribe procedure for dispensing with preliminary evidence of the complainant;

(v) to prescribe procedure for servicing of summons to the accused or witness by the court through speed post or empanelled private couriers;

(vi) to provide for summary trial of the cases under the Act with a view to speeding up disposal of cases;

(vii) to make the offences under the Act compoundable;

(viii) to exempt those directors from prosecution under section 141 of the Act who are nominated as directors of a company by virtue of their holding any office or employment in the Central Government or State Government or a financial corporation owned or controlled by the Central Government, or the State Government, as the case may be;

(ix) to provide that the Magistrate trying an offence shall have power to pass sentence of imprisonment for a term exceeding one year and amount of fine exceeding five thousand rupees;

(x) to make the Information Technology Act, 2000 applicable to the Negotiable Instruments Act,1881 in relation to electronic cheques and truncated cheques subject to such modifications and amendments as the Central Government, in consultation with the Reserve Bank of India, considers necessary for carrying out the purposes of the Act, by notification in the Official Gazette; and

(xi) to amend definitions of 'bankers' books' and 'certified copy' given in the Bankers' Books Evidence Act, 1891.

5. The proposed amendments in the Act are aimed at early disposal of cases relating to dishonoured cheques, enhancing punishment for offenders, introducing electronic image of a truncated cheque and a cheque in the electronic form, as well as exempting an official nominee director from prosecution under the Negotiable Instruments Act, 1881.

6. The Bill seeks to achieve the above objects.

Taking further steps the Parliament made several amendments to give speed to financial transactions in this series and a milestone is being created by the Parliament with the [Amendment and Miscellaneous Provisions), Act 2002 (55 of 2002, dt. 17-12-2002, w.e.f. 6-2-2003 vide S.O. 140 (E), dt. 6-2-2003], by making the liability of the drawer of a cheque more stringent in case of dishonour thereof and simplifying the court procedure for trial of cases summarily.

Prior to insertion of 138 of NI, the aggrieved person had the only remedy of instituting a suit in civil court, which took long time to dispose of the matter and ultimately the growth of the economy gets hampered because of an unscrupulous drawer who normally took various pleas to defeat the genuine claim of the payee.

Section 138 has converted civil liability into criminal offence. The insertion of section 138 was to hold the criminal liability and give speed to the commercial transactions, and trade.

Best part of an Offence u/s 138 is an offence without any mens rea, that is why sometimes it is called quasi criminal or quasi civil in nature. But it constitutes a strict liability of the drawer of the cheque, along with the presumption under section 118, which supports this principle.

Thus, the focal object of this Act is to incorporate faith in the efficacy of financial and banking transactions and reliability in transacting business on negotiable instruments.

Section 138

Section 138 sometimes is being treated synonymous of the NI Act, it seems to be the back bone of the whole act.

138. Dishonour of cheque for insufficiency, etc., of funds in the accounts

Where any cheque drawn by a person on an account maintained by him with a banker for payment of any amount of money to another person from out of that account for the discharge, in whole or in part, of any debt or other liability, is returned by the bank unpaid, either because of the amount of money standing to the credit of that account is insufficient to honour the cheque or that it exceeds the amount arranged to be paid from that account by an agreement made with that bank, such person shall be deemed to have committed an offence and shall without prejudice to any other provisions of this Act, be punished with imprisonment for a term which may extend to one year, or with fine which may extend to twice the amount of the cheque, or with both:

PROVIDED that nothing contained in this section shall apply unless:

(a) the cheque has been presented to the bank within a period of three months from the date on which it is drawn or within the period of its validity, whichever is earlier;

(b) the payee or the holder in due course of the cheque, as the case may be, makes a demand for the payment of the said amount of money by giving a notice, in writing, to the drawer of the cheque, within fifteen days of the receipt of information by him from the bank regarding the return of the cheque as unpaid, and

(c) the drawer of such cheque fails to make the payment of the said amount of money to the payee or, as the case may be, to the holder in due course of the cheque, within fifteen days of the receipt of the said notice.

Explanation: For the purpose of this section, 'debt or other liability' means a legally enforceable debt or other liability.

Comment: As the signature in the cheque is admitted to be that of the accused, the presumption envisaged in section 118 of the Act can legally be inferred that the cheque was made or drawn for consideration on the date which the cheque bears. Section 139 of the Act enjoins on the court to presume that the holder of the cheque received it for the discharge of any debt or liability. The burden was on the accused to rebut the aforesaid presumption. K. Bhaskaran, Appellant *v.* Sankaran Vaidhyan Balan, AIR 1999.

Essential ingredients of sec138

Kerala High Court, Kunjan Panicker *v.* Christudas Alias A.J. Alex and 1999 98 CompCas 235 Ker, observe the necessary ingredients of section 138 as:

The ingredients of Section 138 of the Negotiable Instruments Act have too often been stated. They are:

(1) that the cheque must be drawn by a person on an account maintained by him with a banker for payment of any amount of money to another person from out of that account for the discharge, in whole or in part, of any debt or other liability, and

(2) that the cheque must have been returned by the bank unpaid either because the amount of money standing to the credit of that account is insufficient to honour the cheque or it exceeds the amount arranged to be paid from that account by an agreement made with that bank. But nothing in the above section however would apply unless:

  (a) the cheque has been presented before the bank within a period of six months from the date on which it is drawn or within the period of its validity, whichever is earlier,

  (b) the payee or the holder in due course of the cheque, as the case may be makes a demand for the payment of the said amount of money by giving a notice in writing, to the drawer of the cheque, within fifteen days of the receipt of information by him from the bank regarding the return of the cheque as unpaid, and

  (c) the drawer of such a cheque fails to make the payment of the said amount of money to the payee or as the case may be, to the holder in due course of the cheque within fifteen days of the receipt of the said notice.

It is a prerequisite of the offence under section 138 of the Act, that the cheque drawn by a person must be on an account maintained by him with the banker and if such a cheque has been dishonoured, the drawer of the said cheque will be liable for the said offence. Since, the cheques in question were not drawn on any particular account maintained by the respondent in the bank, and since the O.D. account of the respondent was not in existence in, the said bank by the date on which the said cheques were drawn, no case was made out against the respondent for the offence under Section 138 of the Act.[70]

Likewise Karnataka High Court in the case of Deepa Finance Corporation *v.* A.K. Mohammed on 20 February, 2001 2001 (2) ALD Cri 731, 2002 108 CompCas 636 Kar, 2001 CriLJ 3582, ILR 2001 KAR 4310, observe:

70. Urban Co-Op. Credit Society *v.* State of Gujarat and Anr. II (2004) BC 24, 2003 CriLJ 3292, (2003) 3 GLR 2207.

It is prerequisite of the offence under section 138 of the Act, that the cheque drawn by a person must be on an account maintained by him with the banker and if such a cheque has been dishonoured, the drawer of the said cheque will be liable for the said offence. Since in the instant case, it is found that the cheques in question were not drawn on any particular account maintained by the respondent in Vijaya Bank, Bunder Branch, Mangalore City and since it is further found that O.D. account of the respondent was not in existence in the said bank by the date on which the said cheques were drawn, I find that no case is made out against the respondent for the offence under section 138 of the Act. Even assuming that non-mention of the O.D. account number in the cheques drawn by the respondent is not of any importance when he has mentioned that the cheques were drawn on O.D. account, since it is found that even that O.D. account was not maintained by the respondent in the above said bank by the date on which the above cheques were drawn, it is clear that the above cheques were not drawn on an account maintained by the respondent in the above bank. Further, this is not a case where O.D. account maintained by the respondent in the above bank has been closed by him subsequently after the date on which the said cheques were drawn by him with an intention to cheat the appellant and to prevent him from getting the amount realized. Since it is found that O.D. account was not in existence by the date on which the said cheques were drawn by the respondent, in my view, the provisions of section 138 of the Act are not attracted in the present case. Appellant has to blame himself for not taking care to get the account number mentioned in the cheques issued in this case by the respondent, at the time when the said cheques were drawn and in not verifying with the bankers as to whether really the respondent had any O.D. account in the above said bank by the date on which the cheques were drawn by him. In this view of the matter, I find that no case is made out against the respondent for the offence under section 138 of the Act. Apart from this fact, it is also doubtful whether the appellant is entitled to prosecute the criminal proceedings under section 138 of the Negotiable Instruments Act, when he has chosen to obtain a decree for the same loan amount in a Civil Court and when he is executing the said decree by attachment of the amount payable to the respondent from P.W.D. funds, though the appellant is entitled to contend that as long as the decree amount remained unrealized or unpaid, the cheques in question issued must be taken as the cheques issued for the loan amount due by the respondent. But, I agree with the contention of the learned Counsel for the appellant that the learned Magistrate was not correct in holding that by virtue of the order of the attachment obtained by the appellant before judgment in respect of the amount payable to the respondent by P.W.D. authority, it must be taken that the loan amount is not outstanding and the cause of action does not survive in favour of the appellant to prosecute the respondent for the offence under section 138 of the Act. However, since it is found that the cheques in question have not been drawn by the respondent in respect of any particular account number maintained by him on the Vijaya Bank, Bunder Branch, Mangalore City, I find that no case is made out for the offence under Section 138 of the Act.

Discharge, In Whole Or In Part, Of Any Debt Or Other Liability

Delhi High Court in the case of Rameshwar Dass Devi Dayal (P) Ltd. *v.* Consolidated Steels And Alloys observe:

To understand and appreciate as to what is meant by the expression 'any debt or other liability', it would be appropriate to examine the meaning of the word 'debt'. It has already been pointed out above that the Supreme Court in the case of the Union of India *v.* Raman Iron Foundry (supra) had indicated two concepts of 'debt'. An obligation to pay a sum of money at a future date, is a debt 'owing' but, where the obligation to pay a sum of money in the present is involved, it is a debt 'due'. The Supreme Court also approved the meaning ascribed to the word 'debt' by the cases referred to in Raman Foundry (supra) to the effect that the word 'debt' is as applicable to a sum of money which has been promised at a future date as to a sum now due and payable. It was observed that if a distinction were to be made between the two, the former kind would be known as a 'debt owing' and the latter would be known as a 'debt due'. Clearly, a debt is not only a sum of money which is payable at the present but also includes a sum of money which would become payable in future by reason of a present obligation. There must be a present obligation, the question as to whether it is payable now or later is not of much consequence.

9. The Supreme Court had also examined the expression 'debt' in J. Jermons v. Aliammal in the following manner:

...Ordinarily, 'debt' means money that is owed; an existing obligation to pay a certain amount; a sum of money due from one person to another. Debts can be classified, having regard to the criteria for payment, into three categories:

(i) debt which has become due and is payable at present (debitum in praesenti), e.g., in monthly tenancy, rent becomes due after the expiry of each month like rent for the month of January becoming due and payable on February 1;

(ii) debt which has become due but is payable at a future date (debitum in praesenti solvendum in futuro); in the above example if under an agreement of tenancy rent is payable on the 15th of the following month, the rent for January becomes due on February 1, but is payable on February 15; and

(iii) contingent debt which becomes payable on the happening of a certain event which may or may not occur; in the above instance the rent for the month of January will not be a debt in the preceding month of December for the tenant may or may not reside in the next month. Thus, rent that has not become due is not debt. It follows that rent for the unexpired period of lease is not debt....

Delhi High Court M/S The Jammu & Kashmir Bank *v.* Abhishek Mittal Enunciated as

The language employed in Section 138 of the Act makes it ample clear that this Section does not confine its operation to the cases where cheque had been issued by a person in favour of other in discharge of his own personal debt or other liability. Section 138 of the Act is attracted in relation to cheque issued by a person to another for discharge of any debt or other liability. The explanation further specifies that such debt or other liability shall be legally enforceable. This Section provides for discharge of debt or other liability by a person even if it is a debt or other liability of another.

In ICDS Ltd. *v.* Beena Shabeer & Another (2002) 6 SCC 426, cheque issued by the guarantor to discharge the debt of principal borrower was in question. High Court held that being a cheque from the guarantor it could not be said to have been issued for the purpose of discharging any debt or liability. Supreme Court while reversing this finding held as under:

10. The language, however, has been rather specific as regards the intent of the legislature. The commencement of the section stands with the words 'Where any cheque'. The above noted three words are of extreme significance, in particular, by reason of the use of the word 'any' —the first three words suggest that in fact for whatever reason if a cheque is drawn on an account maintained by him with a banker in favour of another person for the discharge of any debt or other liability, the highlighted words if read with the first three words at the commencement of section 138, leave no manner of doubt that for whatever reason it may be, the liability under this provision cannot be avoided in the event the same stands returned by the banker unpaid. The legislature has been careful enough to record not only discharge in whole or in part of any debt but the same includes other liability as well. This aspect of the matter has not been appreciated by the High Court, neither been dealt with or even referred to in the impugned judgment.

11. The issue as regards the coextensive liability of the guarantor and the principal debtor, in our view, is totally out of the purview of section 138 of the Act, neither the same calls for any discussion therein. The language of the statute depicts the intent of the law-makers to the effect that wherever there is a default on the part of one in favour of another and in the event a cheque is issued in discharge of any debt or other liability there cannot be any restriction or embargo in the matter of application of the provisions of section 138 of the Act. Any 'cheque' and 'other liability' are the two key expressions which stand as clarifying the legislative intent so as to bring the factual context within the ambit of the provisions of the statute. Any contra- interpretation would defeat the intent of the legislature. The High Court, it seems, got carried away by the issue of guarantee and guarantor's liability and thus has overlooked the true intent and purport of section 138 of the Act. The judgments recorded in the order of the High Court do not have any relevance in the contextual facts and the same thus do not lend any assistance to the contentions raised by the respondents.

12. In Komalam Gopi *v.* T.K. Mohankumar and Anr. MANU/KE/0504/2008, wife had issued a cheque in favour of payee in discharge of liability of her husband. Plea taken by her that ingredients of offence under section 138 of the Act were not attracted, since she had not issued the cheque in discharge of her liability, was rejected. It was held as under:

3...It needs to be noticed that section 138 of the N.I. Act comes into play in relation to cheques issued by a person to another person for the discharge, in whole or in part, of any debt or other liability. The explanation at the foot of that section provides that 'debt or other liability' means a legally enforceable debt or other liability. Neither does that explanation, nor the charging provision in section 138 confine its operation to be only in relation to cases where cheques are issued in discharge of debt or liability of the person issuing the cheque. The law provides for discharge of debt by a person, even if it is a debt of another. Such transactions, where one discharges debt of another, is an instance of discharge of debt or other liability. If A discharges a legally enforceable debt or other liability of B, by making a payment to C, then, if that is done by A issuing a cheque to C, it becomes a cheque issued in discharge of the legally enforceable debt or other liability of B and is therefore, debt or other liability for the purpose of section 138 of the N.I. Act. So much so, the arguments on behalf of the accused that she issued the cheque for discharge of liability of her husband DW4 would not save her from the penal provision of Section 138 of the N.I. Act.

13. It is, thus, clear that for whatever reason if a cheque is drawn on an account maintained by a drawer with its bank in favour of any person for the discharge of 'any debt or other liability" the ingredients of offence under section 138 of the Act gets attracted in case the cheque is returned dishonoured for insufficiency of funds and the cheque amount remains unpaid within the statutory period, despite service of notice. Legislature has been careful enough to record not only discharge in whole or in part of any debt but the same also includes other liability as well. The words 'any' and 'other liability' used in the section assumes importance in the sense that if a cheque is issued by a person to discharge any debt or other liability of another person it would attract the penal consequences under section 138 of the Act. Accordingly, the view taken by the Trial Court is perverse being contrary to the settled legal position and has resulted in miscarriage of justice.

In the case of Kamalammal *v.* Mohanan 2007 CriLJ 3124, 2006 (3) KarLJ 972 Kerala High Court observed:

The Supreme Court was only highlighting the expression, 'for the discharge of a debt or liability' in the relevant context to hold that there is a presumption in section 139 of the Act in respect of the purpose for which the cheque is allegedly 'received' by the holder. The presumption available in section 139 is only in respect of the purpose for which the cheque is 'received' by the holder-complainant, i.e., for the discharge of a debt or liability. The presumption which the court can draw under Section 139 confines only to the expression, 'for the discharge of a debt or liability' and not to the factum of issuance, i.e., execution or drawing of the cheque. The court cannot therefore, draw any presumption that a cheque is 'issued/executed' by virtue of Section 139, even if the accused admits his signature in the cheque. The argument that an alleged blank signed cheque can be presumed to be 'executed/issued' for the discharge of a debt, etc., by virtue of section 139, under no stretch of imagination be accepted.

Past Liability No Future Liability

Delhi High Court in the case of Suresh Chandra Goyal *v.* Amit Singhal said:

Section 138 of the NI Act is attracted only if the dishonoured cheque was issued in whole or in part payment of an existing debt or liability, and that the said section does not apply to a cheque issued to meet the future liability, which may arise on the happening of some contingency. It was held that a post-dated cheque, if issued for discharge of a due debt, in the event of dishonour, would attract section 138 of NI Act, but a cheque issued not for an existing debt/liability, but issued by way of a security for meeting some future contingency, would not attract section 138 of NI Act.

Dishonour of Cheques Due to the Insufficiency of Funds

Bombay High Court in the case of Pawankumar *v.* Ashish Enterprises And Another:

The plain meaning of the words 'is returned by the bank unpaid, either because of the amount of money standing to the credit of the account is insufficient to honour the cheque or that it exceeds the amount arranged to be paid from that account by an agreement made with that bank' is that either there is no sufficient amount in the bank in the account to honour the cheque or the demand is of excess amount than the amount standing to his credit. It is, therefore, crystal clear that no amount could be paid nor the cheque honoured if there is no sufficient amount to honour the cheque.

Gujarat High Court in the case of Dada Silk Mills And Ors. v. Indian Overseas Bank And Anr. 1995 82 CompCas 35 Guj, 1994 CriLJ 2874:

On a plain and strictly literal reading of section 138, it becomes clear that the section refers to dishonour of cheques on two grounds, i.e.,

(i) due to the insufficiency of funds in the account to honour the cheque, and

(ii) the amount of the cheque exceeds the amount arranged to be paid from that account by agreement made with that bank.

The question which is raised for consideration of this court is as to whether section 138 deals with dishonour of cheques in all types of cases or whether criminal liability arises only in the aforesaid two contingencies of dishonour of cheques? Return of cheques may be for number of reasons. The specimen return memo as published in Tannan's *Banking Law and Practice in India*, 1989, 18th edition, clearly indicates different types of reasons for a cheque being returned unpaid, and reference to such specimen return memo may be made at this stage.

Jurisdiction

There is a recent (from 1st August 2014) change in the Jurisdiction of the court after the judgment of Hon'ble Supreme Court held in the case of Dashrath Rupsingh Rathod *v.* State of Maharashtra; MANU/SC/0655/2014, as 'it mandatory that the complaint related to cheque bouncing must be filed only where the drawee bank is located.'

With the reference to the above judgment, the Government of India passéd an Ordinance on 15th June 2015 as 'The Negotiable Instruments (Amendment) Ordinance, 2015, No. 6 of 2015. The Ordinance has introduced a new sub-section to section 142 of the Negotiable Instruments Act. The sub-section reads as follows:

(2) The offence under section 138 shall be inquired into and tried only by a court within whose local jurisdiction,—

(a) if the cheque is delivered for collection through an account, the branch of the bank where the payee or holder in due course, as the case may be, maintains the account, is situated; or

(b) if the cheque is presented for payment by the payee or holder in due course, otherwise through an account, the branch of the drawee bank where the drawer maintains the account, is situated.

Explanation: For the purposes of clause (a), where a cheque is delivered for collection at any branch of the bank of the payee or holder in due course, then, the cheque shall be deemed to have been delivered to the branch of the bank in which the payee or holder in due course, as the case may be, maintains the account.

Insertion of new section 142A: Validation for transfer of pending cases

The above noted ordinance also makes the requirenment of section 142 A for the cases which filed during the period August 2014 to June 2015, many cases related to cheque bouncing were returned to the complainants for re-filing at the places where the cheques were issued. All such cases will now head back to the place where the payee has a bank account.

142A. (1) Notwithstanding anything contained in the Code of Criminal Procedure, 1973 or any judgment, decree, order or direction of any court, all cases arising out of section 138 which were pending in any court, whether filed before it or transferred to it, before the commencement of the Negotiable Instruments (Amendment) Act, 2015 shall be transferred to the court having jurisdiction under sub-section (2) of section 142 as if that sub-section had been in force at all material times.

(2) Notwithstanding anything contained in sub-section (2) of section 142 or sub-section (1), where the payee or the holder in due course, as the case may be, has filed a complaint against the drawer of a cheque in the court having jurisdiction under sub-section (2) of section 142 or the case has been transferred to that court under sub-section (1) and such complaint is pending in that court, all subsequent complaints arising out of section 138 against the same drawer shall be filed before the same court irrespective of whether those cheques were delivered for collection or presented for payment within the territorial jurisdiction of that court.

(3) If on the date of the commencement of the Negotiable Instruments (Amendment) Act, 2015, more than one prosecution filed by the same payee or holder in due course, as the case may be, against the same drawer of cheques is pending before different

courts, upon the said fact having been brought to the notice of the court, the court shall transfer the case to the court having jurisdiction under sub-section (2) of section 142 before which the first case was filed and is pending, as if that sub-section had been in force at all material times.

Cognizance of Offences

Section 142: Cognizance of offences

Notwithstanding anything contained in the Code of Criminal Procedure, 1973 (2 of 1974),

(a) no court shall take cognizance of any offence punishable under section 138 except upon a complaint, in writing, made by the payee or, as the case may be, the holder in due course of the cheque;

(b) such complaint is made within one month of the date on which the cause -of-action arises under clause (c) of the proviso to section 138;

(c) no court inferior to that of a Metropolitan Magistrate or a Judicial Magistrate of the first class shall try any offence punishable under section 138.

Supreme Court of India in the case of M/s M.M.T.C. Ltd. & Anr v. M/S Medchl Chemicals & Pharma P held as:

In the case of Vishwa Mitter *v.* O.P. Poddar reported in (1983) 4 SCC 701, held that it is clear that anyone can set the criminal law in motion by filing a complaint of facts constituting an offence before a Magistrate entitled to take cognizance. It has been held that no court can decline to take cognizance on the sole ground that the complainant was not competent to file the complaint. It has been held that if any special statute prescribes offences and makes any special provision for taking cognizance of such offences under the statute, then the complainant requesting the Magistrate to take cognizance of the offence must satisfy the eligibility criterion prescribed by the statute. In the present case, the only eligibility criteria prescribed by section 142 is that the complaint must be by the payee or the holder in due course. This criteria is satisfied as the complaint is in the name and on behalf of the appellant Company. In the case of Associated Cement Co. Ltd. v. Keshvanand reported in (1998) 1 SCC 687, it has been held by this Court that the complainant has to be a corporeal person who is capable of making a physical appearance in the court. It has been held that if a complaint is made in the name of a incorporeal person (like a company or corporation) it is necessary that a natural person represents such juristic person in the court. It is held that the court looks upon the natural person to be the complainant for all practical purposes. It is held that when the complainant is a body corporate it is the de jure complainant, and it must necessarily associate a human being as de facto complaint to represent the former in court proceedings. It has further been held that no Magistrate shall insist that the particular person, whose statement was taken on oath at the first instance, alone can continue to represent the company till the end of the proceedings. It has been held that there may be occasions when different persons can represent the company. It has been held that it is open to the de jure complainant company to seek permission of the court for sending any other person to represent the company in the court. Thus, even presuming, that initially there was no authority, still the Company can, at any stage, rectify that defect. At a subsequent stage the Company can send a person who is competent to represent the company. The complaints could thus not have been quashed on this ground.

Limitations

It is considered that the power of condonation of delay delay as in the case of civil does not arise at all under section 138 as it special piece of legislation with speedy disposal centric.

Strict application of time lines are attached with the section as:

i. 03 months of presentation of cheque to the bank for encashment.
ii. Notice of dishonor/demand must be sent to the drawer of the cheque within fifteen days from the receipt of return memo indicating reason of dishonour cheque.
iii. If the drawer fails to make such payment of dishonoured cheque within 15 days, a complaint thereafter should be filed within 30 days in the relevant court of Metropolitan Magistrate/Judicial Magistrate as the case may be, having jurisdiction.

Punishment

This clause (clause 4 of the Bill) inserts a new Chapter XVII in the Negotiable Instruments Act, 1881. The provisions contained in the new chapter provide that where any cheque drawn by a person for the discharge of any liability is returned by the bank unpaid for the reason of insufficiency of the amount of money standing to the credit of the account on which the cheque was drawn or for the reason that it exceeds the arrangements made by the drawer of the cheque with the bank for that account, the drawer of such cheque shall be deemed to have committed an offence. In that case, the drawer, without prejudice to the other provisions of the said Act, shall be punishable with imprisonment for a term which may extend to one year, or with fine which may extend to one year, or with fine which may extend to twice the amount of the cheque, or with both." ... As rightly pointed out by learned counsel for the accused, section 138 of the Act provides for punishing the drawer of a cheque which is dishonoured only under two eventualities. They are: (i) insufficiency of the amount in the account of the drawer of the cheque to honour the cheque or (ii) the amount covered by the cheque exceeding the amount arranged to be paid from that account by an agreement made with that bank and not on any other ground although there are several eventualities under which a cheque can be dishonoured and one eventuality is the closure of the account of the drawer of the cheque in the particular bank on which he has drawn the cheque, subsequent to the issue of the cheque.

Offence Under 138 by Company

Section 141 talk about the offences by companies

Personal Liability

If the person committing an offence under section 138 is a company, every person who, at the time the offence was committed, was in charge of, and was responsible to the company for the conduct of the business of the company, as well as the company, shall be deemed to be guilty of the offence and shall be liable to be proceeded against and punished accordingly.

Where any offence under this Act has been committed by a company and it is proved that the offence has been committed with the consent or connivance of, or is attributable to, any neglect on the part of, any director, manager, secretary or other officer of the company, such director, manager, secretary or other officer shall also be deemed to be guilty of that offence and shall be liable to be proceeded against and punished accordingly.

The company is also liable to be prosecuted.

Exception

Nothing contained in this sub-section shall render any person liable to punishment if he proves that the offence was committed without his knowledge, or that he had exercised all due diligence to prevent the commission of such offence.

Explanation: For the purpose of this section

(a) 'company' means anybody corporate and includes a firm or other association of individuals; and

(b) 'director', in relating to a firm, means a partner in the firm.

Appendix

The Negotiable Instruments (Amendment) Second Ordinance, 2015

Introduction

The Negotiable Instruments (Amendment) Ordinance, 2015, which was promulgated by the President of India on 15 June 2015, has lapsed on 31 August 2015. Thereafter the said ordinance has not been re-promulgated which was causing uncertainty, as large number of cheque bouncing cases pending before various courts in India and also a large number of cases that are in the process of being filed. To avoid such uncertainty this ordinance has been promulgate.

September 22, 2015 The Negotiable Instruments (Amendment) Second Ordinance, 2015 was promulgated and will be deemed to have been in force from June 15, 2015. The Ordinance amends the Negotiable Instruments Act, 1881. The Ordinance amends & defines promissory notes, cheques and specifies penalties for bouncing of cheques, and other violations. However, the said Ordinance states the jurisdiction of courts where cheque bouncing cases may be filed.

Key features:

Definition of Cheque

The Ordinance also amends the definition of 'cheque in the electronic form'. Under the Act, this was defined as a cheque containing the exact mirror image of a paper cheque and generated in a secure system using a digital signature.

The definition has been amended to mean a cheque drawn in electronic medium using any computer resource, which is signed in a secure system with a digital signature and asymmetric crypto system (pair of a public key and private key to create a digital signature), or electronic system.

The definitions of 'computer resource', 'digital signature', 'electronic system' and 'asymmetric crypto system' are amended to be the same as those assigned to them in the Information Technology Act, 2000.

Jurisdiction

After this ordinance a cheque bouncing case can be filed only in the court at the place where the bank in which the payee has account is located.

Illustration

"A" has an account in a bank in a particular area of Delhi. "A" receives a cheque from "B" who is living in Mumbai. "A" presents his bank account in Delhi. Now, if this cheque is dishonored, then the cheque bounce case can be filed only in Delhi in the court which has jurisdiction over the area where "A" bank is located.

It clarifies the appropriate area of jurisdiction of courts, for filing cheque bouncing cases, the jurisdiction of courts lies over the area of the bank branch where the payee (a person to whom money is paid or is to be paid, especially the person to whom a cheque is made payable.) maintains an account, or

If the payee presents a cheque to a bank in any other way, the jurisdiction lies in the area of the bank branch where the drawer (person who writes the cheque) maintains an account.

Transfer of pending cases

All pending cases of cheque bouncing in any court, before the Ordinance came into force, will be transferred to a court with the appropriate jurisdiction as mentioned above.

If more than one case is filed by the same payee against the same drawer before different courts, the case will be transferred to the court with the appropriate jurisdiction before which the first case was filed.

All subsequent complaints against drawer regarding cheque bouncing will be filed in the same court

All subsequent complaints against drawer regarding cheque bouncing will be filed in the same court, if the payee has filed a complaint against the drawer in a court with the appropriate jurisdiction, irrespective of the mode of presentation of cheque.

रजिस्ट्री सं° डी° एल°—(एन)04/0007/2003—15 REGISTERED NO. DL—(N)04/0007/2003—15

सत्यमेव जयते

भारत का राजपत्र
The Gazette of India

असाधारण
EXTRAORDINARY
भाग II — खण्ड 1
PART II — Section 1
प्राधिकार से प्रकाशित
PUBLISHED BY AUTHORITY

सं° 25] नई दिल्ली, मंगलवार, मई 26, 2015/ ज्येष्ठ 5, 1937 (शक)
No. 25] NEW DELHI, TUESDAY, MAY 26, 2015/ JYAISTHA 5, 1937 (SAKA)

इस भाग में भिन्न पृष्ठ संख्या दी जाती है जिससे कि यह अलग संकलन के रूप में रखा जा सके।
Separate paging is given to this Part in order that it may be filed as a separate compilation.

MINISTRY OF LAW AND JUSTICE
(Legislative Department)

New Delhi, the 26th May, 2015/*Jyaistha* 5, 1937 (*Saka*)

The following Act of Parliament received the assent of the President on the 25th May, 2015, and is hereby published for general information:—

THE COMPANIES (AMENDMENT) ACT, 2015

No. 21 of 2015

[25*th May*, 2015.]

An Act to amend the Companies Act, 2013.

Be it enacted by Parliament in the Sixty-sixth Year of the Republic of India as follows:—

Short title and commencement.

1. (*1*) This Act may be called the Companies (Amendment) Act, 2015.

(*2*) It shall come into force on such date as the Central Government may, by notification in the Official Gazette, appoint and different dates may be appointed for different provisions of this Act and any reference in any provision to the commencement of this Act shall be construed as a reference to the coming into force of that provision.

Amendment of section 2.

18 of 2013. **2.** In section 2 of the Companies Act, 2013 (hereinafter referred to as the principal Act),—

(*i*) in clause (*68*), the words "of one lakh rupees or such higher paid-up share capital" shall be omitted;

(*ii*) in clause (*71*), in sub-clause (*b*), the words "of five lakh rupees or such higher paid-up capital," shall be omitted.

Amendment of section 9.

3. In section 9 of the principal Act, the words "and a common seal" shall be omitted.

Omission of section 11.

4. Section 11 of the principal Act, shall be omitted.

Amendment of section 12.

5. In section 12 of the principal Act, in sub-section *(3)*, for clause *(b)*, the following clause shall be substituted, namely:—

"*(b)* have its name engraved in legible characters on its seal, if any;".

Amendment of section 22.

6. In section 22 of the principal Act,—

(i) in sub-section *(2)*,—

(a) for the words "under its common seal", the words "under its common seal, if any," shall be substituted;

(b) the following proviso shall be inserted, namely:—

"Provided that in case a company does not have a common seal, the authorisation under this sub-section shall be made by two directors or by a director and the Company Secretary, wherever the company has appointed a Company Secretary.";

(ii) in sub-section *(3)*, the words "and have the effect as if it were made under its common seal" shall be omitted.

Amendment of section 46.

7. In section 46 of the principal Act, in sub-section *(1)*, for the words "issued under the common seal of the company", the words "issued under the common seal, if any, of the company or signed by two directors or by a director and the Company Secretary, wherever the company has appointed a Company Secretary" shall be substituted.

Insertion of new section 76A.

8. After section 76 of the principal Act, the following section shall be inserted, namely:—

Punishment for contravention of section 73 or section 76.

"76A. Where a company accepts or invites or allows or causes any other person to accept or invite on its behalf any deposit in contravention of the manner or the conditions prescribed under section 73 or section 76 or rules made thereunder or if a company fails to repay the deposit or part thereof or any interest due thereon within the time specified under section 73 or section 76 or rules made thereunder or such further time as may be allowed by the Tribunal under section 73,—

(a) the company shall, in addition to the payment of the amount of deposit or part thereof and the interest due, be punishable with fine which shall not be less than one crore rupees but which may extend to ten crore rupees; and

(b) every officer of the company who is in default shall be punishable with imprisonment which may extend to seven years or with fine which shall not be less than twenty-five lakh rupees but which may extend to two crore rupees, or with both:

Provided that if it is proved that the officer of the company who is in default, has contravened such provisions knowingly or wilfully with the intention to deceive the company or its shareholders or depositors or creditors or tax authorities, he shall be liable for action under section 447.".

Amendment of section 117.

9. In section 117 of the principal Act, in sub-section *(3)*,—

(i) in clause *(g)*, the word "and" occuring at the end shall be omitted;

(ii) after clause *(g)*, the following proviso shall be inserted, namely:—

"Provided that no person shall be entitled under section 399 to inspect or obtain copies of such resolutions; and".

Amendment of section 123.

10. In section 123 of the principal Act, in sub-section *(1)*, after the third proviso, the following proviso shall be inserted, namely:—

"Provided also that no company shall declare dividend unless carried over previous losses and depreciation not provided in previous year or years are set off against profit of the company for the current year.".

11. In section 124 of the principal Act, in sub-section *(6)*,— Amendment of section 124.

(i) for the words, brackets and figure "unpaid or unclaimed dividend has been transferred under sub-section *(5)* shall also be", the words "dividend has not been paid or claimed for seven consecutive years or more shall be" shall be substituted;

(ii) after the proviso, the following *Explanation* shall be inserted, namely:—

"*Explanation*.—For the removal of doubts, it is hereby clarified that in case any dividend is paid or claimed for any year during the said period of seven consecutive years, the share shall not be transferred to Investor Education and Protection Fund.".

12. In section 134 of the principal Act, in sub-section *(3)*, after clause *(c)*, the following clause shall be inserted, namely:— Amendment of section 134.

"*(ca)* details in respect of frauds reported by auditors under sub-section *(12)* of section 143 other than those which are reportable to the Central Government;".

13. In section 143 of the principal Act, for sub-section *(12)*, the following sub-section shall be substituted, namely:— Amendment of section 143.

"*(12)* Notwithstanding anything contained in this section, if an auditor of a company in the course of the performance of his duties as auditor, has reason to believe that an offence of fraud involving such amount or amounts as may be prescribed, is being or has been committed in the company by its officers or employees, the auditor shall report the matter to the Central Government within such time and in such manner as may be prescribed:

Provided that in case of a fraud involving lesser than the specified amount, the auditor shall report the matter to the audit committee constituted under section 177 or to the Board in other cases within such time and in such manner as may be prescribed:

Provided further that the companies, whose auditors have reported frauds under this sub-section to the audit committee or the Board but not reported to the Central Government, shall disclose the details about such frauds in the Board's report in such manner as may be prescribed.".

14. In section 177 of the principal Act, in sub-section *(4)*, in clause *(iv)*, the following proviso shall be inserted, namely:— Amendment of section 177.

"Provided that the Audit Committee may make omnibus approval for related party transactions proposed to be entered into by the company subject to such conditions as may be prescribed;".

15. In section 185 of the principal Act, in sub-section *(1)*, in the proviso, after clause *(b)*, the following clauses and proviso shall be inserted, namely:— Amendment of section 185.

"*(c)* any loan made by a holding company to its wholly owned subsidiary company or any guarantee given or security provided by a holding company in respect of any loan made to its wholly owned subsidiary company; or

(d) any guarantee given or security provided by a holding company in respect of loan made by any bank or financial institution to its subsidiary company:

Provided that the loans made under clauses *(c)* and *(d)* are utilised by the subsidiary company for its principal business activities.".

Amendment of section 188.

16. In section 188 of the principal Act,—

(*a*) in sub-section (*1*),—

(*i*) for the words "special resolution", at both the places where they occur, the word "resolution" shall be substituted;

(*ii*) after the third proviso, the following proviso shall be inserted, namely:—

"Provided also that the requirement of passing the resolution under first proviso shall not be applicable for transactions entered into between a holding company and its wholly owned subsidiary whose accounts are consolidated with such holding company and placed before the shareholders at the general meeting for approval.";

(*b*) in sub-section (*3*), for the words "special resolution", the word "resolution" shall be substituted.

Amendment of section 212.

17. In section 212 of the principal Act, in sub-section (*6*), for the words, brackets and figures "the offences covered under sub-sections (*5*) and (*6*) of section 7, section 34, section 36, sub-section (*1*) of section 38, sub-section (*5*) of section 46, sub-section (*7*) of section 56, sub-section (*10*) of section 66, sub-section (*5*) of section 140, sub-section (*4*) of section 206, section 213, section 229, sub-section (*1*) of section 251, sub-section (*3*) of section 339 and section 448 which attract the punishment for fraud provided in section 447", the words and figures "offence covered under section 447" shall be substituted.

Amendment of section 223.

18. In section 223 of the principal Act, in sub-section (*4*), in clause (*a*), for the words "by the seal", the words "by the seal, if any," shall be substituted.

Amendment of section 248.

19. In section 248 of the principal Act, in sub-section (*1*),—

(*i*) in clause (*a*), after the word 'incorporation', the word 'or' shall be inserted;

(*ii*) clause (*b*) shall be omitted.

Amendment of section 419.

20. In section 419 of the principal Act, in sub-section (*4*), the words "or winding up" shall be omitted.

Amendment of section 435.

21. In section 435 of the principal Act, in sub-section (*1*),—

(*i*) for the words "trial of offences under this Act", the words "trial of offences punishable under this Act with imprisonment of two years or more" shall be substituted;

(*ii*) the following proviso shall be inserted, namely:—

"Provided that all other offences shall be tried, as the case may be, by a Metropolitan Magistrate or a Judicial Magistrate of the First Class having jurisdiction to try any offence under this Act or under any previous company law.".

Amendment of section 436.

22. In section 436 of the principal Act, in sub-section (*1*), in clause (*a*), for the words "all offences under this Act", the words, brackets and figures "all offences specified under sub-section (*1*) of section 435" shall be substituted.

Amendment of section 462.

23. In section 462 of the principal Act, for sub-section (2), the following sub-sections shall be substituted, namely:—

"(2) A copy of every notification proposed to be issued under sub-section (*1*), shall be laid in draft before each House of Parliament, while it is in session, for a total period of thirty days, and if, both Houses agree in disapproving the issue of notification or both Houses agree in making any modification in the notification, the notification shall not be issued or, as the case may be, shall be issued only in such modified form as may be agreed upon by both the Houses.

(*3*) In reckoning any such period of thirty days as is referred to in sub-section (*2*), no account shall be taken of any period during which the House referred to in sub-section (*2*) is prorogued or adjourned for more than four consecutive days.

(*4*) The copies of every notification issued under this section shall, as soon as may be after it has been issued, be laid before each House of Parliament.".

DR. SANJAY SINGH,
Secretary to the Govt. of India.

CORRIGENDUM

In the Coal Mines (Special Provision) Act, 2015 (11 of 2015), as published in the Gazette of India, Extraordinary, Part II, Section 1, Issue No. 4, dated the 30th March, 2015, at page 6, in line 7 *for* "quesiton", *read* "question".

CORRIGENDA

In the Insurance Laws (Amendment) Act, 2015 (5 of 2015), as published in the Gazette of India Extraordinary, Part II, Section 1, Issue No. 8, dated the 20th March, 2015,—

(i) at page 5, in line No. 41, *for* "sub-section (1)", *read* "sub-section (2);

(ii) at page 7, in lines 40 and 41, *for* ' "the Securities', *read* "Securities";

(iii) at page 35, in line 30, *for* "sub-section (12)", *read* "sub-section (2).

PRINTED BY THE GENERAL MANAGER, GOVERNMENT OF INDIA PRESS, MINTO ROAD, NEW DELHI AND PUBLISHED BY THE CONTROLLER OF PUBLICATIONS, DELHI—2015.

GMGIPMRND—1188GI(S3)—26-05-2015.

Index